INVESTMENT OPPORTUNITIES FOR A
Low-Carbon World

INVESTMENT OPPORTUNITIES FOR A
Low-Carbon World

Edited by Will Oulton
Second edition

Environmental Finance
PUBLICATIONS

Environmental Finance Publications
22-24 Corsham Street
London N1 6DR
UK
Tel: 44 20 7251 9151
Fax: 44 20 7251 9161
E-mail: info@environmental-finance.com
www.environmental-finance.com

PEFC PEFC: Promoting Sustainable Forest Management
PEFC/16-33-293

ISBN 978-0-9572311-0-8

Printed in Great Britain by the MPG Books Group, Bodmin and King's Lynn

© Fulton Publishing Ltd, 2012. All rights reserved. No part of this publication may be reproduced, stored in or introduced into any retrieval system, or transmitted, in any form or by any means, electronic, mechanical, photocopying, recording or otherwise, without the written permission of the publisher.

Every possible effort has been made to ensure that the information contained in this publication is accurate at the time of going to press and neither the publishers nor any of the authors, editors, contributors or sponsors can accept responsibility for any errors or omissions, however caused. No responsibility for loss or damage occasioned to any person acting, or refraining from action, as a result of the material in this publication can be accepted by the editors, authors, the publisher or any of the contributors or sponsors.

Environmental Finance Publications and its authors, editors, contributors, partners, sponsors or endorsing bodies make no warranty, express or implied, concerning the information, and expressly disclaim all warranties. The views expressed in the research materials and publications herein are those of the individual authors or contributors identified as the originators of each specific piece of research or publication and are not necessarily those of Environmental Finance Publications or of any of the other authors, contributors, partners, sponsors or endorsing bodies.

Views expressed within Environmental Finance Publications's print publications do not constitute legal advice or opinion and readers should where relevant seek appropriate legal advice..

Contents

Acknowledgements		ix
About the contributors		x
Foreword		xxi
Sir Mark Moody-Stuart		
Making the transition to a Green Economy		xxiii
Achim Steiner, UN Environment Programme		
Investing in a low-carbon world: a view from the British government		xxv
Gregory Barker, Minister of state, UK Department of Energy & Climate Change		
Introduction		xxvii
Environmental Markets Quiz		xxx

Section 1. Environmental and Low-Carbon Technologies — 1

1	Wind power *Mark Thompson, Tiptree Investments*	3
2	Solar industry – entering new dimensions *Matthias Fawer, Bank Sarasin*	21
3	Hydropower and ocean power *Mark Thompson, Tiptree Investments*	45
4	Geothermal energy *Alexander Richter, Canadian Geothermal Energy Association*	59
5	Biomass *Mark Thompson, Tiptree Investments*	77
6	Energy efficiency as an investment theme *Zoë Knight, HSBC*	93
7	Water technologies and infrastructure *Daniel Wild, Marc-Olivier Buffle, Junwei Haffner-Cai, SAM – Sustainable Asset Management*	101
8	Investment opportunities in renewable energy and environmental infrastructure *Erich Becker, Zouk Capital LLP*	143
9	Heat pumps *Philip Wolfe, Ownergy Plc*	159
10	Sustainable timberland investing *Simon Fox, Mercer*	163
11	Climate change: key issues for institutional investors *Mark Fulton, Bruce Kahn, Deutsche Bank Climate Change Advisors*	173

Section 2. Investment Approaches, Products and Markets   191

12 Environmental technologies within strategic asset allocation   193
    Danyelle Guyatt, Catholic Super; Laureen Bird, Mercer

13 Investment approaches to environmental markets   211
    Ian Simm, Impax Asset Management

14 Capturing the performance of environmental technology companies   219
    David Harris, FTSE Group

15 Exchange traded funds as an investment option   233
    Lillian Goldthwaite, Friends Provident

16 Climate bonds – the investment case   241
    Sean Kidney, Stuart Clenaghan, Padraig Oliver, The Climate Bonds Initiative

17 Carbon risk and carbon trading: considerations for institutional investors   251
    Xinting Jia, Mercer

18 The European carbon emissions market   263
    David Peniket, ICE Futures Europe

19 Measuring carbon intensity and risk   271
    Simon Thomas, Liesel van Ast, Trucost

Section 3. Regulation, Incentives, Investor and Company Case Studies   281

20 Policy regulation: a risk and an opportunity   283
    Kirsty Hamilton, Chatham House

21 Renewable energy incentive mechanisms   295
    Louise Moore, Henry Davey, Herbert Smith LLP

22 An investment portfolio view of the low-carbon world   317
    Professor Michael Mainelli, Z/Yen Group; James Palmer, BP;
    Liang Shi, University of Edinburgh

23 Investor case study: investment issues for public pension funds   333
    Winston Hickox, adviser to CalPERS and the FTSE Group

24 Investor case study: an institutional investor approach to 'clean-tech'   339
    David Russell, Universities Superannuation Scheme (UK)

25 Investor case study: low-carbon investments and considerations   343
    Marcel Jeucken, Pieter van Stijn, PGGM

26 Company case study: the challenge of moving to mass low-carbon automotive transportation   349
    Nissan Motor Company

27 **Company case study: desalination's place in the water cycle**   355
Degrémont (part of Suez Environnement)

Concluding remarks   363
Glossary of terms   371
Appendix: The FTSE Environmental Markets Indices   379
Environmental Markets Quiz: answers   **394**

Dedications

This book is dedicated to my late but great Dad, William John Oulton and to the memory of my uncle, Henry Oulton and friend Neil McEwan.

Finally, to all Tranmere Rovers fans, we are the Super White Army.

Acknowledgements

I would like to thank all the contributors who willingly gave their valuable time and expertise, without which this book would not have been possible. In particular I would like to thank Graham Cooper at *Environmental Finance* and Miles Smith-Morris for all his hard work, patience and support.

I have been fortunate through my career to have benefited from the advice, support and in many cases friendship of a large number of highly talented and passionate people. I would in particular like to express my sincere appreciation and gratitude to the following people who have helped me in many ways over the years and apologise to those I have either forgotten or missed out. They are: Masaru Arai, Mark Makepeace, Paul Grimes, Melvyn Lee, Steve Hull, David Harris, Jayn Harding, Tony Campos, Arisa Kishigami, Danielle Carriera, Danyelle Guyatt, Helga Birgden, Laureen Bird, Susanna Jacobsen, Sarika Goel, Jane Ambachtsheer, Rory Sullivan, Tom Kuh, Penny Shepherd, Hugh Wheelan, Tony Hay, Aled Jones, Giuseppe van der Helm, Davide Delmaso, Ioana Dolcos, Paul Clements-Hunt, Professor Tom Donaldson, Simon Williams, Helen Wildsmith, Reg Green, Yve Newbold, Craig Mackenzie, Peter Webster, Jen Morgan, Rachel Singh, Richard Spencer, Mark Campanale, Martin Hancock, Wendy Chapple, Professor Jeremy Moon, Bill McClory, Donald MacDonald, Howard Pearce, Raj Thamotheram, Matt Christensen, Matthew Kiernan, Nick Robins, Melissa MacDonald, Toby Webb, Adrian Cornwall, Ian Simm, Bruce Jenkyn-Jones, Winston Hickox, Eric Borremans, Mark Thompson, Alice Chapple, Stephanie Pfeifer, David Russell, Dan Summerfield, Frank Curtiss, Lillian Goldthwaite, Patrick Race, Tom Geraghty, Amit Popat and all of the responsible investment team at Mercer.

I am particularly indebted to the late Sir Mervyn Pedelty, who was both a friend and mentor and was instrumental in shaping my views on sustainable and responsible investment.

Finally, I would like to thank my family as they are my foundation and inspiration. So to my Mam Ada, Linda, Toby, Ellis, Jane, Debbie, John, Roy, Neil, Sharon, Amanda, Robyn, Louis, Amy, Charlotte, Ben and all the Oultons wherever they may be. Lastly to my uncle, Harry McWha, who introduced me as a young boy to the art of angling and consequently lit the fire of curiosity in biodiversity and our natural environment that has brought me to do this book (again!).

About the contributors

Liesel van Ast is Research Editor at Trucost. Liesel writes and edits published reports and commissioned research on the investment implications of company environmental impacts. She co-authored the UN PRI/UNEP FI report on Universal Ownership and a chapter on the Canadian oil sands for a WWF Canada/Mercer study, published in 2011. Liesel also advises on environmental policies and regulations. Before joining Trucost in 2007, she was a section and online editor for *The ENDS Report*, the UK environmental business and policy journal. Liesel holds an MSc in business strategy, politics and the environment from the University of London. She also has certificates in environmental management and investment management.

Dr Erich Becker co-leads Zouk Capital's infrastructure team. Zouk Capital, formerly Zouk Ventures, is an independent London-based private equity fund manager with a focus on the European clean-tech market. From a base in process engineering and project finance focusing on power plants and other energy infrastructure assets, Erich has built an exceptional career in the energy industry, working in principal investment, corporate finance, commodity trading and fund management.

Before joining Zouk, Erich was senior managing director at Macquarie Bank; he created and managed a merchant banking approach to commodity markets at this financial institution renowned for its infrastructure investment credentials. Prior to Macquarie, he was an energy sector specialist leading principal investments in energy assets at Och-Ziff Capital Management Group, an alternative asset manager with $28 billion in assets under management. Before working with Och-Ziff, Erich was an executive director at Goldman Sachs, executing a number of principal transactions as well as advising clients in the energy and power sectors.

Erich has a PhD in process engineering from the Technical University of Vienna, focused on financing, design and optimisation of power plants. He also holds an MBA from the Vienna School of Economics and Business Administration.

Loreen Bird is an analyst in Mercer's investment consulting business in London. She is a member of the Responsible Investment business unit, supporting the global and European teams across a range of tasks including manager research, business development and providing input into client reports. Laureen is also involved in coordinating the development of new projects.

Laureen joined Mercer in 2008. She graduated from Queensland University of Technology with an honours bachelor of biotechnology innovation degree.

Marc-Olivier Buffle is a Senior Analyst in SAM's research team, covering the water industry and technology sector, bringing 12 years of related industry experience.

Prior to joining SAM in 2008, he was a business development manager at the Danaher Corporation, where he led the market development efforts for advanced water treatment products. Previously, he was a team leader in the R&D department of Trojan Technologies, a global water treatment technology manufacturer. Marc-Olivier has published numerous articles in peer-reviewed water treatment and environmental science publications, is the recipient of several awards for his work in the field of ozone research, and has patented various processes in water treatment technology. He holds an MSc in engineering from the Swiss Federal School of Technology (ETH) and a PhD in water treatment chemistry from the Swiss Federal Institute of Aquatic Science and Technology (EAWAG).

Stuart Clenaghan is a member of the Climate Bonds Initiative Advisory Panel and a principal at Eco System Services, a consultancy with a focus on developing financing and business models for large-scale sustainable land-use projects. Stuart spent 23 years at Lehman Brothers and UBS as a fixed income specialist and has extensive experience in all aspects of the fixed income markets. including origination, trading and sales. Since leaving UBS in 2004, Stuart has specialised as an early-stage investor in sustainable forestry and environmental enterprises. His investments include the largest planted forest company in Uganda, a forest conservation private equity company and Green Gold Forestry, an FSC-certified sustainable forestry management company in Peru. Stuart takes an active role in contributing to public discussions on developing finance for sustainable forestry and mechanisms to fund REDD+.

Henry Davey is a Partner at Herbert Smith LLP. He has over 17 years' experience in the international energy industry, where he has advised on mergers and acquisitions and projects in Eastern and Western Europe, the CIS, Asia, India, Pakistan and the Middle East. His practice encompasses energy mergers and acquisitions (including oil refineries, oil, gas and power assets), electricity generation, distribution and transmission projects and oil and gas field developments.

Matthias Fawer joined Bank Sarasin and Co Ltd as a sustainability analyst in 2000. He is now Director, responsible for the renewable energies and energy utilities sectors. Since 2004 he has been the main author of the Bank Sarasin annual solar energy study. He has a PhD degree in biotechnology from the Swiss Federal Institute of Technology (ETH) in Zurich. He then worked for the ecology department of the Swiss Federal Materials Testing and Research Institute (EMPA) in St Gallen, where he was senior expert in environmental impact projects on behalf of Swiss and European industry associations. In 1996 he spent a year with Boustead Consulting in the UK. He has also completed training as lead auditor for environmental management systems and social accountability SA 8000.

Simon Fox is a Principal within Mercer's alternatives boutique, part of the investment consulting business. Located in London, he is responsible for manager research and intellectual capital on a range of alternative asset classes and their potential use by clients. Simon has responsibility for research in both 'alpha' driven alternative investments – for example, he leads Mercer's fund of hedge fund research globally – and 'beta' driven strategies, including timberland, farmland and commodity-related strategies.

Simon also provides broader investment advice for a number of institutional clients. This includes investment strategy and structure advice as well as manager selection, and governance considerations.

Simon has a degree in mathematics from Oxford University and a masters in European politics and policy from the London School of Economics and Political Science. He is a Chartered Financial Analyst (CFA) charterholder and has eight years investment experience with Mercer.

Mark Fulton is Managing Director of Deutsche Bank Climate Change Advisors. In his role as global head of climate change investment research, based in New York, Mark co-ordinates a team of analysts who publish white papers on key industry, policy and strategic topics. The research team uses this to advise investment managers on climate change-based strategies across the asset management platform. Mark joined the company in 2006 after 29 years of investment experience in senior roles in research and management at Citigroup in the US, Salomon Smith Barney and NatWest in Sydney and James Capel in London.

Mark is co-chair of the UNEP FI Climate Change Working Group and member of the steering committee, Capital Markets Climate Initiative, UK Department of Energy and Climate Change. He has a BA in philosophy and economics from Oxford University.

Lillian Goldthwaite has more than 18 years' experience in financial services encompassing product management and strategy roles for asset management, defined contribution and index providers. Currently, she heads Friends Provident's fund strategy and selection group, which oversees governance of its unit-linked investments for corporate and individual pension platforms and wealth products. Previously, she led FTSE's equity and alternatives product management including oversight of the firm's index research and design groups and its practitioner governance committees. She has also held product development and strategy roles with Dresdner RCM's Institutional Fixed Income division, Morningstar and Lipper.

Danyelle Guyatt started her career as an economist at the Commonwealth Treasury of Australia before moving to London in the financial sector as a strategist and later a global balanced fund manager with Deutsche Asset Management.

Danyelle graduated with an MSc in investment management with distinction from the Cass Business School and completed a PhD in economic psychology at the University of Bath, researching institutional investors and long-term responsible investing. She was awarded the best PhD thesis for 2006 prize from the French Social Investment Forum.

More recently, Danyelle was global head of research for Mercer's Responsible Investment team, based in London. During that time she established a process to assess fund managers against their ability to integrate environmental, social and governance (ESG) factors into their investment decisions and active ownership practices. She also established and led a collaborative project with large investors from around the world to assess the implications of climate change for strategic asset allocation decisions.

Danyelle is currently an investment manager at the Catholic Super fund based in Melbourne and is focused on making the portfolio sustainable across all asset classes and investment mandates.

Junwei Hafner-Cai is an analyst covering the industrials sector for the SAM Sustainable Water and SAM Sustainable Water Evolution Strategies, with a focus on Asian equities. Prior to joining SAM in 2010, Junwei was a junior portfolio manager at EFG International. Previously, she was an assistant relationship manager within the International Wealth Management Desk at Crédit Suisse Private Banking, Singapore, and was an assistant fixed income portfolio manager at Wegelin & Co, Private Bankers. Junwei holds a bachelor's degree in business (major in banking and finance) from Nanyang Technological University in Singapore, and holds a Certified International Investment Analyst (CIIA) designation from AZEK in Switzerland.

Kirsty Hamilton leads the Renewable Energy Finance Project, as an associate fellow at Chatham House, creating stronger interaction between leading mainstream financiers and senior policy counterparts, to bring about a more effective 'investment grade' policy environment. She has 20 years' experience of the international policy debate as an observer at the UN climate change negotiations, and is on the World Economic Forum's Global Agenda Council on Renewable Energy; the Advisory Board of UNEP Finance Initiative's Climate Change Working Group; the Steering Committee of REN 21, the international renewable energy policy network; as well as an expert reviewer and contributing author to the Intergovernmental Panel on Climate Change (IPCC). Kirsty is also an international policy consultant in these areas.

David Harris has responsibility for FTSE's Responsible Investment (RI) indices, including FTSE4Good, FTSE Environmental Markets and FTSE CDP Carbon Strategy Series. The RI Unit, which he heads, is responsible for RI index management, corporate engagement, managing research partnerships and developing new RI indices and services. David is a vice-chair and a board director for the UK Sustainable

Investment and Finance association (UKSIF), a Forest Footprint Disclosure Project steering committee member, a judge for the FT Sustainable Finance Awards and is on Eurosif's public policy advisory committee. Previously, David worked for ADL's Environment & Risk Practice and PwC's climate change team. David has an MSc in environmental technology, an IMC from the UK Society of Investment Professionals, and a first-class degree in biological sciences from Oxford University.

Winston H Hickox joined California Strategies LLC as a partner in 2006, bringing with him unparalleled experience in environmental policy and regulation, as well as a strong background in public finance, including pension fund investment management. He served as a member of the Governor's Cabinet for five years as secretary of the California Environmental Protection Agency (CalEPA); seven years as a special assistant for environmental affairs to Governor Jerry Brown; and two years as an alternate to the California Coastal Commission, appointed by the speaker of the assembly. Winston recently completed a two-year assignment with the California Public Employees' Retirement System (CalPERS) Investment Office, assisting in the design and implementation of a series of environmental initiatives in the private equity, real estate, global public equity, as well as corporate governance segments of the fund's $211 billon investment portfolio. Winston was asked by the Schwarzenegger administration to chair the Market Advisory Committee (MAC) in 2007. The committee advised the California Air Resources Board about the use of market mechanisms to reduce greenhouse gas emissions.

Dr Marcel Jeucken is Head of Responsible Investment and member of the Management Team of the portfolio managers' unit at PGGM Investments. PGGM Investments is the fiduciary manager for, among others, Pensioenfonds Zorg en Welzijn, the second largest pension fund in the Netherlands and Europe, and has approximately €100 billion under management. Marcel is also a member of the PRI board and member of the steering committee of the Institutional Investors Group on Climate Change (IIGCC). For the 10 years before joining PGGM, Marcel was a director at Dutch Sustainability Research, sales and marketing director at SiRi Company, and a senior economist at Rabobank Group. Marcel holds a PhD in economics on sustainability issues and the financial sector. He has written numerous papers and is author or editor of several books, including *Sustainable Finance and Banking* (2001) and *Sustainability in Finance* (2004).

Dr Xinting Jia is a Senior Associate with the Responsible Investment Unit of Mercer's investment consulting business. Xinting works very closely with clients in implementing the United Nations Principles for Responsible Investment (PRI) and in formulating strategies for taking environmental, social and governance (ESG) issues into investment processes. Xinting also researches RI thematic funds – renewable energy, water, agriculture, waste and carbon – and provides client advice.

Xinting co-authored the Mercer and International Finance Corporation (IFC) report, *Gaining Ground: integrating environmental, social and governance (ESG) factors into investment processes in emerging markets*, and co-authored Mercer's white paper on carbon risk and carbon trading. Xinting's book *Corporate governance and resource security: The transformation of China's global resources companies*, was published by Routledge in 2010 in New York. Xinting was also a contributor to the Mercer *Climate Change Scenarios and Asset Allocation Report* (2011).

Xinting holds a PhD in corporate governance from Victoria University and an MBA from Melbourne Business School.

Bruce M Kahn is Director and Senior Investment Analyst for Climate Change Strategies at Deutsche Bank Climate Change Advisors, based in New York. He joined the company in 2008 with 20 years of experience in environmental research, most recently as it relates to investments. Prior to joining Deutsche Bank, he managed assets for high-net-worth and institutional investors at CitiSmith Barney's Private Wealth Management Group. Previous experience includes investment and market research for IC Value (previously Center for Sustainable Systems Studies, Miami University of Ohio), management consulting and corporate sustainability strategist for Cameron-Cole LLC and environmental research positions for the University of Wisconsin, Madison, The Ecological Society of America and Auburn University, and service in the US Peace Corps as an agricultural agent and provincial representative.

He has a BA in ecology and evolutionary biology from the University of Connecticut; an MS in fisheries and allied aquacultures from Auburn University; a PhD in environmental science from University of Wisconsin, Madison; and is the recipient of both a J William Fulbright Scholarship and a National Science Foundation Fellowship in ecological economics.

Sean Kidney is co-founder of the Climate Bonds Initiative. His background is in stakeholder communications, social issues strategy and pension fund marketing. He is a director of one of the Climate Bonds Initiative parents, the Network for Sustainable Financial Markets, an international, non-partisan network of finance sector professionals, academics and others who see the need for fundamental changes to improve financial market integrity, stability and efficiency. He is also a steering committee member of the TransformUK business/NGO coalition, pushing for a rapid shift to a low-carbon economy and chair of the UK Local Energy Efficiency Coalition, developing "scalable and sustainable financial solutions" suitable for climate bond financing at an institutional investor scale. Sean's background is in stakeholder communications, social issues strategy and as a marketing adviser to a number of the largest Australian pension funds.

Zoë Knight is a senior analyst at HSBC, responsible for climate change strategy. She has been an investment analyst at global financial institutions since 1997. She is a regular speaker at industry events, including the 51st awards ceremony of the Belgian Society of Financial Analysts and conferences in Tokyo, Singapore and Moscow, as well as for the Environment Agency national conference in London. Prior to joining HSBC, she was responsible for SRI at Bank of America Merrill Lynch and a pan-European small and midcap strategist at UBS. Throughout her career she has been ranked in Extel and Institutional Investor. She holds a BSc (Hons) in economics from the University of Bath.

Professor Michael Mainelli PhD FCCA FSI leads Z/Yen, the City of London's leading think-tank, which he co-founded in 1994 to promote societal advance through better finance and technology. Educated at Harvard, Trinity College Dublin and the London School of Economics and Political Science, as a scientist in the 1970s Michael conceived and delivered the first global environmental mapping project, Geodat, in 1984. He became a leading accountancy firm partner in the 1980s and served on the board of Europe's largest research and development organisation in the 1990s. Michael is Emeritus Professor of Commerce at Gresham College, Visiting Professor at London School of Economics, non-executive director of the United Kingdom Accreditation Service, trustee of the International Fund for Animal Welfare and Ocean Alliance, and principal adviser to the London Accord.

Louise Moore is a partner at Herbert Smith LLP. She specialises in environmental law and heads the Herbert Smith environment, health and safety practice. Louise advises on a wide range of environmental issues (national and international) including nuclear liability, waste, emissions trading, asbestos liability and control, contaminated land and environmental and health and safety risk management. Her work ranges from advising on specialised regulatory EHS matters (in both contentious and non-contentious contexts) to advising on the environmental aspects of projects and corporate transactions. Louise has advised on environmental issues affecting rail, nuclear, chemical, pharmaceutical, waste, automotive, and oil and gas sector clients among others.

Padraig Oliver is Research Manager at the Climate Bonds Initiative. Padraig has worked as a clean energy and climate strategy consultant for four years with experience in China and Europe. He has extensive experience in international project management and clean energy analysis for such clients as the European Commission, the International Finance Corporation, WWF and the UK government and with partners such as the International Energy Agency, major international banks and NGOs. Padraig holds an MSc in environmental technology from Imperial College London.

Will Oulton BSc DipM, FRSA has over 10 years of experience working in sustainable and responsible investment. He is currently the Head of Responsible Investment for Mercer Investments across Europe, the Middle East and Africa, advising institutional investors on environmental, social and corporate governance related matters.

Before joining Mercer, Will was the director of responsible investment at FTSE Group, where he led the development of FTSE's global sustainability indices and services including the FTSE4Good, Environmental Markets and Carbon Strategy benchmark indices and was involved in the development of the FTSE ESG Ratings service.

In February 2010 he was appointed vice president of the European Sustainable Investment Forum (Eurosif) and, in the same year, was also appointed to the board of the UK Sustainable Investment Forum.

Will is also a fellow of the Royal Society of Arts, a special lecturer at Nottingham University Business School's International Centre for Corporate Social Responsibility and sits on a number of investment industry advisory committees.

James Palmer was seconded to support the London Accord from BP Australia, where he works within BP's Supply and Trading business as an asset economist, responsible for the commercial optimisation of BP refineries. Since 1999, James has performed a variety of engineering and commercial roles within BP Refining and BP Integrated Supply and Trading. James holds a BE in mechanical engineering from the University of Queensland.

David Peniket has served as President of ICE Futures Europe since October 2005 and as its Chief Operating Officer since January 2005. Prior to assuming the role of COO, he served as director of finance from May 2000. Before joining ICE Futures Europe (then the IPE) in 1999, he worked for seven years at KPMG, where he trained as an accountant and was a consultant in its financial management practice. He was research assistant to John Cartwright MP from 1988 to 1991. He holds a BSc (Econ) degree in economics from the London School of Economics and Political Science and is a chartered accountant.

Alexander Richter is Director and Board Member of the Canadian Geothermal Energy Association. In this role he also represents the association, among others, as a board member (alternate) at the International Energy Agency Geothermal Implementing Agreement (GIA). He has been a speaker at many of the major geothermal energy events internationally.

Previously, he was a Director in the Geothermal Energy Team of Icelandic bank Islandsbanki. As a founding member of the team, he focused on business development, origination and research in geothermal energy for the bank over a six-year period.

A German national, Alexander has a law degree from the University of Konstanz, Germany, with additional legal studies at Queen's University and the University of Ottawa, Canada, and graduated with a master's in electronic commerce from Dalhousie University, Canada.

He is also founder and principal of the leading news service for the global geothermal energy industry, www.thinkgeoenergy.com.

David Russell is Co-Head of Responsible Investment for the Universities Superannuation Scheme (USS). USS is the second largest pension fund in the UK, with assets of over £32 billion and approximately 280,000 members. USS has a responsible investment team of five who work with USS's fund managers and other market participants on extra financial issues. USS's responsible investment strategy focuses on integrating extra-financial factors into its investment processes across asset classes, and on engaging with companies where these issues pose a risk to the fund's investments. David is a steering committee member of the Institutional Investors Group on Climate Change (IIGCC), a board member for the Principles for Responsible Investment Association and a member of the British Venture Capital Association RI Advisory Board.

Liang Shi studied at Shanghai University (BSc in Mathematics and Applied Mathematics) and the University of Edinburgh (MSc in Operational Research with Finance). Liang obtained prizes in mathematical modelling contests during his undergraduate studies in Shanghai University and a master's degree with distinction from Edinburgh University. He also did voluntary work for the Red Cross, museums, middle schools, and the 7th China Universities Games. Liang is currently working in Beijing with the China Securities Company in its department of fixed income.

Ian Simm is the Founder and Chief Executive of Impax Asset Management Group plc (IAM), an investment management firm managing or advising around £2 billion in the alternative energy and related environmental sectors on behalf of more than 100 institutional investors worldwide. Ian has been responsible for building IAM since its launch in 1998, particularly the firm's listed equity and infrastructure teams and investment products. In addition to his role as chief executive, Ian heads the firm's investment committees.

Prior to Impax, Ian was an engagement manager at McKinsey & Company in the Netherlands, where he led teams providing advice to clients in a range of environmentally sensitive industries. He has a first class honours degree in physics from Cambridge University and a master's in public administration from Harvard University.

Pieter van Stijn is a responsible investment adviser and has been a member of PGGM Investments' Responsible Investment team since 2007. Pieter is responsible for engagement and overlay activities of PGGM Investments in the field of climate change and for the exclusions activities relating to controversial weapons. Previously, Pieter worked at SNS Asset Management for five years as ESG analyst. After graduating from Tilburg University as a development economist, Pieter started his career as a policy adviser in communications and lobbying for trade organisations in the wood processing and chemical industries.

Simon Thomas is a Founder Director of Trucost Plc, an environmental data company he jointly founded in January 2000. He has overseen the development of Trucost's methodology by its research team, with the support of an international advisory panel of leading academics in the fields of economics and the environment.

Simon is a regular commentator on the quantification of environmental impacts, reporting and analysis and he frequently addresses the investment and corporate community on these issues. Trucost has undertaken research projects on behalf of the Department for Environment, Food & Rural Affairs, the Environment Agency, the Carbon Disclosure Project and many leading financial institutions worldwide.

Simon previously worked in the finance and publishing sectors holding senior positions with LCF Edmond de Rothschild, Swiss Bank Corporation, Nomura International and Reed International.

Mark Thompson has been financing environmental technologies since 1997. He is currently a director of Tiptree Investments, which provides management and financial resources for environmental technology companies. Previously, he was a director of equity research, at Cannacord Adams, in London and the portfolio manager for a global environmental technology fund. Mark has been instrumental in listing companies on AIM and the TSX, as well as completing numerous secondary financings and venture investments in Europe, China and North America. He is a CFA charter holder, a chartered engineer and has an MSc in finance from London Business School. His early career was spent as an officer in the British Army.

Daniel Wild is Head of Research at SAM and has been covering the water-related industries and technology sectors as a senior analyst. Daniel studied chemical engineering at the Swiss Federal Institute of Technology (ETH) in Zurich. For his PhD he studied at the Swiss Federal Institute of Aquatic Science and Technology (EAWAG) under the supervision of Professor Willi Gujer.

After postdoctoral research studies in the civil and environmental engineering department of Stanford University from 1997–99, he joined the engineering and consulting firm Ernst Basler and Partners in Zollikon, as head of the environmental technology department, and carried out consulting mandates in Switzerland, Eastern Europe and Asia. From 2004–06, he worked as programme manager in the Infrastructure Financing Department at the Swiss State Secretariat for Economic Affairs (SECO), where he was in charge of infrastructure investments in Macedonia, Kosovo, Poland and Vietnam. He joined SAM in 2006.

Philip Wolfe is one of the pioneers of the UK renewable energy industry. He recently founded Ownergy Plc, to provide renewable electricity and heating systems to businesses and consumers, supported by the government's new Renewable Energy Tariffs. He is also a director of the Renewable Energy Association and the Aldersgate Group.

He has installed renewable energy in his home for all of its heating and part of its electricity.

A Cambridge first-class engineering graduate, Philip has been involved in the sector since the 1970s when he became the first chief executive of what is now BP Solar. He later established his own renewables company Intersolar Group, which from 1993–02 was the sole UK manufacturer of photovoltaic cells. He has served on the boards of European and British industry, academic and advisory bodies, and advised the European Commission and the British government.

Foreword

Sir Mark Moody-Stuart

Edited by Will Oulton, the second edition of this book brings together up-to-date information on clean technologies from a wide range of authors, including specialists in different fields, investors and, not least, company practitioners. Will Oulton has used his long experience in the field to select contributors who can provide a review of the current state of the full range of clean technologies as well as reviewing the various investment vehicles and methods. It thus provides a guide for those investors who look to profit from and contribute to the rapid growth of this field or those who need to understand the drivers of investment. The book also has a number of corporate case studies.

It is a timely contribution to a field that is not only growing very rapidly, but in which different technologies compete to meet the common objective of a low-carbon economy in a landscape that is changing fast. One needs an understanding not only of the changes in technology, but of the barriers to growth and future opportunities for cost reduction through learning curves. The economic environment is also changing rapidly. The regulatory frameworks necessary to guide this industry evolve and subsidies come under pressure from the straitened budgets of today. On top of all of this, public opinion and essential consumer support can change rapidly.

The book is helpfully divided into three parts. In the first, each technology is reviewed in a chapter written by a relevant expert. It is encouraging to see the often-neglected topic of heat pumps well covered. It is difficult to understand how this important technology has gained such widespread use in Scandinavian countries, while remaining relatively unknown in the UK. Perhaps this book will do something to redress that balance. It is also encouraging to see the attention paid to energy efficiency, an area where investment can deliver high returns but which often loses out in the competition for capital to growth in other areas. Energy efficiency is at least half of the solution to a lower-carbon economy and is an essential partner to almost every technology.

The second part of the book covers the development of various investment vehicles, from bonds to exchange-traded funds, as well as the question of asset allocation. There is a thorough review of carbon markets in general and the European market in particular.

The third section covers the regulatory framework. An understanding of this essential driver of investment and of how frameworks may evolve is essential to both practitioners and investors. The likely evolution of frameworks presents both risks and opportunities to what are long-term investments. This section also contains case studies by different investors ranging from public pension funds to other institutional investors. There is also a chapter making the link through desalination to that other great resource challenge of our time – water.

I welcome this contribution to increasing the knowledge and understanding of investors in what is an important part of our future.

Sir Mark Moody-Stuart KCMG, PhD, MA, FGS, is Chairman of the Global Compact Foundation and former chairman, Shell Group and Anglo American plc

Making the transition to a Green Economy

Achim Steiner

The world and the financial world are both going through one of the most challenging moments in history. Climate change is accelerating and, unless checked, promises to be the greatest market failure of all time. This is also a time of reflection on the urgent need for all countries to catalyse a defining and definitive response to the sustainability challenges which now face 7 billion people.

The world of the here and now is light years from the world of the late 20th century – geopolitically, socially, economically and environmentally. It underlines that a transition to a Green Economy is the responsibility of not only central, but also local and regional governments, as well as the private sector and civil society – a central consideration for Rio+20 and a litmus test of leadership at all levels.

Rio+20's two themes are a Green Economy in the context of sustainable development and poverty eradication and an institutional framework for sustainable development. UNEP's Green Economy report[1] underlines that if the world invested 2% of GDP in 10 key sectors, backed by the right enabling policies, economies could grow but without the shocks and risks inherent in the current economic model.

The report, compiled in collaboration with economists and a multitude of partners, comprehensively challenges the myth of a trade-off between environmental investments and economic growth and instead points to a current "gross misallocation of capital".

For example, investing about 1.25% of global GDP each year in energy efficiency and renewable energies could cut global primary energy demand by 9% in 2020 and close to 40% by 2050, says the report. In addition:

- Employment levels in the energy sector would be one-fifth higher than under a business-as-usual scenario as renewable energies take close to 30% of the share of primary global energy demand by mid-century.
- Savings on capital and fuel costs in power generation would, under a Green Economy scenario, be on average $760 billion a year between 2010 and 2050.

Several 'big ticket' items are also being examined and proposed by countries, companies and civil society, including:

- Phasing down or phasing out more than $600 billion worth of annual fossil fuel subsidies; and

---

1 UNEP, 2011, *Towards a Green Economy: Pathways to Sustainable Development and Poverty Eradication*, www.unep.org/greeneconomy.

- Accelerating green procurement by governments. By some estimates, if government spending is over 20% in an economy, it could, if directed into environmentally-friendly products and services, tip the rest of the economy into the sustainability space.

The world is at one of those proverbial crossroads where some tough and transformative choices need to be made. Choices that will be remembered by future generations as representing a time when today's world leaders took up the challenge, decided upon the means of implementation and seized the opportunity for a sustainable 21st century so that the ideas and ideals of nearly 20 years ago are finally fulfilled.

The challenge is to encourage, accelerate and scale up these transitions to a low-carbon, resource-efficient Green Economy that is manifesting itself everywhere. When UNEP launched its Global Green New Deal/Green Economy initiative in 2008, I do not think we or anyone else could have imagined how far and how fast it would evolve and become a hot currency of international discourse.

While the formal climate negotiation process struggles, climate science continues to consolidate – with shortening timelines and escalating risk implications for the planet, its people and their economies. Notwithstanding the science gaps and uncertainties, we need to insure our futures through rational risk management.

Climate actions are gaining pace across regions, sectors and actors but are insufficient to prevent average global temperatures rising by more than 2°C. While encouraging trends can be found in areas from renewable energies, hybrid cars and improved energy efficiency to sustainable forestry and waste recycling they are still marginal to the overall emissions footprint of our global economy.

Addressing climate change needs to be understood in the broader context of reorienting our economies and delivering multiple benefits, for the same investment, from increased and decent job opportunities to reduced air pollution as well as a low-carbon world – in short a transition towards a low-carbon, resource-efficient Green Economy

A Green Economy needs to be understood as relevant to developing as it is to developed countries and offer transformational policy levers applicable at the national level but also as part of a cooperative deal between nations. One thinks of phasing down or phasing out fossil fuel and other subsidies to energy diversification; faster energy access, REDD+ and green public procurement.

The Green Economy also offers a pathway to mobilise the necessary finance, re-directing financial flows into the 'real economy'. Global investors will play a key role in providing the capital required for sustainable growth and the transition to a low-carbon economy.

I welcome the second edition of this publication as an important resource for the many global institutional and individual investors who are yet to realise the potential that will arise from the creation of a more sustainable world.

Achim Steiner, UN Under-Secretary-General and Executive Director of the UN Environment Programme (UNEP)

Investing in a low-carbon world: a view from the British government

Gregory Barker

The green economy offers a massive new business opportunity for the UK. This coalition government fully understands this potential and is determined to show real and global leadership on this agenda and to make good on Prime Minister David Cameron's pledge to be the greenest British government ever.

When we came into government we made it our urgent priority to reduce the fiscal deficit and put the UK on the path to sustainable growth both financially and environmentally. I firmly believe that these are not mutually exclusive goals and the early signs are indeed encouraging.

Britain's low-carbon environmental goods and services market is the sixth largest in the world and grew by 4.3% in 2009. It is now worth £112 billion ($175 billion), employing over 900,000 people. Over the next decade we will see tens of billions of pounds of investment heading for this sector, which will generate tens of thousands of new green jobs. The shift to a low-carbon economy represents a huge opportunity for UK exports too. The global market for low-carbon goods and services is currently worth £3.2 trillion and is estimated to grow to more than £4 trillion by 2015.

What is crucial is that the right framework is put in place to drive green growth across all sectors of the economy. Thriving, innovating and high-growth low-carbon businesses will be and should be the hallmark of a globally competitive, 21st century economy in Britain.

To make this happen this government is focusing on four key areas:

- Firstly, we are using policy to create new markets that will stimulate new investment. The Green Deal will mobilise billions of pounds of private sector investment to improve the energy efficiency of our building stock and create up to 150,000 green industry jobs by 2015.
- Secondly, we are making existing markets work better. Our reforms of the electricity market will reduce risks and increase certainty for investors to bring forward the £110 billion needed in electricity generation infrastructure.
- Thirdly, we need to make the most of the expertise that we have in the City of London to develop innovative green and low-carbon finance and break

down the barriers to global green investment. In 2010 I launched the Capital Markets Climate Initiative, bringing together key players from the City of London with international financiers and policy-makers, to discuss practical steps to unleash private capital and make green investment the best option in all economies. I see no reason why the City of London, with its unique expertise in innovative financial products, can't lead the world and become the global hub for green growth finance.
- Finally, we're clear that we can't achieve this low-carbon transition alone. This is a global push and one that can only succeed if governments, economies and companies work together to provide investors with the greatest certainty to invest in low-carbon technologies.

The move to a new low-carbon economy offers great opportunities that we in Britain are serious about capturing. Britain stands ready to work with business and investors from all corners of the globe to make a prosperous and sustainable new economy a reality.

GREGORY BARKER
Minister of State, UK Department of Energy and Climate Change

Introduction

We are now living at an unprecedented point in time where public and political awareness of our environment and the power of our climate to cause significant risk to humanity and the societies we live in has never been higher. A core part of many political leaders' messages to their citizens is that long-term and sustainable economic growth can be achieved, in part, by increasing investment in the technologies, infrastructure and services that will form a central part of the transition to a low-carbon world.

It is also increasingly clear that corporations will have no choice but to pay for their negative environmental impacts and externalities by governments and consumers. This will have implications for profitability and creditworthiness and will therefore have a direct effect on the market value of their securities, affecting the risk and expected returns of investors' multi-asset portfolios. The implications of this for the global economy are immense and the opportunities that this will create for investors from global institutional pension funds, insurance companies and fund managers, as well as individual investors, are becoming more and more apparent. This book's objective is to provide a view, from leading global experts, on the key features, risks and investment outlooks for the leading environmental technologies that are pointing the way to a low-carbon global economy.

The book is arranged, for ease of reading, into three sections. The first section is dedicated to some of the established and leading low-carbon technologies and services, the second looks at some of the tools and investment vehicles that are available to investors and the third section contains a view on the regulatory and political outlook as well as case studies from institutional investors and leading companies that are committing capital and investing in developing environmental products and services.

As readers will no doubt become aware as they read through this book, the positions of governments on supporting this transition by policy, incentives and taxation will have a direct bearing on the confidence of investors in the sector. The British government has long been seen as a leader in the development of climate related policy initiatives and I am grateful to the Minister of State for Climate Change, Gregory Barker, for kindly providing an overview of the UK's policy.

Section 1
Section 1 highlights the main environmental technologies and their investment cases. Mark Thompson provides a detailed overview of the key features and growth potential of the wind, hydro and biomass energy sectors. Dr Matthias Fawer provides a detailed overview of the technologies and outlooks for the global solar power indus-

try and discusses the key differences between solar photovoltaic and solar thermal, commenting on the drivers and relative potential of each. Alexander Richter examines the opportunities for geothermal energy, highlighting the US market as a key example of the potential for this renewable clean energy source.

Dr Daniel Wild, Marc-Olivier Buffle and Junwei Hafner-Cai provide a fascinating view of the global water market, which is of increasing interest to many investors as clean potable water becomes a resource at risk in many parts of the world. Water is one natural resource that is expected to be profoundly affected by climate change in terms of availability, access and quality. This is of great interest to investors as many companies across many different industry sectors are reliant on access to water for their products and services. Erich Becker of Zouk Capital then outlines the wide range of investment opportunities in renewable energy and environmental infrastructure and the various drivers and risks facing this sector.

Philip Wolfe provides an insight into the potential for heat pumps as an emerging technology for heating domestic and commercial residences and discusses some of the key features of these systems. Mark Fulton and Bruce Kahn of Deutsche Bank Climate Change Advisors examine climate change as a 'megatrend' and explore the impacts on a range of asset classes. Improved energy efficiency has been described as critical in reducing global emissions. Zoë Knight discusses the role of energy efficiency products and services, how they are developing and the role of political and regulatory incentives. Simon Fox of Mercer Investment Consulting covers the opportunities for sustainable timberland investment.

Section 2

Section 2 provides the reader with information on the ways that investors can identify, analyse and track the performance of those companies operating in and providing services to environmental markets.

Firstly, Dr Danyelle Guyatt and Laureen Bird cover the issues for integrating climate risk and low-carbon investment opportunities into institutional investors' long-term asset allocation processes. Ian Simm of Impax Asset Management then provides an overview of the investment characteristics of environmental markets and different investment strategies. David Harris discusses the performance measurement tools for environmental markets, including how to identify and track the performance of companies. Lillian Goldthwaite provides an easy to understand description of how exchange traded funds work and how investors can utilise these increasingly popular instruments to gain access to the performance of environmental markets. Sean Kidney, Stuart Clenaghan and Padraig Oliver examine the issues and the investment case for 'Green Bonds' and the emerging standards around definitions of green projects. Dr Xinting Jia discusses carbon risk and carbon trading and the considerations for institutional investors.

David Peniket of ICE Futures Europe provides an overview of the European carbon emissions market, including how that market functions and operates. Simon Thomas and Liesel van Ast discuss the merits of carbon intensity as a measurement of the carbon efficiency of companies and how this can be used by investors.

Section 3
The final section of the book takes a longer-term view from a regulatory risk and opportunity perspective. In addition, there are a number of case studies from both corporates and investors, looking at what leading investors are doing today about their approaches to the investment opportunity from low-carbon technologies.

Kirsty Hamilton provides the all-important policy and regulatory overview. Louise Moore and Henry Davey highlight the various renewable energy incentive mechanisms in place around the world. Professor Michael Mainelli, James Palmer and Liang Shi discuss how to structure an investment portfolio for a low-carbon world. David Russell, Marcel Jeucken and Pieter van Stijn, and Winston Hickox all provide case studies from leading institutional investor perspectives in the UK, Netherlands and US respectively.

Also highlighted are case studies from major industry players Nissan and Degrémont, which discuss their environmental technology services, the business rationale and the technological developments and challenges to be overcome by them in the motor transport and desalination sectors.

The purpose and objective of this book is to raise the awareness and knowledge of a wider pool of potential investors and advisers to the exciting investment potential that the transition to a global low-carbon economy will bring. Although many technology and service businesses are still in their relative infancy, there are many mature and well-managed businesses in the sector. There are also a number of multinational companies that have, within their business portfolios, growing and profitable environmental businesses. All of these companies will benefit from the private capital provided from the public markets, where they can access a diverse group of investors, with long-term investment interests who will act as supportive shareholders to company boards and executive management. In return, shareholders should benefit from long-term and sustainable earnings growth.

There are many environmental technologies and services that have been developed or are under development; however, this book focuses on those that are of most interest and are most accessible to investors in public markets. Other asset classes to which investors may also look for exposure to the performance of environmental market opportunities – such as timberland – which are also covered in the book.

I hope that readers enjoy learning more about the growing and exciting investment opportunities emerging from the technological and innovative approaches to address the world's serious environmental challenges. I invite you to start that journey by testing your knowledge with a short and fun 'Environmental Markets Quiz. The answers can be found at the end of the book on page 394.

Environmental markets quiz

Provided by Mark Thompson, Tiptree Investments

1. Which was the warmest year, in the warmest decade, in the warmest century during the last millennium?
   A. 1862   B. 1998   C. 1976   D. 1799

2. Low-E windows prevent warmth escaping in winter and block heat from the sun in summer. A low-E coating can reduce energy use by?
   A. 25%   B. 35%   C. 50%   D. 60%

3. Incandescent light bulbs are being replaced with compact fluorescent lights (CFLs) to save energy – how much less energy does a CFL use?
   A. 25% less   B. 50% less   C. 67% less   D. 75% less

4. Recycling one aluminium can saves enough energy to power a TV for?
   A. 3 seconds   B. 3 mins   C. 3 hours   D. 3 days

5. According to the US National Center for Disease Control, what percentage of all childhood illnesses is related to air quality?
   A. 10%   B. 40%   C. 85%   D. 5%

6. An average American produces 4.4lbs of rubbish every day – what fraction of this is produced by the average European and the average Indian respectively?
   A. 36%/15%   B. 48%/22%   C. 60%/27%   D. 72%/33%

7. In 1995, how many tons of volatile organic compounds (VOCs) were emitted in the US from hair-care products?
   A. 180   B. 18,000   C. 185,000   D. 1,800,000

8. Air pollution shortens the life expectancy of the average Briton by how many months?
   A. 18   B. 3   C. 12   D. 8

9. GM was the proud maker of the Hummer. What was the official EPA mileage rating for the Hummer H1?
   A. Unknown   B. 14mpg   C. 18mpg   D. 8mpg

10. How much carbon dioxide (CO$_2$) is created per passenger on an average flight from London to New York?
    A. 47kg   B. 251kg   C. 728kg   D. 989kg

11. The US has 4.6% of the world's population. What proportion of the world's oil is consumed by Americans?
    A. 10%   B. 40%   C. 7.5%   D. 25%

12. How many photocopies could be produced from the energy used by a photocopier left on overnight?
    A. 100   B. 10,000   C. 1,500   D. 50

13. On average, what percentage of revenue goes into wasted energy costs for UK businesses?
    A. 2.3%   B. 0.7%   C. 4.5%   D. 1.5%

14. Which country has the highest CO$_2$ emissions per capita?
    A. Kuwait   B. UAE   C. Australia   D. US

15. The heat energy in the top 10km of the Earth's crust is equivalent to how many times the total energy stored in all the world's oil and gas?
    A. 50,000×   B. 500×   C. 5×   D. 0.5×

16. Emissions trading is a key concept in reducing greenhouse gases. Which country invented it?
    A. Germany   B. Sweden   C. Norway   D. US

17. For many years California has actively encouraged energy efficiency. An average person in the US consumes ~12,400 kWh/year. What percentage of this does the average Californian consume?
    A. 17%   B. 57%   C. 77%   D. 107%

18. How many litres of water are required on average to produce each of the following products?
    1kg of beef:
    A. 15   B. 155   C. 1,550   D. 15,500
    1kg of roasted coffee:
    A. 21   B. 210   C. 2,100   D. 21,000
    One bushel of maize:
    A. 23   B. 229   C. 2,290   D. 22,900

19. Approximately what percentage of the energy contained in one barrel of oil extracted from Canada's tar sands is required to extract and upgrade that oil to usable synthetic crude?
    A. 8%   B. 18%   C. 28%   D. 38%

20. The UK estimates its first 19 nuclear sites will cost £74 billion to decommission over the next 100 years, or £44 billion in present value terms. The 12 power stations had an effective capacity of almost 4.3GW. Approximately what percentage of the UK's current 80GW of generating capacity would £44 billion invested in wind farm shares represent?
    A. 153%   B. 53%   C. 35%   D. 5.3%

21. The 'neon' adverts above Piccadilly Circus are world famous and each one nets the landlord around £2 million per year in rent. How much CO_2 is released each year from generating the electricity required to power them?
    A. 1,900kg   B. 19 tonnes   C. 190 tonnes   D. 1,900 tonnes

22. Carbon intensity measures tonnes of CO_2 emitted each year per dollar of GDP created. This reflects a country's energy efficiency and energy mix (and degree of industrialisation). Trinidad & Tobago is worst at 6.29t/$, while Namibia is 'best' at 0t/$. The worst developed country is Australia at 2.07t/$, followed by the US at 1.77t/$. Switzerland is best – how much more efficient is it than Australia?
    A. 1.4×   B. 3.4×   C. 5.4×   D. 7.4×

23. It takes 70% less energy to recycle paper than to make it from virgin fibre. How much Christmas wrapping paper does the UK throw away each year (Hint: it could cover an area larger than Guernsey)?
    A. 8,300m²   B. 83,000m²   C. 830,000m²   D. 83km²

24. Assuming it could be captured, how much of the sunlight falling on the Earth would need to be captured to provide the energy needs of the entire population for one year?
    A. One hour   B. Two days   C. Three weeks   D. Four months

Section 1

Environmental and Low-Carbon Technologies

Chapter 1

Wind power

Mark Thompson, Tiptree Investments

Introduction

Wind is a vast source of energy that should never run out. Wind energy, after being harnessed for thousands of years, has grown spectacularly in recent years. The first wind powered electricity was generated in 1888. By the end of 2010, global wind turbine capacity was over 199 gigawatts (GW)[1] and it provided ~2.4% of global electricity, or 409TWh[2].

Wind power is favoured since it is widely available, clean and easily integrated with existing infrastructure. Although it is intermittent, it is not unpredictable and

Figure 1. Global installed wind capacity and annual growth rates

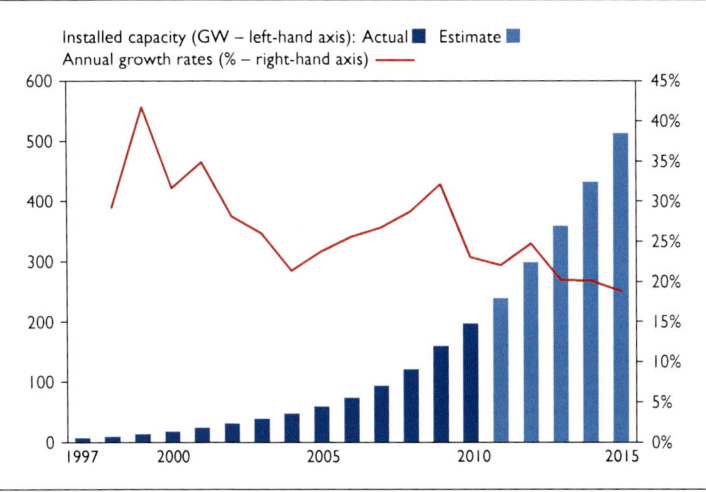

Source: BTM Consult/Tiptree Investments

---

1 One GW equals 1,000 megawatts (MW) and 1MW equals 1,000 kilowatts (kW). On average, 1MW is sufficient to support 750–1,000 western homes. A terawatt (TW) is 1,000GW. Gigawatts, megawatts and kilowatts are all measures of power and represent a rate of energy conversion.
2 One terawatt hour (TWh) is 1 million megawatt hours (MWh) or 1 billion kilowatt hours (kWh). These are all units of energy.

the existing grid can usually cope with penetration rates of up to 20%, with higher percentages possible through relatively simple grid upgrades. Globally, wind energy is forecast to reach 2,300GW of installed capacity by 2030. Europe alone expects to reach 230GW of wind capacity by the end of 2020 (190GW onshore and 40GW offshore), or some 14–17% of the EU's electricity.

In 2010, China increased its annual installation by 37.7% and was the world's leader for the second year running after adding 18.9GW of new wind power capacity, to reach a total installed capacity of 44.7GW. Historically, the other large market was the US, but wind turbine installation fell from 9.9GW in 2009 to 5.1GW in 2010 due to the impact of the recession and financial crisis on project financing. At the time of writing, 83 countries are using wind power commercially and the wind sector generated around €40 billion in 2010. Denmark, Spain and Germany currently lead the world in terms of the proportion of their electricity obtained from wind power.

Commercial wind power began seriously in the 1980s, and over the past 20 years the average turbine size grew by a factor of over 100, while per megawatt costs fell more than 90%. From machines of 20–60kW in the early 1980s, with rotor diameters of 20 metres, wind turbines have grown to 7MW with rotors of over 120 metres. The dramatic increase in size, technology and economies of scale from growing production volumes has reduced wind power's cost to the point where

Figure 2. Global installed capacity by country

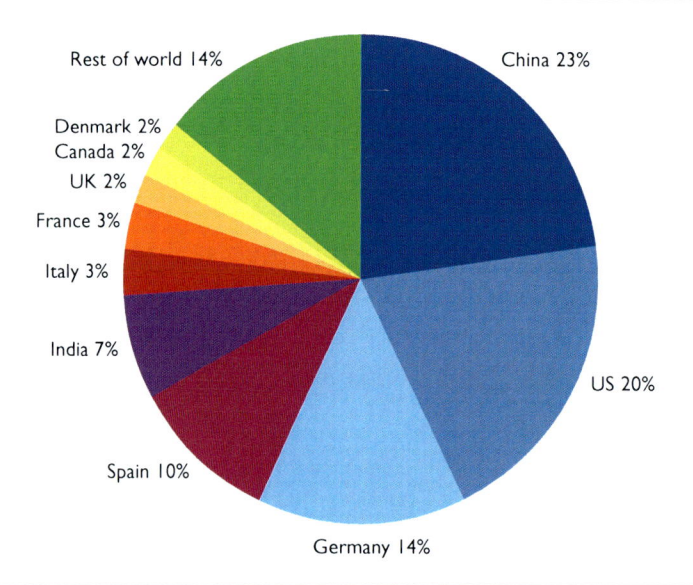

- China 23%
- US 20%
- Germany 14%
- Rest of world 14%
- Spain 10%
- India 7%
- Italy 3%
- France 3%
- UK 2%
- Canada 2%
- Denmark 2%

Source: Global Wind Energy Council

many onshore wind farms are price competitive with conventional generation, especially in markets such as India.

RISE OF THE EMERGING MARKETS

As western economies slowed following the credit crunch, the market shifted to China and subsequently India. Favourable policies, encouraging energy independence and manufacturing growth supported the move, especially in China. In parallel, India introduced a range of pragmatic renewable energy incentives, that are now seeing the market rapidly accelerate.

What is a wind turbine?

Wind turbines are a natural evolution from traditional windmills, but are now designed to generate high-quality, network frequency electricity, while operating continuously, unattended and with little maintenance, for more than 20 years. An operational turbine will typically have running costs of less than $0.01 per kWh.

Rotors usually consist of three blades, with the speed and power controlled by stall or pitch regulation. The rotor can be attached to the generator via a gearbox and drive train, or directly through an arrangement known as 'direct drive'. Turbines that operate at varying speeds are becoming increasingly common, because of their higher efficiency. Rotor blades are typically made from glass polyester or

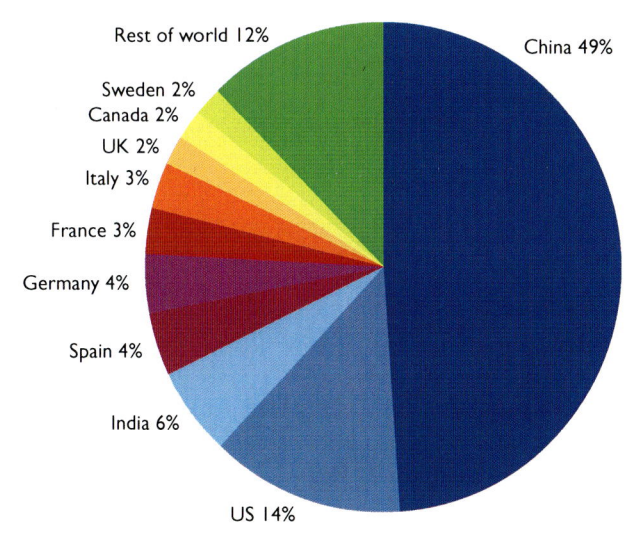

Figure 3. New capacity installed in 2010 by country

Source: Global Wind Energy Council

Figure 4. Components of a typical wind turbine

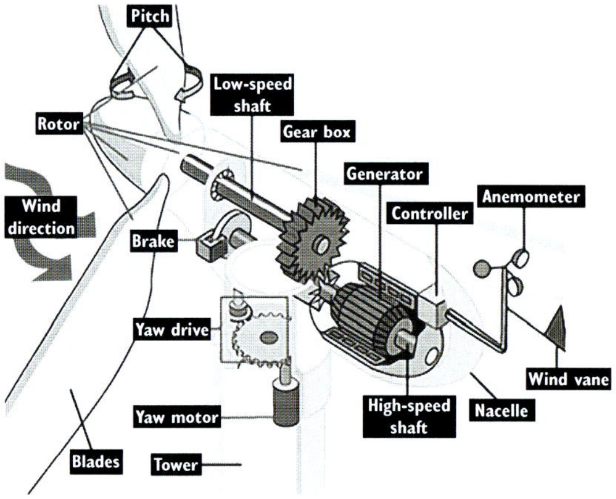

Source: US Department of Energy

glass epoxy, sometimes in combination with wood or carbon fibre.

The tubular towers supporting the nacelle and rotor are typically made of steel and taper from their base to the nacelle at the top. Wind turbines are mounted on high towers to optimise energy capture, as the wind is generally stronger, more consistent and less turbulent higher up.

Instruments on the nacelle include anemometers and a wind vane to measure wind speed and direction. When the wind changes its direction, motors turn the nacelle, and the blades along with it, to face into the wind, thereby maximising energy extraction. All this information is recorded by computers and transmitted to a control centre that is often located many kilometres away, meaning that the wind turbines are not physically staffed, although each gets a periodic mechanical check. The onboard computers also monitor the performance of each turbine component, especially the blades, and automatically shut down the turbine if problems are detected.

HOW BIG IS THE RESOURCE?
Wind is primarily caused by the uneven heating of the Earth by the sun: the poles receive less energy than the equator and dry land heats up (or cools down) faster than the oceans. This differential heating drives global atmospheric convection from the Earth's surface to the stratosphere. Most of the wind's energy is found at high altitudes, where continuous wind speeds of over 160 kilometres per hour (100 mph) occur. However, even modest changes in height can materially increase the available resource. Research by Stanford University suggests that 72TW of wind power could be commercially viable, compared to the 16TW of energy that the world currently consumes on average.

TURBINE POWER

Most turbines start generating electricity at wind speeds of 3–4 metres per second (m/s), generate their maximum 'rated' power at approximately 13 m/s and shut down to prevent damage around 25 m/s[3]. Large areas of the world have mean annual wind speeds above 4–5 m/s, which makes wind power widely available and flexible.

A turbine's power is proportional to:
- the cube of the wind speed;
- the area swept by the blades; and,
- the density of the air (which varies with altitude, temperature and humidity).

Wind speed is the most important factor, as doubling the speed increases the energy eight-fold. However, blade length is also important, as doubling the blade length increases the swept area by a factor of four and hence the power output goes up by a factor of four. As a result, the size of the average wind turbine has increased significantly, with most recent demand for megawatt-class machines, due to economies of scale and the ability to target regions with lower average wind speeds.

Nowadays, wind turbines of over 5MW are running, though most new turbines are still in the 1–2MW range. Larger machines bring economies of scale and, for a

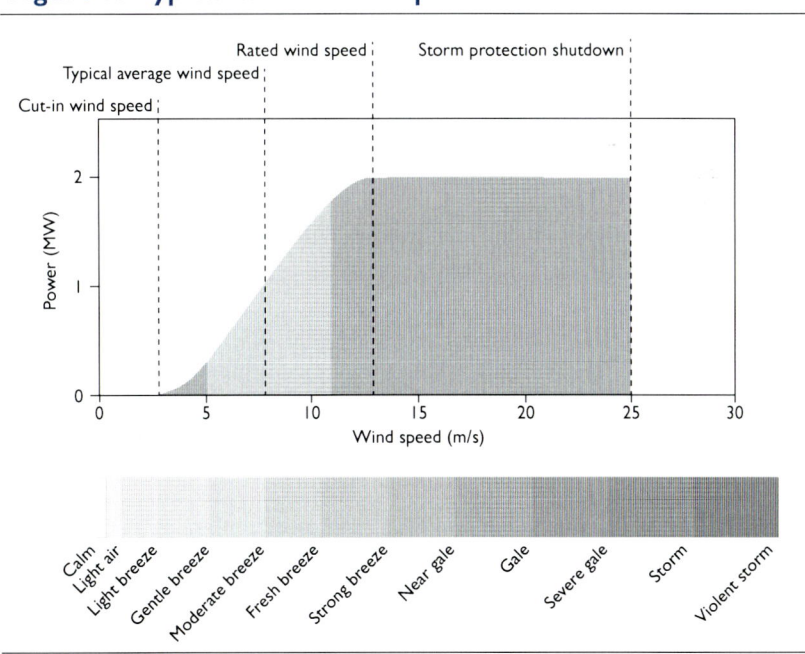

Figure 5. Typical wind turbine power curve

Source: British Wind Energy Association

---

[3] Start at 7–9 miles per hour, maximum power at 33 mph and shut down at 56 mph.

Figure 6. Rotor size and height impact on output relative to a 10-metre hub

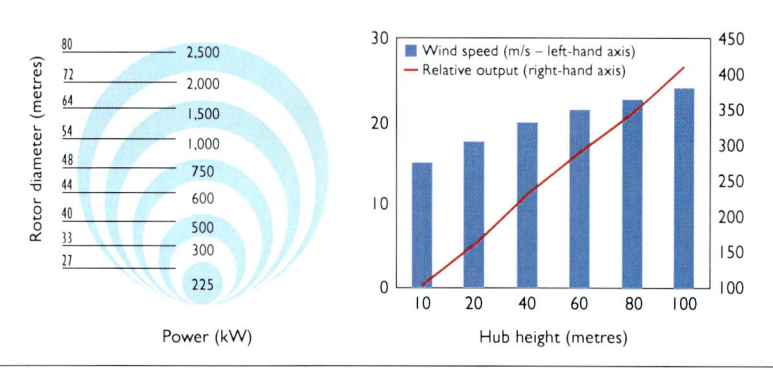

Source: Airtricity

given capacity, they are less visually intrusive than numerous smaller machines. Figure 6 illustrates the relationship between rotor size and power output – a 40-metre rotor generates 0.5MW of power, while an 80-metre rotor generates 2.5MW of power. It also shows the substantial difference an increase in hub height brings due to the faster and less turbulent air found further off the ground.

There are several turbine designs, but the most common operational design is the upwind, three-bladed, stall-controlled, constant-speed machine. However, most new projects are now using pitch-controlled, variable-speed machines, with a small, but growing number of turbines using direct drive. Niche manufacturers continue to produce two-bladed turbines and other concepts, such as the vertical axis ('eggbeater') design.

Since wind turbines are designed to produce electricity as cheaply as possible, they usually reach their maximum output at wind speeds of 30 knots (35 mph). Designing for maximum output at higher speeds is uneconomic, as these winds are rare, but when they do occur, it is necessary to prevent damage to the turbine through some form of power control:

- *Pitch control* uses a computer to actively adjust the angle of blades, to maximise the extracted power or, if the wind is too fast, to reduce their aerodynamic efficiency. Pitch-controlled machines are variable speed and require more complex engineering, which increases their cost.
- *Stall control* is a passive system with the blades set at a permanent angle of attack and no moving parts required to adjust their pitch. The blade's twist and thickness vary along its length and its aerodynamics set the power output. The design increases the turbulence behind the blades as the wind speed increases, which reduces the power the turbine can extract. Stall control avoids moving parts in the rotor and a complex control system, but it requires complex aerodynamics,

it is less efficient across the power curve and stall-induced vibration may impact the entire turbine.
- *Active stall control* uses a few fixed blade pitch angles to maximise power at low wind speeds. When its rated speed is reached, the angle of attack is increased (the opposite of pitch-controlled machines) to put the blades into a deep stall, thereby using up excess energy. Active stall can control its power output more accurately than passive stall and offers power curve efficiency between passive stall and pitch control. As with pitch control, it is economics that decide the value of the additional complexity.

It is expected that more variable-speed machines will be produced in the coming years with the growth in utility-scale plants. While the power electronics are more challenging, the machines tend to generate more power for any given wind speed and there is less system wear.

Turbine design and production

Turbine manufacturing was a concentrated market. In 2007, six suppliers covered 84% of the market. Since then, the rise of Chinese manufacturers on the back of domestic incentives has fragmented the market, with 10 suppliers in 2010 covering 83% of the market. This has expanded the number of manufacturers quoted on the stock market and driven down returns. Vestas is still considered the market leader,

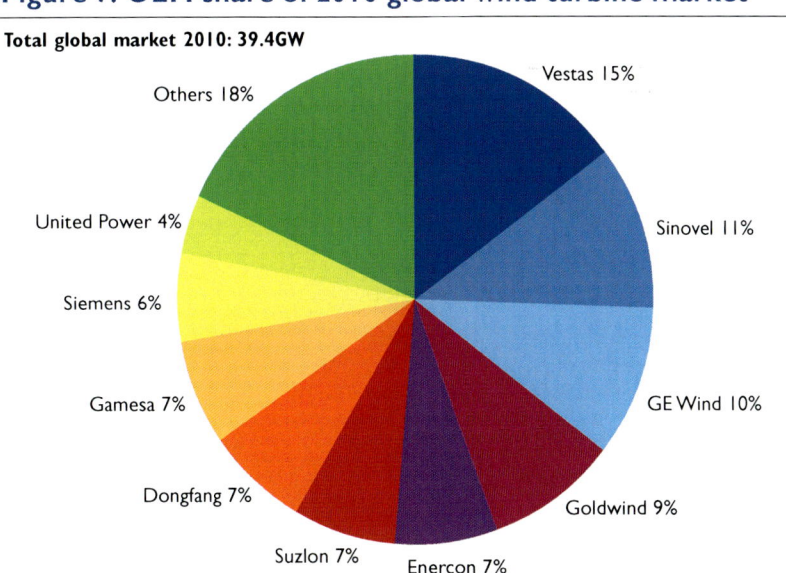

Figure 7. OEM share of 2010 global wind turbine market

Total global market 2010: 39.4GW

- Vestas 15%
- Sinovel 11%
- GE Wind 10%
- Goldwind 9%
- Enercon 7%
- Suzlon 7%
- Dongfang 7%
- Gamesa 7%
- Siemens 6%
- United Power 4%
- Others 18%

Source: BTM Consult

as it has one of the best technology portfolios and, with over 40,000 turbines operating, it is the most established supplier. In general, turbine makers need a minimum sales base to afford the warranties required by the project finance market and to spread the substantial research and development costs across a large revenue base.

NEW ENTRANTS
The cost of bringing a turbine to commercial maturity limits the opportunity for new entrants to the global original equipment manufacturer (OEM) wind turbine market, outside of controlled markets such as China. Several new entrants are still trying to establish themselves, by offering incremental improvements and an alternative to the dominant players. However, there are concerns over their ability to achieve scale, as:
- most project developers require a proven technology, with verifiable operational data over several years, credible after-sales support and a balance sheet able to support the warranty;
- sales are only likely to developers (ie, utilities) able to fund projects on their balance sheets, or government-sponsored projects, due to the difficulty in securing credit for unproven technology;
- the technical challenges of designing a machine that withstands continually variable mechanical loads, is lightweight and able to operate on a vibrating platform should not be underestimated; and
- public market disclosure can make technology development unusually difficult, as normal engineering setbacks may disproportionately impact a company's reputation, compared to a private company.

DIRECT DRIVE
Since the first edition of this book, direct drive turbines have increased their market share, primarily through Goldwind's success in China, but also as a couple of manufacturers developed the technology as a means to improve reliability and broaden

Figure 8. Direct drive pros and cons

Advantages	Disadvantages
No gearbox and less wear on mechanical components	Larger nacelle makes installation harder
Simpler design, fewer parts and more reliable	Higher top mass weight – tower costs go up
Permanent magnets offer higher electrical efficiency	Expensive permanent magnets with supply chain risk. Risk of losing magnetism at high temperatures
Improved thermal efficiency (no field losses)	More advanced cooling system required
Full power conversion improves grid compatibility	Full power conversion increases capex

product offerings. Direct drive technology has gained traction as permanent magnet generators became more readily available and power electronics improved their ability to cope with variable frequency power.

At present the economic case for direct drive remains to be established unequivocally. Direct drive turbines are generally heavier than conventional turbines and gearboxes have become far more reliable, while permanent magnet supply chain risk has increased with China's near monopoly on the neodymium needed in their manufacture.

COMPONENT MANUFACTURING

In the supply chain there are few pure play investment opportunities, as most turbine manufacturers keep strategic manufacturing in-house and the vast number (~8,000) of small components creates little pricing power. Most suppliers are part of larger industrial companies and tend to produce 'commoditised' goods, since the main turbine manufacturers keep key intellectual property-related production in-house.

Blades and control systems are typically produced in-house, while generators, gearboxes and inverters are sourced externally. The reliability problems that the whole industry faced with gearboxes have tended to keep this contracted to a few major providers. Overall, the trend is towards more in-house production, as manufacturers seek to control quality and internalise margins, but notable component

Figure 9. Main component suppliers for leading OEMs

OEM	Blades	Gearboxes	Generators	Controllers	Towers
Vestas	*IH*, LM Glasfiber	Bosch, Hansen, Winergy, Moventas	*IH*, Elin, ABB, LeroySomer	*IH*	*IH*
GE	LM Glasfiber, Tecsis, MFG, TPI	*IH*, Winergy, Bosch, Eickhoff, Moventas, China High Speed	*IH*, ABB, VEM	*IH*	DMI, Omnical, Siag
Gamesa	*IH*, LM Glasfiber	*IH*, Winergy, Hansen, Bosch	*IH*, ABB, Ingeteam	*IH*, Ingeteam	*IH*
Enercon	*IH*	na	*IH*	*IH*	KGW, SAM
Siemens	*IH*	Winergy, Hansen	*IH*, ABB	*IH*, KK Electronic	Roug, KGW
Suzlon	*IH*	Hansen, Winergy, China High Speed	*IH*, Siemens	*IH*, Mita Teknik	*IH*
Sinovel	LM Glasfiber, Zhongfu	Hansen, Dalian, Wikov, China High Speed	Dalian, Lanzhou, Yongji, Elin	Windtec	nk
Goldwind	LM, Huiteng, Sinoma	Chongqing, China High Speed	CSR, Yongji	*IH*	nk
Nordex	*IH*, LM, Sinoi	Bosch, Eikohoff, Winergy, China High Speed	VEM, Winergy, Elin	*IH*, Mita Teknik	nk

IH = In-house; Winergy is owned by Siemens, Source: BTM Consult

suppliers are LM Glasfiber, with a 27% market share in blade manufacturing, along with Hansen Transmissions and China High Speed Transmissions in gearboxes. Other minor players include Hanwei Energy Services, which is using its experience in GRP (fibre glass/plastic) pipe to produce blades; Zoltek, which provides carbon fibre for blades (and other industries), and a host of Chinese manufacturers surging straight into megawatt-class machines, with some licensed European designs (such as Goldwind/Vensys).

PRODUCTION COSTS
In 2007–08, strong global demand, due to rising energy prices and new tariffs, along with increases in commodity prices (steel and cement) meant that turbine prices on a per megawatt basis rose materially, after 20 years of falling prices. This subsequently reversed as production capacity outstripped demand and China's local content rules kept its growth in the hands of domestic players. These companies subsequently achieved critical mass and drove margins down. While quality remains an issue, along with questions over warranties, Chinese manufacturers have reshaped the industry and shattered the comfortable oligopoly that had developed.

Historically, wind power's costs per unit of electricity have fallen by 9–17% each time total capacity doubled. For example, on a reasonable wind site on the coast, the cost has dropped from €92/MWh using a 95kW turbine in the 1980s to €45/MWh for a modern 2MW machine. Typically, the turbine manufacturers expect production costs to fall by 3–5% for each new generation of machine.

Wind project development

Numerous wind farm developers and operators are now active in the market. Some are publicly quoted, others are venture backed. Utilities are also making their presence felt. Historically, development was best done by small, entrepreneurial firms that could balance cash against development pipeline risk. Most large wind power companies still depend on these companies, as utilities have a poor record in building small, but economically attractive, renewable energy projects.

In some markets, small wind farm development has stalled, as utilities concentrate their resources on much larger projects. This is most noticeable in the UK, where the offshore opportunity has dragged in resources, creating a gap in the market between utility-scale projects and small, local community-scale projects.

Development is an area that the quoted market finds difficult to value sensibly, partly due to a lack of experience and partly the inevitable disclosure limitations on projects still in development. As a result, private equity firms and trade investors have a real advantage in their ability to do thorough due diligence on a development portfolio. While the development process offers some of the best returns in the sector, the quality of disclosure varies substantially and headline figures between portfolios are rarely comparable.

THE DEVELOPMENT PROCESS
Taking a green field site through to construction typically offers the best returns. Wind project development has several well-defined steps. These include prospecting, optioning land, wind and environmental studies, securing a power purchase agreement (PPA), finance and construction:

- Prospecting involves finding a site with good wind resources. Several wind atlases have been created so far to help this process. However, prospecting also requires an on-site topographical assessment to identify features that might reduce the resource (woods, towns) or cause planning problems (airfields, TV masts). Once the site is identified, it is typically secured under option for three to four years.
- A detailed wind study typically requires several measurement devices (wind speed, direction, temperature, humidity) installed at the site. Measurements run for at least one full year and preferably longer. These measurements are then correlated with local data (such as from an airport) going back 20-plus years, to assess the site's long-term potential and to develop a resource forecast. Poor measurement and resource modelling have been consistent factors behind the few wind farms that have underperformed.
- Environmental studies include the effects on local wildlife, noise and vibration, while visual impacts are often a complaint of local community groups. Over the past few years, environmental assessments have tended to delay, rather than stop, wind farm development.
- The most economic projects are those able to secure long-term PPAs (other than in India), as these can often attract project debt finance up to 80%. This will depend on the site quality and the turbine provider.
- The final step is construction, typically via an engineer-procure-construct (EPC) 'turnkey' contract. More experienced developers do their own project management and save ~10% of the EPC cost. Typically, a 20–100MW wind farm can be built inside nine months, depending on the availability of cranes and reasonable weather.

Once a wind farm is running, operations and maintenance costs are relatively low (around 1.5% of capital costs). A design life of 25 years is typically assumed for financial and permitting purposes. In reality, the life of a wind farm is potentially far longer, as repowering turbines can significantly extend the economic operation and the sunk cost of a grid connection makes it unlikely that a site will be abandoned. Once operational, a wind farm can be monitored and controlled remotely with roughly two maintenance people for every 20–30 turbines.

HOW MUCH LAND IS NEEDED?
Even though a wind farm only uses a fraction (3–5%) of its total land area, wind dynamics and equipment size mean that turbines need to be well spaced. Depending on the wind regime, topography and other structures in the area, turbines are

placed three to five rotor diameters apart (300–500 metres). This makes wind farms attractive to many landowners, as livestock can continue using the land, while the rental income amply offsets the small loss of grazing. In other words, an area of 20 × 50 kilometres could have enough turbines to provide 25% of Britain's nameplate capacity, assuming a 5MW machine. This is a large land area for Britain, but small in an offshore context.

WIND TURBINE OPTIMISATION AND RISKS
The revenue created by a wind turbine depends on three factors:
- *Windiness of the site* – the power available from the wind is a function of the cube of its speed. Therefore, a site with an average wind speed of 7 m/s produces around 30% more power than a 6 m/s site. Careful location can substantially change the site's effectiveness. While computer models are becoming more sophisticated, experience and detailed anemometry across the whole site play a major role.
- *Equipment availability* is the ability to operate when the wind is blowing – an indication of the turbine's reliability. This is typically 98% or above for modern machines, although manufacturers tend to warrant less than this (~96%) to reduce their costs.
- *Site layout* is important, so that one turbine does not steal the wind from another. The ideal position for a wind turbine is a smooth hilltop, with a flat clear fetch, at least in the prevailing wind direction.

A number of site constraints could affect the layout of a wind farm, such as land ownership, positioning in relation to roads or overhead lines, the location of inhabited buildings and avoidance of sites of environmental importance. Once these constraints have been determined, the layout of the wind turbines themselves can be set to maximise electricity production while minimising infrastructure and operations and maintenance (O&M) costs. Specialist software has been developed to produce visualisations of how the turbines may appear in the landscape, enabling developers and planners to choose the best visual impact solutions before the project is constructed and model the potential output. Aside from the turbines, the other principal components of a wind farm are foundations for the turbine towers, access roads and the electrical infrastructure to connect with the grid.

OBJECTIONS TO WIND FARMS
Objections to wind farms usually centre on three issues: aesthetics, noise or bird kill. While objections are often driven by the 'Not In My Back Yard' syndrome, rather than objective analysis, there is also an element of truth in all three concerns that is compounded by the industry's unthinking behaviour in the past. Certainly, compared to the impact of conventional energy, the environmental impact of wind power is tiny: it uses no fuel, emits no chemical pollution and the energy used in cre-

ating a wind farm is usually recovered within months of full operation. On average, the whole life cycle[4] of wind power produces about 18kg of carbon dioxide (CO_2) per megawatt hour, compared to coal-fired generation at ~1,000kg CO_2/MWh or nuclear at ~40kg CO_2/MWh.

The risk to birds and bats is often the main objection, as poorly sited wind farms can cause unacceptable mortality rates. However, these wind farms are usually located on flight paths or near feeding or roosting sites. The advent of larger turbines, with slow moving blades, higher hub heights, more widely spaced towers and the avoidance of lattice towers (great perching spots), means that bird kills are negligible compared to other man-made problems, such as pollution. To put the problem in context, on average, for every 1,000 birds killed by anthropogenic causes, 550 are killed by buildings, 100 by domestic cats, 70 by cars, 70 by pesticides and less than one by wind turbines.

Aesthetics may also be an issue. Projects have been delayed for years due to aesthetic concerns – although some, such as the Ardrossan Wind Farm in Scotland, reputedly enhance the area. Beauty is certainly in the eye of the beholder, but careful design and the trend to fewer, but larger, machines means that the worst visual blight found in parts of Spain or California's Altamont Pass can be avoided.

Technological advances have meant that mechanical noise has been practically eliminated and aerodynamic noise vastly reduced. The comment is often made that the only people who hear noise from a wind farm are those not receiving rent from it. Modern turbines are generally very quiet and onshore machines usually have their aerodynamics designed to minimise noise in return for a small loss of efficiency. Older machines can be noisier, although the overall effect is insignificant at a range of a few hundred metres and nothing compared to a conventional generating plant. Good design plus the careful location of any sub-station ('transformer hum') means that noise concerns should not prevent the approval of a wind farm.

What happens when the wind stops?

Electricity is not generated when there is no wind. Although wind power is intermittent, making it non-dispatchable (ie, generation must be taken when it is available), it is not unpredictable. The idea of intermittent generation is often cited as a disadvantage, with a popular question being 'what happens when the wind stops blowing?' The answer is not a lot, as electricity continues to be provided by other forms of generation and utilities can use wind power as a fuel saver, rather than a capacity saver. The electricity system is mostly made up of large power stations and it already copes when one of these large plants goes off line unexpectedly. Equally, the system is used to dealing with fluctuations in demand throughout the day, so that the fluctuations caused by non-firm generation from wind turbines are not noticeable above the normal rises and falls in demand on the system.

---

4 Life cycle analysis calculates the emissions related to construction, process, materials and decommissioning, as well as operation.

WIND ENERGY PENETRATION

Wind energy penetration is the fraction of energy produced by wind compared to the total available generating capacity. There is no set maximum and the limit for a particular grid system depends on existing generating plants, storage capacity, demand management systems, transmission losses and pricing mechanisms. Although there are some technical challenges when incorporating wind power into the grid, studies show that up to 20% of grid power can come from wind power using current systems.

A 2004 study in Minnesota found that adding 1,500MW of wind power to Xcel Energy's system only needed an additional 8MW of conventional generation to deal with the increased variability. Stanford University backed this up in a study that showed that when 10 or more wind farms are interconnected, a third of their total energy can be used as reliable, baseload power. Future improvements, such as increasing the level of grid interconnection, the use of storage technologies or demand-side management, should allow even greater penetration.

Wind economics

Although wind energy economics have changed dramatically over the past 20 years, as the cost of wind power has fallen ~90% over that period, the industry remains relatively immature. Production volumes are tiny compared to the forecast growth and the factors affecting the cost of wind energy are still changing rapidly. The move to large wind farms is also reducing costs due to the spreading of fixed costs (grid connection, transaction costs, operations and maintenance) across a larger revenue base. For instance, with an 8 m/s (~18 mph) average wind speed and identical wind turbine sizes, a 3MW wind project delivers electricity at $59/MWh, while a 51MW project delivers it at $36/MWh – a drop of nearly 40%.

The main cost of producing wind power comes from its construction, as there are no fuel costs. Turbines make up most of the capital cost (~64% onshore and ~50% offshore), although civil works and grid connections are significant. Therefore, the cost per unit of production mainly depends on the construction cost, the cost of capital, the average capacity factor and the total service life, since the marginal cost of wind energy for an operating plant is typically less than $0.01/kWh. As the cost of capital plays a large part in projected cost, risk (as perceived by investors) plays a major role in determining wind power's actual cost. Therefore, low political/policy risk and the availability of predictable power purchase agreements have a disproportionate impact on cost.

Wind power's cost per unit of energy produced in 2006 was estimated for the US to match new generating capacity using coal and natural gas: wind was estimated at $55.80/MWh, coal at $53.10/MWh and natural gas at $52.50/MWh. However, existing conventional power capacity is a sunk cost and its cost of production depends on its future marginal cost (mainly fuel, maintenance and pollution), so that the price of new wind power may be lower than new coal, but higher than old coal.

Wind Power | 17

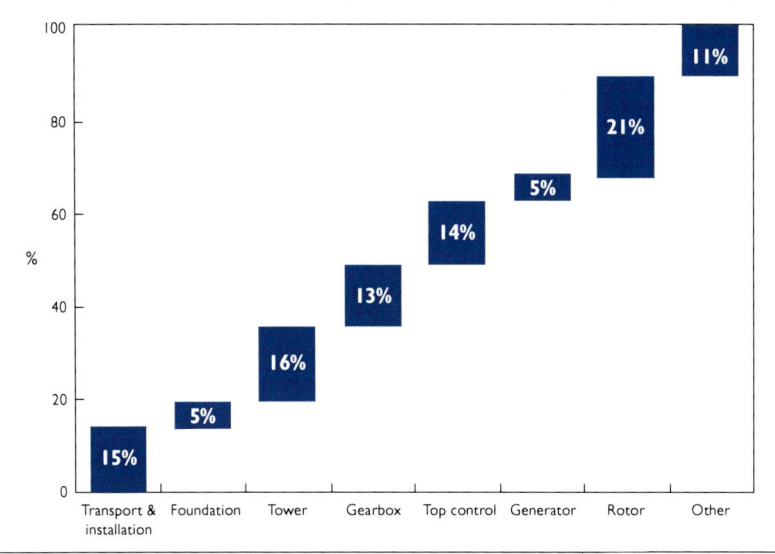

Figure 10. Turbine cost breakdown

[Chart showing turbine cost breakdown with the following components and percentages:
- Transport & installation: 15%
- Foundation: 5%
- Tower: 16%
- Gearbox: 13%
- Top control: 14%
- Generator: 5%
- Rotor: 21%
- Other: 11%]

Source: Gamesa/Tiptree Investments

CAPACITY FACTORS

Due to variability of the wind, a wind farm's capacity is usually qualified by a capacity factor, which is the ratio of the actual production in one year compared to the theoretical maximum. This measures the expected power generated and allows the comparison of different site types, so that a low wind speed site with consistent winds can be compared to a high wind speed site with highly variable winds. Typical capacity factors are in the 20–40% range and a wind turbine will generate electricity for approximately 80% of the year. In broad terms for onshore wind, a capacity factor under 25% is rarely economic, 30% is adequate and more than 35% is good.

FINANCIAL METRICS

There is no doubt that wind power is economic on good sites and has the ability to further reduce its costs – by anything up to an additional 30% over the next 15 years – through incremental technology improvements. This should increase the range of sites that are commercially viable, without subsidy, to capacity factors of ~30% or more, provided suitable PPAs are available.

ENERGY PORTFOLIO IMPACT OF WIND

Studies show that the cost of wind power is often less than expected, since adding wind power to the grid can reduce the overall cost of power. On a windy day, the marginal cost of wind power is almost zero, since there is no fuel cost. That

Figure 11. Wind power financial summary

Performance	
Duty cycle	Varies with resource
Typical capacity factor (%)	24–40
Economics	
Project costs ($m/MWe)	1.3–2.1
Fixed O&M ($'000/MW/year)	25–35
Variable O&M ($/MWhe)	5–20
Levelised cost ($/MWhe)	50–100

Source: Tiptree Investments

power displaces generation from other sources and usually the highest cost power is switched off first. Nuon calculated that in 2005 the average spot price was €45/MWh when there was no wind and €30/MWh when the average wind speed exceeded 13 m/s. In 2007, for the first time, wind power gave consumers a net saving in Denmark. Within Europe, wind turbine output correlates with demand. For example, in 2003, the average capacity factor of UK wind farms was 31%. In the summer, the capacity factor was 17%, but during the winter it was 45%, just as demand peaked.

THE OFFSHORE WIND OPPORTUNITY

Wind turbines can be sited offshore, where the wind blows harder, more consistently and larger turbines can be installed. Many offshore wind farms are being proposed and developed in Europe, where there is limited space on land, relatively large offshore areas with shallow water and a strong wind resource. The Baltic and North seas are the main areas for development, with the UK's 1,341MW of installed capacity leading the market and comparing to 1,100MW installed across the rest of the world.

The offshore potential is substantial. Figure 12 shows the opportunity around Europe, with the UK unsurprisingly having a disproportionate resource. Around the US, there is ~90GW of capacity in 30 metres or less of water and ~273GW in less than 60 metres.

For several years, the offshore market was expected to drive wind market growth. So far, expansion has been slower than forecast, and several companies remain sceptical of any major offshore impact until the many unknown costs are better quantified. Offshore wind needs to achieve a 35% compound annual growth rate (CAGR) over the next few years to hit the European Wind Energy Association's 60GW target for 2020. Although challenging, this is not impossible, as onshore wind had achieved a 33% CAGR between 1994 and 2008. Reducing costs and risks are the main issues, with current estimates sitting around €2,000/kW (a crane barge costs ~€15 million, or €25,000–30,000 per day), along with uncertainty over foundations, grid connections and the harsh marine climate. These should all reduce with scale and experience, so that interest in offshore wind development is maintained, despite the increased costs, due to:

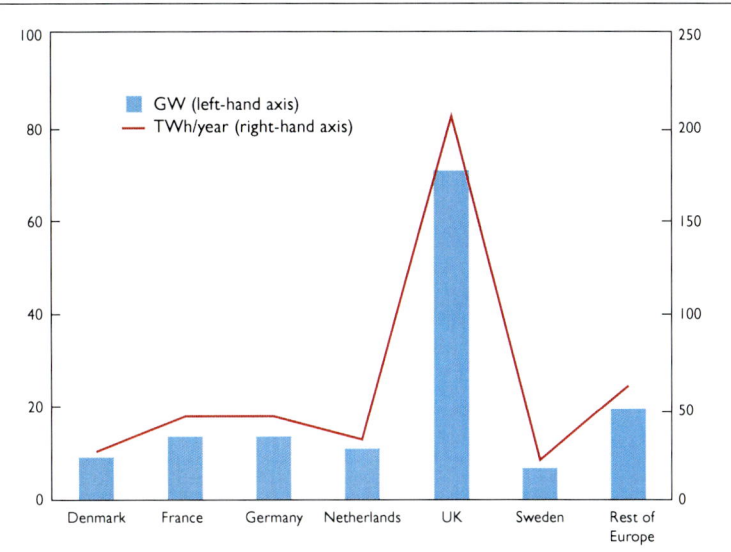

Figure 12. European offshore wind potential

Source: EU

- better capacity factors, as it is windier at sea and the wind is less turbulent. Offshore capacity factors are typically expected to be around 40%;
- unsightliness and lack of space are less of an issue; and,
- noise is not an issue, meaning the aerodynamics can be optimised for power production.

SMALL-SCALE WIND TURBINES

Small wind turbines are usually considered to have a capacity of between one and 50kW. They are typically used to provide power to isolated regions, places where the cost of a grid connection is excessive, or to reduce the dependence on expensive diesel fuel. Recently, demand has also come from individuals, to reduce their reliance on the grid or their carbon footprint. These systems are sometimes coupled to battery storage or feed the power back to the grid via 'net metering'.

Small wind turbines are still a disproportionately expensive source of power, but with several companies now manufacturing them, volume growth has been substantial and prices are likely to fall. Between 2005 and 2010, 43MW of small wind turbines were installed in the UK, which includes 14MW in 2010. Renewable UK estimates that the small wind turbine sector could provide up to 1.7TWh per year of electricity in the UK (0.5% of total consumption), which equates to around 900MW of capacity.

Summary
- Substantial growth is likely for the next 10-plus years and wind is competitive with conventional generation at good sites, with further cost reductions possible.
- It is the most investable sector, with the best risk-adjusted returns from developers with existing capacity.
- Size is a competitive advantage in turbine production in order to manage warranty risk and spread R&D costs. Most new entrants to the OEM market are likely to be found in the developing world.
- Most technical developments are focused on incremental improvements to reduce weight and vibration or improve blade aerodynamics, monitoring systems or drive train efficiency.
- Improvements in aerodynamics, wind prediction and control systems are likely to provide the best efficiency gains over the next five years.

Chapter 2

Solar industry – entering new dimensions

Matthias Fawer, Bank Sarasin

Introduction

The Earth receives 174 petawatts (PW, 10^{15} watts) of incoming solar radiation at the upper atmosphere, of which approximately 30% is reflected back into space, the remainder being absorbed by clouds, oceans and land masses. The absorbed solar light heats the land surface, oceans and atmosphere. It is this light that is harnessed to create energy.

Over the past few years the solar industry has shown itself to be incredibly resilient to the general economic crisis. Supported by cost-cutting and efficiency improvements, the photovoltaics (PV) industry managed to achieve a growth rate of 87%, or 13.8GW, of newly installed capacity in 2010. However, individual companies are feeling strong price and margin pressure, and intensifying competition. At least eight new PV markets with a potential annual capacity of 500MW are expected to be added over the next two years. The PV industry will therefore acquire the stability and political autonomy it needs to be able to continue to grow unimpeded and to enter new dimensions.

Photovoltaics supply and cost trends

SLIGHT MARKET CONSOLIDATION IN 2009

After the difficult autumn of 2008, with the start of the financial crisis and the cap imposed on the Spanish PV market, expectations for 2009 were much more subdued. This new situation triggered a slump in demand and consequently an excess supply of modules. Many therefore feared there would be significant consolidation among the 250 or more manufacturers of solar wafers, cells and modules.

Looking back, we can see that these pessimistic predictions were never fully realised. Obviously almost every PV company had a challenging first half in 2009. Well-known companies such as Q-Cells, REC, Solon, BP-Solar, United Solar, Suntech Power and others were forced to restructure and shed jobs. A number of smaller firms were also bought up. MEMC purchased SunEdison, while First Solar acquired Next Light and Optisolar. There was also a series of mergers between producers of wafers, cells and modules. Only a few actually went out of business. Sunfilm and Signet Solar, key clients of Applied Materials (the 'Sunfab' production line of amorphous silicon modules) had to file for bankruptcy in April 2010. In addition, BP Solar and General Electric (GE) shut down their production facilities in Spain and in Delaware, US.

In fact, the market consolidation process in 2009 was not as brutal as expected. Despite the challenging conditions, demand and installed PV capacity still rose by 24% during the year. The bulk of this growth came from the German market (+2.3GW$_p$[1]) as well as from Italy (+0.4GW) and the Czech Republic (+0.35GW). The feed-in tariffs in these countries were still high enough for companies to be able to generate an attractive return from PV projects. Political announcements warning that feed-in tariffs would be cut more drastically in 2010 also generated a strong pull-forward effect in the fourth quarter of 2009. Furthermore, project financing was easier to secure in the second half of the year. The unexpectedly strong demand for solar modules could not ultimately be entirely satisfied by low-cost module manufacturers, such as First Solar, Suntech Power, Yingli Solar and Trina Solar. Because of this, the more expensive producers were also able to sell their modules. This situation continued up to the end of June 2010.

SOLAR CELL PRODUCTION IN 2009

In 2009 global PV cell production reached a total of 12.3GW$_p$, an increase of 52% on the previous year's figure of 8.1GW. China (+2.1GW), Malaysia (+0.63GW) and Taiwan (+0.58GW) enjoyed the biggest year-on-year growth in absolute terms. The combined global market share of these three countries now stands at 66% (Figure 1). Other up-and-coming production countries include the Philippines, South Korea and India. The offshoring of solar cell production to Asia occurred mainly at the expense of the Europeans and Japanese. Germany still managed to increase its cell production by 22%. Although Japanese producers raised their cell output by 320MW, their share of the global market shrank from 16% to 12.5%. By way of comparison, only five years ago, half of the world's entire solar cell production was concentrated in Japan.

Global capacity for PV module production is still being continuously expanded and at the end of 2009 stood at 25GW, with thin-film technologies accounting for around 4.2GW.

In general, production capacities seem to have developed in a relatively synchronous fashion along the entire value chain. We therefore think the risk of a severe bottleneck occurring is relatively small. Furthermore, there is still some room for improvement in capacity utilisation for specific production lines. With module prices continuing to fall and a low utilisation level, there is still pressure to close down

---

[1] GW$_p$ – Gigawatt Peak: unit of measurement for the maximum potential output of PV modules. Measured under standard test conditions (STC). Throughout the rest of this chapter the 'p' is omitted.

Solar industry – entering new dimensions | 23

Figure 1. Regional shift in solar cell production
MW cells, 2005–09

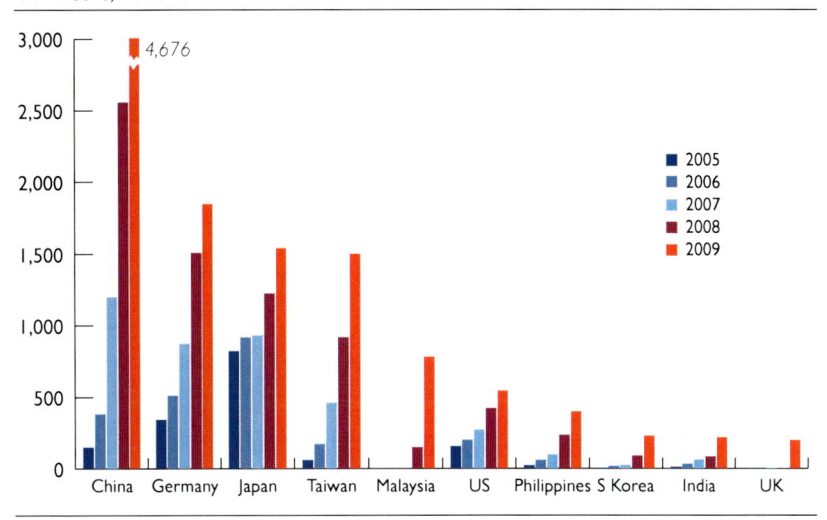

Source: GTM Research, IEA-PVPS, Bank Sarasin, November 2010

Figure 2. Comparison of annual cell production and PV installation
GW, 2006–12

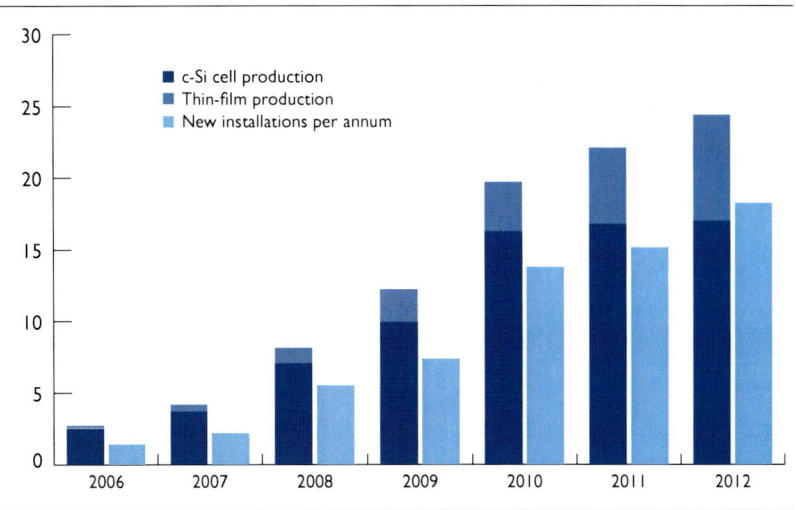

Source: IEA-PVPS, Bank Sarasin, November 2010

24 | Investment Opportunities for a Low-Carbon World

unprofitable production facilities or, where technically feasible, to upgrade them and to ensure that the most cost-efficient lines operate at full capacity.

MODULE PRICES STABLE IN 2010 – BUT NOT FOR LONG
In 2009, solar module prices fell by 30–50%. In previous years the price fall averaged only around 5–10% (Figure 3). The steep drop was caused, on the one hand, by the collapse of the Spanish PV market and, on the other, by the mounting glut of solar module supply. Rising demand in Germany in the first half of 2010 was the result of pre-emptive activity ahead of further cuts in feed-in tariffs in July and October. This helped to stabilise module prices temporarily. Price pressure was set to rise again significantly for the first quarter of 2011 in response to the announcement of further reductions in feed-in tariffs. We therefore expect PV module prices to drop by between 10 and 20% per annum over the next few years.

MARGIN PRESSURE STILL HIGH
Falling prices have put pressure on companies' margins, but not to the same extent for all cell and module manufacturers. Figure 4 shows the development of the EBIT (earnings before interest and taxes) margin of six leading solar players for the period 2006–12. It is interesting to note that margins fell sharply in some cases in 2009. With the exception of First Solar, the EBIT margin for all companies has shrunk compared to 2006. The reasons for this development are to be found in the rapid increase in the number of providers and the associated expansion of production

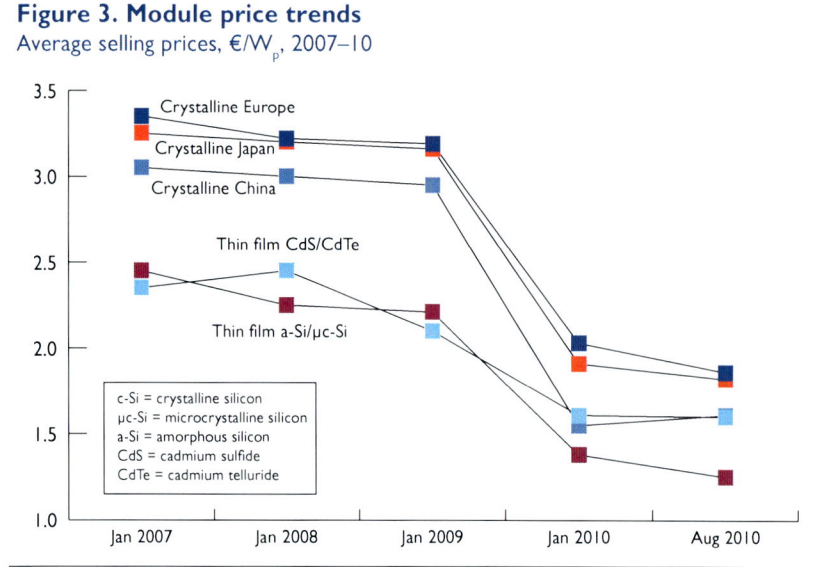

Figure 3. Module price trends
Average selling prices, €/W$_p$, 2007–10

c-Si = crystalline silicon
μc-Si = microcrystalline silicon
a-Si = amorphous silicon
CdS = cadmium sulfide
CdTe = cadmium telluride

Source: solarserver/pvXchange, Bank Sarasin, November 2010

Figure 4. EBIT margin at six PV companies
%, 2006–12

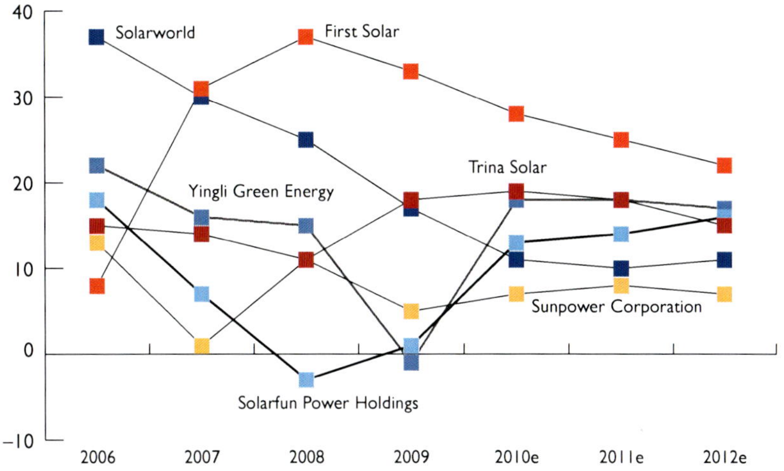

[Chart showing EBIT margins for Solarworld, First Solar, Yingli Green Energy, Trina Solar, Sunpower Corporation, and Solarfun Power Holdings from 2006 to 2012e]

Source: Datastream, Bank Sarasin, November 2010

capacities. Competitive pressure has also intensified due to the market entry of Asian (especially Chinese) companies, which benefit from specific cost advantages compared with their European counterparts. The overall effect of this has been that companies have had to reduce their prices more rapidly than their production costs in order to expand their market share.

With the sudden change from a market supported by generous subsidies in 2008 to more stunted growth in 2009, almost every company has been forced to improve its cost structure. This allowed some PV companies to increase their margins again in 2010. Margins of well over 20% seen in the boom years are virtually inconceivable now. In the longer term, however, we think margins between 10 and 15% are perfectly realistic. They should be attainable for both Western and Asian producers. This is compatible with the normal development of a mature industry with competitive mass production.

This trend can also be highlighted by analysing the stock market performance of the entire solar industry over a given time period. To this end, we examine the relationship between enterprise value and sales. Figure 5 shows the average valuation of selected silicon producers, PV manufacturers (wafer, cell and module producers) and manufacturers of production equipment, compared with the valuation of selected semiconductor and electronics companies. This clearly brings to light the high growth expectations placed on the solar industry during 2006 and 2007. These valuations were many times higher than those of comparable industries that were already mature. In the wake of the financial crisis, these expectations were reined

Figure 5. Stock market valuation of solar sector, compared with semiconductor and electronic industry
Enterprise value/sales

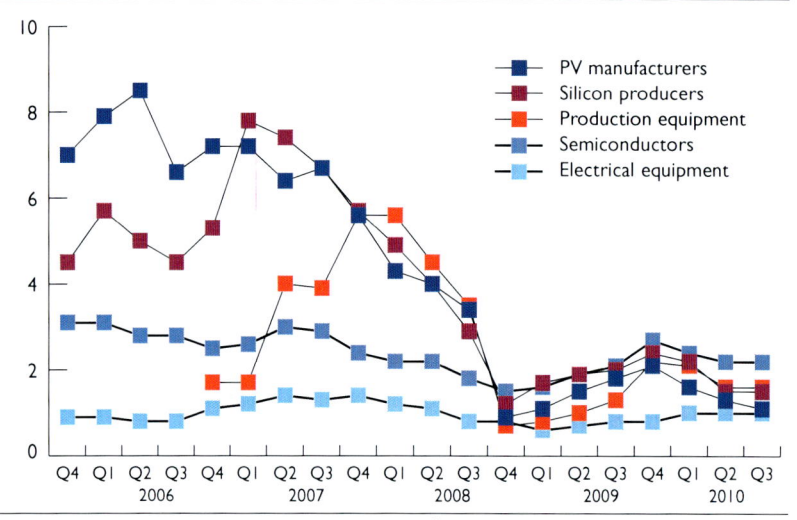

- PV manufacturers
- Silicon producers
- Production equipment
- Semiconductors
- Electrical equipment

Source: Datastream, Bank Sarasin, November 2010

in significantly; within the space of a year, the valuation of solar companies dropped back to the same level as more mature companies and industries. Since then, silicon producers and PV manufacturers have moved more or less in parallel with the related semiconductor firms. At the same time, the manufacturers of production equipment seem to be shadowing electronics companies, which share similar characteristics. This is another reason for concluding that the former high-growth solar industry should in future be valued more along the lines of a mature, conventional industry.

PV INDUSTRY: CONCENTRATION AND GLOBALISATION

As the size of the market increases and competition intensifies, the PV industry is increasingly turning into a mass market.[2] Solar cells and modules are already highly standardised products, relatively speaking. Rivals are therefore competing increasingly on price. To remain competitive, cell and module producers primarily need to cut their costs. The industry's production structures are therefore developing in the direction of bigger units in order to exploit cost degression effects. The trend towards larger production units means that financially strong companies able to finance the rapid expansion of significant production capacities will succeed in the market over the longer term. At the moment we can see, for example, that a number of big players from the electronics industry, such as Samsung and LG Electronics, are

[2] Bank Sarasin (August 2010), *Renewable energies: Evolving from a niche to a mass market.*

investing in the construction of their own large production facilities. Big Japanese corporations such as Sharp and Sanyo are also keen to be involved in the mass production of solar modules. But the established, more specialised producers, such as First Solar, are also moving into new dimensions. This company, the largest module manufacturer, is now represented on the S&P 500 index. We also expect the trend towards mass production to accelerate merger and acquisition activity in the sector. This mass production will mainly be built up in Asia, as was shown in Figure 1.

In a further trend in the offshoring and streamlining of production, the PV industry is following the lead of the electronics industry by outsourcing production to specialised contract manufacturers (OEM production). The US's SunPower, for example, has entered a joint venture with Taiwan's AU Optronics, while Germany's Q-Cells is collaborating with Flextronics, one of the world's biggest contract manufacturers in the electronics industry.

However, certain political requirements imposed on local content have to be taken into consideration when choosing new production locations. There are stories coming out of China and India of conditions being imposed requiring up to 70% local content.

FOCUS ON NON-SILICON-BASED COSTS

The significant shift in production quotas among regions reflects the cost trap that companies currently face. Established European producers suffered heavy losses in 2009 and could not keep pace with the aggressive pricing policy and cost structure of Chinese manufacturers. In the current competitive market environment, with a polysilicon price of around $50/kg, non-silicon-based costs are becoming increasingly important.

In the case of polysilicon, procurement prices are now more or less the same for both European and Chinese cell and module producers. When it comes to non-silicon-based costs, however, the top company in China can produce a module at a cost of $0.90/W compared with around $1.50/W for European companies. This difference is split into $0.35/W material- and energy-related costs, and $0.25/W labour costs.

In this context, however, the question arises as to whether the advantages enjoyed by Chinese manufacturers in non-silicon-based costs are of a permanent nature. If the generous subsidies from the Chinese government were to be taken away, it could significantly undermine these companies' cost advantages. Also, the labour cost advantage of approximately $0.25/W could come under pressure in the longer term. With a premium brand strategy, however, European solar companies can achieve a higher price, making up for this disadvantage on the cost side.

Current foreign exchange rate movements have also helped to reduce the cost differential. The weakness of the euro puts European production locations in a more favourable position than those in China. At the end of June 2010, the Chinese government officially removed the yuan's peg to the US dollar, even though for the time being it is making absolutely sure that its central bank closely monitors the exchange rate. The advantages China gains from other cost components could also decline in the near future. For example, there is now upward pressure on labour costs. Cheap labour is in short supply in some regions and there has recently been an increasing number of labour disputes, with workers demanding better working conditions and higher wages. After companies such as Foxconn and Honda were forced to raise the basic salaries of their employees, other manufacturers are coming under mounting pressure as well. The Chinese government's subsidy of energy prices has also come under increasing fire.

MARKETING AND SERVICES AS KEY FACTORS
In the current buyer's market, the expansion of marketing and distribution activities is becoming a vital success factor for PV cell and module producers. Additional services such as training, consulting and after-sales support are also very important to ensure that price is not the only assessment criteria. Furthermore, a number of companies, such as First Solar, Q-Cells, Suntech Power, Solarwatt and Solon, have entered the project business. The flipside of this forward integration is the potential danger of paper transactions with a firm's own project company or competing with its own clients. Another strategy would be to focus on higher-priced niche products or on the premium segment.

Due to growing domestic market demand, China certainly remains an attractive location for the solar industry. For an internationally active company, however, it will become increasingly important in future to have a local presence, in the form of a production facility, in all three of the world's biggest markets: North America, Europe and Asia. Producing modules in Europe still makes economic sense, particularly while oil prices and transport costs continue to rise.

VERY FEW BANKS STILL OFFER PROJECT FINANCING
Since the financial crisis in 2008 the conditions imposed by financial institutions for granting loans for PV projects have become much tougher, while the financing terms themselves have deteriorated. The number of banks offering finance, and the volume of credit available, have both fallen dramatically. Financing terms did improve slightly in 2009. Nevertheless, the stress test introduced in 2010 by the Committee of European Banking Supervisors obliges some of the banks active in the renewable energy sector to review their loan portfolios to bring their core capital quotas into line with the required limits. The following criteria are crucial for the bankability of a large-scale PV project:
- financial strength and good track record of sponsors and investors;
- an attractive, stable political and regulatory environment (eg, subsidised feed-in tariffs, tax advantages, etc);

- geographic and climatic conditions;
- track record and references of local installers;
- high technical quality of modules, inverters and the overall system (balance of system – BOS); and
- transparent calculation of costs and returns. BOS costs are becoming increasingly important as module prices drop – ie, greater focus on erection costs and inverter prices.

PV market trends

INSTALLED PV CAPACITY IN 2009

Around 7.5GW of new photovoltaic capacity was installed worldwide in 2009.[3] This corresponds to an impressive growth rate of 24% compared with the previous year. Admittedly, this is very much lower than the growth rate of 150% achieved in 2008. However, many expected a growth rate as low as zero. The cumulative PV capacity at year-end 2009 therefore stood at around 21GW. This equates to around 7% of total global installed electricity capacity from renewable sources of 305GW[4], generating around 31.5TWh of electricity per year.

For the European solar energy market the decline in market growth from 170% in 2008 to 18% in 2009 was, admittedly, drastic. However, it was not as severe as originally feared. The booming market in Germany (+155%) and above-average growth in Belgium (+500%), France (+139%), Italy (+144%) and the Czech Republic (+560%) were able to compensate for the collapse in the Spanish market.

2010: GROWTH DESPITE LOWER REMUNERATION RATES.

In 2010, too, the number of new installations in many markets came as a positive surprise. Despite the lowering of remuneration rates in double figures in percentage terms, we expected a growth rate of 87% or 13.8GW worldwide. Europe would see growth of 86% or 10.6GW in 2010. Germany's huge market again grew by 79% or 6.9GW.

GLOBAL MARKET TRENDS TO 2015

We have analysed the following core data for our market forecast:
- PV market data for each country, from trade associations and the International Energy Agency's Photovoltaic Power Systems Programme (IEA-PVPS);
- national targets for PV installations and production capacities; and
- data on capacity expansion in thin-film technologies and information from companies on their reliability.

---

3 IEA Photovoltaic Power Systems Programme – Task 1 (September 2010), *Trends in PV applications; survey report of selected IEA countries between 1992 and 2009.* www.iea-pvps.org.
4 REN 21 (June 2010), *Renewables Global Status Report: 2010 Update.*

30 | Investment Opportunities for a Low-Carbon World

Figure 6. Sarasin's long-term forecast for the global PV market

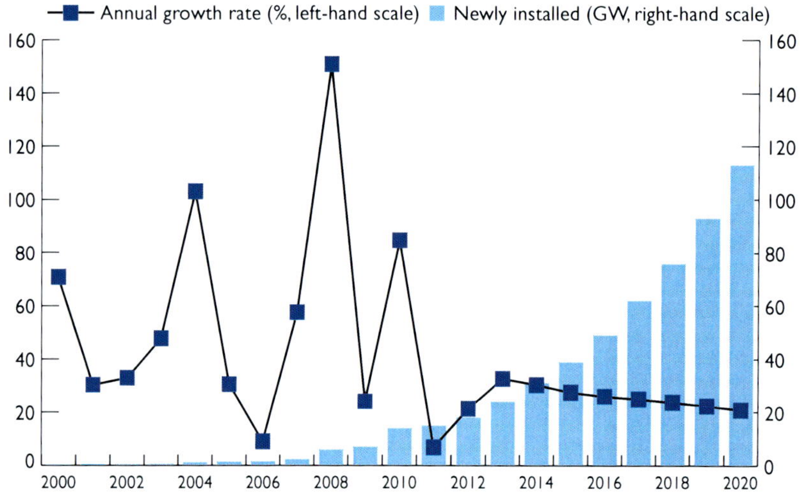

— Annual growth rate (%, left-hand scale) ■ Newly installed (GW, right-hand scale)

Source: Bank Sarasin, November 2010

Taking into account the attractiveness rating for each country, we anticipate the market trends shown in Figure 6 for the period to 2015. Globally, our forecast for 2009–15 produces annual average growth of 33%. This results in newly installed PV capacity of 13.8GW for 2010, 15.2GW for 2011 and 18.3GW for 2012. The growth rates for individual countries and years vary enormously, however. Following 87% growth in 2010, we expect global growth of just 10% in 2011, rising to 20% in 2012.

In Europe, the strongest growth countries for the period to 2015 are primarily Spain (compound annual growth rate 2009–15 of 69%), France (55%), Greece (51%) and Portugal (42%). The US will grow by on average 70% per year over the same period, and will also gain massively in importance in terms of volume (an additional 11.3GW in 2015). Other important growth markets are China (CAGR 2009–15 of 77%), India (76%), Japan (30%), the rest of Asia (35%) and other countries (64%).

116GW OF NEWLY INSTALLED PV CAPACITY IN 2020

Several markets will achieve an annual volume of over 500MW of newly installed PV capacity in 2010 or over the next two years. This is a decisive factor, because it will mean that the PV industry is less susceptible to changes to the general operating conditions in individual key markets. A globally based PV industry of this kind will therefore grow in a more stable manner. We expect average annual growth of 28% for the period 2009–20. This will produce newly installed PV capacity of 116GW in 2020. The tendency will be for sunny, non-European markets to grow more rapidly in the period to 2020, as they still have a great deal of catching up to do in terms of solar power generation. Over the past two years the solar industry has demonstrated that it can survive and continue to grow even in a challenging economic and political environment. We are convinced that costs can also be reduced by on average 10% per year over the coming years, and that our scenario can therefore be realised in practice.

The new solar energy report from the European Photovoltaic Industry Association (EPIA) also forecasts that solar electricity will see double-digit percentage growth over the coming years. Compared with Sarasin's 30.3GW forecast, the moderate EPIA scenario expects global newly installed PV capacity of 13.8GW for 2014. The additional policy-driven scenario predicts 30GW of new PV capacity. Our forecast is higher for 2010, and from 2014 onwards, while for 2011, 2012 and 2013 we are lower. This is certainly not out of any hope for greater support from policymakers, but because of the growing economic arguments for photovoltaics.

For 2011 and beyond, the industry has prepared itself for further cutbacks in subsidies for solar power. There will be a significant reduction in tariffs in Italy, Germany and in the Czech Republic. The politicians responsible fear, among other things, a rise in energy prices and instability in their power distribution grids. This will intensify competition among module manufacturers across Europe.

GRID PARITY ARRIVING SOONER THAN EXPECTED
The solar industry has already achieved incredible things. Since as recently as 2006, prices for solar electricity have fallen by 40% and, over the coming years, will converge with the level of consumer electricity tariffs. The key goal at present is to ensure an efficient and sustainable broadening of the photovoltaic market and to secure both the investments already made and those still required by this forward-looking industry. It will only take a few more years before the solar industry can survive without subsidy programmes in many key markets. Even in Germany, the electricity produced by solar panels on one's own roof will match the price charged for electricity by conventional energy suppliers or regional public utilities from 2013 onwards. This will mark an important milestone on the road to commercial competitiveness. For this reason, the industry is developing a road map towards further successful development of the photovoltaic market, and in the course of this process will demonstrate ways in which this commercial competitiveness may be achieved in a speedy manner. In addition, the solar industry is making efforts to underscore its positive economic and commercial achievements, and is increasingly bringing hard facts and figures to bear to counter one-sided arguments centred around cost.

Grid parity will be an important driver for demand in future. Compared with feed-in tariffs – which are continually being reduced, forcing house owners and investors into rash decisions – where grid parity applies the returns become better the longer one waits. A market with grid parity will therefore tend to see more gradual

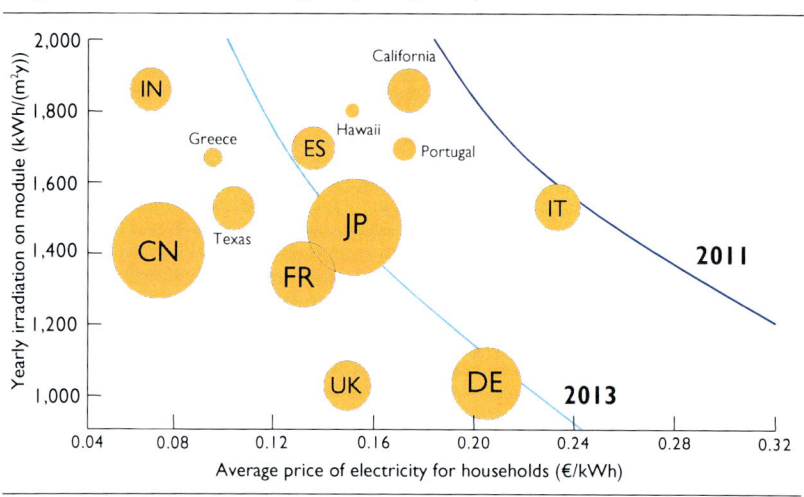

Figure 7. Trend towards grid parity for private customers

Source: EPIA, REC, Bank Sarasin, November 2010

progress, and will not create a 'gold-digger' mentality, as is the case in subsidised markets.

In sunny regions of the world such as Italy, California, Hawaii and Spain we expect this household grid parity to be achieved as early as 2010–12 (Figure 7). In Japan, too, with the highest electricity prices in the world, PV systems on the roof of a private home will soon become the norm, simply because it makes economic sense. From 2013 onwards, solar electricity will be as cost-effective as conventional grid power even in the countries of central Europe.

Concentrating solar power

CSP PLANTS READY FOR MARKET

Solar thermal electricity (STE) has been in a critical stage of commercial development during the past two years. Efforts in the areas of innovation and cost reduction are leading to a proven and attractive form of electricity generation based on solar energy. Furthermore, the industry has improved its organisation. The leading European industry association, the European Solar Thermal Electricity Association (Estela), has grown increasingly active. Current reports indicate possible developments in concentrating solar power (CSP) regarding cost reduction and power station construction.[5] As a result STE has gained stronger perception among the media and in the broader population.

---

[5] Estela/A T Kearney (June 2010), *Marketability of solar thermal electricity.*

CSP WITH HUGE PROJECT PIPELINE

In 2009, roughly eight power stations with a total capacity of 350MW were brought on line. One plant each was erected in Algeria, Italy and Mexico, while the remaining construction occurred in Spain. Some 18 power stations with a capacity of 1,000MW were due for completion in 2010.

The current global pipeline for STE projects amounts to around 3,500MW, with some large-scale power stations having a capacity of more than 50MW. The focus of activity continues to lie in Spain and the US. Additional CSP plants are either under construction or in planning in Sudan, South Africa, the Middle East, India and Australia.

CSP technology has gained further momentum especially in the sunny US Southwest, where it is the preferred form of renewable energy. The world's largest parabolic trough system, a power station with a capacity of 1GW, is slated for construction by Solar Millennium and Chevron Energy Solutions in Blythe, California. The $6 billion project consists of four power stations, each with a capacity of 250MW, and is due on line in 2013. Blythe Solar services an area of 28.5km^2 some 350km east of Los Angeles.

In October 2010, US Secretary of the Interior Ken Salazar approved additional CSP projects in California and Nevada having a total generation capacity of 1.8GW. For comparison, one megawatt of CSP capacity (2,700MWh/a) meets the electricity consumption needs of 400 average American households.

In the summer of 2010 construction also began on the Shams-1 CSP plant in Abu Dhabi. Chosen for this 100MW plant was the joint venture of Masdar with Abengoa Solar and Total. The plant is due on line in 2012. Onsite experts have discovered in the meantime that direct solar radiation is considerably reduced due to airborne sand particles, impairing the performance of the parabolic troughs. The array of mirrors will therefore be enlarged.

In the current list of CSP projects worldwide of 900MW in operation, parabolic trough technology dominates, with a 93% share of the market, followed by solar towers at 5%, Fresnel at 1% and Dish-Sterling at less than 1%. For CSP plants currently under construction this distribution will not change markedly. Only for those power stations scheduled for 2015 will solar towers, Fresnel and parabolic mirrors emerge more strongly.

ATTRACTIVE FEED-IN TARIFFS FOR CSP

The feed-in tariffs for CSP plants are only marginally affected by the current discussion regarding compensation rates for photovoltaics. Various countries have established subsidy programmes for CSP technology. Spain launched a feed-in tariff for solar thermal electricity as early as 2002. Since then such tariffs have also been provided in Greece, Portugal, Italy, France, Israel, Algeria, India and Turkey, as well as in South Africa since March 2009. Alongside this, in the US subsidies are granted in the form of tax reductions of up to 30% (investment tax credits – ITCs).

CONSOLIDATED CSP INDUSTRY

Solar thermal power plants are huge capital investment projects, the supply chain for which also requires expensive infrastructure. In contrast to the PV industry, in which more than 400 companies are still active, there are in the CSP industry only a few vertically integrated major enterprises. In view of banks' continued rather conservative lending activities and the high capital requirements for a CSP project, the key financial data must meet very high criteria. As a result, financially strong companies such as Chevron, Alstom, Areva and Siemens are increasingly entering the fray. Alstom announced an investment of $55 million in a partnership with BrightSource Energy (BSE) in May 2010. Combining Alstom's experience in turbine construction with BSE's know-how in CSP technology, the firms will build power stations in the Mediterranean region, in Africa and the US. BSE has a project pipeline in the US amounting to 4GW.

Energy utilities' engagement also continues, helping to develop CSP to an established technology for renewable energy. In particular, the possibilities of energy storage or combined use with a fossil fuel (hybrid operation) make CSP plants suitable for peak as well as baseload electricity production.

First Solar has substantially strengthened its engagement in project business in recent years. The company has acquired one engineering and project planning company after another. The most recent was NextLight Renewable Power with a project pipeline of 1.1GW. This yields an important sales channel for the company's thin-film modules. With new projects, including some with capacities exceeding 500MW, First Solar is clearly playing in the big league among CSP plants.

PV and CSP – the battle of lower costs

As a result of the significant price reduction among PV modules (c-Si-based and thin-film) in recent months, electricity generation costs per generated kilowatt hour by large-scale PV plants have also dropped substantially. On a cost basis, a CdTe thin-film installation has surpassed a parabolic trough system using a storage medium. The former achieves electricity generation costs of €0.14/kWh. Newly installed CSP plants, though they appear to have contributed experience to the industry, have not been able to reduce generation costs per kWh to the same extent. The two solar technologies were presented in detail within the scope of Sarasin's 2008 solar energy study.[6]

CSP WITH COST REDUCTION PLANS

CSP plants can nevertheless achieve further advances in the future to regain the cost leadership position. According to industry representatives,[7] electricity production could become 30–50% cheaper by 2015. Thus electricity generation costs of €0.08–0.10/kWh would be achieved.

---

6 Bank Sarasin (November 2008), *Solar energy 2008 – Stormy weather will give way to sunnier periods*.
7 Abengoa Solar: Michael Geyer, director of international development.

This should be reached principally due to steam temperatures of up to 580°C. In comparison with current temperatures of 380°C, the higher level can increase the efficiency of the steam cycle by 20%. An initial pilot power plant with a capacity of 5MW using molten salt not only for heat storage but also as a transfer medium was started up in Sicily during summer 2010. This should achieve a steam temperature of 500°C. In addition, it enables a simplified design of power plant which eliminates oil-to-molten salt heat exchangers, resulting in fewer safety and environmental concerns within the context of synthetic oil use. This pilot project has a current high price of €60 million for 5MW. Despite the previously low net efficiency of 13%, the technology could gain a footing in the market. The heat storage mentioned and the option of constructing a hybrid power station remain additional benefits of CSP technology. Cost reduction potential consists primarily in the leverage of scale. The investment per kilowatt of electrical capacity drops by roughly 15% upon doubling the size of the power plant. Until now the standard size for such CSP plants stood at 50MW. New projects in the US now often range above 200MW. In Spain funding for CSP would need to be adjusted accordingly, as it has previously promoted power plants of 50MW.

CURRENT COST COMPARISON

Over the past two years we have compared the various technologies for large-scale solar power plants. Figure 8 compares the costs of two PV installations, one with polycrystalline Si-modules and the other with CdTe thin-film modules, as well as two CSP plants, one with a parabolic trough solar array and the other with linear Fresnel technology.

Since the last solar energy study in 2008 the specific total investment for CdTe thin-film has fallen by some 25%, and that for a c-Si-module installation by roughly 14%. For parabolic trough systems we assume a reduction of about 3%. Data for the linear Fresnel CSP plant continue to be based on the previous year's project; costs have incurred only slight reduction due to moderately improved financing conditions. Thus a CdTe thin-film installation with electricity generation costs of €0.14/kWh lies clearly ahead of the polycrystalline PV installation at €0.16/kWh, and of the parabolic trough system with generating costs of €0.17/kWh. The Fresnel technology, at €0.21/kWh, has the highest electricity generating costs. By comparison, electricity from a coal-fired plant costs roughly €0.042/kWh. The peak efficiency of CSP plants at 25% is higher than that of photovoltaics. The average efficiency of polycrystalline Si-modules lies at some 15%, and that of CdTe modules at 11%.

CSP project developers in California are battling increasing risks simultaneously with decreasing electricity tariffs. Twenty-two of the total 29 CSP projects in California with power purchase agreements (PPAs) are negotiating with only two energy utilities: Pacific Gas & Electric (PG&E) and Southern California Edison (SCE). The two energy utilities have the much better negotiating position and shift additional costs to the project developers – for example, for power transmission.

Figure 8. Pros, cons and cost comparisons of large-scale Si-PV, thin-film PV and CSP installations, 2010

Pros/cons of individual technologies	Photovoltaics (PV) Multi-crystalline silicon module	Photovoltaics (PV) CdTe thin-film module	Concentrating solar power (CSP) Parabolic trough solar field	Concentrating solar power (CSP) Linear Fresnel technology
Typical size (MW)	2–50	2–50	50–200	1–30
Project phase	Short; systems are scalable	Short; systems are scalable	Lengthy planning and construction times	Lengthy planning and construction times
Surface area required per kW	Medium	Large	Medium, but even surface	Medium, but even surface
Irradiation	Direct irradiation	Diffused light	Direct irradiation required	Direct irradiation required
Storage	Not usual, expensive at present	–	Simple to implement	Possible
Steam cooling	–	–	Water or air	Water or air
Suitable for hybrid operation	–	–	Hybrid operation with gas possible	Hybrid operation with gas possible
Adjustability of power	Not usual, expensive at present	Not usual, expensive at present	Yes	Yes
Service life (years)	25	25	25	25
Cost comparison				
Contractor/construction costs (€/kW)	2,800	2,200	3,900	3,600
Financing (€/kW)	280	242	429	396
Total investment (€/kW)	3,080	2,442	4,329	3,996
Electricity conversion (kWh/kW)	2,000	1,800	2,700	2,000
Peak efficiency (%)	15	11	25	19
Maintenance per annum (% of total investment)	1.3	1.4	2.1	1.3
Electricity generating cost (€/kWh)	0.16	0.14	0.18	0.21

Location of solar energy installations: southern Spain, receives annual solar radiation of 2,000kWh/m²

Source: companies, Bank Sarasin, November 2010

SPEEDIER IMPLEMENTATION OF MID-SIZED PV PROJECTS
From an investor's standpoint, the swift realisation of a project is also significant. In this instance, mid-sized PV installations of 2–20MW have the lead. They can be built very rapidly, in 18–24 months, without major environmental impact studies. This occurs preferably in the vicinity of an existing network (medium voltage) in the sense of a decentralised electricity generation and without excessive burden to power transmission capacities. Such an installation size has become the specialty of – among others – American Recurrent Energy. This company has recently been acquired by Sharp.

CSP projects require up to five years' development time, since they must fulfil a greater number of environmental regulations and because a link to the electrical power network might need to be built. For example, the environmental approval process for BrightSource Energy's 400MW Ivanpah CSP project in California took two and a half years.

NEW CSP TECHNOLOGIES
The development of new technologies is exposed to very high financial and political risks. Banks are currently refraining from financing power plants based on sparsely proven technologies. The guarantee of a public authority or of a major energy utility is thus almost essential.

Three technologies that may achieve a breakthrough are as follows:
- Stirling Energy Systems (SES) is attempting a less conventional technology based on parabolic mirrors in combination with a Stirling engine. This is driven by the heat of concentrated solar radiation, and through a generator delivers 25kW. According to information from SES such installations achieve an efficiency of 31%. Recently in Arizona a 1.5MW park with 60 parabolic disks was dedicated. Far larger power plants are being planned by SES to 2012. A 250MW power plant is slated for Phoenix at a cost of €525 million–700 million. Two further projects of 750MW and 850MW are now in planning in California. Apparently a power purchase price as low as €0.07–0.09/kW has been agreed upon.
- Fresnel technology has also made decisive progress. In particular, the Compact Linear Fresnel Reflector (CLFR) technology received a powerful boost due to the acquisition of CLFR expert Ausra by Areva Solar. This CSP technology should derive 1.5–3 times as much electricity from one square kilometre of desert as parabolic trough arrays, a solar tower or a thin-film PV installation, largely as a result of the sophisticated design of the mirror and the receiver.
- Innovative Swiss company Airlight Energy (ALE)[8] presented the details of its novel, cost-effective solar collector in 2009. The system is based on pneumatic mirrors and uses air as a heat transfer medium. Independent university and industry certifications were successfully concluded. Following the completion of

---
8 www.airlightenergy.com.

this prototype test phase, the construction of a pilot plant is being expedited. The new dual-axle receiver promises especially high power station efficiency – significantly higher than current parabolic trough systems. The gravel bed heat accumulator enables low-cost electricity production, suitable for the market. The integrated rain water collection system employing air-cooled condensors to cool steam induces a positive hydrological balance.

OPPORTUNITIES FOR SOLAR HYBRID POWER STATIONS
With an increasing proportion of solar-derived electricity in the network, a disadvantage of solar energy becomes apparent, namely intermittency, the swiftly altering quantity of electricity that can be generated from sunlight.

CSP has bridged this difficulty with the storage of heat, which can also drive a turbine after sundown. Some developers are working on hybrid power stations in which solar energy is applied along with gas, coal or diesel fuel. CSP technology is highly suited to this, since it also operates with steam turbines and generators, which can be activated by both energy sources, depending upon the availability of solar radiation. At the moment, hybrid power stations based on CSP are being developed in a number of countries in the Middle East (Israel, United Arab Emirates) and North Africa (Egypt, Algeria, Morocco). These countries can thus gain initial, low-risk experience with solar technology. Solar hybrid systems offer persuasive arguments, since they generate fewer emissions and require less fossil fuel, at the same time facilitating the integration of solar electricity into the network.

In appropriate locations such CSP technologies can be retrofitted to existing power stations comparatively easily and inexpensively. They could in future become acknowledged competition to planned carbon capture and storage (CCS) power stations. In contrast to CCS technology, the efficiency of the fossil-fuelled portion of the power station is markedly less reduced by the solar portion.

The above-mentioned CSP pilot plant employing molten salt as heat transfer medium and higher steam temperatures will further simplify linkage to an existing power station. With the higher temperatures it is possible to employ a steam turbine with standard pressure and temperature parameters that is in use in conventional power stations today. In combination with a heat storage unit, a competitive, efficient power station generating dispatchable power can be created.

Market outlook for CSP systems

The project pipeline for CSP installations in the coming years will be strongly dependent on development programmes in the aforementioned countries and on individual innovative energy utilities. More than 70% of installations planned in 2010 and 2011 are located in Spain and the US. Countries in the Middle East and North Africa (MENA) region as well as in southern Europe will realise projects, including hybrid power stations, with a total capacity of over 700MW. Experience gained

Figure 9. Predicted expansion of CSP systems

New capacity in MW	Spain	US	MENA	Rest of world	Total
Cumulative 2009	345	435	80	30	890
Annual additional capacity					
2010	455	265	170	120	1,010
2011	600	600	250	150	1,600
2012	700	1,300	350	200	2,550
2013	900	2,300	460	290	3,950
2014	700	1,600	1,200	350	3,850
2015	500	1,200	700	450	2,850
2016	450	1,200	850	400	2,900
2017	450	1,200	950	400	3,000
2018	400	1,100	1,200	400	3,100
2019	500	1,000	1,200	400	3,100
2020	500	1,100	1,250	350	3,200
Cumulative 2020	6,500	13,300	8,600	3,540	32,000

Source: Estela, Bank Sarasin, November 2010

thus far with new installations is encouraging and critical for a broader deployment of CSP technology. Our forecast projects a cumulative CSP capacity of 32GW by 2020 (Figure 9). For the period from 2010–20 this corresponds to an average annual growth rate in newly installed capacity of 12%. This forecast is of a similar order of magnitude to the report by A T Kearney, prepared for Estela in June 2010. This assumes capacity of 30GW by 2020 and 60–100GW by 2025.

SOLAR COLLECTORS
Decentralised heat generation using solar collectors for hot water and space heating represents the third application area of solar energy. The prices of fossil fuels (normally heating oil or natural gas) are more significant for solar thermal energy than for photovoltaics, since development programmes play a smaller role. As a result of the economic crisis oil prices are now far below their high of $150 a barrel in 2008 and are not stimulating additional use of solar thermal energy.

Nevertheless solar thermal energy is being supported by many governments through financial incentives and legislation. The EU target to increase its proportion of energy supply from renewable sources to 20% by 2020 includes space heating and warm water. The International Energy Agency (IEA) estimates that solar hot water and space heating systems could replace 60–70% of gas and electricity consumption for this purpose. In comparison with other renewable energies (excluding hydropower) solar collectors deliver a substantial portion of energy supply. Already 70 million households supply themselves with hot water

40 | Investment Opportunities for a Low-Carbon World

Figure 10. Cumulative renewable capacity and energy generated
End 2010

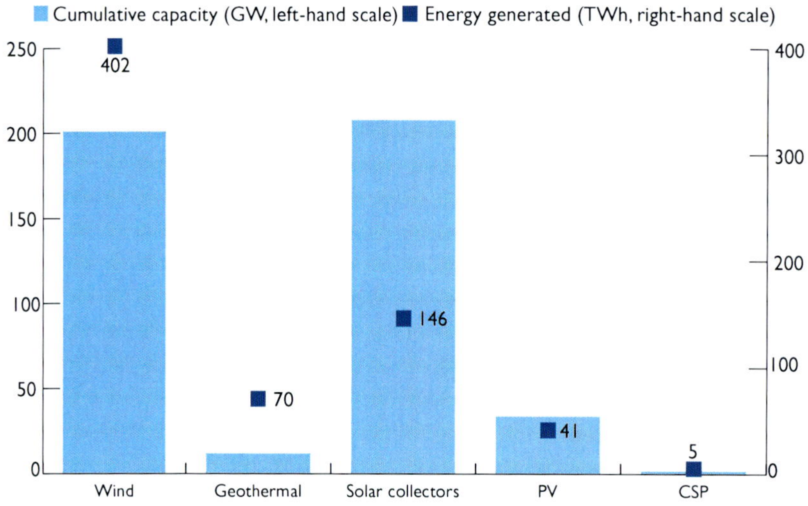

■ Cumulative capacity (GW, left-hand scale)   ■ Energy generated (TWh, right-hand scale)

- Wind: 402 (cumulative capacity ~200 GW)
- Geothermal: 70
- Solar collectors: 146 (cumulative capacity ~210 GW)
- PV: 41
- CSP: 5

Source: Bank Sarasin, November 2010

using solar rooftop installations. This portion is the largest energy contribution among all solar technologies. Figure 10 shows the projected cumulative electrical or thermal capacity ($GW_{el/th}$) at year-end 2010 for wind, solar collectors, geothermal power, photovoltaics and CSP, as well as the energy generated from it in 2010 ($TWh_{el/th}$).[9]

Global market trends

GLOBAL GROWTH OF 23% IN 2009

Across the world, regional differences regarding newly installed collector surface area remained large. Global newly installed capacity in 2009 registered $34.1 GW_{th}$ (48.8 million m² – Figure 11). Around 82% was installed in China, which corresponds to a surface area roughly 10 times larger than that installed in Europe. In 2009 the Chinese market again recorded growth of 29%. Demand in China is mainly driven by the central government programme 'Household appliances for the rural population'. This was responsible for some 58% of installations. The European market shrank in contrast by 10%. Besides the Chinese home market there are other major markets in Europe (Germany, Austria and Greece) as well as in Latin America, in Turkey, India, and Australia/New Zealand.

---

9 In this report the installed solar collector capacity is not expressed in square metres, but in kilowatts of thermal energy based on the conversion factor $0.7 kW_{th}/m^2$. For more details visit www.iea-shc.org.

Figure 11. Global newly installed collector capacity GW$_{th}$, 2009

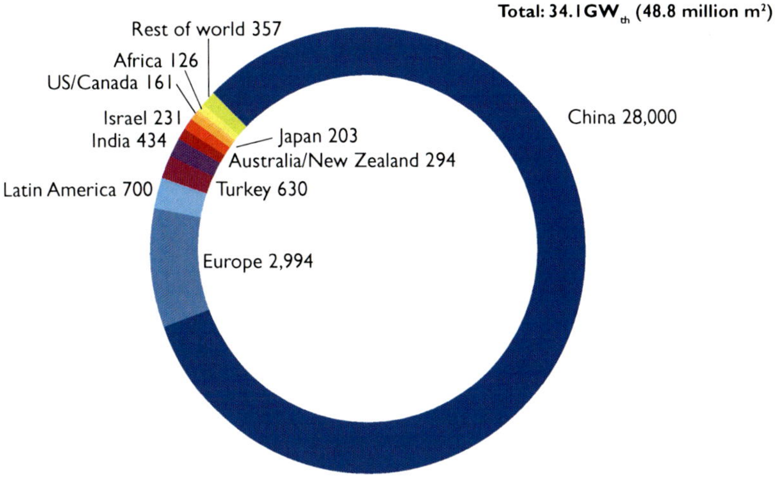

Total: 34.1GW$_{th}$ (48.8 million m²)

- Rest of world 357
- Africa 126
- US/Canada 161
- Israel 231
- India 434
- Japan 203
- Australia/New Zealand 294
- Turkey 630
- Latin America 700
- Europe 2,994
- China 28,000

Source: W B Koldehoff, November 2010

NATIONAL GROWTH RATES FLUCTUATE

Markets for solar collectors in individual countries are not very stable, and fluctuate from year to year. Growth rates in 2009 in Australia/New Zealand (50%), Africa (43%) and China (29%) were all above the global rate of 23%. In Latin America (13%), Japan (12%), Israel (14%) and India (13%) there was positive growth below the global average, Turkey recorded zero growth, whereas markets in Europe (–10%) and the US and Canada (–15%) showed negative growth.

In 2008 growth rates looked completely different: Australia/New Zealand (6%), India (–15%), Africa (–1%), Europe (60%), Israel (4%), Turkey (29%), Japan (13%), and US/Canada (50%).

Figure 12 shows the cumulative collector capacity in operation in individual countries and regions at the end of 2009. In comparison with 2008 this capacity has grown worldwide by 11% to a total of 158GW$_{th}$ (226 million m²). China has increased its share from 68% to 71% and is clearly the largest market with an operational solar collector capacity of 112GW$_{th}$. The percentage shares of total collector surface area are regionally very stable, despite fluctuating annual growth rates.

MARKET TRENDS IN EUROPE

After the European solar thermal energy market experienced extraordinary growth of 60% in 2008, newly installed solar collector capacity dropped by 10% in 2009.[10]

---
[10] European Solar Thermal Industry Federation (Estif – June 2009), *Trends and Market Statistics 2009*; EU 27 + Switzerland; www.estif.org.

42 | Investment Opportunities for a Low-Carbon World

Figure 12. Global total operational solar thermal energy capacity
%, 2009

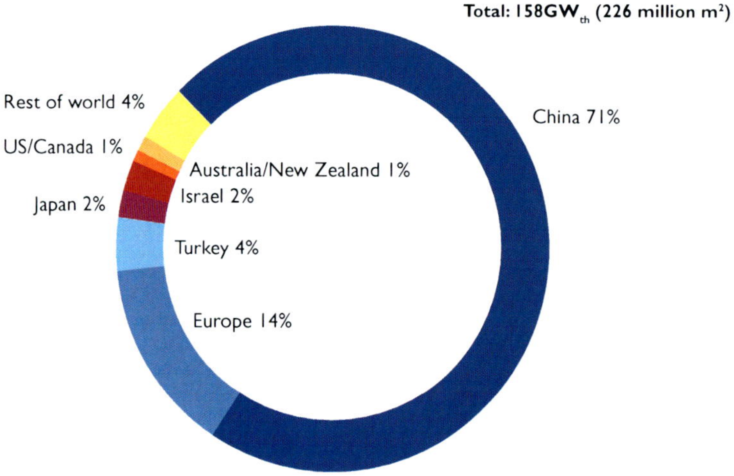

Total: 158GW$_{th}$ (226 million m^2)

- China 71%
- Europe 14%
- Turkey 4%
- Rest of world 4%
- Japan 2%
- Israel 2%
- US/Canada 1%
- Australia/New Zealand 1%

Source: W B Koldehoff, November 2010

Sales declined in five of the six top markets. Besides the financial crisis, the solar thermal energy market was also affected by the turbulence in the building and construction sector as well as in the real estate market. A clear correlation exists between the solar thermal energy market, energy costs and the general economic situation. Despite this, the installed surface area in 2009 amounted for the second time to more than 4 million square metres. Furthermore, the European market has diversified and is now less dependent on developments in Germany. In 2009, Italy, Spain, Austria, France and Greece together achieved a market share of newly installed collector surface area of 39% – for the first time more than Germany with 38%. Markets did not grow in those countries, however, but merely shrank less severely than in Germany (–23%). Due to tax credits in Italy, sales fell by only 5% in comparison with the previous year. With the collapse of the building boom in Spain the solar thermal energy market also succumbed, since building codes are its central pillar. There was a similar plunge in Greece of nearly one third in comparison with the previous year. The market in France declined 15% year-on-year. Only in Austria, as a result of environmentally conscious private home owners, was there a sliver of growth (3%).

There is nevertheless positive news to report from smaller markets. An above-average amount of solar collector surface area was installed in Romania (150%), Hungary (127%), Portugal (103%), the Netherlands (76%), Denmark (65%), Switzerland (48%) and Slovenia (38%).

PROSPECTS FOR EUROPE

In 2008 we predicted the collapse of the European solar thermal energy market in 2009 with a fall of 20% – larger than the –12% that eventually occurred. For 2010 we expect another market decline of 12%. Once again the major markets will shrink. In contrast, Eastern European countries exhibit stable growth, as do Switzerland, Belgium and Sweden. The French solar market could gain slightly.

In 2011 Germany can once more expect 15% growth, provided that market parameters there align. In the rest of Europe, the Eastern European countries will continue to advance. Portugal could achieve slight growth in conjunction with its current subsidy policy (coupling with PV feed-in tariff and large-scale systems). Growth of some 5% is also possible in France. Sizeable uncertainty exists in Spain and Italy. For the entire European solar energy market, we predict moderate growth of roughly 10% for 2011 (Figure 13).

GLOBAL FORECAST UP TO 2020: ANNUAL 20% GROWTH

At 34.1 GW$_{th}$ (48.8 million m²), global newly installed collector capacity in 2009 was some 23% higher than in 2008. For 2010 we assume a global newly installed capacity of 41 GW$_{th}$ (58 million m²), or an increase of around 20%. This growth continues to be carried by China, but is now also boosted by Africa, Oceania, Japan and India. In Europe and the US we again expect a decline in installations in 2010. For a number

Figure 13. European solar thermal energy market
2000–12, EU-27 + Switzerland

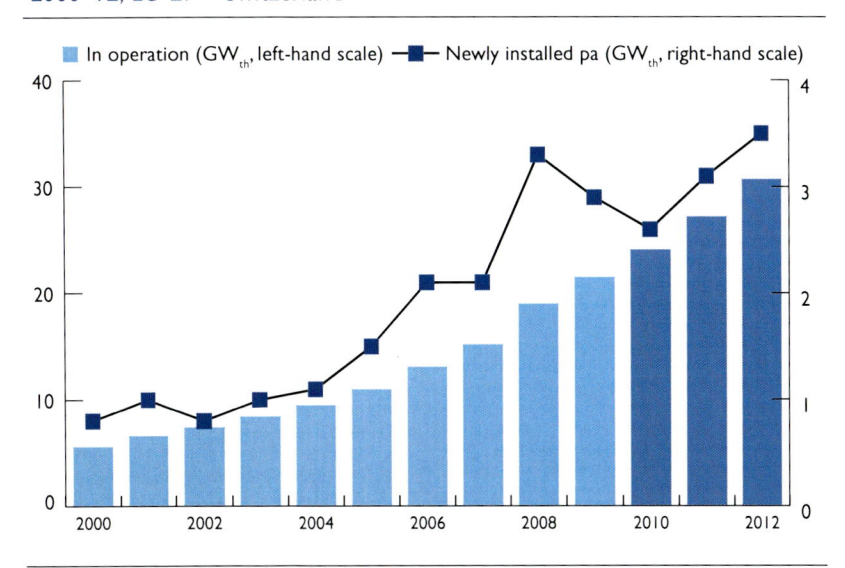

Source: Estif, June 2010, W B Koldehoff, Bank Sarasin, November 2010

Figure 14. Sarasin's forecast of solar collector market 2000–20

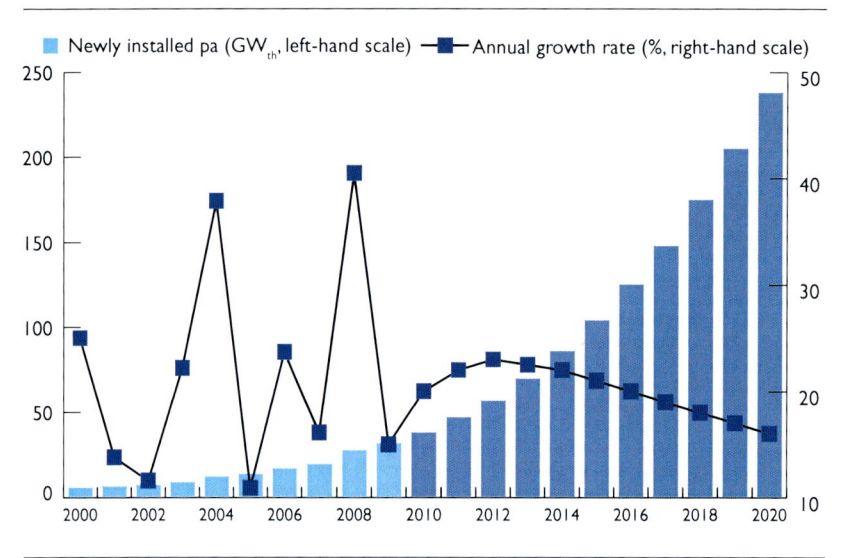

■ Newly installed pa (GW$_{th}$, left-hand scale) ■ Annual growth rate (%, right-hand scale)

Source: W B Koldehoff, Bank Sarasin, November 2010

of years China has demonstrated itself to be the stablest, most dynamic market, with annual growth rates exceeding 20%. With this growth, the Chinese government can presumably achieve its own objectives in the area of solar thermal energy for 2020.

In 2011 the global growth rate of the solar collector market (newly installed capacity of 50GW$_{th}$) should again approach 22%. In 2012 we expect market volume of 61GW$_{th}$. This corresponds to a monetary value of roughly €16 billion. Thus, by the end of 2012, 320GW$_{th}$ of cumulative collector capacity would be in operation globally. For the entire period from 2010–20 we continue to predict an average annual growth rate for newly installed capacity of approximately 20%. The global market for newly installed solar collectors would have, in consequence, a volume of roughly 254GW$_{th}$ by 2020 (Figure 14).

We are convinced that the trend toward solar thermal energy worldwide will also continue. It can be expected that in future the dynamics of markets in sun-drenched countries will increase considerably – for instance, in southern European countries, the US, South America and Australia as well as other emerging countries such as India, Indonesia, Mexico, Brazil, South Africa and the countries of North Africa. This prognosis rests – besides the high growth possibilities among current primary applications – in particular on the enormous potential of new applications such as solar cooling, solar water treatment/desalination and the broad field of industrial process heat.

Chapter 3

Hydropower and ocean power

Mark Thompson, Tiptree Investments

The incredible energy of moving water has been harnessed for thousands of years, the density of water making substantial amounts of useable energy available in a relatively small volume. This energy is generally predictable and provides an important element of any generating portfolio. Although hydropower technology for rivers and dams is mature, innovation continues to improve efficiencies, reduce costs and open more sites for economic development. Conversely, ocean power technology is still at an early stage of development and could offer massive new sources of power, especially with 60% of the world's population living within 100km of the coast.

Hydropower

Hydropower was first harnessed to generate electricity in 1882. Today it supplies around 880 gigawatts (GW)[1] of power, or 20% of the world's electricity. Projects range in size from a few kilowatts to China's massive 22.5GW Three Gorges Dam. Hydropower is economically viable, an important element of any power portfolio, a (very) long-lived asset (50-plus years operating life) and an excellent source of carbon savings as well as being pollution-free.

HOW IT WORKS
Hydropower is by far the best-established form of renewable energy generation. A typical hydropower station includes a dam, reservoir, penstocks (pipes), a powerhouse and substation. The dam stores water and creates the head; penstocks carry water from the reservoir to turbines inside the powerhouse; the water rotates the turbines, which drive generators that produce electricity. The electricity is then transmitted to the grid, via a substation.

Turbines placed within the flow of water use its kinetic energy to drive a generator and convert it to electrical energy. The power generated is determined by the volume of water flowing and the vertical distance (known as 'head') that it has fallen[2].

---
[1] One GW equals 1,000 megawatts (MW) and 1MW equals 1,000 kilowatts (kW). On average, 1MW is sufficient to support 750–1,000 western homes. A terawatt (TW) is 1,000GW. Gigawatts, megawatts and kilowatts are all measures of power and represent a rate of energy conversion. One terawatt hour (TWh) is 1 million megawatt hours (MWh) or 1 billion kilowatt hours (kWh) and these are all units of energy.
[2] The power in 1 cubic metre per second of water falling 10 metres is the same as 10 cubic metres per second of water falling 1 metre.

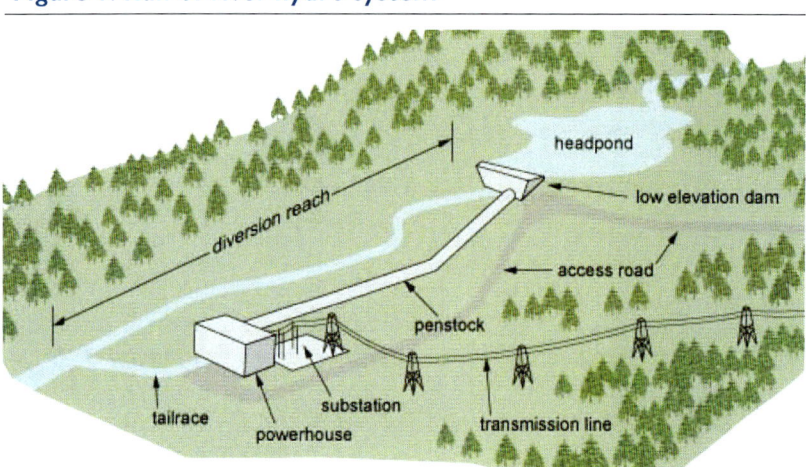

Figure 1. Run-of-river hydro system

Source: Watershed Watch (T Douglas)

Most hydropower stations simply use one-way water flow to generate electricity and are typically divided into run-of-river or storage schemes. The third type of scheme is pumped storage, which recirculates water:

- *Storage* schemes use a dam to impound water in a reservoir that feeds turbines and generators, usually located within the dam itself. These plants have enough storage to cope with seasonal fluctuations and large dams can often store several years of water.
- *Run-of-river* schemes use the natural flow of a river, with negligible storage other than a small weir to improve the consistency of generation. Run-of-river plants usually have widely varying generation across the seasons and some may only operate for a few months a year.
- *Pumped storage* links two reservoirs at different elevations. At times of high power demand, water is released from the upper reservoir, through the turbines to generate electricity and into the lower reservoir. During off-peak hours (typically overnight), cheap electricity from 'always on' base-load generation (such as nuclear) is used to pump the water back to the upper reservoir. Pumped storage projects are highly sought after, as they are the only commercial means of large-scale grid energy storage.

Storage and run-of-river schemes may use a 'diversion', whereby water is channelled to a remote powerhouse containing the turbine and generator, before being returned to the river. Such schemes usually aim to divert 20–50% of the river, in order to maintain environmental flows through the diversion reach.

HYDROPOWER TURBINES

There are three main turbine types: the Kaplan (invented by Viktor Kaplan in 1913), the Pelton (invented by Lester Pelton in the 1870s) and the Francis (invented by James Francis in 1848)[3]. Each design is optimised for a particular combination of flow rate and head (pressure), although innovative new designs are appearing for ultra-low-head sites. All these turbines usually operate at 90%-plus efficiency and most sites apply a degree of customisation to improve efficiency.

Turbines can run for several decades without major maintenance – the most common problem being waterborne material that abrades the turbine blades, although these are relatively easily replaced.

HYDROPOWER USE

Today around 125 countries use hydropower and it provides around 87% of global renewable power, although this share is declining as other renewables are growing much faster. Other than the few countries with abundant hydropower, it is usually used for peak load demand, as it is easily stopped or started, which also makes it an ideal complement to intermittent generating sources, such as wind, wave, tidal or solar. Twenty-five countries depend on hydropower for over 90% of their electricity and 12 of these are completely reliant on hydropower.

FUTURE GROWTH

In 2005, the most recent year for which data is available, the total investment in hydropower was about €18 billion and of this, the equipment component was ~€3 billion in China and €4 billion for the remainder of the world. Although hydropower

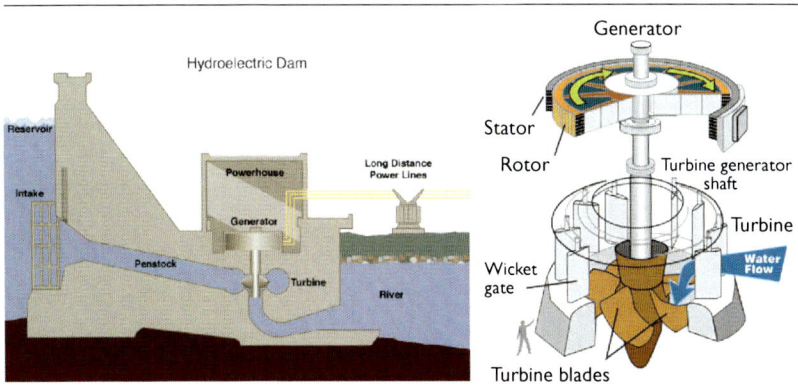

Figure 2. Typical dam cross-section and a Kaplan turbine

Source: Tennessee Valley Authority; US Army Corps of Engineers

---

3 Kaplan – low head, high flow; Pelton – low–medium head, medium-high flow; Francis – high head, low flow.

Figure 3. Leading users of hydropower, 2010

	Annual hydropower production (TWh)	Hydro capacity (GW)	Capacity factor (%)	% of total electricity
China	652.5	196.8	37.0	22.3
Canada	369.5	89.0	59.0	61.1
Brazil	363.8	69.1	56.0	85.6
US	250.6	79.5	42.0	5.7
Russia	179.0	45.0	42.0	17.6
Norway	140.5	27.5	49.0	98.3
India	115.6	33.6	43.0	15.8
Japan	83.6	27.2	37.0	7.2
Sweden	66.2	16.2	46.0	44.3
France	63.6	25.3	25.0	11.2

Sources: industry sources

is growing more slowly than other renewables, only one third of the global technically and economically feasible resource has been developed.

Opportunities for large, new projects are limited in the developed world, as most sites are either already exploited or unavailable for reasons such as environmental constraints. However, there remain many opportunities for small low-head, or run-of-river projects. Canada is home to over 475 hydropower plants with a capacity of 89GW and produces about 370TWh each year. But Canada's untapped potential remains substantial. It is estimated to have ~2.5 GW (ie, C$8 billion of investment) of economic small hydro sites available for development, while Scotland has 650MW of usable potential and the Department of Energy reports that the US has 400GW untapped (34% with conventional turbines, 50% in micro-hydro and 16% requiring unconventional systems). In the developing world there is greater scope for large projects and hydropower will be an important source of new generation in South America, China, India, Africa and South-East Asia.

A relatively small proportion of dams are primarily used for hydropower: 11% in North America, 6% in Africa and 7% in Asia. Only 2,400 of the 80,000 US dams are currently used for hydropower. Therefore, one of the most economic development routes is the retrofit of power systems to dams built for other purposes. For example, the Three Gorges Dam should cover its construction costs within five to eight years of full operation, as it was also designed for flood control.

IS LARGE HYDRO RENEWABLE?
In the past, large hydro projects were considered a renewable source of power. However, negative impacts associated with the environmental and social consequences of large-scale hydropower development – including possible impacts on climate change, particularly in the tropics – now mean fewer international organisations consider large hydropower to be 'clean' energy.

Hydropower and Ocean Power | 49

Figure 4. Large versus small hydro

Small hydro	Large hydro
Fewer 'eggs in one basket'	Most efficiently meets central needs
Power to remote communities	Economy of scale (cheaper per kilowatt)
Less capital	Security of supply, with storage
More private sector and local involvement/ownership	Able to provide ancillary services
Assists grid stability	Improves thermal generating performance and helps other renewables
Greater political acceptability	

The World Bank considers that 'large hydro' should be excluded from its commitment to financing renewable energy and uses a *de facto* limit of 50MW. However, many organisations consider anything over 10MW to be 'large hydro'. The UK government's Renewables Obligation only considers a hydro plant of less than 20MW to be renewable. While the 50MW threshold provides a useful rule of thumb, large run-of-river projects typically have far lower environmental and social impacts than an equivalent storage-based plant. As such, these often qualify for Clean Development Mechanism credits based on a formula that measures output relative to head pond area.

RUN-OF-RIVER
Most new projects in the developed world now tend to be run-of-river, as this uses little or no impoundment and the natural river flow is utilised with no seasonal regulation. This reduces the environmental impact and such projects are common for:
- large flows in flat river reaches;
- flows where a large head is obtainable;
- installed capacities below the maximum potential for the site;
- rivers with major sediment or bed loads; and,
- sites unsuitable for dam construction.

As a rule of thumb, the capacity factor (the ratio of the net electricity generated,

Figure 5. Construction cost split

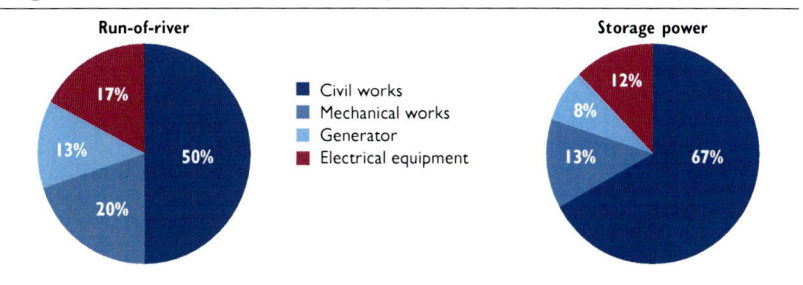

Run-of-river: Civil works 50%, Mechanical works 20%, Generator 13%, Electrical equipment 17%

Storage power: Civil works 67%, Mechanical works 13%, Generator 8%, Electrical equipment 12%

Source: Andritz VA Tech

for the time considered, to the energy that could have been generated at continuous full-power operation during the same period) for a run-of-river project should be around 50%. Much greater than 60% suggests that the turbine is undersized, and less than 40% suggests the plant is bordering on uneconomic.

ENVIRONMENTAL AND SOCIAL ISSUES

Hydropower generates no greenhouse gases or other pollutants and it can increase the percentage of intermittent renewables the transmission grid can handle. However, there are environmental and social issues to consider, especially with large storage projects. These can change eco-systems, limit fish migration (fish ladders can offset this) or change downstream flow (sediment, oxygenation, flow rates) and new designs of dam or turbine that ameliorate this are being actively researched.

The creation of a reservoir may also create greenhouse gases, as the plant life decays in a low oxygen environment, when it is first inundated. In the tropics, the World Commission on Dams reports that, with a large reservoir relative to the power capacity (under 100 watts per square metre of surface) with no preliminary clearing of vegetation, emissions matching fossil fuel generation may occur. However, boreal reservoirs create only 2–8% of the emissions from a corresponding fossil fuel plant.

Finally, forced relocation of the population when a reservoir is created causes significant problems. Some 40 million–80 million people are estimated to have been displaced due to dam construction. Because of the complex problems this causes, most large lenders now avoid such projects.

ECONOMICS

The main attraction of hydropower is the elimination of fuel costs, its long service life and ability to turn on/off rapidly. With very low running costs, the economics of hydro power primarily depend on the construction cost, cost of capital and power prices. Even small run-of-river power is commercial and it has the potential to cut costs further through turbine improvements and better control systems, although increased environmental costs (environmental assessments, fish ladders, etc) may

Figure 6. Run-of-river financial summary

Performance	New	Incremental
Duty cycle	Varies with resource	Varies with resource
Typical capacity factor (%)	40–60	40–60
Economics		
Project costs ($m/MWe)	1–4	0.5–3
Fixed O&M ($'000/MW/year)	5–25	5–25
Variable O&M ($/MWhe)	4–6	3–6
Levelised cost ($/MWhe)	40–120	5–90

Source: Tiptree Investments

Hydropower and Ocean Power | 51

limit this. Therefore, some of the most attractive projects are likely to be re-powering existing sites or adding capacity to existing dams.

A project's revenue depends on its capacity and capacity factor, but its economic return depends on revenue and construction cost. Figure 7 shows two high-quality run-of-river projects in India that both use similar water volumes (design ~26m^3/sec). However, the Malana project has an output of 86MW, as the gross head is

Figure 7. Two Indian run-of-river plants
Bhilwara Energy's 86MW Malana plant in Himachal Pradesh

Bhoruka Power's 4.5MW Madhavamantri plant in Karnataka.

Photos: Mark Thompson

480m, while the Madhavamantri project has an output of 4.5MW, since its gross head is only 4.7m. Both are economically attractive projects, but the challenges of building a project in the foothills of the Himalayas somewhat offset the extra energy collected, compared to building on the Deccan Plateau.

INVESTMENT RISKS

The risks facing hydropower divide neatly into pre- and post-commissioning. As with any development project, the early stage issues of permitting, grid connection, power purchase agreements, resource assessment and design create uncertainties for the investor. Construction risks also tend to be greater than for other renewables, given the large component of on-site civil works, along with unexpected geology or abnormal river levels that may delay construction. Most small run-of-river projects will take two to three years to build, exposing them to at least two winter seasons.

Post-construction, the main risk comes from variability in water flows – either too much or too little. Extremely high water flows may cause 'overtopping', which can damage infrastructure, while unexpected periods of low flow may stretch financial covenants. Technical operating risks tend to be minor and plants generally run with minimal supervision.

THE INVESTMENT OPPORTUNITIES

Companies that are all subsidiaries of major multinationals currently dominate the large hydro sector and there are no credible 'pure play' hydro technology investments available on the quoted markets. Small hydro projects are difficult to follow reliably, given their position in the larger, mature sector. However, these are potentially attractive investment opportunities, along with technology developers focused on micro hydro, low-head hydro, improved efficiency and environmental integration (ie, fish friendly). One of the only established developers of small hydro projects on the public market is Canadian Hydro Developers, based in Alberta.

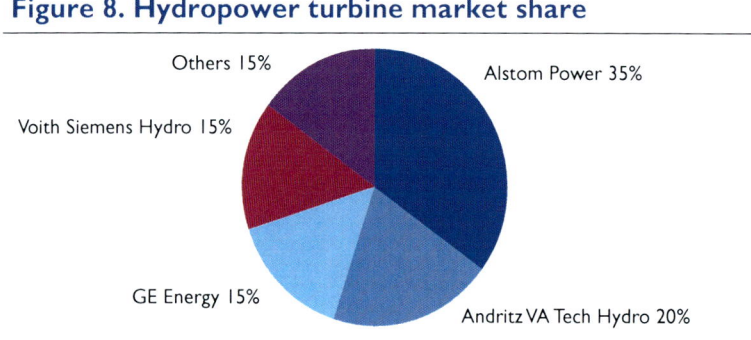

Figure 8. Hydropower turbine market share

- Alstom Power 35%
- Andritz VA Tech Hydro 20%
- GE Energy 15%
- Voith Siemens Hydro 15%
- Others 15%

Source: Company and Tiptree Investments estimates

Ocean power

Ocean power is a broad term encompassing several energy sources: wave, marine and tidal currents, tidal potential energy and nascent sources such as thermal or saline inclines. Other than a small number of tidal barrages, ocean power is one of the least developed sources of renewable energy. However, it is attracting substantial interest due to its massive potential and the fact that 60% of the world's population lives within 100km of the coast.

Of all the intermittent renewable sources, ocean power could be closest to providing a predictable generating profile and water's density means that lots of energy can be extracted from a relatively small area. Significant developments in ocean power are expected over the coming decade, with over 1,000 patents existing for ocean power generators. Tidal and wave power is at a similar development stage to wind power 25 years ago, with capacity forecast to grow from 1TWh in 2002 to 35TWh in 2030, with the UK currently in the early development stage and hosting 2.4MW of capacity (~12GWh).

According to the Douglas-Westwood report, *The World Wave and Tidal Market Report 2011-2015*, installations in 2011 are more than double those in 2010 and a total of 150MW of wave and tidal current stream capacity is forecast to be installed between 2011 and 2015. The three largest markets are the UK, Canada and the US. The UK leads with 110MW of installations forecast. This report expects $1.2 billion to be spent on wave and tidal current stream sectors over the next five years, with an annual capital expenditure estimated at $52 million in 2010 rising to $500 million in 2015.

TYPES OF OCEAN POWER
- *Tidal power* captures energy from the vertical change in the sea's height, typically by capturing the flow with a barrage – the incoming tide raises the water level and at low tide the water is released through a turbine. This has long been used in France, Canada and Russia.
- *Wave power* uses the energy in waves to move pontoons, buoys or columns of air/water up and down to generate electricity. Many locations provide a surface wave energy density of over 40MW/km of coastline, which is enough for economic wave energy.
- *Tidal stream power* captures energy from the flow of tides or marine currents, often using the underwater equivalent of a small wind turbine.
- *Ocean thermal energy conversion* (OTEC) uses the temperature difference between the warm surface and the cold depths to create power. This is still at a research stage, as the costs of the piping to move the water and the parasitic energy losses have proved prohibitive, as has the difficulty of finding sites close enough to shore to make it economic.
- *Blue energy* uses the difference in the salt concentration between seawater and fresh water to generate power. Technologies include reverse electro-dialysis and pressure-retarded osmosis, but both are still at an early research stage.

WHAT MAKES A GOOD OCEAN ENERGY TECHNOLOGY?
Wave and tidal power are renewable energy technologies that should offer substantial growth. However, in order to bring prices down to a commercial level, devices need economies of scale and robust economics. Tiptree Investments's criteria for a world-class, investable technology are that it needs to be:
- scaleable and easy to fabricate or transport onshore;
- useable at any site, without customisation;
- storm proof;
- simple; and,
- easy to maintain on site and in almost any weather conditions.

Only two designs are approaching these criteria at the moment: the Pelamis and power buoy designs. This is not to dismiss tidal designs, which have great potential but may never achieve the necessary scale due to geographic limitations. Other technologies requiring extensive infrastructure or civil engineering may be attractive on a case-by-case basis (for example, when incorporated in a new harbour), but these are unlikely to interest an investor seeking the venture capital-type returns expected from a young technology.

Wave power

Waves have the potential to provide a completely sustainable source of energy that can be captured by a wave energy converter. These can be deployed on the shoreline, near the shore or in deep offshore waters. Wave power has long been recognised as an energy source: the first wave energy patent was issued in 1799 and by 1909 harbour lighting was wave powered in California. However, numerous technical problems have frustrated progress and a clearly successful design is yet to emerge.

LONG-TERM SUSTAINABLE ENERGY RESOURCE
Waves are created by the wind interacting with the sea. The size of wave depends on the wind speed, its fetch (the distance over which the wind excites the waves), seafloor bathymetry and currents (which can focus or disperse the energy). The resource potential is enormous, although estimates are not yet robust, so Figure 9 shows the average wave energy available across the globe. As an indication, consultancy firm ETSU believes the lower 48 US states have the potential for 860TWh per year, Alaska offers 1,250TWh per year and the UK offers 58TWh per year.

WAVE ENERGY CONVERTERS
A wave power machine needs to resist the motion of the waves in order to generate power. There are five main designs:
- A partially submerged, hollow structure is open to the sea below the water line and encloses a column of air on top of a column of water. Waves cause the water column to rise and fall, which in turn pushes the air through a turbine that spins in the same direction, regardless of the airflow direction (Oscillating Water Column.

Hydropower and Ocean Power | 55

Figure 9. Global wave energy, MW/km of wave front

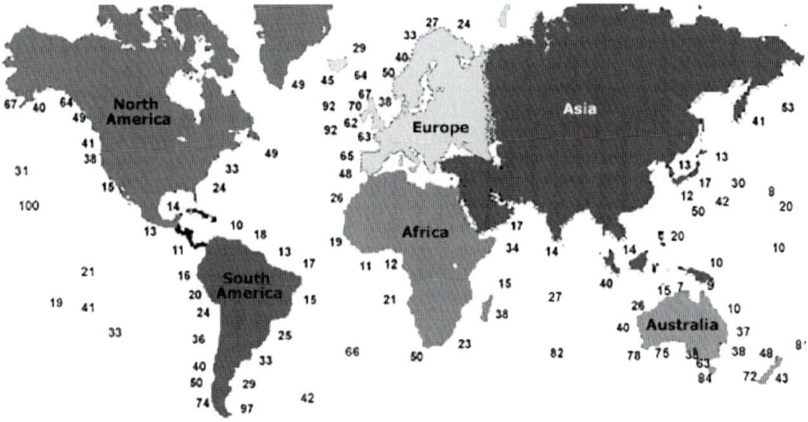

Source: IMechE 1991

- A floating device moored to the seabed that reacts to the change in water level. The floating part of the device can be either segmented with components hinged together (ie, Pelamis) or a single component that bobs up and down (a Wave Pump).

Figure 10. Wave power devices

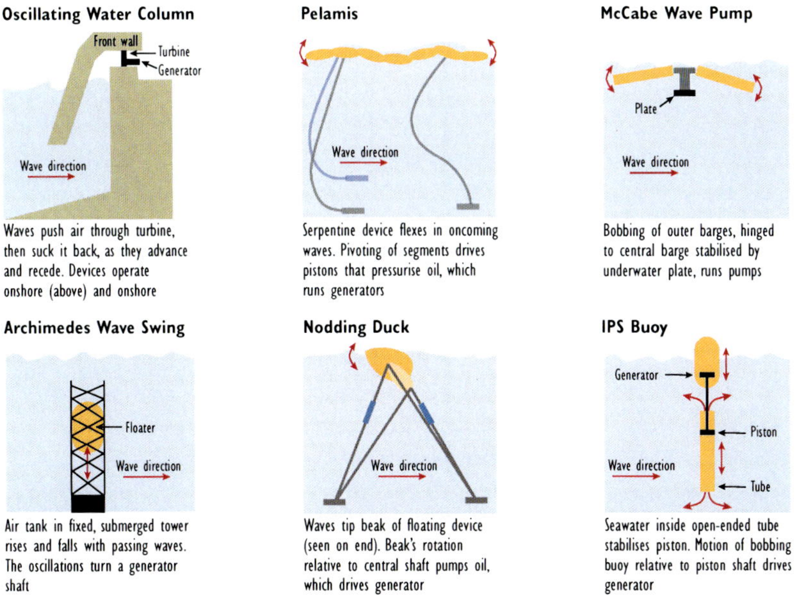

Oscillating Water Column
Waves push air through turbine, then suck it back, as they advance and recede. Devices operate onshore (above) and onshore

Pelamis
Serpentine device flexes in oncoming waves. Pivoting of segments drives pistons that pressurise oil, which runs generators

McCabe Wave Pump
Bobbing of outer barges, hinged to central barge stabilised by underwater plate, runs pumps

Archimedes Wave Swing
Air tank in fixed, submerged tower rises and falls with passing waves. The oscillations turn a generator shaft

Nodding Duck
Waves tip beak of floating device (seen on end). Beak's rotation relative to central shaft pumps oil, which drives generator

IPS Buoy
Seawater inside open-ended tube stabilises piston. Motion of bobbing buoy relative to piston shaft drives generator

Source: P Weiss and R Savidge

- An underwater buoyant device rigidly moored to the seabed that reacts to the variations in the water pressure, so that the single moving part bobs up and down (Archimedes Wave Swing or IPS Buoy).
- A hinged flap that is bottom-mounted. Waves cause the buoyant paddle to oscillate, pushing hydraulic fluid through hydraulic pumps to generate electricity, with the device reacting to changes in water velocity (Nodding Duck).
- Overtopping devices that physically capture water from waves and hold it in a reservoir above sea level, before being returned to the sea through conventional low-head turbines (Tapchan or Wave Dragon).

Wave energy devices are one of the most promising new renewable energy technologies, although no clear favourite exists. The wide availability of suitable wave climates, both near and far offshore, makes this an attractive resource. Unfortunately, technical problems over reliability, efficiency and cost have limited testing to a small number of prototypes. Several government supported test centres are now operational, which should reduce the set-up costs for new technologies and encourage venture capital investment.

Tidal energy

Tidal energy conversion devices use the natural rise and fall of the sea level to create energy. The gravitational interaction of the moon, the sun and the earth's rotation creates this change and provides an inexhaustible form of renewable energy. The local shape of the seafloor or coastline may accentuate this effect, such that Canada's Bay of Fundy has a tidal range of 17 metres and Britain's Bristol Channel a range of 15 metres.

TIDAL POWER

Tidal power accesses the potential energy created by the difference in height between high and low tides, typically via a tidal dam or barrage. As the water level changes with the tides, a difference in height develops across the barrage, creating a strong current through the barrage's turbines on each ebb and flow. The tidal cycle means that power can be generated for a large part of the day, on a predictable basis and as a barrage uses similar technology to a conventional hydropower plant, the investment risk is primarily during construction of the barrage.

Barrages are typically built across an estuary, although designs involving partial enclosure, or a tidal lagoon within an estuary, have all been proposed. The 240MW La Rance barrage in France uses an 8 metre tidal range and is the best-known project, although barrages also exist in Canada and Russia. However, estuaries are among the world's most productive and sensitive ecosystems. Flooding and flow changes caused by a barrage could disrupt the natural processes and ecosystems. As a result, the technology's global potential is constrained by its environmental impact, the massive civil engineering costs and the limited number of viable sites.

TIDAL STREAM

Rather than using a dam, marine current turbines are placed directly in-stream and work much like submerged windmills driven by flowing water, rather than air. They can be installed in the sea where there are high tidal current velocities, or in the few places with fast continuous ocean currents. These devices can extract energy from the huge volumes of flowing water, which have the major advantage of being as predictable as the tides that cause them. Some limited development is also occurring in major rivers, such as the Mississippi, which is deep enough to accommodate the technology.

Currents created by the tides are often magnified by topographical features, such as headlands, inlets and straits, or by the shape of the seabed, forcing the sea through a narrow channel. The UK and Canada have some of the largest potential resources in the world (Pentland Firth and Bay of Fundy[4]); according to Natural Resources Canada, its tidal resources could supply two-thirds of the country's electrical demand.

Compared to wind turbines, marine current turbines are smaller (water is 800 times denser than air), and can be sited closer together (tidal streams are normally bi-directional whereas wind is multi-directional). Most designs use a horizontal axis, although some innovative vertical axis designs (cross flow turbines), using drag or lift, are being tested (Figure 12).

Figure 11. A tidal barrage and tidal stream converter

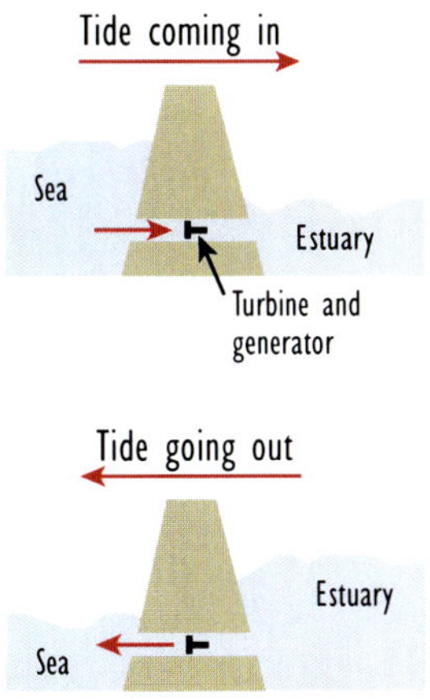

Source: Marine Current Turbines; Darvill

---

4 The Pentland Firth has a tidal race of 16 knots (~30kph) and the Bay of Fundy runs at 8 knots.

Figure 12. Tidal stream technologies

Horizontal axis, bottom mounted

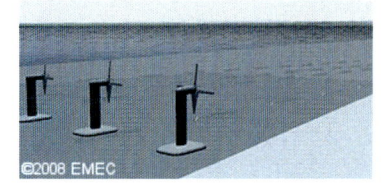

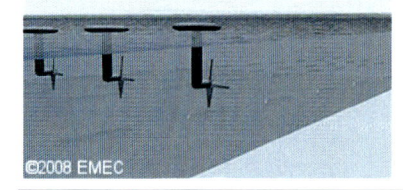

Horizontal axis, surface piercing

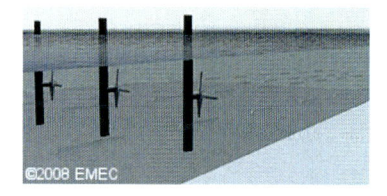

Horizontal axis, floating

Vertical axis

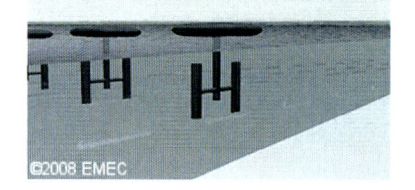

Source: Greenpeace

All tidal stream technologies are currently at a development stage, as issues of reliability, maintenance, survivability, security and cost are resolved. One or two companies are testing quasi-commercial scale products, although production models are unlikely to appear for several years. Today, tidal stream is a promising area, but one suited to venture capital and research funding, rather than the public markets.

Summary

Wave and tidal power will become increasingly interesting to investors due to the:
- high degree of predictability of such power;
- the density of water creating a massive resource (according to the International Energy Agency, 100,000TWh per year, or five times the current global electrical demand) of concentrated renewable energy;
- high levels of population (~60% of the world) living near the coast; and,
- indications that cost parity is achievable in the medium term, once many of the technologies come through the development stage.

Chapter 4

Geothermal energy

Alexander Richter, Canadian Geothermal Energy Association

What is geothermal energy?

'Geothermal' literally means 'earth's heat'. The temperature at the earth's core is estimated to be 5,500°C – about as hot as the surface of the sun. Geothermal energy is a clean, renewable resource that can be tapped by many countries around the world, especially those located in geologically favourable areas. Geothermal energy can be harnessed from underground reservoirs (conventional geothermal) containing hot rocks saturated with water and/or steam. Wells of typically 2km in depth or more are drilled into the reservoirs. The hot water and steam are then piped up to a geothermal power plant, where they are used to drive electric generators to create power for businesses and homes.

Geothermal energy is considered a renewable resource because it exploits the abundant interior heat of the earth; the water, once used and cooled, is piped back to the reservoir. It can be utilised for electricity production and for direct use, for example, for heating and industrial purposes.

In areas with no hydrothermal fluid circulation, there is traditionally no potential for conventional geothermal systems, but with enhanced geothermal systems (EGS) that "allow some form of engineering to develop the permeability necessary for the circulation of hot water or steam and the recovery of the heat for electrical power generation" (US Geological Survey – USGS), geothermal energy could be utilised far beyond the possibilities of today's technologies.

Comparison to other renewable energies

While depending heavily on political and financial support, geothermal energy represents the only real base-load capacity alternative to fossil fuels, such as coal or oil (Figure 1). The biggest potential and prospects for the shorter term are in the direct use of geothermal energy, particularly for heating and other applications that use heat directly.

With technological developments – for example, in binary systems and engineered geothermal systems – geothermal energy could provide all the electricity needed worldwide.

Beyond cost and other factors, the capacity factor – the ratio of actual power

Figure 1. Capacity factors of selected renewable energies
Average net capacity, %

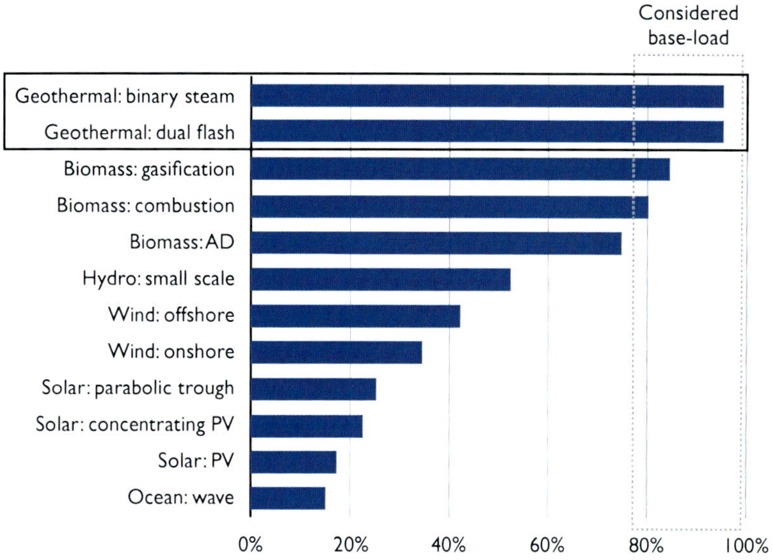

Geothermal: binary steam	~95%
Geothermal: dual flash	~90%
Biomass: gasification	~85%
Biomass: combustion	~80%
Biomass: AD	~75%
Hydro: small scale	~50%
Wind: offshore	~40%
Wind: onshore	~35%
Solar: parabolic trough	~25%
Solar: concentrating PV	~22%
Solar: PV	~18%
Ocean: wave	~15%

Considered base-load: Geothermal binary steam and dual flash

Source: Íslandsbanki Geothermal Research

output over a period of time and its output if it operated at full capacity around the clock – is probably one of the most convincing arguments for geothermal energy. Geothermal energy can be utilised nearly around the clock with average capacity factors of around 90–95%.

Global overview and potential

Today, geothermal energy generates approximately 67,000GWh of electricity, with an installed capacity of about 11,000MW. The main producing countries are the US, the Philippines, Mexico, Indonesia and Italy, which produce approximately 80% of the world's total geothermal electricity generation.

The top 10 countries produce approximately 95% of geothermal electricity. As of 2010 there were 24 countries generating electricity from geothermal energy and three nations deriving more than one fifth of their electricity from geothermal: Iceland, the Philippines and El Salvador.

Geothermal direct-use applications generate approximately 121,700GWh (thermal). China, Sweden, the US, Turkey and Iceland produce approximately 60% of the world's direct-use GWh thermal. The top 10 countries account for approximately 70% of the world's direct use.

The largest potential for geothermal electricity generation lies in the hot regions of the planet or the tectonic plates – for example, along the Pacific 'ring of fire'. Look-

Figure 2. Installed capacity by region: current and potential MW

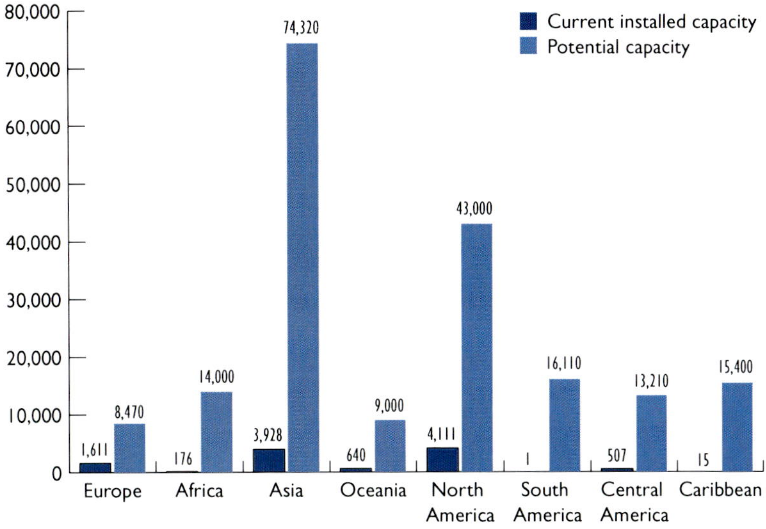

Bar chart showing current installed capacity and potential capacity (MW) by region:
- Europe: 1,611 / 8,470
- Africa: 176 / 14,000
- Asia: 3,928 / 74,320
- Oceania: 640 / 9,000
- North America: 4,111 / 43,000
- South America: 1 / 16,110
- Central America: 507 / 13,210
- Caribbean: 15 / 15,400

Source: IGA, Bertani, Íslandsbanki estimates 2010

ing at conventional technology only, the overall potential lies at around 200,000MW installed electricity generation capacity. The largest potential is in Asia (Figure 2). Indonesia, in particular, has the largest potential of around 28,000MW. The Americas follow closely, primarily Latin America and the US. Regions like the Horn of Africa and Oceania also show great potential for geothermal electricity generation.

Geothermal energy – market, players and project timeline

It is not uncommon for geothermal power projects to take five to seven years before the actual operation of the installation, depending on project size and technology. An additional one or two years may be required, depending on permits and other licensing issues.

Projects for direct use of geothermal heat need less time. Both applications depend greatly on the success of drilling and available resources. As in any other industry, depending on a drilling for success in raising capital can be difficult. The success is defined by a proven resource – sufficient reservoir volume, fluid temperature and rock parameters.

The geothermal energy market is heavily dependent on a number of specialised services and suppliers – for example, specific engineering services and technology suppliers, which demand high expertise and are in short supply (Figure 3).

The market also depends heavily on clear legislation and administration – for

Figure 3. Geothermal energy market and players

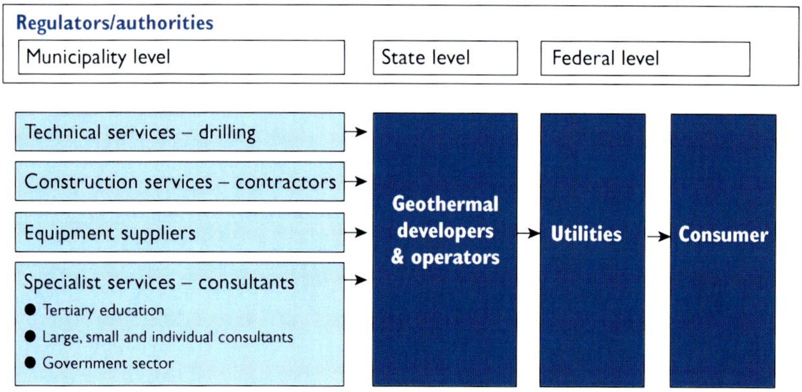

Regulators/authorities
- Municipality level
- State level
- Federal level

- Technical services – drilling
- Construction services – contractors
- Equipment suppliers
- Specialist services – consultants
  - Tertiary education
  - Large, small and individual consultants
  - Government sector

→ Geothermal developers & operators → Utilities → Consumer

Source: Íslandsbanki Geothermal Research

example for permits and land use issues, not only from domestic governments, but also at local and municipality levels. It also requires strong knowledge and experience on the site of the development, as well as a concrete understanding of geothermal development on the side of the off-taker.

Generally, a geothermal project can be divided into five different phases (Figure 4). Any concrete time estimate for the individual phases is difficult, as this is strongly dependent on local and national legal requirements and the availability of services and supplies needed – for example, for drilling.

Figure 4. Geothermal project timeline

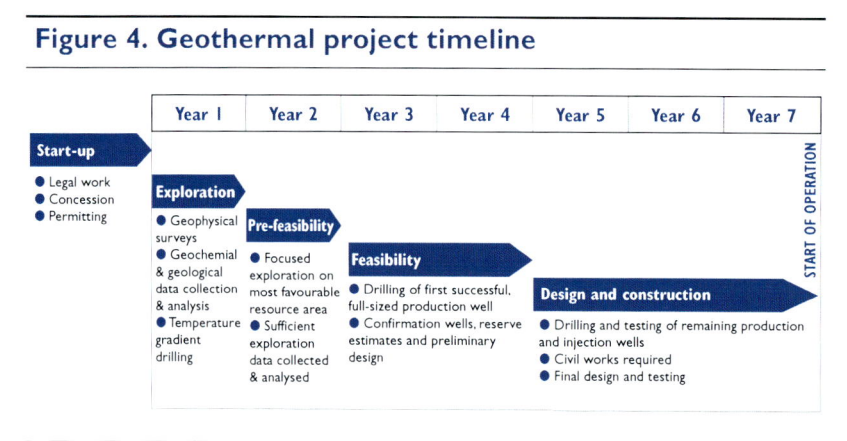

Years 1–7

Start-up (Year 1)
- Legal work
- Concession
- Permitting

Exploration (Year 1–2)
- Geophysical surveys
- Geochemical & geological data collection & analysis
- Temperature gradient drilling

Pre-feasibility (Year 2–3)
- Focused exploration on most favourable resource area
- Sufficient exploration data collected & analysed

Feasibility (Year 3–4)
- Drilling of first successful, full-sized production well
- Confirmation wells, reserve estimates and preliminary design

Design and construction (Year 5–7)
- Drilling and testing of remaining production and injection wells
- Civil works required
- Final design and testing

START OF OPERATION

Source: Íslandsbanki Geothermal Research

Geothermal energy in the US

CONSUMPTION, GENERATION AND RESOURCE LOCATIONS

The US remains the leading country in installed geothermal power generation capacity, representing nearly a third of the world's geothermal capacity (Figure 5).

Today, geothermal energy represents approximately 0.3% of total US energy consumption and 7.7% of renewable energy resources (excluding hydro) in the country's primary energy supply mix (Figure 6). For US electricity production, geothermal energy represents 0.4% of the total production and 13.5% of electricity generation through renewable resources (excluding hydro).

The main geothermal resources are located in the Western states (Figure 7),

Figure 5. Geothermal power generation capacity 2010
Installed capacity, MW

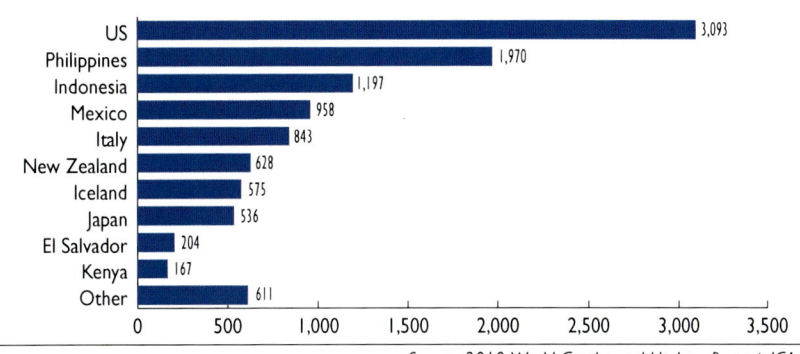

Country	MW
US	3,093
Philippines	1,970
Indonesia	1,197
Mexico	958
Italy	843
New Zealand	628
Iceland	575
Japan	536
El Salvador	204
Kenya	167
Other	611

Source: 2010 World Geothermal Update, Bertani, IGA

Figure 6. US energy consumption and electricity generation
By source, rolling 12 months as of June 2009

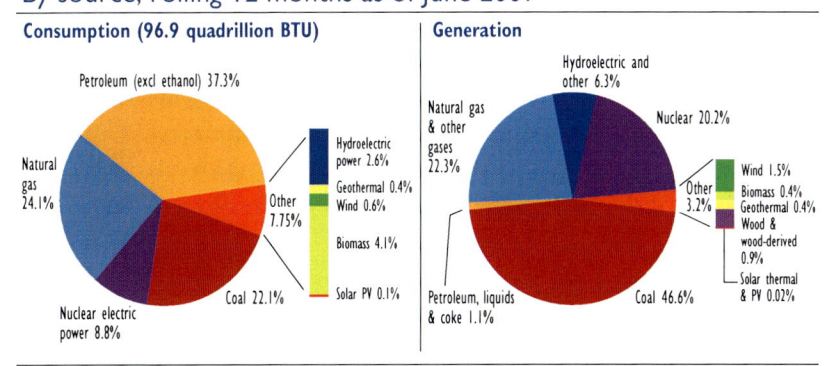

Consumption (96.9 quadrillion BTU)
- Petroleum (excl ethanol) 37.3%
- Natural gas 24.1%
- Nuclear electric power 8.8%
- Coal 22.1%
- Other 7.75%
  - Hydroelectric power 2.6%
  - Geothermal 0.4%
  - Wind 0.6%
  - Biomass 4.1%
  - Solar PV 0.1%

Generation
- Hydroelectric and other 6.3%
- Natural gas & other gases 22.3%
- Nuclear 20.2%
- Coal 46.6%
- Petroleum, liquids & coke 1.1%
- Other 3.2%
  - Wind 1.5%
  - Biomass 0.4%
  - Geothermal 0.4%
  - Wood & wood-derived 0.9%
  - Solar thermal & PV 0.02%

Source: US Energy Information Administration

64 | Investment Opportunities for a Low-Carbon World

Figure 7. Geothermal resources in the US
Estimated earth temperature at 5km depth

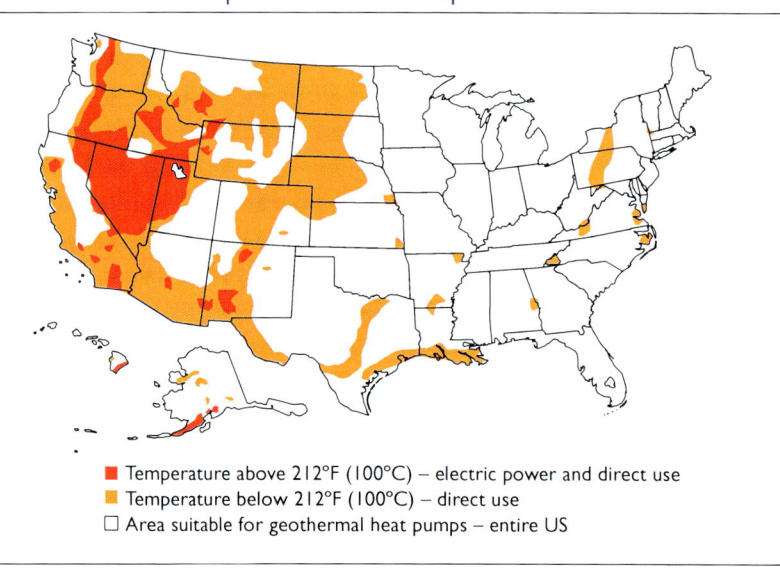

■ Temperature above 212°F (100°C) – electric power and direct use
■ Temperature below 212°F (100°C) – direct use
☐ Area suitable for geothermal heat pumps – entire US

Source: NREL

with installed capacity in seven states: Alaska, California, Hawaii, Idaho, Nevada, New Mexico and Utah. All these states have projects in development, as do Arizona, Colorado, Florida, Oregon, Texas, Washington and Wyoming.

California represents 83% of the total installed and operating capacity, Nevada 14%. Utah 1.4% and Hawaii 1.1%, with other states combined providing only a marginal percentage with installations of less than 1MW each.

Today, there are 80 geothermal plants in operation in the US. The majority of

Figure 8. US geothermal power capacity by state
Installed capacity online, MW, %

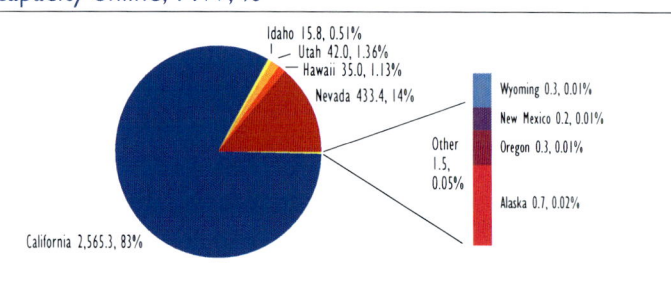

California 2,565.3, 83%
Nevada 433.4, 14%
Idaho 15.8, 0.51%
Utah 42.0, 1.36%
Hawaii 35.0, 1.13%
Other 1.5, 0.05%
Wyoming 0.3, 0.01%
New Mexico 0.2, 0.01%
Oregon 0.3, 0.01%
Alaska 0.7, 0.02%

As at April 2010. Source: Geothermal Energy Association

Figure 9. US geothermal power plants

State/plant	Start year	Type	Number of units	Installed capacity (MW)
Alaska				
Chena Hot Springs	2006	Binary	3	0.7
California				
Aidlin	1989	Dry steam	2	20.0
Amedee	1988	Binary	2	1.6
Bear Canyon	1988	Dry steam	2	20.0
Big Geysers	1980	Dry steam	1	97.0
BLM	1989	Double flash	3	90.0
Bottle Rock	2007	Dry steam	1	55.0
Calistoga	1984	Dry steam	1	80.0
CE Turbo	2000	Single flash	1	10.0
Cobb Creek	1979	Dry steam	1	110.0
Del Ranch (Hoch)	1989	Dual flash	1	38.0
Eagle Rock	1975	Dry steam	1	110.0
Elmore	1989	Dual flash	1	38.0
Gem Resources II	1989	Double flash	1	18.0
Gem Resources III	1989	Double flash	1	18.0
Gould	2006	Binary	2	–
Grant	1985	Dry steam	1	113.0
Heber	1985	Dual flash	2	52.0
Heber II	1993	Binary	7	48.0
Heber South	2008	Binary	1	10.0
Honey Lake	1989	Hybrid: biomass	1	1.5
Lake View	1985	Dry steam	1	113.0
Leathers	1990	Dual flash	1	38.0
Mammoth Pacific I	1984	Binary	4	10.0
Mammoth Pacific II	1990	Binary	na	15.0
McCabe	1971	Dry steam	2	106.0
Navy I	1987	Double flash	3	na
Navy II	1988	Double flash	3	na
NCPA I	1983	Dry steam, low pressure reaction	2	110.0
NCPA II	1983	Dry steam, low pressure reaction	2	110.0
North Brawley	2009	Binary	7	50.0
Ormesa I	1986	Binary	1	44.0
Ormesa IE	1988	Binary	1	10.0
Ormesa IH	1989	Binary	1	13.2
Ormesa II	1987	Binary	1	18.0
Quicksilver	1985	Dry steam	1	113.0
Ridgeline	1972	Dry steam	2	106.0
Salton Sea I	1982	Dual flash	1	10.0
Salton Sea II	1990	Dual flash	3	20.0
Salton Sea III	1989	Dual flash	1	50.0 ▶
Salton Sea IV	1996	Dual flash	na	40.0
Salton Sea V	2000	Dual flash	1	49.0
SIGC Binary	1993	Binary	6	40.2
Socrates	1983	Dry steam	1	113.0 ▶

Figure 9. US geothermal power plants (continued)

State/plant	Start year	Type	Number of units	Installed capacity (MW)
California (continued)				
Sonoma	1983	Dry steam	1	72.0
Sulphur Springs	1980	Dry steam	1	109.0
Vulcan	1986	Dual flash	1	34.0
West Ford Flat	1988	Dry steam	2	27.0
Wineagle	1985	Binary	1	0.7
Hawaii				
Puna Geothermal Venture	1993	Hybrid: single flash/binary	10	35.0
Idaho				
Raft River	2007	Binary	1	15.8
Nevada				
Beowawe	1985	Double flash	1	16.6
Brady Hot Springs	1992	Double flash/binary	3	27.0
Desert Peak	2006	Binary	1	na
Dixie Valley	1988	Double flash	1	67.2
Faulkner I, Blue Mountain	2009	Binary	–	49.5
Galena 2	2007	Binary	1	15.0
Galena 3	2008	Binary	1	20.0
Jersey Valley	2010	Binary	–	15.0
Richard Burdett	2005	Binary	2	30.0
Salt Wells	2009	Binary	1	24.0
San Emidio (Empire)	1987	Binary	4	4.8
Soda Lake I	1987	Binary	4	5.1
Soda Lake II	1990	Binary	6	18.0
Steamboat Hills	1988	Single flash	1	14.4
Steamboat I	1986	Binary	7	8.4
Steamboat IA	1988	Binary	2	3.0
Steamboat II	1992*	Binary	2	29.0
Steamboat III	1992	Binary	2	24.0
Stillwater	2009	Binary	4	47.3
Wabuska	1984	Binary	3	2.2
New Mexico				
Lightning Rock	2008	Binary	1	–
Oregon				
OIT	2009	Binary	–	60.0
Utah				
Blundell I	1984	Single flash	1	23.0
Blundell II	2007	Binary	1	9.0
Cove Fort 1**	1990	Dry steam	1	8.5
Cove Fort 2**	1990	Binary	3	2.3
Hatch, Thermo no 1	2009	Binary	–	60.0
Thermo Hot Spring	2009	Binary	50	10.0
Wyoming				
Rocky Mountain Oilfield Testing Center	2009	Binary, co-production	–	0.3

*upgrade 2006; ** Shut down for redevelopment in 2003 and 2004   As at April 2011. Source: GEA

those can be found in California (48). Nevada has 20 plants operating today, Utah six plants, with Alaska, Hawaii, Idaho, New Mexico, Oregon and Wyoming each having one plant in operation.

GEOTHERMAL DEVELOPMENT
In the US, the development of wind energy has been more prominent than development in the geothermal sector. However, this will change because of the large number of projects in development in the geothermal sector, and there will be a strong increase in electricity generation from geothermal sources in the years to come (Figures 10 and 11). As it takes longer to develop geothermal power capacity than wind or solar installations, many projects in development today will not generate electricity until 2011–14.

Most geothermal development in the US is taking place in Nevada (86 projects) and California (35), which together account for nearly two-thirds of all development by capacity. Utah (21), Oregon (15) and Idaho (12) represent the second group of states with sizeable geothermal projects in development. Other states with projects in development are Alaska (7), New Mexico (two), Colorado, Louisiana, Mississippi, Texas and Wyoming (one each).

GEOTHERMAL DIRECT USE IN THE US
Geothermal direct use relates to utilising geothermal hot water for a variety of applications that require heat. It includes, among other things, heating of pools and spas, greenhouses and aquaculture facilities, space and district heating, snow melting, agricultural drying, industrial applications and ground-source heat pumps.

In the US, geothermal direct use is approximately 31,200 terajoules (TJ) a year,

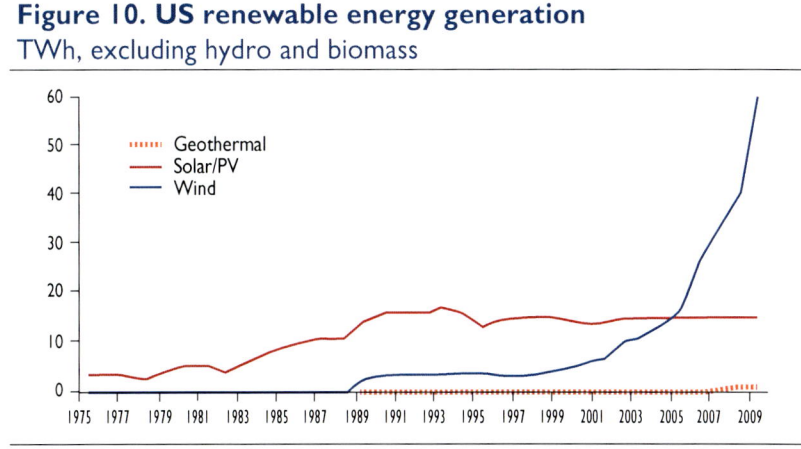

Figure 10. US renewable energy generation
TWh, excluding hydro and biomass

Source: Energy Information Administration

68 | Investment Opportunities for a Low-Carbon World

Figure 11. US geothermal plants and confirmed projects

Year	Value
2006	51
2007	69
2008	97
2009	132
2010	152

Source: GEA, 2010

of which traditional direct use accounts for approximately 9,000TJ. Geothermal heat pumps account for the vast majority of direct use of geothermal heat, with approximately 22,200TJ a year (Figure 12). Total thermal installed capacity is approximately 8,000MW. There has been a continuing increase over the years, but by far the largest annual growth has been in geothermal heat pump applications.

Over a five-year time frame (2000–05) heat pumps have seen an 11% increase, followed by agricultural drying (10.4%) and space heating (9.3%).

There are an estimated 600,000 12kW geothermal heat pumps installed today,

Figure 12. US geothermal direct use
Based on annual use, TJ/year

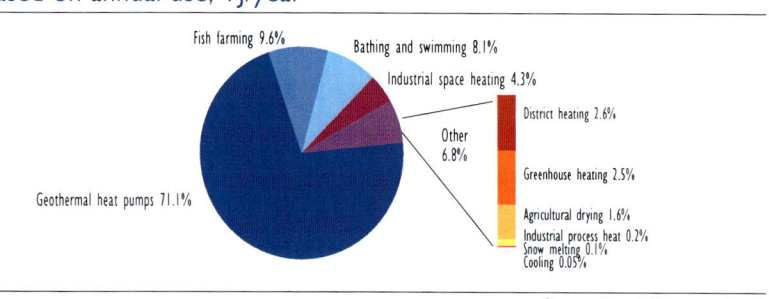

- Geothermal heat pumps 71.1%
- Fish farming 9.6%
- Bathing and swimming 8.1%
- Industrial space heating 4.3%
- Other 6.8%
- District heating 2.6%
- Greenhouse heating 2.5%
- Agricultural drying 1.6%
- Industrial process heat 0.2%
- Snow melting 0.1%
- Cooling 0.05%

Source: Lund, Freeston, Boyd

Figure 13. Traditional direct-use categories

Category	Installed capacity, MW	Annual use, TJ
Individual space heating	146	1,335
District heating	84	788
Cooling	<1	15
Greenhouse heating	97	766
Fish farming	138	3,012
Agricultural drying	36	500
Industrial process heat	2	48
Snow melting	2	18
Bathing and swimming	112	2,543

most of which are located in the mid-west, mid-Atlantic and southern states (from North Dakota to Florida).

Examples of direct-use applications in the US include small district heating system in northern California and a greenhouse operation to raise tree seedlings added to the district heating system in Klamath Falls, Oregon (Figure 13).

With the tremendous potential of geothermal direct use, the numbers could be significantly higher, given that the oil price could increase further in the years to come. Particular growth is expected in space heating and greenhouse projects, along with increased countrywide interest in geothermal heat pumps.

US GEOTHERMAL ENERGY POTENTIAL
Geothermal potential in the US is undeniably considerable. Projects now in development in the US alone could more than double the installed capacity. Different estimates for resource potential are given below.

The biggest potential by far lies in California, with approximately 11,340MW in undiscovered geothermal resources, according to the USGS. Nevada, Hawaii, Oregon, Idaho and Alaska also have tremendous undiscovered resources.

The figures in this section give an overview of current installed capacity as provided in the Geothermal Energy Association's (GEA's) *Power and Development Update*, April 2010. Two other organisations, the Western Governors' Association (WGA) Geothermal Task Force and USGS, give resource estimates for individual states with geothermal development potential (Figures 14, 15 & 16).

The WGA estimates a short- and long-term development potential based on electricity prices and technological development. The USGS, in its most recent *US Geothermal Resources Assessment* (September 2008), looks at "conventional geothermal" (hydrothermal) based on identified geothermal systems, at undiscovered resources based on a "series of geographical information system (GIS) statistical models" and also at enhanced geothermal systems.

The overall potential for geothermal power generation is very promising. The min-

70 | Investment Opportunities for a Low-Carbon World

Figure 14. US geothermal capacity, projects and potential
Installed capacity, MW

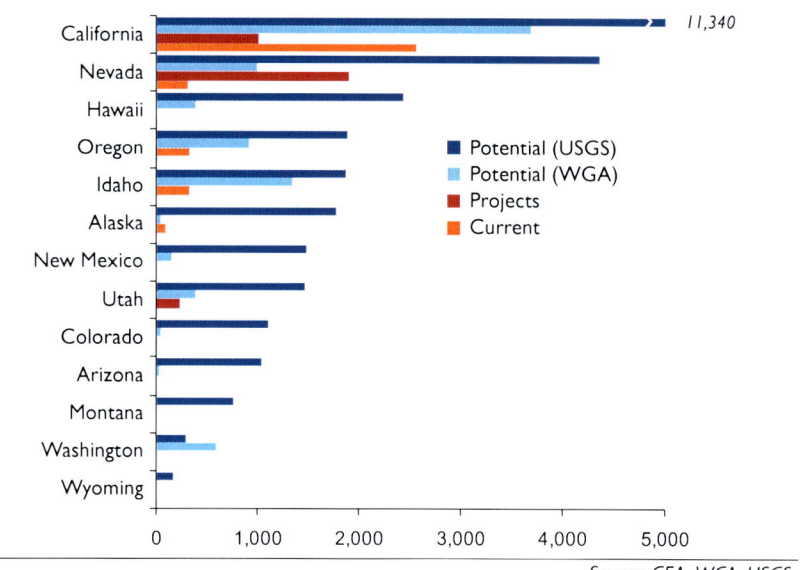

California 11,340
Nevada
Hawaii
Oregon
Idaho
Alaska
New Mexico
Utah
Colorado
Arizona
Montana
Washington
Wyoming

Legend:
- Potential (USGS)
- Potential (WGA)
- Projects
- Current

Source: GEA, WGA, USGS

Figure 15. Capacity, projects and resource estimates
Installed capacity, MW

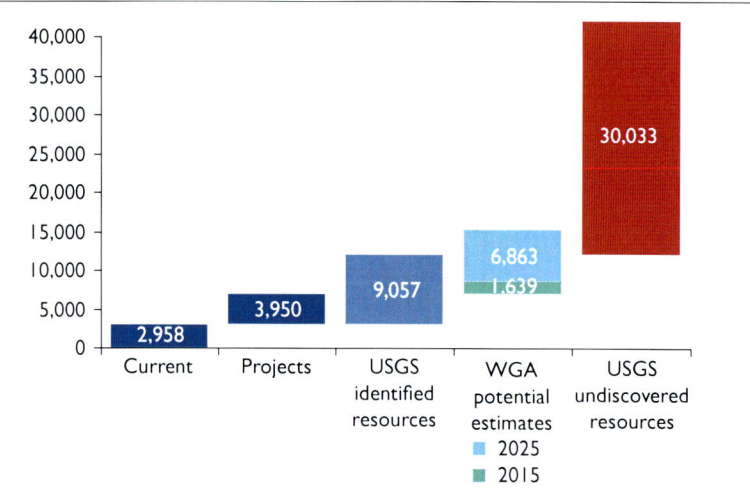

Category	MW
Current	2,958
Projects	3,950
USGS identified resources	9,057
WGA potential estimates 2025	6,863
WGA potential estimates 2015	1,639
USGS undiscovered resources	30,033

Source: GEA, WGA, USGS

Geothermal Energy | 71

Figure 16. Projects and resource assessments

State	GEA update Installed capacity Today	Projects in development phase I–IV* Low	High	Projects* Number	WGA estimates Near market 2015	Longer term 2025	USGS estimates Identified resources Mean	Undiscovered resources Mean	EGS systems Mean
Alaska	0.7	60.0	80.0	7	20	150	677	1,788	na
Arizona	—	2.0	20.0	1	20	50	26	1,043	54,700
California	2,565.5	1,609.7	1,997.7	35	2,375	4,703	5,404	11,340	48,100
Colorado	—	10.0	10.0	1	20	50	30	1,105	52,600
Hawaii	35.0	8.0	8.0	2	70	400	181	2,435	na
Idaho	15.8	413.0	676.0	12	855	1,670	333	1,872	67,900
Louisiana	—	0.1	5.3	2	—	—	—	—	—
Mississippi	—	0.1	0.1	1	—	—	—	—	—
Montana	—	—	—	—	—	—	59	771	16,900
Nevada	426.8	2,130.4	3,686.4	86	1,488	2,895	1,391	4,364	102,800
New Mexico	0.2	35.0	35.0	2	80	170	170	1,484	55,700
Oregon	0.3	342.0	473.0	15	380	1,250	540	1,893	62,400
Texas	—	—	—	1	—	—	—	—	—
Utah	42.0	628.0	848.0	21	230	620	184	1,464	47,200
Washington	—	—	—	1	50	600	23	300	6,500
Wyoming	0.3	0.3	0.3	1	0	0	39	174	3,000
Total	3,086.6	5,238.6	7,839.8	188	5,588	12,558	9,057	30,033	517,800

Source: GEA, April 2010; * with unconfirmed | Source: WGA, January 2006 | Source: USGS, September 2008

Figure 17. Capacity in development
MW

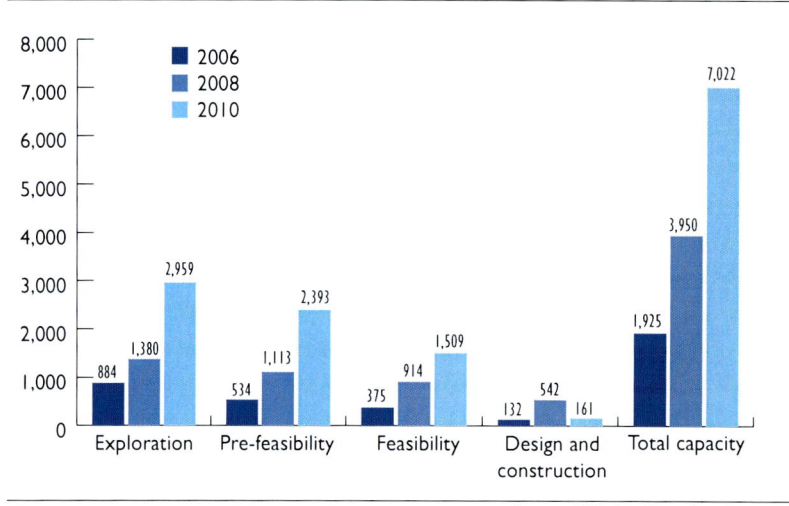

Stage	2006	2008	2010
Exploration	884	1,380	2,959
Pre-feasibility	534	1,113	2,393
Feasibility	375	914	1,509
Design and construction	132	542	161
Total capacity	1,925	3,950	7,022

Source: GEA (confirmed projects only)

imum potential is a four-fold increase in installed capacity compared to today (WGA) and a maximum of a ten-fold increase for conventional geothermal systems (USGS).

The WGA and USGS estimates already draw a promising picture of the overall potential. However, other organisations have either looked at EGS alone or are bolder in their estimates of the potential not only for energy generation but also for the positive aspects regarding climate change.

These include:
- The Massachusetts Institute of Technology, which estimates up to 100,000MW installed capacity by 2050.
- The National Renewable Energy Laboratory, which refers to a base-case scenario of co-produced potential of 71,600MW and an overall potential of 126,300MW (including EGS).
- The World Wide Fund for Nature, which stresses not only the importance of geothermal energy in providing a clean energy supply but also the major importance of direct use in the overall sustainable energy mix for the future.

Investment and development needs

GEOTHERMAL FINANCING OPTIONS

The development cycle for geothermal energy projects requires equity and debt finance at various stages and very different profiles. The risks involved require sound knowledge and experience and generally attract very different types of in-

Geothermal Energy | 73

Figure 18. Geothermal financing options

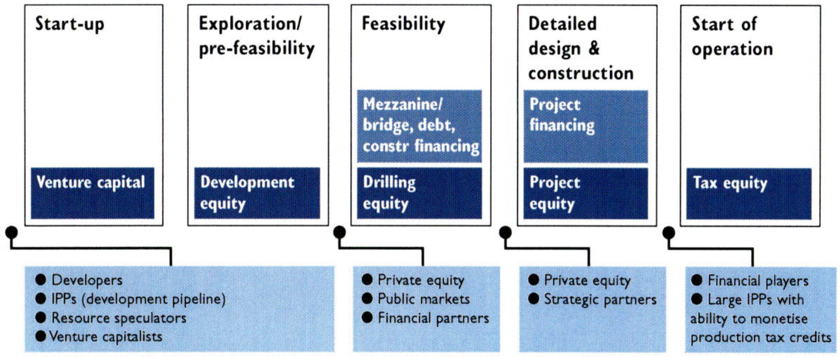

Source: Íslandsbanki Geothermal Research

vestors and financial institutions. An overview of the different stages is shown in Figure 18.

ESTIMATES OF GEOTHERMAL ELECTRICITY SALES

Although more recent statistics are not available, sales prices for 2007, for both residential and industrial sales, show the electricity sales potential. Around $3 billion in electricity sales was generated from geothermal energy in the eight states with geothermal generation capacity (Figure 19).

Current price levels for electricity sales should reach at least similar, if not higher

Figure 19. Geothermal electricity sales estimates
Based on 2007 sales, industry/residential, $ million

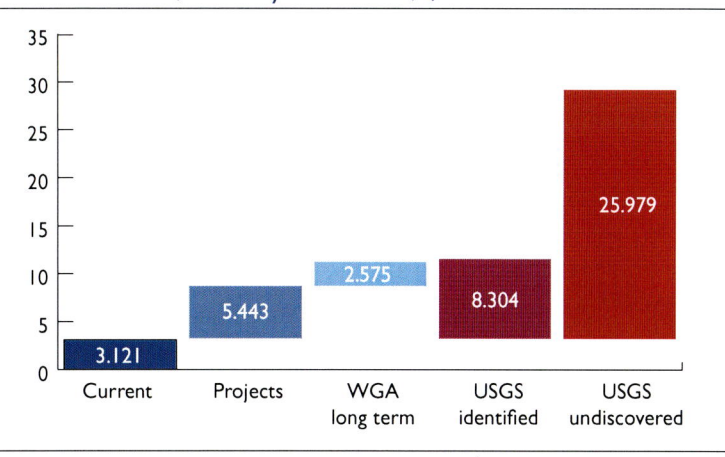

Current	3.121
Projects	5.443
WGA long term	2.575
USGS identified	8.304
USGS undiscovered	25.979

Source: Íslandsbanki Geothermal Research

74 | Investment Opportunities for a Low-Carbon World

levels, as 2008 saw a big hike in prices, particularly in states with renewable portfolio standards in place.

With ongoing projects, sales could more than double to $8.5 billion, by 2015 at the latest. The resource estimates from WGA and USGS indicate that the overall outlook looks even more promising.

The WGA's long-term estimates could add a further $2.5 billion, bringing the total to $11 billion by 2025. Looking at the undiscovered resources estimated by USGS, the overall electricity sales potential for geothermal could be $29 billion.

INVESTMENT NEEDS OF CURRENT PROJECTS

Íslandsbanki estimates the overall investment needed just for current projects at $26 billion. The largest investment is clearly needed for the drilling campaign and the actual construction of power plants. As a large number of projects are in the early stages of development, the major investments needed to drive today's projects forward will be required in 2012 and 2013, both of which years represent around half of total investment needs for current projects. The largest investment needs for drilling are likely to be in 2011, with $3.4 billion needed for projects at this stage of development. By 2012 the industry will need large construction financing, which will see a large increase again in 2013, maintained at the same level in 2014.

Looking at the development pipeline, the industry needs a total of $11 billion in equity investments and about $15 billion in construction financing until 2015.

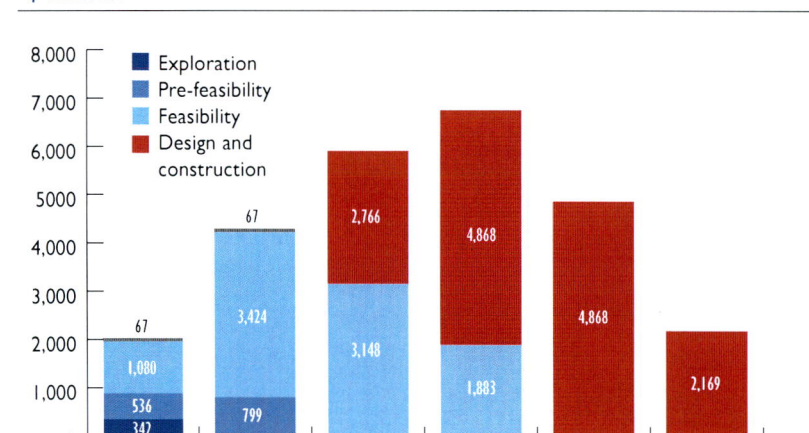

Figure 20. Investment needs for current US projects
$ million

As of September 2009. Source: Íslandsbanki Geothermal Research

US geothermal energy opportunities, challenges and risks

CHALLENGES AND RISKS
- Financing and the availability of equity will remain the key challenge for the geothermal sector.
- Smaller players continue to find it extremely difficult to attract financing for their projects.
- Falling electricity prices could also hit geothermal developers, despite the increase in financing costs, hitting the return for players and investors.
- Current press coverage of EGS and earthquake fears could reflect negatively on the sector and also affect conventional geothermal projects. The industry will still have to work on promoting itself and educating the general public, politicians and the marketplace.
- Some elements of the stimulus legislation are extremely short term – too short for the majority of projects. This applies particularly to loan guarantees.
- Oil and gas sector players are entering the market, providing competition for some players.
- The increased number of projects in the US also means an increase in competition for scarce expertise and staff, creating a shortage of qualified people.

OPPORTUNITIES
- The Obama administration's stimulus package and the allocation of much-needed resources to current development, as well as R&D, have increased awareness of geothermal energy. Interest in geothermal energy as a base-load capacity renewable energy resource has increased as a result.
- Political support has increased.
- Some consolidation in the market has attracted attention and will have a positive impact on how the industry is perceived.
- There are still opportunities to develop stronger companies in the market.
- Overall resource estimates show huge geothermal energy opportunities in the US.
- Oil and gas companies are showing increased interest in the sector, increasing the availability of drilling rigs.

For a complete overview of geothermal energy and comparisons with other renewable energies, see Íslandsbanki's *Fact Sheet on Geothermal Energy*, which can be downloaded from www.islandsbanki.is/energy under 'Research & Publications'.

Sources

GEOTHERMAL ENERGY
Geothermal Energy Association (GEA): Kagel, A, *Socioeconomics and Geothermal Energy*, www.geo-energy.org/reports/Socioeconomics%20Guide.pdf
National Renewable Energy Laboratory (NREL), www.nrel.gov/analysis/power_databook/docs/pdf/db_chapter12_2.pdf

GLOBAL GEOTHERMAL ENERGY: OVERVIEW & POTENTIAL
Bertani, R, 'World Geothermal Generation in 2007', *GHC Bulletin*, September 2007, http://geoheat.oit.edu/bulletin/bull28-3/art3.pdf (accessed 23 September 2009).
Lund, J W, D H Freeston and T I Boyd (2005), 'Direct application of geothermal energy: 2005 worldwide review.' *Geothermics*, Vol 34, pages 690–727.

GEOTHERMAL ENERGY IN THE US: TODAY
Renewable Energy Portfolio Standards
Database of State Incentives for Renewables & Efficiency (DSIRE), www.dsireusa.org (accessed 23 September 2009).
Geothermal energy direct use
Energy Information Administration (EIA), electric power monthly, electricity data and others, www.eia.doe.gov (accessed 23 September 2009).
Lund, J W, D H Freeston and T I Boyd (2005), 'World-Wide Direct Uses of Geothermal Energy 2005', published in *Proceedings of the World Geothermal Congress 2005*, Turkey, 24–29 April 2005.

GEOTHERMAL ENERGY IN THE US: PROJECTS & POTENTIAL
Bertani, R (2003), '"What is Geothermal Potential', *International Geothermal Association Quarterly* No 53 (July–September 2003), http://www.geothermal-energy.org/308,iga_newsletter.html (accessed 23 September 2009).
Geothermal Energy Association (2010), *Geothermal Power Production and Development Update*, April 2010.
Massachusetts Institute of Technology (MIT), *The Future of Geothermal Energy – Impact of Enhanced Geothermal Systems (EGS) on the United States in the 21st Century*, www1.eere.energy.gov/geothermal/future_geothermal.html (accessed 23 September 2009).
NREL (2006), *Geothermal – The Energy Under Our Feet: Geothermal Resource Estimates for the United States*, Technical Report, November 2006, www1.eere.energy.gov/geothermal/pdfs/40665.pdf.
NREL (2007): Petty, S and G Porro, *Updated US Geothermal Supply Characterization*, Presented at the 32nd Workshop on Geothermal Reservoir Engineering, January 2007, www.nrel.gov/docs/fy07osti/41073.pdf (accessed 23 September 2009).
Open Congress, *American Clean Energy And Security Act of 2009 – US Congress*, www.opencongress.org/bill/111-h2454/show (accessed 24 September 2009).
US Geological Survey (2008), *Assessment of Moderate- and High-Temperature Geothermal Resources of the United States*, September 2008, http://pubs.usgs.gov/fs/2008/3082/pdf/fs2008-3082.pdf (accessed 23 September 2009).
Western Governors' Association (2006), *Geothermal Task Force Report*, January 2006.
World Wide Fund for Nature (WWF), "Climate Solutions – WWF's Vision for 2050", wwf.panda.org/about_our_earth/all_publications/?122201/Climate-Solutions-WWFs-Vision-for-2050

GEOTHERMAL ENERGY ASSOCIATIONS
US Geothermal Energy Association (GEA), www.geo-energy.org
Geothermal Resources Council (GRC), www.geothermal.org
International Geothermal Association (IGA), www.geothermal-energy.org

Chapter 5

Biomass[1]

Mark Thompson, Tiptree Investments

Introduction

Since the advent of fire, people have used biomass fuels in the form of solid biofuels for heating, light and cooking. Following the discovery of electricity and the steam engine, it became possible to use biomass to generate electrical power.

Biomass is material derived from recently living organisms. This includes plants, animals and their by-products. For example, manure, garden waste and crop residues are all sources of biomass. It is also a renewable energy source that is 'carbon neutral'. As plants grow, they absorb carbon dioxide (CO_2) from the atmosphere. When this biomass material is used as a fuel, the CO_2 is returned to the atmosphere through a 'carbon neutral' cycle. If biomass displaces fossil fuels instead of decomposing naturally, it limits the emission of 'old' CO_2 and methane from decomposition, although with most biomass plants having lower energy conversion efficiency than conventional generation, the comparison is not straightforward.

Biomass is one of the largest sources of renewable energy and mainly used in direct combustion. Approximately 65 gigawatts (GW)[2] of biomass power are operational worldwide, with 8.5GW in the US, according to the Sustainable Energy Coalition. Depending on the statistics used, biomass produces around 14–17% of global primary energy, although in some developing countries this can reach 90%. Unfortunately, much of the biomass used in developing countries is used inefficiently and derived from unsustainable sources, with a corresponding impact on human health and the environment.

Most countries have the potential to produce a sustainable and efficient source of biomass given structural changes in agriculture, forestry and municipal solid waste (MSW) management. Locally produced biomass reduces the need to import fossil fuels and improves energy security. To this end, biomass resources are generally most efficiently used when they are grown for a primary purpose – such as food – and energy is subsequently extracted from the residue. With growing energy demand, high oil

---
1 Excluding biofuels for transport.
2 1GW equals 1,000 megawatts (MW) and 1MW equals 1,000 kilowatts (kW). On average, 1MW is sufficient to support 750–1,000 western homes. A terawatt (TW) is 1,000GW. Gigawatts, megawatts and kilowatts are all measures of power and represent a rate of energy conversion. One terawatt hour (TWh) is 1 million megawatt hours (MWh) or 1 billion kilowatt hours (kWh) and these are units of energy.

prices and the urgent risks from global warming, biomass is an essential energy option for a range of applications as part of a mix that includes energy efficiency, intermittent renewables, such as wind or solar, and changing consumption

WHAT IS BIOMASS?
Biomass is derived from plant- or animal-based organic matter and may include:
- animal wastes;
- agricultural feed crops, waste and residues;
- aquatic plants;
- municipal and other organic waste materials; and,
- trees, wood waste and residues.

A wide range of biomass can be used to produce heat, electricity, liquid, solid and gaseous fuels, and chemicals, which are all considered renewable.

RESOURCE BASE
The annual global primary production of biomatter is ~220 billion oven dry tonnes or 4,500 exajoules[3]. The theoretically harvestable bioenergy potential is estimated to be 2,900 exajoules, of which 270 exajoules (equivalent to ~2,300GW of gross capacity) are considered technically available on a sustainable basis. Here, the challenge is not availability but logistics: sustainable management, conversion and delivery to the market. As biomass resources can be converted into chemical fuels or electricity through several routes, the role of biomass in the future energy supply of industrialised countries is based on several considerations:

- The development of competitive production, collection and conversion systems to create biomass-derived fuels that can substitute for fossil fuels in the existing energy supply infrastructure.
- The potential resource base is substantial, given the existence of land not needed or unsuitable for food production, as well as agricultural food yields that continue to rise faster than population growth.
- Biomass is bulky and often has a high water content. Fuel quality is variable, and physical handling of the material can be challenging. But technologies for biomass fuel upgrading (into pellets or briquettes, for example) and the development of energy crops may improve consistency.
- For biomass to become a major fuel, energy crops and plantations will have to become a significant land-use category. Land requirements depend on crop yields, water availability and the efficiency of biomass conversion to usable fuel. Assuming an optimistic 45% conversion efficiency and yields of 15 oven dry tonnes per hectare per year, four square kilometres (400 hectares) are needed per installed megawatt of electrical capacity.

---
3 One exajoule is equivalent to 2.78 × 10^8 megawatt hours (MWh).

In some ways, biomass appears simple compared to other alternative technologies, as it primarily uses conventional equipment and can generate a predictable output, unlike wind or solar power. This is incorrect. Biomass has probably been responsible for more 'problem projects' than any other renewable energy technology. However, when done properly, it delivers substantial returns, its use as base-load generation provides an important component of any generating portfolio and the opportunity for new generating capacity is almost unlimited.

TECHNOLOGIES
There are several techniques for harnessing biomass to generate electricity. The next section focuses on the production of electricity and divides this into three groups:
- *direct combustion* typically using mass burn processes. This is currently the largest source of biomass power;
- *advanced thermal treatment* typically using pyrolysis or gasification. This is currently at the development stage, with no economically robust designs available;
- *biogas* produced by anaerobic digestion (AD) or as landfill gas (LFG) via microbes that turn organic material into methane ('natural gas'). LFG is well established and one of the cheapest sources of renewable energy. AD systems are widely used in Denmark and Germany but have room for further development.

Apart from large conventional wood-chip plants, almost every other biomass technology has been developed as a waste treatment solution, with energy recovery used to reduce the cost. Waste regulations continue to be the main driver of biomass economics. Demand for biomass treatment could increase substantially if some proposed regulations for agricultural waste are ever enforced. The widespread deployment of electric cars might also change the demand for biomass power, as the University of California reports that a small sport utility vehicle (SUV) could do 9,000 highway miles (14,480km) on the energy produced from an acre of switchgrass converted into ethanol, but 14,000 miles (22,530km) if the same fuel were converted into electricity and used with a battery-powered SUV.

Direct combustion
Most biomass plants use traditional solid fuel technology (moving grate/steam boiler), with some additional equipment for fuel handling. This is used in energy from waste plants and most large biomass plants using straw, wood or energy crops.

BIOMASS POWER
Most biomass capacity comes from large wood-burning boilers that use waste wood products generated by the agriculture and wood-processing industries. These plants tend to be in the 10–50MW range and use conventional solid fuel processing equipment, with specialised fuel-handling equipment. These plants are usually one-offs and depend on the availability of sufficient fuel in the immediate area. Plants have been built to burn paper sludge, chicken litter and straw, among other fuels.

ENERGY FROM WASTE

Energy from waste (EfW) is a term describing the technologies used to recover energy in a carefully controlled combustion environment. The technologies are relatively well established and range from moving grate systems to circulating fluidised beds. EfW plants mirror conventional generation systems, along with pollution control systems for the combustion gases.

EfW accounts for 8% of MSW treated in the UK and plays a crucial role at the end of the waste hierarchy. Currently, 270MW of electricity is generated in 27 EfW plants in the UK, with a further two in construction. These facilities range from 26,000 tonnes a year (Lerwick) to 600,000 tonnes a year (Edmonton). Since 2001, the UK's rate of recycling has more than tripled (to 9.4 million tonnes), reducing the demand for EfW, with a government target of 25% of municipal waste to be combusted and turned into energy in the next 10 years.

The potential health impacts of EfW have dominated the discussion on incineration. While public surveys have typically shown that the role of EfW is acknowledged when integrated into a balanced waste management strategy, individual applications to build such facilities are often met with suspicion. Consequently, EfW is one of the most tightly regulated industrial processes, often with emission requirements that exceed comparable thermal processes in other industries.

EMISSIONS

Emissions from mass burn/EfW are comparable with other solid fuels, although this completely depends on the fuel mix: wood can burn cleanly, while mixed waste and plastics produce a range of unpleasant pollutants. However, any combustion process that is not tightly controlled will produce pollutants and efficient flue gas treatment systems are routinely specified for most combustion systems.

CO-FIRING

Some coal-fired power plants mix biomass into their coal-burning process (known as co-firing) to reduce the emissions produced by burning the coal. Co-firing may require the boiler to be modified and only a small amount of biomass is typically added (no more than 15% of the fuel going into the boiler) to maintain the boiler's efficiency. However, emissions are reduced, green credits are often available on a *pro rata* basis and the biomass combustion efficiency may improve significantly, compared to a state-of-the-art, pure biomass plant.

ECONOMICS OF DIRECT COMBUSTION

Direct combustion of biomass can be economic where the delivered fuel price is effectively zero and this only occurs where waste or environmental regulations dictate a disposal route and where long-term (15 years or more) power purchase agreements (PPAs) are readily available. Some economies of scale exist in terms of plant

Figure 1. Biomass direct combustion financial summary

Performance	Direct-fired	Co-fired
Duty cycle	Base load	Base load
Typical capacity factor (%)	60–90	60–85
Economics		
Project costs ($m/MWe)	1.5–3.5	0.3–0.5
Fixed O&M ($'000/MW biomass/year)	70–90	5–15
Variable O&M ($/MWh biomass)	10–15	1–3
Levelised cost ($/MWhe)	70–120	5–30
Commercial status		
Time to commercial operation	Now	Regulatory-driven

Source: Tiptree Investments

size, although these tend to be capped at 50MW by fuel logistics. Real savings are capped by limited market demand and an on-site construction process, meaning improvements are most likely to come from operating experience or regulations changing the fuel supply dynamics.

Advanced thermal technologies

Pyrolysis and gasification are widely proposed as alternative thermal treatment processes for biomass and MSW. However, gasification and pyrolysis are yet to prove themselves when running on waste-derived fuels. The task is to create a synthesis gas of sufficient quality to make the economics work, but at the moment, the incentives for taking the technical risk are marginal. However, their status as 'advanced' and 'not incineration' has given significant impetus to the sector.

GASIFICATION

Gasification is a thermo-chemical process that heats biomass in a low-oxygen environment. This produces a relatively low-energy gas, compared to natural gas, that contains hydrogen, carbon monoxide and methane. The gas can fuel a turbine, combustion engine or conventional steam boiler to generate electricity – or possibly get converted into ethanol or hydrogen. Oxygen-blown gasifiers tend to produce a higher calorific gas than air-blown gasifiers, albeit with an operating cost penalty.

Gasifiers using coal have been used for many years and are now being developed to accept more varied fuels. Gases generally burn cleaner and more efficiently than solids, which allows removal of toxic materials. New gas clean-up technology ensures that the resulting gas can be used in different gas engines, with a decent emissions profile.

PYROLYSIS

Pyrolysis has many characteristics of gasification but, instead of partial oxidation, pyrolysis heats the biomass in an oxygen-free atmosphere to produce gas, olefins,

Figure 2. Typical product yields by weight from dry wood

Mode	Temperature (°C)	Residence time	Liquid (%)	Char (%)	Gas (%)
Fast pyrolisis	500	~1 sec	75	12	13
Pyrolisis	500	~10–20 sec	50	20	30
Carbonisation	400	Very long	30	35	35
Gasification	800	Long	5	10	85

Source: Pyrolisis Network

liquid and char. The gas and oil can be processed, stored and transported, if necessary, and burnt in an engine, gas turbine or boiler. Char can be recovered from the residue and used as a fuel or passed through a gasifier.

TECHNOLOGY TRADE-OFFS
Pyrolysis is always the first step in combustion and gasification processes, which is followed by total or partial oxidation of the primary products. Lower process temperature and longer vapour residence times favour the production of charcoal. High temperature and longer residence time increase the biomass conversion into gas, and moderate temperature and short vapour residence time are optimum for producing liquids. Fast pyrolysis for liquid production is of particular interest as the liquids are transportable and easily stored. The product distribution obtained from different process modes is summarised in Figure 2.

ALTERNATIVE PRODUCTS
Bio-oil can substitute for fuel oil or diesel in many static applications, including boilers, furnaces, engines and turbines for electricity generation, although the economics depend more on government incentives than energy prices. There is also a range of chemicals that can be extracted or derived including food flavourings, resins, agrichemicals, fertilisers and emission control agents.

Upgrading bio-oil to transportation fuel is feasible but currently not economic, although most current research is looking at its fuel applications. The near-term production of bio-oil will depend on its use as a chemical feedstock due to the following:

- Bio-oil is easier to transport than biomass, meaning that pyrolysis plants could be located near low-cost feedstock while reforming occurs at a site with existing hydrogen infrastructure.
- The production of higher value co-products from bio-oil could help the economics, with the lignin-derived fraction used as a phenol substitute and the carbohydrate-derived fraction catalytically steam-reformed to produce hydrogen. If the phenolic fraction could be sold for $0.44/kg (approximately half of the price of phenol), the estimated cost of hydrogen would be $7.70 per gigajoule, which is at the low end of current prices.

ADVANCED THERMAL TREATMENT OF WASTE

Many of the perceived benefits of gasification and pyrolysis over simple combustion are unproven for waste treatment, as there is no real track record. There is real technology risk, and neither stand-alone gasification nor pyrolysis are commercially proven for residual MSW. These technologies might offer potential if:

- renewable incentives make the economics far more robust;
- a municipality is willing to take the technology risk to overcome negative public perception of mass burn; and
- the waste stream is homogenous or consists of small quantities of high-value clinical/hazardous waste.

Biogas

Biogas is primarily methane and carbon dioxide that occurs from the decay of wet organic matter such as manure, sewage sludge, MSW or any other (wet) biodegradable feedstock, under anaerobic (ie, low-oxygen) conditions. These conditions typically occur in a landfill or a purpose-made anaerobic digester.

Biogas from a landfill can be flared, used to power a gas engine that drives a generator or, more recently, purified and sold into the natural gas grid. Since methane is a greenhouse gas (GHG) that is ~21 times more damaging than carbon dioxide, its recovery and use from landfills/digesters reduces GHG emissions, as well as offsetting electricity generated by polluting sources.

Large amounts of biogas are produced globally. Historically, most of this has been flared or used to provide heat in sewage works. Over the past couple of decades, waste legislation and renewable energy incentives have increased the amount of biogas used for generating power. As biogas production is (usually) a continuous process, anaerobic digestion (AD) and landfill gas (LFG) provide predictable, base load, generation.

LANDFILL GAS

The capture and conversion of LFG into carbon dioxide is expected to produce approximately 10% of Kyoto Protocol certified emissions reductions in 2012, due to

Figure 3. European biogas (GWh)

Country	Total	Landfill	Sludge	Other	Electricity
Germany	22,370	6,670	4,300	11,400	7,338
UK	19,720	17,620	2,100	0	4,997
Italy	4,110	3,610	10	490	1,234
Spain	3,890	2,930	660	300	675
France	3,640	1,720	870	50	579
EU	62,200	36,250	11,050	14,900	17,272

Source: Biogas barometre 2007, EurObserver

methane's GHG potency. MSW typically contains a large proportion of biodegradable organic material that produces LFG from anaerobic bacteria, causing decay in the organic waste fraction amid the sub-optimal conditions of a landfill. Under ideal conditions, one tonne of waste produces 150–300 cubic metres of gas. Depending on the phase of the breakdown process, the gas produced is mainly methane (~60%) and carbon dioxide (~35%). These are the major constituents for most degradation, and this process can continue at commercial rates for up to 30 years. A LFG system has three basic components (Figure 4):

- *Gas collection* typically occurs via a series of wells, as gas from decomposing garbage exists at all levels of the landfill. The number and spacing of wells depends on landfill aspects such as volume, density and geometry. Each well is created by drilling into the landfill, inserting a perforated plastic pipe and filling the space around the pipe with gravel, to prevent refuse plugging. The wells are connected by a series of pipes leading to larger header pipes that deliver the gas to the processing stations. The pipes are under partial vacuum created by blowers at the processing station, causing LFG to migrate towards the wells, while the landfill itself has an impermeable capping. Typically, a simple collection system captures ~10% of the gas generated, while modern systems capture up to 80%.
- *Gas processing* occurs once blowers deliver the gas to a central point where it can be processed or converted. At a minimum, the gas needs to be filtered to remove any particles and condensate that may be suspended in the gas stream.
- *Conversion equipment* such as internal combustion engines or turbines can be used to power on-site generators that convert the gas into saleable electricity.

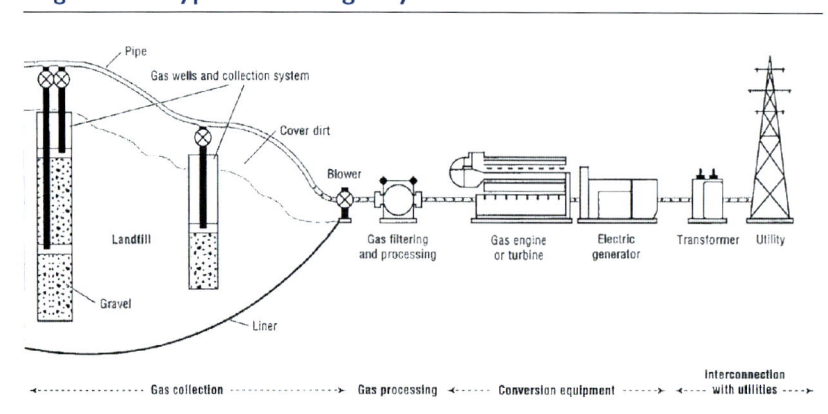

Figure 4. A typical landfill gas system

Source: Rhode Island Solid Waste Management Company

BIOGAS ECONOMICS

Methane is flammable, an asphyxiant in confined spaces and also kills vegetation when soil is infiltrated. It was the need to minimise these risks that led to the development of LFG control systems and recovery over the past 20 years. While some landfills simply flare LFG, the US has 519 operational projects, in 46 states, supplying 13TWh of electricity each year. The UK has 421 landfill gas sites, with capacity of 985MW and annual generation of approximately 4.9TWh. The US Environmental Protection Agency estimates that more than 600 additional landfills could support LFG energy projects cost-effectively.

In many developing countries, general standards of solid waste management are low. Considerable volumes of methane continue to be released from dumps or poorly controlled landfills. Regulatory requirements do not normally require full control of LFG and, therefore, adding a gas destruction system can make the project eligible for emission reduction credits under the Kyoto Protocol's Joint Implementation or Clean Development Mechanism.

Undiluted LFG has a calorific value of 15–21 megajoules per cubic metre, and in the UK, 357 plants generated 4.2TWh in 2006, with an average capacity factor of 60–65%. LFG production continues for 20–30 years after a landfill is closed. Therefore, as long as landfills continue to be used, LFG will continue to be a resource for producing electricity.

Since landfills are already obliged to capture biogas in the EU and most developed nations, the fuel supply is effectively free. This reduces the economic decision to a trade-off between the returns from flaring, converting into electricity or purifying for the gas grid. This means that LFG has tended to be one of the cheapest sources of renewable power, and projects with long-term PPAs can make economic sense at prices of $50/MWh.

FINANCIAL METRICS

LFG is clearly economic where regulations require methane capture and, with a reasonable PPA term, it is economic where drilling is required, provided appropriate control over landfill operation is possible. There are some options to cut costs further, although the technology is effectively mature.

Figure 5. Landfill gas financial summary

Performance	
Duty cycle	Baseload
Typical capacity factor (%)	70–95
Economics	
Project costs ($m/MW)	0.75–2
Variable O&M ($/MWh)	15–20
Levelised cost ($/MWh)	40–80

Source: Tiptree Investments

LFG INVESTMENT

This is a mature technology, which has been a major contributor to renewable energy generation and its operation is increasingly outsourced to specialist operators such as Infinis or Novera. LFG has investment interest when it is held as part of a wider renewable energy generating portfolio. In the UK, for example, the industry is fragmented, divided largely between large waste management companies that manage generation at their own sites and numerous small independent operators. Opportunities for consolidation clearly exist.

ANAEROBIC DIGESTION

The biological processes that take place in a landfill site can be harnessed in a specially designed vessel known as an anaerobic digester to accelerate the decomposition of wastes. AD is typically used on wet wastes, such as sewage sludge or animal slurries, but the biodegradable fraction of municipal wastes can be added to wetter wastes to increase the biogas output.

An anaerobic digester produces biogas that can be converted into heat and electricity, with the digestate creating a soil improving material. AD is the preferred stabilisation process for wastewater sludges and organic wastes. The process provides volume, odour and mass reduction, renewable energy and predictable pathogen kills. The digestate also displaces energy-intensive chemical fertilisers and helps store indigestible carbon in the soil.

AD is primarily a waste treatment process but, as it is a living system, digesters require dedicated staff, meaning that farmer-run solutions have often failed in the past. As a result, a minimum scale is required to make this investable (~100,000 tonnes per annum feedstock/3,600 dairy cattle) and the economics only make sense when natural gas is over $5 per million British thermal units (BTUs), or the equivalent in power prices.

Farmers in many developing countries use small biogas plants to provide household gas and fertiliser from animal manure. Larger anaerobic digesters are more common in Europe and are starting to appear in North America. Many of these digestion plants use manure from cattle feedlots or swine operations, as biogas plants provide an excellent method for disposing of waste that is becoming increasingly regulated.

The main issue for an AD system is feedstock. Digesters can typically accept any biodegradable material; however, the level of putrescibility is key. Anaerobes break down biological material to varying degrees: short-chain hydrocarbons such as sugars are easily digested; longer molecules such as cellulose or hemi-cellulose take longer to digest; and long-chain woody molecules such as lignin cannot generally be broken down. Anaerobic digesters were originally designed for use with sewage sludge and manures, although this is rarely the best material, as the animal has already extracted most of its energy content.

Figure 5. Anaerobic digestion financial summary

Performance	
Duty cycle	Baseload
Typical capacity factor (%)	70–90
Economics	
Project costs ($m/MWe)	4–6
Variable O&M ($/MWhe)	15–20
Levelised cost ($/MWhe)	70–130

Source: Tiptree Investments

Two conventional operating temperatures exist for anaerobic digesters:
- *Mesophilic* bacteria thrive at 37–41°C. These micro-organisms are relatively robust but have slower digestion rates.
- *Thermophilic* bacteria thrive at approximately 50–52°C. These micro-organisms are more sensitive to their environment but have higher digestion rates and meet most standards for pathogen kill levels.

FINANCIAL METRICS

AD is commercially viable if regulations constrain animal waste disposal, or if a generous power price makes it attractive to secure the waste. It is unlikely that farm-scale projects can attract useful levels of investment unless funded by a major user further along their value chain with specific environmental obligations. There are some options to cut costs with design standardisation, although the technology is approaching maturity.

BIOGAS INVESTMENT OPPORTUNITIES

Significant interest in AD has come from countries where intensive dairy and hog farming occurs, as manure disposal is becoming difficult due to environmental regulations and land restrictions limiting traditional disposal routes. To put the opportunity in context, the US hog and dairy industry produces ~1.5 million tonnes of manure a day, and the power potential of one animal is:
- dairy cow – 100 watts/head/day
- hog – 28 watts/head/day
- layer chicken – 1 watt/head/day.

Global biogas development was led by Germany in 2006, following the introduction of favourable power prices. In that year, ~650 systems were installed, taking the total installed base to 3,500 plants and 1.1GW of capacity (ie, average plant size of 0.3MW), although sales growth has subsequently slowed following increases in construction costs. In addition to Germany's renewable energy incentives, biogas receives a bonus for using renewable raw materials, innovative technology or using a combined heat and power system.

Biomass issues

FUEL SUPPLY

The key to any biomass project is the fuel supply, which is usually only economically sourced from the local area and exhibits substantial variation in its characteristics. This variation is partly a function of the inevitable differences in a natural material, partly the different collection/harvesting techniques used and partly due to seasonal variation.

Fuel is a major logistical challenge and it is rarely economic for a plant to source its fuel beyond an 80km radius. This exposes the plant (a 30-year asset) to changes in the local area, where biomass is often on a five-year cycle. Unlike coal, biomass is a living fuel that continually changes over time and significant variation can occur between batches. This requires careful fuel management and skilled operators.

ENERGY CROPS

Energy crops are a form of biomass that uses crops planted solely for energy production. This includes switch grass and high-yield varieties of poplar and willow. Wood-based fuels are usually known as short rotation coppice (SRC), with saplings planted at a high density of ~15,000 per hectare for willow and 12,000 per hectare for poplar.

Saplings are grown for a year before being coppiced. The first three years are part of the establishment phase and do not yield much biomass. After four years, the plantation is ready for harvest on a two- to five-year cycle. It should yield 8–18 tonnes of dry woodchip per hectare per year and can be harvested for up to 30 years. The price of dry willow as a heating fuel is around €45 per tonne in most of Europe. This is not a relatively high-return crop, but it is low-maintenance and is a way of using difficult fields. Correctly managed, SRC has little need for pesticides or treatments.

The carbon costs associated with SRC are the planting, farming and chipping of the plantation. However, energy from SRC provides three to six times the CO_2 reduction of bioethanol from cereal crops. A power station requires approximately 100 hectares (1 square kilometre) of SRC for 1MW of capacity. The primary barrier to establishing plantations is the cost, as there is no financial reward for the initial four years from a large initial investment. The current nature of the power industry generally requires flexibility in energy supply, which is incompatible with the long-term commitment that SRC requires.

FOOD VERSUS FUEL

Much discussion occurs about the trade-off between food and fuel, most often when considering transport biofuels. Measuring the impact of biomass demand on food prices is complex, with many second-order effects. While biomass production may change the availability and price of food, by competing with food crops, the issue is more complex than it appears.

Energy crops represent a small proportion of total land use. For instance, approximately 1% of Brazil's arable land is used for ethanol production, but it supplies approximately 40% of the country's gasoline demand. Studies have shown that the 40% rise in food prices in 2007 was partially caused by biofuel demand; however, estimates vary from a 10% to an 80% impact. What is certain is that changes in diet across the developing world, weather-related poor harvests and high oil prices all contributed significantly. In practice, the agricultural industry will grow whichever crop gives the highest return. With much of the world's agriculture remaining woefully inefficient, biomass has the ability to contribute significantly to the energy mix, without disturbing the food markets, provided incentives are structured effectively.

CARBON NEUTRALITY

Unlike fossil fuel, biomass is carbon neutral, provided the greenhouse gases produced during its use are absorbed from the atmosphere during growth. However, the detailed calculation depends on a range of factors such as fertiliser use, energy used in planting/harvesting, the energy conversion efficiency and the type of land used. Inappropriate changes in land use, such as deforestation, are particularly damaging and create a carbon debt even before the first biomass crop is planted. The most notorious example is the clearance of Indonesian peatland for oil palms used in biodiesel. The CO_2 released in clearing the land will take 423 years of biodiesel production just to get back to carbon neutral. Cutting down Amazonian rain forest to plant soybeans is almost as bad, with a 319-year carbon debt. This means biomass needs careful sourcing and that waste or by-product material is likely to offer the most attractive carbon savings.

COMMISSIONING RISK

Compared to wind or hydro plants, biomass generators are more complex, with substantial on-site fabrication. A one- to two-year build period is usual, which tends to be followed by a prolonged commissioning programme, as many issues can only be resolved sequentially. Most biomass plants take at least one year post-commissioning to achieve their full output; however, there are several plants that have taken over three years to achieve their design output.

GAS VERSUS POWER

If biogas is suitably purified, the resulting methane can be sold to the natural gas grid, rather than being burnt locally to create power. Rises in natural gas prices have made this an attractive option and some jurisdictions attach green certificates to the gas, meaning a utility can claim a portion of renewable electricity generation at a combined-cycle gas turbine plant (~50% efficient) or combined heat and power plant (~70% efficient) rather than using on-site generation (20–30% efficient).

The economics are predicated on the availability of a gas grid and the price of

90 | Investment Opportunities for a Low-Carbon World

Figure 6. Gas versus power sales trade-off

	AD and 600kW power	AD and PSA gas sales
Total system cost ($m)	1.6	1.45
Gas engine and generator cost ($)	700,000	550,000
Local power price (¢/kWh)	5.5	5.5
Local gas price ($/m BTU)	6–7	6–7
Annual revenue ($)	300,000	380,000

Source: QuestAir and author's estimates

local power. However, companies that sell gas purification systems (typically based on pressure swing adsorption – PSA) have indicated that on a small AD site, the gas engine and generator trade-off typically occurs with gas at ~$6/million BTUs. Figure 6 gives an example using a current project.

BASE-LOAD GENERATION

Biomass power is almost constant all year round. Wet weather can reduce output if the delivered fuel has increased moisture content, while cold dry weather can increase output as the cooling systems operate more efficiently. Biomass plants are exposed to hydrocarbon fuel price risk to a modest extent, as they often use gas or oil to help control the combustion process. In the worst cases, this can reach 10% of the energy content, although 1–3% is more usual.

ENERGY BALANCES AND BIOMASS PRODUCTIVITY

Biomass production depends on factors such as climate and agronomy. Examples of net energy yields – output minus energy inputs for agricultural operations, fertiliser, harvest and the like – are given in Figure 7. Generally, perennial crops perform better than annual crops, as perennials have lower inputs and thus lower production costs as well as lower ecological impacts. Different management situations – irriga-

Figure 7. Biomass productivity

	Yield (oven dry tonnes/hectare/year)	Energy factor	Net energy yield (Gigajoules/hectare/year)
Short rotation crops (willow, poplar)	10–12	10×	180–200
Tropical crops (eucalyptus etc)	2–10	10×	30–180
Miscanthus	10–12	12×	180–200
Sugar cane (Brazil, Zambia)	15–20	18×	400–500
Commercial wood	1–4	20–30×	30–80
Sugar beet (Europe)	10–16	10×	30–100
Rapeseed (NW Europe)	4–7	4×	50–90

Assumes no genetic enhancement and standard agronomy *Source: UN World Energy Assessment*

tion, fertiliser application, genetic plant improvements or some combination of the three – can also increase biomass productivity, by a factor of up to 10.

In addition to production and harvesting, biomass requires transportation to a conversion facility and the logistical challenges of managing a crop that may only be produced for a limited time each year (such as straw) should not be underestimated. The energy used to transport biomass over land averages about 0.5 megajoules per tonne per kilometre, depending on the infrastructure and vehicle. This means that land transport of biomass can become a significant energy penalty for distances of over 100km. But such a radius covers a surface of hundreds of thousands of hectares and is sufficient to supply enough biomass for conversion facilities with hundreds of megawatts of thermal power.

Biomass investment summary

Biomass as an investment is challenging and relatively risky. The fuel is challenging, economies of scale are rare and few companies are consistently successful. However, its ability to provide baseload power and a wide range of potential projects means that it is likely to form a core component of any renewable energy portfolio.

LFG is the easiest and lowest risk option, with a substantial opportunity in the developing world to secure uncapped landfills or improve *in-situ* operations. The use of AD is growing, with second-generation technologies providing substantially better gas yields (on an annualised basis) and government incentives being increased. However, the economics of AD struggle at a farm scale and need professional operation, supported by robust waste disposal regulations that create gate fees, before it becomes an attractive investment without well above-average green power prices. Wood and waste-fired incineration can offer large projects but are unlikely to provide venture capital-type returns as a result, without taking development risk. Advanced thermal treatment processes are some way off being commercial, and we can expect the most successful processes to be those that offer niche products, such as bio-oil. Investors should be wary about the technical risks facing advanced thermal treatment when used for waste disposal or on a very large scale. However, biomass is:

- a massive resource that is 'carbon neutral' and can use waste products or be grown on marginal land;
- able to deliver consistent baseload power;
- subject to issues around fuel logistics, managing a bulky and 'living' fuel; and,
- competitive with conventional generation:
    - LFG – now;
    - direct combustion/AD – when waste regulations are supportive; and
    - advanced thermal treatment – development stage.

Market acceptance of biomass will increase as the true cost of conventional energy sources becomes apparent and the relative economics of biomass improve.

Conventional energy costs that are not always apparent include the low price of pollution and the numerous subsidies paid for conventional energy. Internalising the cost of pollution and reforming subsidies for energy and agriculture would rapidly increase the economic attractiveness of biomass.

Chapter 6

Energy efficiency as an investment theme

Zoë Knight, HSBC

It is becoming increasingly difficult to deliver policy for emissions trajectories consistent with the scientific recommendation to stay below 2°C warming against a preindustrial baseline. There is already 0.7°C of warming 'in the system' and a further 0.6°C would occur even if we halted emissions today. The policy delivery hurdles have been cost, economic uncertainty, political commitment and uncertainty over the credibility of climate science. The solution to low-carbon economic growth is two-fold: decoupling energy use from growth, by implementing best available technology to improve energy efficiency, and taking the carbon out of energy by reducing emission-intensive energy use. This is not only desirable for developed economies, it is imperative for developing countries to reduce poverty without the polluting side effects of growth.

Energy-efficiency measures are the most cost-effective tool to invoke the changes required to induce decoupling and sustain the low-carbon scenario. Energy-efficiency measures result in a reduced dependency on fossil fuels, improved energy security and reduced investments in energy infrastructure. In addition, they are a low-cost strategy, which has an immediate impact and is, therefore, popular politically. The International Energy Agency (IEA) estimates that, on average, an additional $1 spent on more efficient electrical equipment, appliances and buildings avoids more than $2 in investment in electricity supply.

These arguments are not new, yet the implementation of energy-efficiency measures has been slow. For example, the EU is not on track to deliver its 20% energy saving target by 2020, yet will achieve the 20% greenhouse gas reduction and renewable energy goals. There has been some progress, however. The IEA notes that, for 16 IEA countries since 1990, approximately half of the increased demand for energy services has been met through higher energy consumption, and the other half through gains in energy efficiency. All sectors achieved efficiency improvements, which averaged 0.9% per year between 1990 and 2005, with improvements translating into fuel and electricity cost savings of $180 billion in 2005. In addition, the IEA estimates that proposed actions (if implemented globally, without delay) could save around 8.2Gt of carbon dioxide per year by 2030.

Energy usage is key to our economic functionality, but some sectors are more

Figure 1. Global total final energy consumption

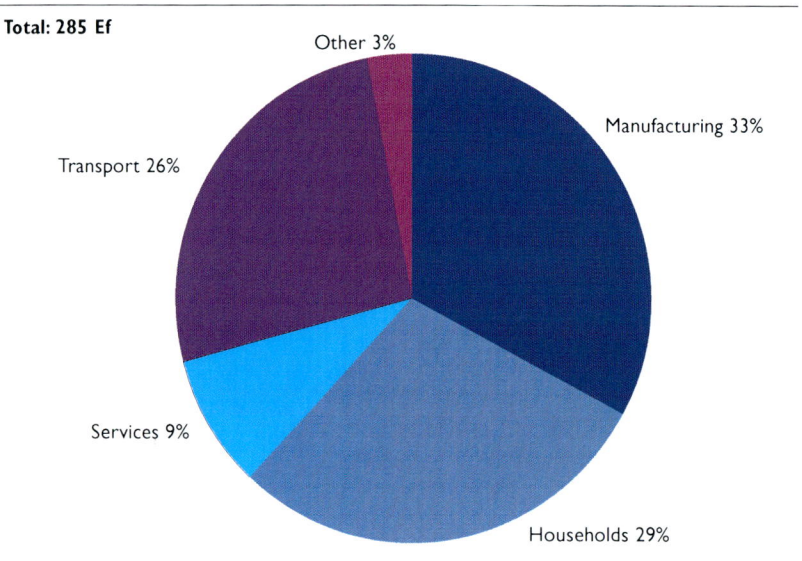

Total: 285 EJ

- Manufacturing 33%
- Households 29%
- Transport 26%
- Services 9%
- Other 3%

Source: International Energy Agency (IEA), Worldwide trends in energy use and efficiency

Figure 2. Global total direct and indirect CO_2 emissions

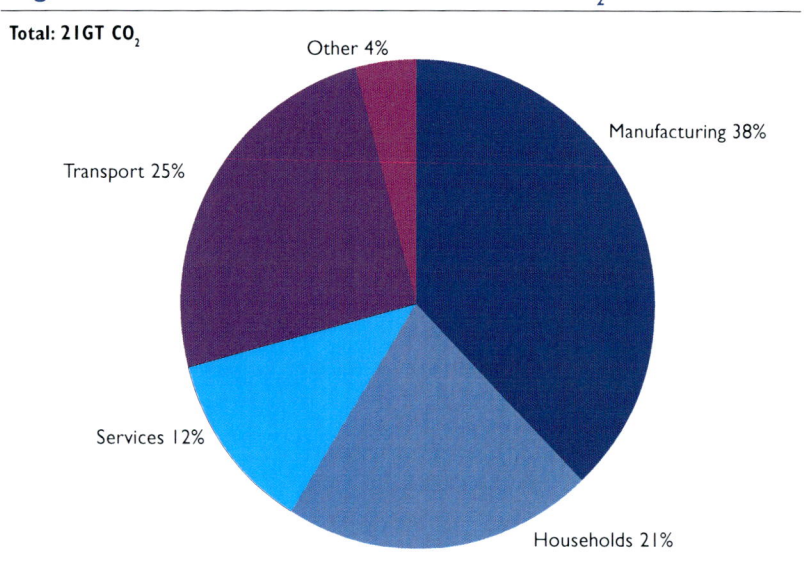

Total: 21 GT CO_2

- Manufacturing 38%
- Transport 25%
- Households 21%
- Services 12%
- Other 4%

Source: International Energy Agency (IEA), Worldwide trends in energy use and efficiency

energy-intense than others. Figure 1 shows global total final energy usage and figure 2 shows global total carbon dioxide emissions. The sectors have different proportions within the mix according to the energy commodities used, and so have different average levels of carbon dioxide emissions per unit of energy consumption. For example, households are greater consumers of energy in the total mix, at 29%, but are responsible for only 21% of global carbon dioxide emissions.

Consequently, the priority areas for most government policies are in transport, buildings, improved energy-efficiency requirements for equipment and industry along with technology and innovation and improving consumer energy-saving behaviour.

Government policy is key

In economic terms, the effects of greenhouse gases on society are defined as externalities. An externality is 'an effect of a use of resources on parties that did not have a choice in the use of resource and whose interests were not taken into account. The term refers to situations where human activities generate side effects of some sort that affect the welfare of others in society'.

Economic theory on externalities points to taxes and quotas as solution providers, which need to be implemented by a third party – usually government. For energy efficiency, government needs to provide the legislative backdrop to invoke behavioural change. Legislative drivers play an important role in sending signals for accurate pricing of investment decisions – in this case, to incorporate the externality cost of carbon.

Many governments have already implemented legislation to achieve the climate change-related targets for reducing emissions, even into a post-Kyoto Protocol time frame. For example, in Europe the commitment is for a 20% reduction in carbon dioxide emissions from a 1990 base by 2020, with a 30% reduction if other nations match the commitment. In addition, even governments that have not stated a quantitative target have finally bought into a carbon reduction framework and are implementing initiatives targeting environmental protection. Much legislation is already targeted towards energy efficiency. However, the reason that energy efficiency measures have not been scaled up as quickly as hoped for is because, for the most part, they are not legally binding. Perversely, because they are the most cost-effective solution and do not require subsidies, there has been lethargy towards large-scale implementation, which is in contrast to renewable energy, where feed-in tariffs have provided the economic incentive.

EUROPEAN LEGISLATIVE DRIVERS
The EU has had a strategy of achieving a 20% increase in energy efficiency by 2020 from 2008. It published directives, or non legally binding guidelines, for EU states to achieve the goals. In Europe, the policies related to energy efficiency include:
- the eco-design of energy-using products directive;

- the energy end-use efficiency and energy services directive;
- the labelling directive; and
- the energy performance of buildings directive.

The aim of the eco-design of energy-using products directive is to ensure free movement of those products within the internal market and prevent poor inefficient products from reaching the European market. This directive came into force in 2005, but was adopted by the Commission from the end of 2007 for many products. Generic eco-design requirements aim at improving the environmental performance of energy-using products (such as mobile phones, TVs, household appliances, computers), focusing on significant environmental aspects thereof without setting limit values. In reaction to this, the mobile manufacturers launched a star-rating system to compare the energy consumption of chargers. This was developed and supported in conjunction with industry, and provides a good example of proposed legislation changing behaviour without a large cost impact.

The energy end-use efficiency and energy services directive was adopted on 30 November 2005, and requires member states to save at least an additional 1% of their final energy consumption each year for the next nine years, starting from 2008. To achieve these savings, member states must adopt targets, impose obligations on their energy suppliers and prepare national energy-efficiency action plans. Savings will be achieved in both the private and public sectors, using a framework of measures. The directive will have a major impact not only on the work of national governments but also on local and regional energy actors in important areas such as energy-efficient and cost-effective lighting, heating, hot water, ventilation and transportation. It also improves the market uptake of energy-efficient technology and integrates energy efficiency into public procurement practices. The adoption of National Energy Efficiency Action Plans (NEEAPs) is one of the core elements of this directive. NEEAPs have been prepared by the member states. These action plans present the national strategy on how each member state seeks to achieve its energy savings objective. Member states need to speed up their efforts, however.

The EU revisited the energy efficiency directive in 2011. The revisions did not make the 20% energy-efficiency target legally binding, but they did focus on utilities and public sector retrofits. Now, energy-efficiency obligations mean that member states will introduce regulations to require energy utilities to achieve annual savings equivalent to 1.5% of their slates. In addition, the public sector has to carry out annual energy saving renovation in buildings covering 3% of the floor area.

SECTOR DRIVERS

Government legislation plays an important role in invoking behavioural change but corporates can also benefit from revenue opportunities in new markets. HSBC estimates that the annual market size for energy-efficiency and energy-management goods and services will reach $1.2 trillion by 2020, which includes goods and services in transport, building and industrial efficiency.

Investors will be rewarded by innovative companies if they can profitably capitalise on the opportunities proffered from energy-efficiency initiatives. There are different opportunities in different sectors.

Manufacturing (33% of total energy consumption)
The IEA estimates that the global manufacturing industry could improve its energy efficiency by 18–26% overall. This is based on the global adoption of best practices and technologies currently available. At the same time, this would reduce the sector's carbon dioxide emissions by 19–32%. New power plants that are being established in the emerging world are 8–10% more efficient than Western facilities.

Industrial productivity has always been one of the key drivers for capital goods demand, including the need to improve the energy efficiency of the equipment that is being used. Capital goods companies make many of the products or solutions that are used to achieve the carbon reduction goal. Efficiency has always been a factor in the replacement cycle, but the pace of renewal should accelerate going forward, which in turn gives a structural driver to companies in the capital goods space, which has historically been cyclical. One of the main opportunities for savings is in improving the efficiency of transmission and distribution.

Within an industrial facility, the biggest energy wastages occur as a result of inefficient machine drives (refrigeration, fans, pumps, compressors, materials processing), and suppliers of energy-efficient components (variable-speed drives, motors, controls) going into these products should be beneficiaries. Other areas within the industrial plant where energy can be saved include minimising heat transfer losses from local generation and steam plant.

Households (29% of total final energy consumption)
Among households, there is opportunity for saving energy though improvements in building standards. For households, hot water and central heating generation are likely to be the largest energy-intense activities. Heat generation through efficient boilers is one area to target, as well as heat retention, through wall and roof insulation and window and door glazing. These initiatives are encouraged through the European energy performance buildings directive. Implementing efficiency into new build is already work in progress; however, retrofitting the existing building stock is moving at a glacial pace. Building industry associations would like the retrofit rate in Europe to be increased from 1% of the building stock to 3% per year.

In addition, lighting accounts for 19% of all electricity used in the world (heat and light). Some 75% of all lighting is used in professional applications like street lighting and buildings, while 25% is used in homes. If new efficient lighting technologies were adopted globally, the world could achieve an energy saving of 40%. This would save €106 billion in energy costs per year, equivalent to 555 million tonnes of carbon dioxide.

The most popular light bulbs, incandescent bulbs, are the least energy-efficient because only 5% of the electric energy they use is transformed into light; the remaining 95% of the energy consumed is given off as heat. These bulbs tend to have a lamp life of about 1,000 hours, with an efficacy of about 10 lm/W.

The later generation of light bulbs, compact fluorescent bulbs (CFLs) are more efficient but are environmentally unfriendly as they contain small amounts of mercury.

Light-emitting diodes (LEDs) are small particles (the size of a grain of sand) that emit a very bright light (usually red, amber, green or blue, depending on the material) when an electrical current is applied. LEDs were first developed in the 1960s but were only recently used in indicator applications. The first LEDs, for example, were red and used for on/off switches on consumer applications like video recorders. The breakthrough for LED potential usage came in 1989, when white light was created by mixing a blue LED with red and green. This enabled a wider range of applications. Now the best white LED products can meet or exceed the efficiency of CFLs. Lighting is also a relatively easy sector in which to implement change because of the shorter replacement cycle.

In recent years, advances in brightness and efficiency have resulted in the implementation of LEDs for use in general illumination purposes, in applications such as toys, indicators for PCs, mobile backlights, LCDs, traffic lights, signs and displays, and downlight applications.

High brightness LEDs have already been widely adopted in mobile phones, signs/displays, illumination products and automotive applications. The high brightness segment growth has been outperforming the wider LED market and this trend is likely to accelerate in our view. LEDs have a lower power consumption than incandescent lighting, which offers a variety of benefits. The lower voltage results in low maintenance, which is beneficial in areas where public spending is required (eg, traffic signs). Additionally, a variety of colours means that there is improved visibility and safety in applications like traffic signals, and there are plenty of applications in 'mood' lighting (hotels, shops). Medical devices are also an area of opportunity as the long life is clearly a significant benefit. Finally, the lack of lead and mercury is a key environmental benefit.

Other areas where technology plays a role in energy efficiency is in chips for power conversion and motor control, by reducing standby power on devices and lowering heat loss in power supplies. In addition, smart metering systems to monitor energy usage would reduce consumption.

Transport (26% of energy consumption)
The IEA estimates that, between 1990 and 2005, global final energy use in transport increased by 37%, with road transport (passenger and freight) accounting for

89% of the total. The automotive industry has been reasonably proactive in the fight against climate change. In 1998, the European Automobile Manufacturers' Association (ACEA) and the EC agreed to the ACEA Agreement, a collective undertaking by the association and its members voluntarily to reduce the carbon dioxide emissions rates of vehicles sold in the EU. However, few of the top 20 car brands in Europe met the voluntary targets, and taxation legislation on emission levels of cars has subsequently been introduced, which is changing consumer behaviour towards lower-emission models. Against this backdrop, the suppliers with niche products tackling efficiency benefit the most from tightening legislation.

How do investors access the energy-efficiency theme?
Investors can access the theme through single stock selection of the companies that are exposed to the sectors above. For many companies, however, the energy-efficiency drivers are a small part of the business model. Therefore, investors need to identify whether the theme is a material enough earnings driver to warrant stock selection or whether there may be other factors that will drive valuation of the stock (like the state of the economy or currency exposure, for example), outweighing the positive structural drivers from increased investment at a government level into energy efficiency. As with any equity investment, positive long-term structural drivers may differ from short-term trading cyclicality.

Financial institutions also structure products that offer investors broad exposure to the theme through a certificate. Some investment banks have developed energy-efficiency indices comprising stocks that are exposed to energy-efficiency drivers. Investors can then choose to buy the index, or a sub category basket of stocks (eg, stocks related only to transport efficiency) through a single certificate.

Conclusion
Energy-efficiency legislation provides structural drivers to ensure the growth of markets in energy-efficient products and services. Investors can access this theme by single stock ideas or structured products but should be aware that, at present, the energy-efficiency theme is unlikely to be the sole earnings driver for these companies.

Chapter 7

Water technologies and infrastructure

*Daniel Wild, Marc-Olivier Buffle and Junwei Hafner-Cai,
SAM – Sustainable Asset Management*

Introduction

Supplying water of adequate quality and in sufficient quantities is one of the major challenges facing modern society. In many countries the available water reserves are now being overexploited to such an extent that the negative consequences can no longer be ignored. Countries located in arid regions are finding it particularly difficult to irrigate the crops they need to feed their population. At the same time many people still do not have access to safe drinking water, because water resources are limited or polluted by domestic and industrial wastewater. The situation will become even more critical in the years ahead. Four megatrends are shaping the development of the water market:

- Global population growth. Demand for water is soaring, and not just to cater for the personal needs of individuals. In the coming years even more water will be needed to produce food for the world's burgeoning population.
- In many countries the infrastructure for supplying the population with drinking water and wastewater treatment is badly run down. Major investments will therefore be required in the short term to upgrade ageing water mains and sewer systems in particular.
- Higher standards for water quality. One major priority is to ensure that people living in developing and newly industrialised countries have access to clean drinking water. In addition, solutions need to be found to meet the fresh challenges arising from new micropollutants that are becoming a problem in industrialised countries, in particular.
- Climate change will cause significant variations in the hydrological regime in many regions, culminating in a water crisis in some areas.

These megatrends will intensify the pressure to manage existing water resources far more efficiently in the years ahead. The associated investments will inevitably have an impact on the markets in question. This situation opens up attractive opportunities to all businesses offering products and services for the treatment, supply or use of water. Those companies that are capable of offering sustainable solutions stand to benefit the most. Based on an analysis of the current situation and an assessment of future market demand, SAM has identified four investment clusters that promise attractive upside potential:

- *Distribution and management:* Companies active in this cluster offer solutions for upgrading water mains and sewer infrastructure, develop systems for supplying freshwater and removing wastewater, act as utilities, or are involved in the management of water resources.
- *Advanced water treatment:* This cluster includes companies that play a key role in the disinfection of drinking water, the treatment of wastewater or the desalination of seawater, or which provide the necessary control systems and analytical instruments.
- *Demand-side efficiency:* This cluster includes companies offering products and services that boost the efficiency of water use in households or industry.
- *Water and food:* Companies in this group develop products that improve water efficiency and reduce pollution in crop irrigation and food production.

Many people do not have access to safe drinking water, because water resources are limited or polluted by domestic and industrial wastewater.

As the overall social, economic and environmental climate changes, corporate sustainability has become an increasingly crucial success factor. This study lays the foundation for an attractive and all-inclusive investment strategy that is geared toward the sustainable development of the water industry.

Water – a global challenge

A KEY ROLE IN OUR FUTURE
Water is essential for life. We need water for everything: for our personal use, to grow food and to produce virtually all the goods required for our daily existence. It is impossible to imagine our lives without an adequate water supply.

Yet water is not just a life preserver: it can destroy life as well. It can spread waterborne infectious diseases, for example. Millions of people worldwide suffer from serious diseases because they do not have access to clean drinking water.

Water is also vital for economic prosperity. The sale of water-related equipment and services is now a business with an annual turnover of more than $480 billion. Although water has become a precious commodity in many areas of the world, the price of water charged to consumers in most countries is still too low to reflect its value accurately.

Economic importance steadily growing
Over the coming years the economic importance of water will continue to increase for a number of reasons:

- Global demand for water is soaring. To meet this demand, a whole range of water services needs to be expanded and made to operate more efficiently.
- To meet the current challenges, enormous investments are required to upgrade

and expand the water infrastructure.
- For poorer and rapidly growing nations in particular, new technologies need to be developed for treating, distributing and using water.
- It is unlikely that water can be made available for all applications in the future at the same low cost as it is today. If the price of water does increase due to supply bottlenecks, this will have dramatic consequences for all areas of our lives that essentially depend on water. These areas include virtually all of society's commercial activities, from agriculture through to the production of everyday consumer goods.

Companies that identify these changes at an early stage and subsequently take steps to exploit the resulting opportunities will be better positioned in the market and will achieve greater commercial success.

SUPPLY AND DEMAND

There are two dominant features in current global water consumption patterns:
- The supply of fresh water is limited, but demand is growing steadily.
- Many countries are failing to satisfy the basic need to provide sufficient quantities of water of acceptable quality.

Limited water reserves

Every year about 90,000–120,000km^3 of precipitation falls on the world's continents and islands (Figure 1). About two-thirds of this precipitation reverts directly to the atmosphere through evaporation. Of the remaining 35%, two-thirds flows into wa-

Figure 1. Global water cycle

Figures in boxes represent the reservoirs of water (in 1,000km^3); the others show water flows (in 1,000km^3/year)

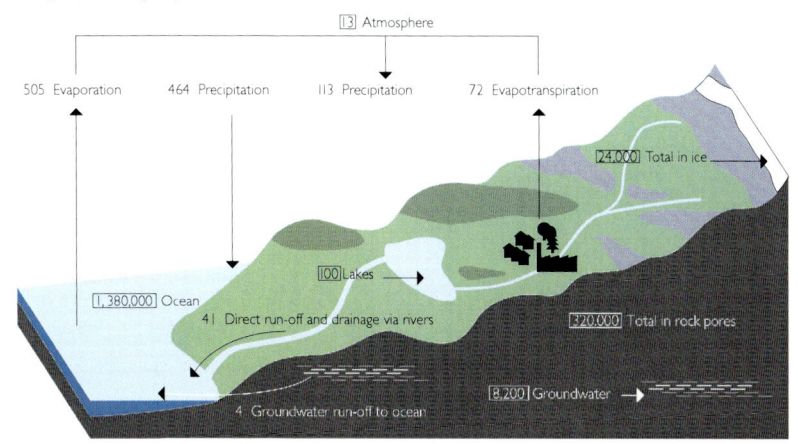

Source: A J B Zehnder, R Schertenleib and C Jaeger (1997), Herausforderung Wasser. EAWAG Jahresbericht

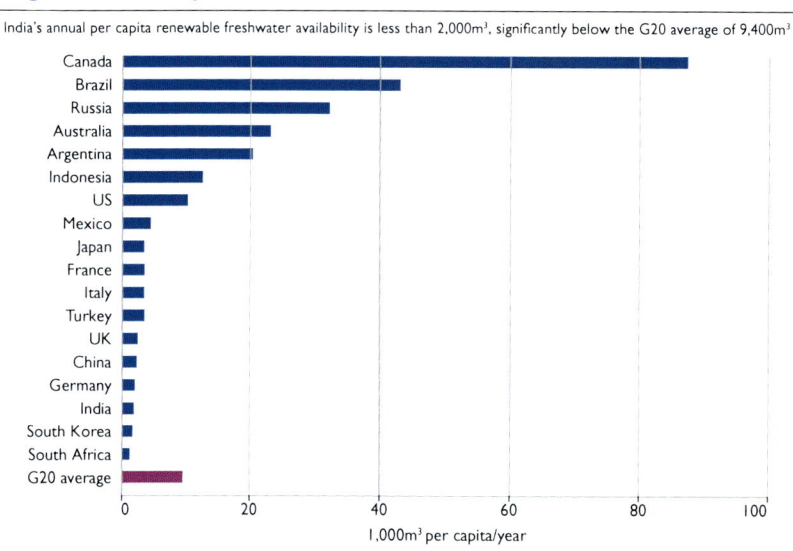

Figure 2. Per capita renewable water resources

India's annual per capita renewable freshwater availability is less than 2,000m³, significantly below the G20 average of 9,400m³

Country	1,000m³ per capita/year
Canada	~90
Brazil	~43
Russia	~32
Australia	~23
Argentina	~20
Indonesia	~13
US	~10
Mexico	~4
Japan	~3
France	~3
Italy	~3
Turkey	~3
UK	~2
China	~2
Germany	~2
India	~2
South Korea	~1
South Africa	~1
G20 average	~9

Source: Responsible Research (2010). Water in China

tercourses and is not fit for human use. A total of some 9,000–12,000km³ of water is therefore available for drinking, agricultural irrigation and industrial use.[1]

However, there are significant regional differences in the distribution of the effectively usable water.[2] In countries with ample rainfall, such as Switzerland, more than 7,000m³ of water are available per person per annum. In arid regions, however, sometimes only a few hundred cubic metres are available per person per annum (Figure 2). One worrying trend is the sharp decline in the quantity of water available to each person in many countries in recent years. The situation is especially critical in low rainfall countries.

Demand continues to rise

Water use can be roughly divided into three areas: urban water management, agriculture and industrial production. Worldwide, 10% of water flows into domestic use, 70% into agriculture and 20% into industrial production. There are, however, major regional differences in water use: in developed countries, about half the water consumption is destined for industrial uses, whereas in developing countries, agriculture is the biggest consumer of water, at about 80% (Figure 3).

Overall, water consumption has risen sharply in recent decades. In 1900, annual water extraction volumes totalled approximately 770km³. By the middle of the

---
[1] Zehnder, A J B, R Schertenleib and C Jaeger (1997), Herausforderung Wasser. *EAWAG Jahresbericht*.
[2] UNESCO (2006), *Water – a shared responsibility*, the second United Nations World Water Development Report. www.unesco.org/water/wwap (accessed 5 October 2007).

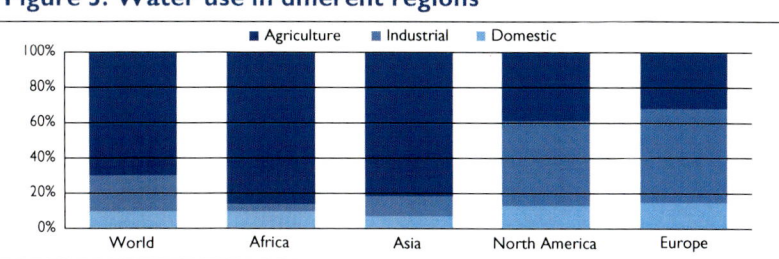

Figure 3. Water use in different regions

[Bar chart showing Agriculture, Industrial, and Domestic water use percentages for World, Africa, Asia, North America, and Europe, with y-axis from 0% to 100%.]

Source: FAO: Aquastat. www.fao.org/nr/water/aquastat (accessed 5 October 2007)

century, this figure had doubled to 1,480km³. Current consumption is estimated at 4,500km³.[3]

This trend is likely to continue in coming years, with consumption surpassing 6,500km³ in 2030. The extra demand can be explained by relentless population growth as well as higher per capita consumption due to improved living standards.

Water shortage is already a serious problem in many regions of the world, including southern Spain, the Maghreb, the Middle East, Central Asia, Pakistan, southern India and northern China. In the Americas, the US Midwest, Mexico and the Andes are the worst-hit areas. Eastern Australia is also badly affected by drought.

Countries such as Yemen, Uzbekistan and Israel are currently consuming more water than can be replenished by natural means. China and India – the two countries with the largest populations – are also heavily exploiting their available water resources.

The availability of water in individual countries is measured by the Water Exploitation Index (WEI). This index records water consumption as a percentage of annually renewable water reserves. A WEI of 20% is a critical value that signals the beginning of a water shortfall. Nine countries in Europe – Belgium, Bulgaria, Cyprus, Germany, Italy, Macedonia, Malta, Spain and the UK (England and Wales) – have a WEI of more than 20% (Figure 4). Countries with a WEI of more than 40% suffer from extreme water shortages and no longer use their available reserves in a sustainable way.

But there are also some regions where the situation has improved. This is particularly the case in Eastern Europe, where water consumption has dropped significantly since 1990, mainly thanks to infrastructure improvements and more efficient use of water.

Private consumption: water brings prosperity

An average European uses between 150 and 400 litres of water every day for his personal requirements. Consumption in the US is almost twice as high, at 580 litres per person per day. In China, by contrast, the figure is only 90 litres per day on average. In many developing countries, individual consumption is well below the limit

---

[3] 2030 Water Resources Group (2009), *Charting our Water Future.*

106 | Investment Opportunities for a Low-Carbon World

Figure 4. Water Exploitation Index for European countries

The Water Exploitation Index (WEI) specifies the percentage of renewable water resources consumed. If it moves above the 20% threshold, this is an alarm signal. Countries with a WEI of more than 40% suffer from extreme water shortage.

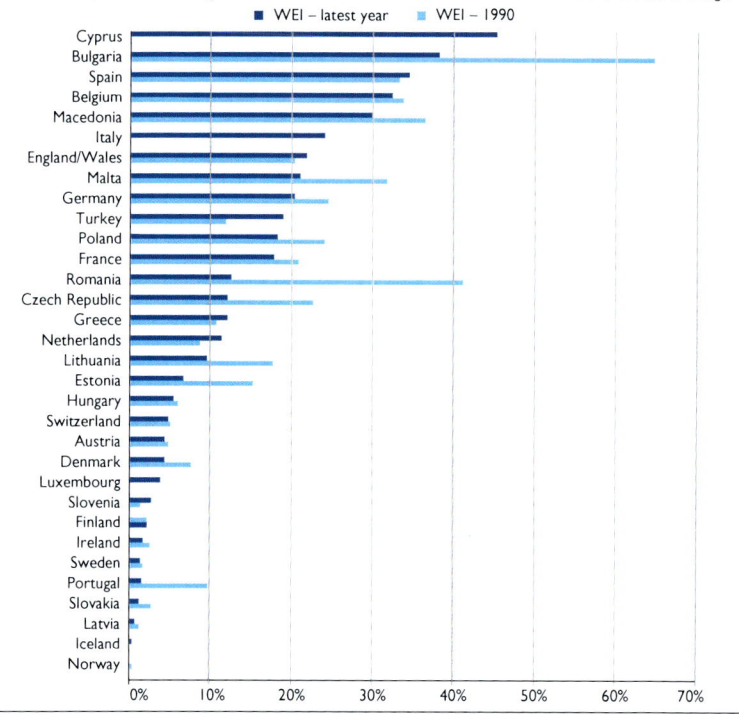

■ WEI – latest year   ■ WEI – 1990

Cyprus, Bulgaria, Spain, Belgium, Macedonia, Italy, England/Wales, Malta, Germany, Turkey, Poland, France, Romania, Czech Republic, Greece, Netherlands, Lithuania, Estonia, Hungary, Switzerland, Austria, Denmark, Luxembourg, Slovenia, Finland, Ireland, Sweden, Portugal, Slovakia, Latvia, Iceland, Norway

Source: European Environment Agency: EEA Signals 2009 Climate Change Adaptation: Water and Drought

Figure 5. Use of water resources in different regions

The map shows river basin areas where the available water reserves are being overexploited by humans. In these regions, the long-term survival of the ecosystems is under threat

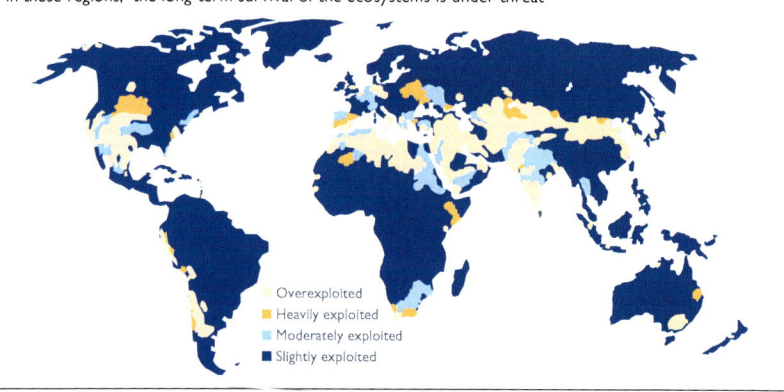

- Overexploited
- Heavily exploited
- Moderately exploited
- Slightly exploited

Source: UNDP (2006), Human Development Report.

Figure 6. Water use and global population, 1900–2025

A comparison of global water consumption since 1900 and predicted water consumption up to 2025 against global population trends demonstrates that water consumption has increased more rapidly than the overall population

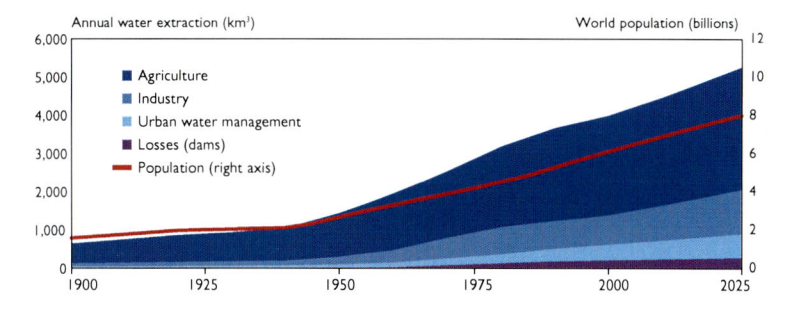

Sources: FAO: Aquastat, www.fao.org/nr/water/aquastat (accessed 5 October 2007); UN Secretariat, The World Population Prospects, 2006

Figure 7. Percentage of population with access to sanitation

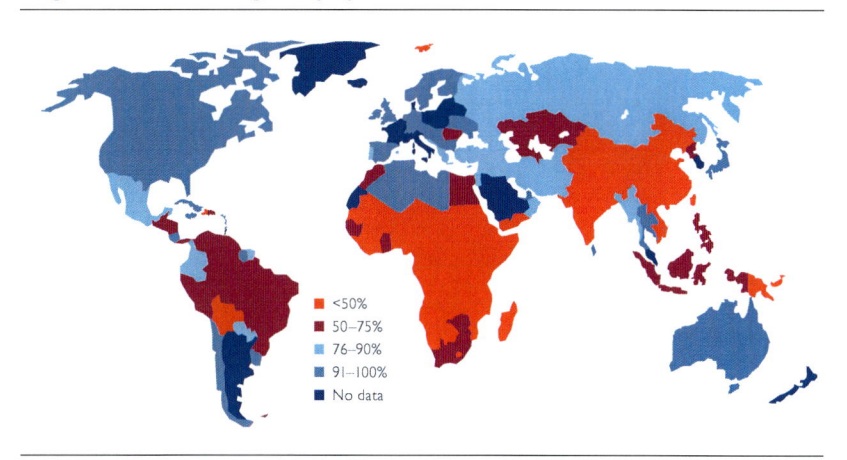

Source: UNDP (2006), Human Development Report

of 50 litres per day specified as the critical threshold by the Food and Agriculture Organization (FAO).[4]

In many countries, wastewater is not adequately treated (or not treated at all) before being channelled back into the water cycle. These countries therefore have to cope with undesirable impacts on human health and the environment. About 2.4 billion people worldwide have no access to adequate sanitation. The situation is particularly critical in Africa, Southeast/Central Asia and parts of South America.[5]

---
4 UNDP (2006), *Human Development Report*.
5 UNDP (2006), *Human Development Report*.

Countries with an efficiently run urban water management system have invested large sums in their infrastructure in recent decades. In Switzerland, the specific repurchase value of the entire public and private sewer system, along with all the wastewater treatment facilities, comes to almost Sfr100 billion. This works out to Sfr13,600 per head of population.[6] Many of these installations are now decrepit, and need to be replaced within the next few years.

Agriculture: the major consumer
Agriculture is easily the world's heaviest consumer of water, most of which is used for irrigation. It takes about 2,500kcal per day to meet one adult's energy requirements. One kilogram of bread contains about 3,500kcal, and it takes roughly 1,000 litres of water to produce this bread under optimum growing conditions. Based on this assumption, it takes about 260m³ of water to feed one person for one year with a vegetarian diet.

The more meat contained in a person's diet, the higher the associated water consumption. Where meat accounts for 20% of a person's diet, twice as much water is consumed for its production.[7] This calculation does not take into account the fact that conditions for food production are seldom ideal. Much of the water used is wasted due to crop failures and losses in irrigation. If production losses are factored in as well, it takes 550m³ of water to provide one person with a purely vegetarian diet for one year.

Because rainfall is distributed so unevenly, not all countries are able to produce enough food for their own population. Many governments therefore have to resort to importing food, which in some cases accounts for up to 35% of all imports.

The situation becomes even more critical for these countries if food prices are forced higher by adverse weather conditions or competition from biofuel produc-

Figure 8. Water quantities used in food production

Volume of water (in litres) needed to produce 1 kg of the food specified

Food	Litres
Beef	15,500
Lamb	6,100
Pork	4,800
Goat	4,000
Rice	3,400
Soybeans	1,800
Wheat	1,300
Corn	900

Source: UNESCO – IHE, www.waterfootprint.org (accessed 5 October 2007)

---

6 Herlyn, A (2007), Status quo der Schweizer Abwasserentsorgung. *Gas Wasser Abwasser* 3, 171–176.
7 Zehnder, A J B, R Schertenleib and C Jaeger (1997), Herausforderung Wasser. *EAWAG Jahresbericht*.

Figure 9. Cropland per person trends

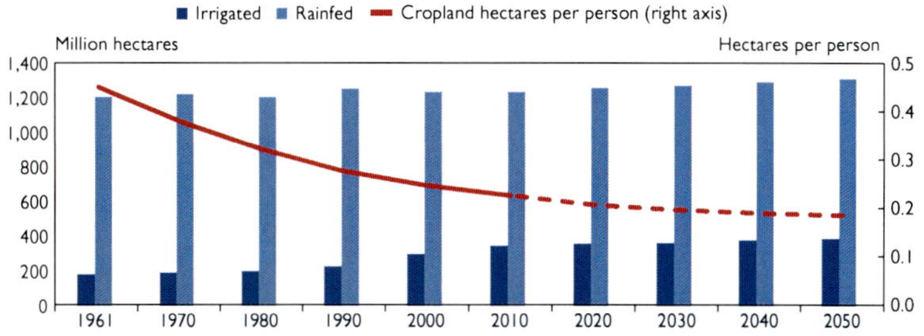

Source: UN Secretariat: World Urbanisation Prospects: The 2007 Revision Population Database; SAM

tion. It is perhaps surprising to find that arable farmland registered only an insignificant increase worldwide in the period from 1960 to 2000. As a consequence, the area of cropland required per person fell from around 0.45 to 0.23 hectares from 1960 to 2010 (Figure 9).

This reduction has been achieved through massive intensification of farming methods. This has included not just the use of fertilisers and crop protection agents, but also crop irrigation. A total of 275 million hectares of land is now under irrigation, equivalent to over 20% of the total area under cultivation.[8]

Industry: consumption stabilised at a high level
Water also plays a crucial role in industrial production, whether it be for paper production, tyre manufacture, electricity generation, mining or oil exploitation. In Europe, industry accounts for just over half of water consumption, while in the US the figure is just below 50%.

In contrast to agriculture and urban water management, where consumption is steadily rising, the situation is slightly more positive for industrial water use. Global water consumption by industry rocketed from about 150km^3 per year in 1950 to over 800km^3 in 1990.[9] Since then, industrial water consumption has continued to rise worldwide, but at a much slower pace than in previous decades. Industrial water withdrawal is projected to be 1,500km^3 in 2030.[10] At the same time, there are significant regional differences. In Europe and North America, industrial water consumption after 1980 settled at about 200 km^3 per annum (Europe) and 300 km^3 per annum (North America). The annual increase in industrial water consumption has been much more gradual in Asia.

---

[8] UNESCO (2009), *Water in a Changing World*, the third United Nations World Water Development Report.
[9] UNESCO (2006). *Water – a shared responsibility*, the second United Nations World Water Development Report. www.unesco.org/water/wwap
[10] 2030 Water Resources Group (2009). *Charting our Water Future*.

Global trends impacting the water market
The global crisis threatening the management of water resources is likely to intensify in the coming years. Four trends are shaping the future development of the water sector:
- Demand for water is increasing further as a result of demographic changes.
- In many cases, the ageing water infrastructure needs to be replaced.
- Water quality improvements are necessary in many places.
- Climate change is altering the availability of water resources.

DEMOGRAPHIC CHANGES
There are three ways in which demographics are affecting water consumption:
- The world's population will continue to grow in future decades.
- More and more people are moving from the countryside to towns.
- General living standards are improving, especially in the two countries with the largest populations, China and India.

Continuing boom in global population
The world's current population of approximately 7 billion people will continue to swell over the coming decades. The UN predicts a global population of 9.2 billion people by 2050. Demand for water will of course escalate purely in response to this population growth. Experiences in recent decades even show that water consumption has grown at a faster rate than the general population. This trend is mainly attributable to continuous improvements in living standards. In 1950, per capita annual water consumption averaged 580m^3. This figure had already risen to 660m^3 by 2009. Given the improving living standards in regions such as Asia, in particular, this underlying trend is unlikely to be reversed for some time.

Increasing urbanisation
Rapid population growth is occurring in tandem with increasing urbanisation. More and more people are moving from the country to the city, usually because of a real or perceived lack of employment opportunities in rural regions. The urbanisation trend is clearly reflected in the number of megacities. In 1950 there were only 86 cities with a population of more than 1 million, but this figure rose from 387 to 431 cities between 2000 and 2007 (Figure 10).

The number of megacities is increasing rapidly in Asia, Africa and Latin America, in particular. The cities are growing not just in number, but also in size. In 2007, the world's 100 largest cities had an average population of more than 7 million people.

UN forecasts indicate that almost 60% of the world's population will be living in urban areas by 2030. The proportion is roughly 50% at present, compared with 29% in 1950. Rapid growth of cities creates a huge challenge for the water sector.

Figure 10. Demographic trends and urbanisation of population

No. of cities >1 million inhabitants	1950	2000	2007
World	86	387	431
Africa	2	35	42
Asia	31	194	218
Europe	30	62	63
Latin America	7	49	54
North America	14	41	46
Oceania	2	6	8
Avg size of 100 largest cities (1,000 inhabitants)	2,200	6,300	7,000
% of population in urban areas	29	47	50
World population (million inhabitants)	2,530	6,125	6,600

Source: UN Population Division Department of Economic and Social Affairs (2007), The Urban Agglomerations; SAM

Demand for water services, especially for wastewater treatment, is booming. Extending basic sanitation will require huge investments in the coming years. Over the next five years, approximately an additional 880 million people will require access to improved drinking water sources and approximately 1.4 billion will need to be connected to proper sewage treatment facilities to meet the 2015 Millennium Development Goals (MDG) targets.[11]

The world seems to be on track to meet the MDG drinking water target, even though some countries face enormous challenges, especially in sub-Saharan Africa. While water supply goals seem achievable, it appears that the MDG sanitation target will be difficult to reach.

Soaring demand for food
The rise in the world's population and the improvement in living standards are also having an impact on food production. The FAO expects demand for food to be 55% higher in 2030 than in 1998. Food production must increase by 1.4% per annum in order to meet this demand. The surge in demand will be driven mainly by developing countries. Intensifying the farming methods used in these countries should help to meet most of the increased demand for food. The FAO expects the overall area under cultivation to expand. At the same time, the amount of cropland under irrigation is likely to increase by 20%. This will in turn push up water consumption by 14%, potentially causing local bottlenecks in areas such as the Middle East and North Africa, where there is likely to be less water available for agricultural use. These countries will therefore be forced to import even more food than at present.

---
[11] United Nations (2009), *The Millennium Development Goals Report*.

Overexploitation of resources
The consequences of overexploiting water resources are already manifesting themselves in different parts of the planet. Once mighty rivers now carry only a fraction of their former water volume, and the groundwater table is steadily falling. Eleven countries accommodating almost half the world's population – including China, India, Pakistan, the US, Israel, Egypt, Libya and Algeria – currently have a negative groundwater balance.[12]

Overexploitation of water has dramatic consequences at local level:
- In the region around the Spanish city of Huelva the water table has been steadily falling for some years because many farmers illegally siphon off water to irrigate their fruit crops. This overexploitation is posing a threat to the Doñana national reserve in particular, which contains one of the most important marshlands in Europe.[13]
- On occasion, China's second-largest watercourse, the Yellow river, does not even reach the sea, or peters out into no more than a stream.[14]
- In the southern Indian state of Tamil Nadu, the expansion of agriculture has led to a situation where the Kaveri river, once 300m wide, dries up on occasion. In some places the water table has fallen between 300 and 400m.[11]
- Farmers in the southwest of the US are feeling the effects of the overexploitation of groundwater. The level of the Ogallala aquifer, the world's third-largest underground water table, has fallen several metres in recent years. This has caused many fertile regions to dry out. Many farmers have had to revert to more basic crops, which generate less income. Although the size of the irrigated area has shrunk again, it will take only another 20–30 years before the Ogallala aquifer dries up completely.[11]

In view of these problems, some countries have plans for large-scale canal systems to divert water and alleviate the shortage in arid regions (Figure 11). India has launched a river-linking project to combine 14 rivers flowing from the Himalayas with rivers from the south. China has started work on a huge project to divert water away from the Yangtze into the arid regions of the north at an estimated investment cost of $60 billion. And Spain also has plans for channelling water from the north to the south. One common thread of these numerous projects is that they are often a source of public controversy and are bound to have serious consequences for the environment.

Tapping into new water sources
Although the water supply infrastructure is in a very dilapidated state in many countries, with large volumes of water being wasted through leakage, countries where water is scarce are increasingly trying to expand freshwater supplies through the

---
12 Lanz, K (2006), *Wem gehört das Wasser?* Lars Müller Publishers.
13 Reye, B (2007), Knallrote Früchte mit üblem Beigeschmack. *Tages-Anzeiger*, www.tagi.ch (accessed 5 October 2007).
14 Den Flüssen den Weg weisen (2006), *Neue Zürcher Zeitung*, www.nzz.ch (accessed 5 October 2007).

Figure 11. Major water transfer projects

Country	Project	Capacity (million m³/day)	Capital cost (billion)
Libya	Great Man-Made River	6.5	$11
China	South to north water diversion	110	$58
Spain	River Ebro diversion	2.9	€18
Kuwait	Karun transfer (from Iran)	0.75	$2
Jordan	Disi Amman water conveyor	0.27	$0.95

Source: GWI (2010), Global Water Market 2011

use of desalination plants. The installed capacity of these plants has increased enormously in recent decades.

In 1970, the amount of water desalinated globally per day was less than 0.8 million m³. This figure has increased to well over 59 million m³ per day in 2009. There is no sign of this trend abating, given that installed capacity is constantly increasing.

There are now over 14,000 desalination plants online, with a further 244 known to be under contract or in construction, which represent an additional capacity of 9.1 million m³ per day.[15]

One reason for the boom in desalination plants is that production costs have dropped dramatically in recent years. Especially for plants using reverse osmosis membrane technology, operating costs are now three to four times lower than they were 30 years ago. With production costs of less than $1 per cubic metre of water, these plants are achieving price levels that are getting much closer to conventional water sources.[16]

Saudi Arabia is already the world's largest producer of desalinated water, with 1,420 plants online providing a total capacity of over 10 million m³ per day.[17] One of the largest projects is a 1 million m³ per day plant at Ras Azzour.

Israel continues to expand its desalination and water recycling programmes and has planned projects including the Red Sea-Dead Sea canal. The project is a 180km aqueduct consisting of tunnel and channel sections, which would carry 1.8 billion m³ of seawater from the Red Sea to the Dead Sea area each year. Of this total, 800 million m³ would be desalinated to use as drinking water for Israel, Jordan and the Palestinian Authority, and 1 billion m³ a year would be pumped into the Dead Sea, which has been drying up.

Apart from facilities to desalinate seawater and brackish water, plants are also being built that are capable of treating wastewater for reuse in other applications. California's Orange County Water District and Orange County Sanitation District

---
[15] The International Desalination & Water Reuse Quarterly industry website, www.desalination.biz /news/news_story.asp?id=5121 (accessed 8 November 2009).
[16] Pacific Institute (2006). *Desalination, With a Grain of Salt – A California Perspective.*
[17] GWI (2010), *Global Water Market 2011.*

together have invested approximately $481 million in a water supply project to expand the county's water purification and seawater intrusion barrier facilities, as well as to install a 13-mile pipeline along the Santa Ana river for the reuse of advanced treated wastewater. The reuse of treated wastewater helps Orange County recharge its groundwater basin, protecting it from further degradation due to seawater intrusion. This represents a more cost-effective and energy-efficient solution, compared to importing water from northern California.[18]

AGEING INFRASTRUCTURE

In contrast with many developing countries, where many people still do not have adequate access to safe drinking water, industrialised nations originally built their water mains back in the early 20th century. In many areas huge investments are now required to repair and upgrade the aging infrastructure. Water supply and sewer systems have a service life of roughly 60–80 years and in many cases have reached the end of their useful lives. Furthermore the water mains are not being adequately maintained in some countries:

- The standard of maintenance for the US water mains and sewer system – like many other areas of the infrastructure – is far too low. Leaking pipes mean that large volumes of precious drinking water are wasted. The City of San Diego, for example, buys in 300 million m^3 of water every year, 25 million m^3 of which is never actually used, costing the city approximately $22 million.[19] The total water loss nationwide is probably in the region of 23 million m^3 per day, which is equivalent to the combined water consumption of America's 10 biggest cities.
- The US Environmental Protection Agency (EPA) has identified a huge financing gap for the maintenance of drinking water and wastewater treatment facilities over the next 20 years. If spending continues at the current level, the total gap by the end of that period will amount to some $540 billion. Even if investments rose by 3% per annum in real terms, the shortfall would still come to $76 billion.[20]
- London loses 30% of its fresh water through leaks in its antiquated pipe system.[21] Under pressure from the industry regulator, the network operator Thames Water is replacing more than 1,500km of the ageing supply network within five years. In 2010, the company also opened a £250 million desalination plant which can produce 140 million–150 million litres/day – enough for around 1 million people.
- Water use is also inefficient in France and Spain. Around 30% of water is lost before it reaches the end consumer.[22]

---

18 *Groundwater Replenishment System Progress Report*, 2008.
19 Davis, R (2007), The case of San Diego's vanishing water, www.awwa.org/publications/MainStreamArticle.cfm? itemnumber=29525 (accessed 5 October 2007).
20 US EPA (2002), *Clean Water and Drinking Water Infrastructure Gap Analysis Report*.
21 Dow Jones Newswires (2010), SAM sees steady growth in world water sector.
22 European Environment Agency, www.eea.europa.eu/themes/climate/ (accessed 5 October 2007).

Water Technologies | 115

Figure 12. State of the US water supply system

If the standard of maintenance of the water supply system continues at its current level, more than half of the pipework will be in a poor condition or worse by 2020

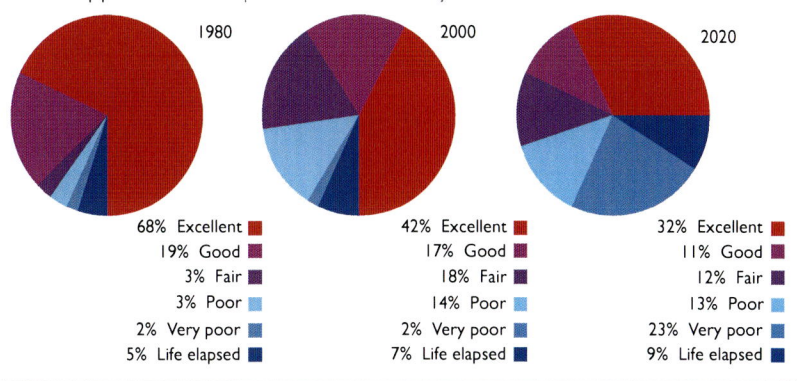

1980
- 68% Excellent
- 19% Good
- 3% Fair
- 3% Poor
- 2% Very poor
- 5% Life elapsed

2000
- 42% Excellent
- 17% Good
- 18% Fair
- 14% Poor
- 2% Very poor
- 7% Life elapsed

2020
- 32% Excellent
- 11% Good
- 12% Fair
- 13% Poor
- 23% Very poor
- 9% Life elapsed

Source: US EPA (2002), Clean Water and Drinking Water Infrastructure Gap Analysis Report

Figure 13. Yearly maintenance capital expenditure in Swiss canton of Schwyz

The sewer network in the Canton of Schwyz is a good example of the expected capital expenditure required for maintenance of the sewer infrastructure in Switzerland. The black curve reflects the projected capital investments needed to maintain the existing network.

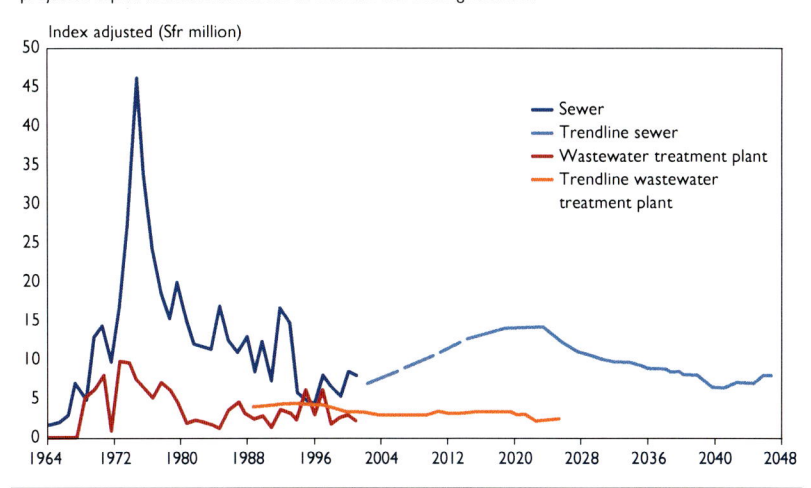

Index adjusted (Sfr million)

- Sewer
- Trendline sewer
- Wastewater treatment plant
- Trendline wastewater treatment plant

Source: Environmental Protection Agency, canton of Schwyz

- There is also a continuous effort to renovate the sewer system in Switzerland, most of which was constructed in the second half of the 20th century and needs to be renewed over the next few decades.[23] About 23% of the sewer network

---
23 Lehmann, M (1994), Volkswirtschaftliche Bedeutung der Siedlungswasserwirtschaft. *Gas Wasser Abwasser* 6/94.

currently has significant or serious defects and needs to be renovated in the mid term.[24] The situation is even more critical in the residential property sector, where up to 85% of the pipe-work is substandard.[25]

HIGHER WATER QUALITY STANDARDS
In many countries, the population is suffering not only from a shortage of water, but also from the poor quality of the water that is available. More than 1 billion people worldwide have no access to safe drinking water.

This situation is mainly caused by three factors:
- In developing countries, many residents of urban areas are not connected to a proper sewer system. The wastewater from these households is released into the environment without any form of treatment, polluting groundwater and surface waters in the process. Solid waste is also frequently dumped into watercourses.
- In many countries, industrial effluent is inadequately treated. This is a critical problem in China, for example.
- The fact that farmers have managed to increase their food production so significantly in recent decades is mainly due to the increased use of crop protection agents and fertilisers. In many regions, these substances are now contaminating the water and polluting the groundwater.

The range of potential pollutants is enormous: organic matter decomposing in the water removes the oxygen that is vital for sustaining life; faeces contaminate the water with bacteria and microorganisms that spread disease; the run-off from overfertilised fields floods rivers and lakes with harmful nutrients; overwatering and excessive groundwater extraction increases soil salinity; acid rain changes the pH value; heavy metals and toxic compounds from industrial processes contaminate drinking water; and inappropriate cultivation methods release large quantities of fine particulates into the water, which also causes the water quality to deteriorate.

The lack of adequate sanitation facilities in countries with poor infrastructure is one of the major causes of widespread gastrointestinal disorders. This can have fatal consequences for children, in particular. The number of deaths caused every year by contaminated water is estimated at up to 5 million worldwide. The installation of a comprehensive sanitation system as typically found in industrialised nations is not feasible within a reasonable timeframe, mainly because cities in these countries are growing so rapidly. Because of this, simpler solutions to the sanitation problem in these countries are being sought.

One point worth raising in this context is that a correlation has been found to exist between water treatment and economic prosperity. A comparison of different

---

24 Herlyn, A (2007), Status quo der Schweizer Abwasserentsorgung. *Gas Wasser Abwassser* 3, 171–176.
25 Gränicher, H U (2006), Die neue VSA-Richtlinie – Baulicher Unterhalt von Abwasseranlagen. Kanalisationsforum, Bern.

Figure 14. Water treatment and the creation of industrial value added

The higher the value created by manufacturing industry, the higher the level of spending on water treatment tends to be.

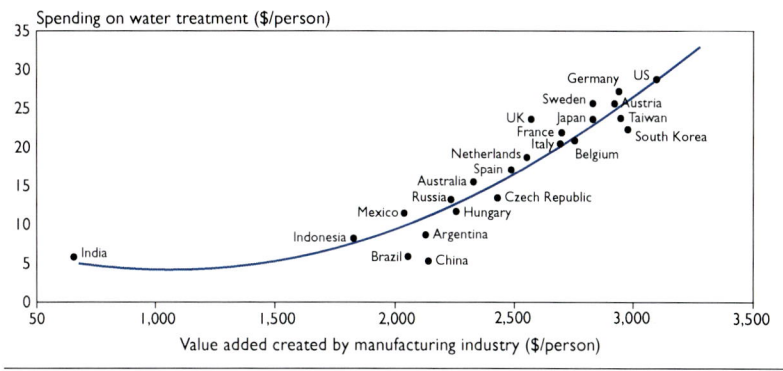

Source: Nalco; Freedonia, 2006

countries shows that those with a high level of value-added spend more money per capita on water treatment than less prosperous countries (Figure 14).

It is interesting to note from this comparison that China spends comparatively little on wastewater treatment.[26] The growing number of reports about severely polluted watercourses in the world's most populous country is less surprising. Many rivers in China are so badly polluted that not even industry can use the water. More than 75% of rivers flowing through urban areas in China are considered unsuitable for drinking or fishing. About 700 million people drink water that is contaminated with animal or human waste and water pollution causes about 60,000 premature deaths every year.[27]

New pollutants in the water
In industrialised countries, decent water quality is more or less guaranteed nowadays thanks to the provision of advanced water and wastewater treatment. But these countries are increasingly facing new challenges. Investigations in Switzerland have shown that, despite the construction of new sewage treatment plants, hazardous chemicals are still entering the watercourses. Especially in times of heavy rainfall, acute concentrations of toxic nitrogen compounds, such as nitrites and ammonium, are being detected at sewer overflows and large quantities of pesticides and nitrate find their way into the groundwater when they are used in farming.[28]

Another problem is the constant stream of new substances and compounds

---
26 Nalco, Freedonia (2006).
27 Responsible Research (2010), *Water in China*.
28 EAWAG, Dübendorf; BUWAL, Bern (2004), *Fischnetz – Dem Fischrückgang auf der Spur*. Schlussbericht des Projekts Netzwerk Fischrückgang Schweiz.

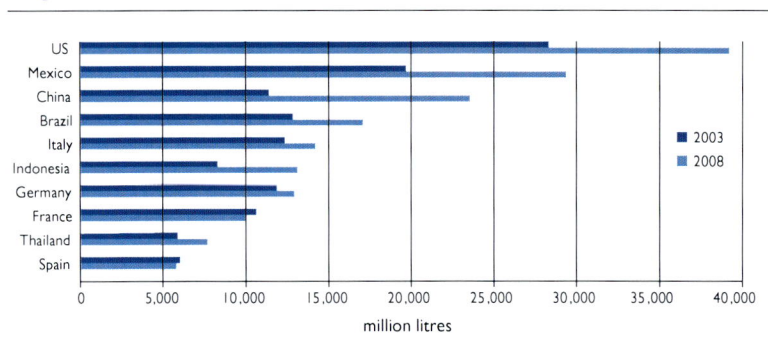

Figure 15. Annual consumption of bottled water

US	
Mexico	
China	
Brazil	
Italy	■ 2003
Indonesia	■ 2008
Germany	
France	
Thailand	
Spain	

million litres (0 – 40,000)

Source: CLSA Asia-Pacific Markets (January 2010), Thirsty Asia 2

entering the water cycle that wastewater treatment systems are unable to remove entirely. The trickiest are endocrine-active substances, which can have a negative impact on any living organisms in the water.[29] Another problematic aspect as far as wastewater treatment is concerned is that many of these substances are excreted in human urine. The water used for flushing heavily dilutes these substances, thereby making it more difficult to remove them, even with the help of the latest technologies in sewage treatment systems.[30]

Greater health awareness
For increasing numbers of people in developed countries, water is not only a basic commodity but also a lifestyle product. In Germany, for example, today's consumer can choose from about 500 different domestic water brands, all of them different in terms of taste and origin. And these are complemented by many other types of mineral water imported from abroad.[31]

In many countries, people rely on drinking bottled water due to the insufficient quality of local tap water. Growth in this industry has been very strong for many years now, averaging 8% by volume per annum for the past 10 years, even though the growth rate is now slowing or even negative in certain countries such as the US (Figure 15).

On the other hand, demand for bottled water is growing faster in developing countries, driven by contaminated and unsafe drinking water. During the period 2003–08, demand for bottled water in China grew at a compound annual growth rate (CAGR) of 15.6%, while consumption in the US grew by 6.7%.[32]

---
[29] Buffle, M-O (2007), Treatment of endocrine disrupting compounds by mean of advanced oxidation, EDC workshop, Montgomery Watson, London, UK.
[30] European Environment Agency, www.eea.europa.eu/themes/climate/ (accessed 5 October 2007).
[31] Informationszentrale Deutsches Mineralwasser, www.mineralwasser.com/ (accessed 5 October 2007).
[32] CLSA Asia-Pacific Markets (2010), *Thirsty Asia* 2.

CLIMATE CHANGE

In many regions of the world, climate change will have a significant impact on global water resources in the coming decades. In its latest report, the Intergovernmental Panel on Climate Change (IPCC)[33] anticipates the following trends:

- In the high latitudes and in some tropical regions, the average annual run-off will increase by between 10% and 40% by the middle of this century.
- It is likely that even more areas will be affected by drought and water shortages will be more common.
- An overall increase in the frequency of heavy downpours is predicted. This also makes it more likely that human settlements will experience severe damage.
- The volumes of water stored in glaciers and the snow pack will decline over the course of the next century. This means that after a phase of increased discharge there will be less water available in regions supplied by meltwater running off from major mountain chains. This is an ominous development, because more than one-sixth of the world's population currently lives in these regions.

Impact will vary from one region to the next

In addition to these general statements, the IPCC also provides forecasts on the effects of global warming on specific regions:

- Within Europe, the Mediterranean countries will be most heavily affected by climate change. The IPCC predicts that Southern Europe will generally have to cope with far more difficult conditions, including high temperatures, extreme drought, poor water availability and subsequently limited potential for exploiting water as an energy source.

Figure 16. Run-off volume from the Indus river under changing climate conditions

The run-off pattern could vary widely, depending on how quickly the average global temperature changes in the coming years. Even if drastic measures are taken to combat climate change, the run-off volume will still drop significantly over the course of this century.

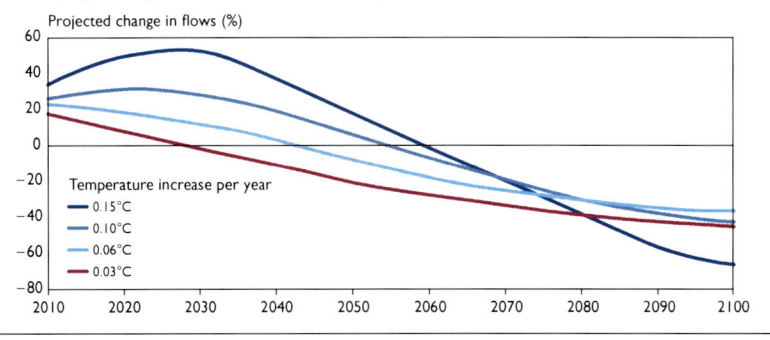

Source: UNDP, Human Development Report 2006

---

33 IPCC, WMO/UNEP (2007), *Climate Change 2007: Summary for Policymakers.*

Figure 17. Changes in water availability in Europe

The map shows which regions will have more or less water available in 2020 than at present as a result of climate change

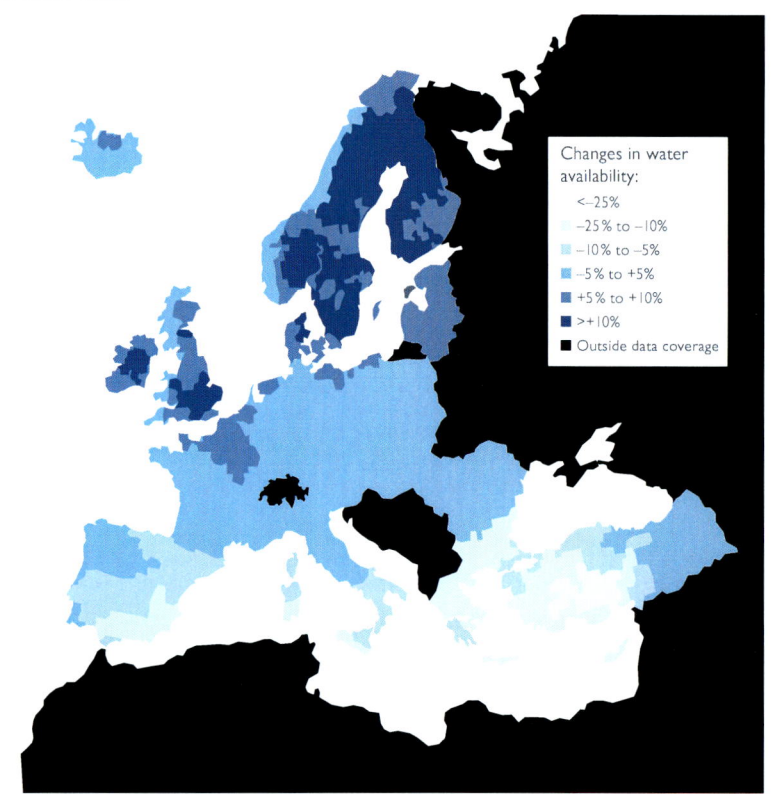

Source: The European Environment – State and Outlook 2005

- In Central and Eastern Europe, IPCC predicts less rainfall in the summer. This could spell trouble, since some parts of this region already experience relatively low rainfall throughout the summer.
- In Central, Southern, Eastern and Southeast Asia the volume of freshwater available in the large river basins is predicted to fall.
- The water supply problems in southern and eastern Australia, as well as in New Zealand, are likely to deteriorate up to 2030 due to evaporation and less rainfall.
- In North America, it will mainly be the west of the country that will be affected by the impact of climate change on the hydrological regime. Rising temperatures in the western mountains will make the snow pack shrink, in-

crease flooding in winter and result in lower run-off volumes in summer. This is likely to intensify competition for the overexploited water resources in that region.
- Even countries that do not directly experience water shortages as a result of changing weather conditions will feel the ripple effects of climate change. In Switzerland, low-lying areas can expect to experience more frequent and in some cases more devastating flooding in winter and spring as a result of climate change.[34] At the same time, unusually dry spells in the summer are likely to increase significantly.[35]

Investment opportunities

The many different challenges surrounding the use of water resources present a number of attractive opportunities for investors. Based on the global trends that will shape the water sector in the coming years, we can identify four investment clusters that offer great potential:
- distribution and management;
- advanced water treatment;
- demand-side efficiency; and
- water and food.

A successful investment strategy is based on three key principles: it complies with the basic principles of sustainability, it adheres to a set of general investment principles, and it takes the entire value chain into consideration. In the case of domestic water supply, for example, this includes a whole series of elements: forecasting natural disasters and providing protection against them; exploring, extracting and transporting water reserves; treating and disinfecting drinking water; distributing water to end consumers; measuring the volume of water sold; domestic water use; drainage into the sewer system; treating the wastewater in sewage plants; reusing the greywater for other purposes or channelling it back into natural watercourses.

If we look at the entire value chain, the spectrum of investment opportunities is actually very broad and encompasses companies that at first sight appear to have little direct connection with the theme of water, but are closely linked indirectly to the sector: food production is one example.

The global water market and the financial crisis
The latest estimates put the size of the global water market at over $480 billion in 2010, including $175 billion for municipal and industrial water and wastewater

---
34 OcCC/ProClim (2007), *Klimaänderung und die Schweiz 2050 – Erwartete Auswirkungen auf Umwelt, Gesellschaft und Wirtschaft.*
35 Bundesamt für Umwelt (BAFU – 2007), *Klimaänderung in der Schweiz – Indikatoren zu Ursachen, Auswirkungen, Massnahmen.*

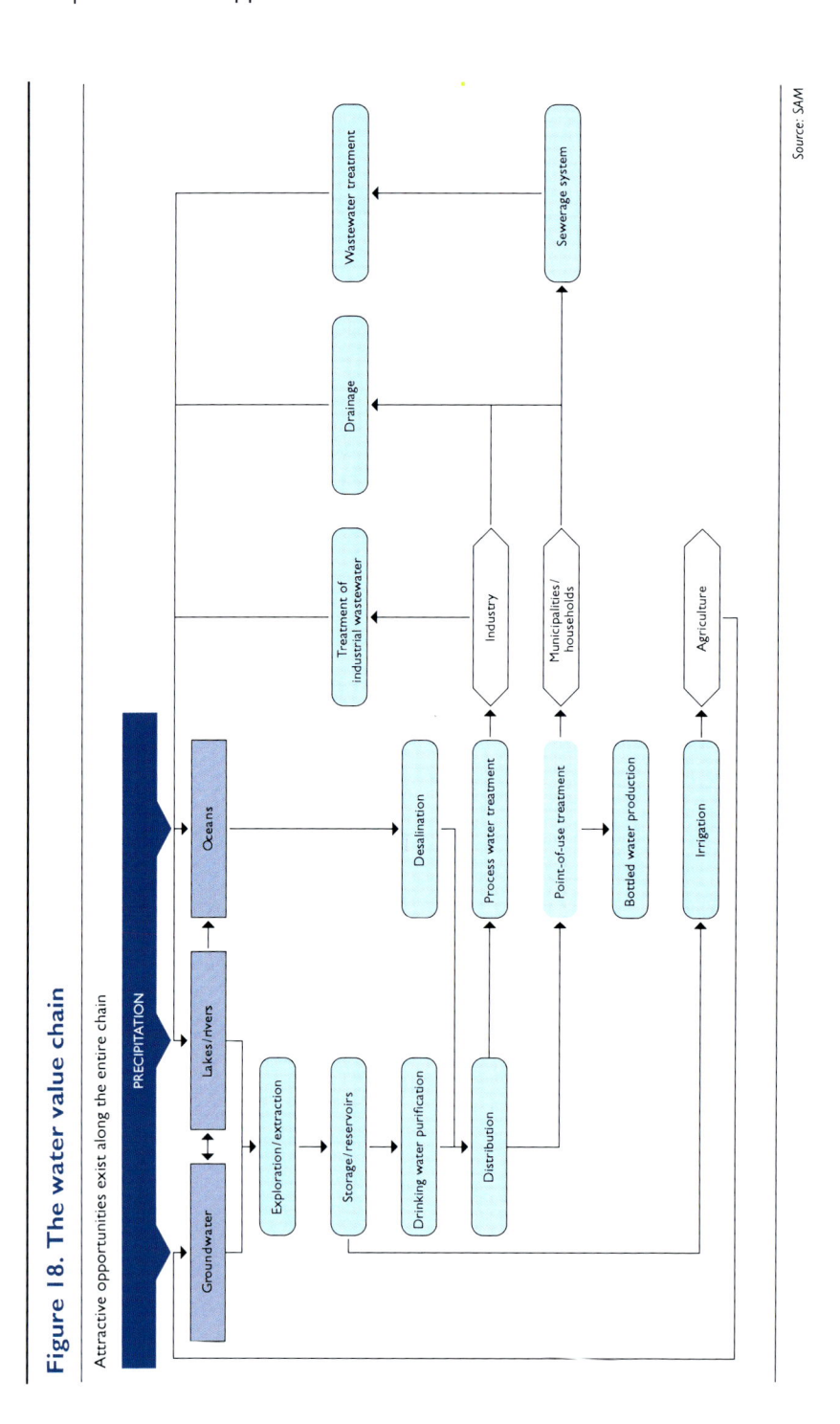

122 | Investment Opportunities for a Low-Carbon World

Figure 18. The water value chain

Attractive opportunities exist along the entire chain

Source: SAM

Figure 19. Global forecast for water, wastewater and desalination expenditure

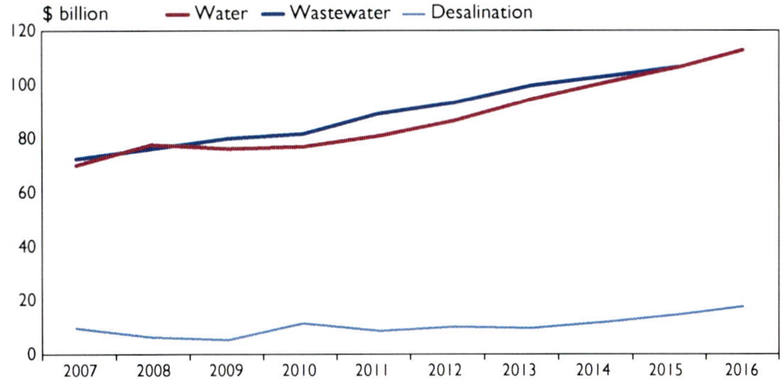

Source: GWI (2010), Global Water Market 2011

capital expenditure.[36] Services, engineering, operation, maintenance and chemicals make up the rest of the market.

Over the past few years, the financial crisis has caused a dramatic economic downturn, with weak residential and commercial construction markets, delays in large infrastructure projects and a decline in industrial production. Against this backdrop, it became more challenging for water companies, utilities and municipalities to find funding for investment projects. Public finance for infrastructure maintenance and upgrades was temporarily impaired due to, for example, the difficulty in issuing municipal bonds. Tightened liquidity and higher costs of borrowing forced companies to postpone necessary asset improvements.

As consumers faced the fear of unemployment it was politically difficult to raise water tariffs in line with the need for infrastructure investments. But it was also recognised that the vicious circle of low tariffs, leading to poor profitability, poor services and ultimately low consumer willingness to pay, should be avoided.

Consequently the global recession has caused a decrease in water capital expenditure growth, but continuation of growth at the pre-crisis rate is expected for the years after 2010. Ongoing water scarcity and increasing pressure on limited global water resources remain the secular drivers of growth in the water sector. Including the impact of the financial crisis, global water capital expenditure is therefore still expected to grow at a CAGR of 6.2% in the period 2010–16.

Furthermore, the financial crisis also triggered a number of positive changes. Some countries have incorporated water infrastructure spending into stimulus packages as a direct response to the economic crisis. In the context of the American

---

36 GWI (2010), *Global Water Market 2011*.

Recovery and Reinvestment Act of 2009, more than $14 billion was dedicated to water, sewerage and federal water projects. Many of the projects to be funded were already in the pipeline for execution over the next several years and are now being brought forward.

The Chinese government looks set to double the amount it is committing to environmental protection in the 12th Five-Year Plan for 2011–15; $450 billion is estimated to be earmarked for environmental protection and pollution control, including a significant proportion for water and wastewater treatment. This amount represents almost 1.5% of China's projected five-year GDP figure.

In water-scarce California, legislators passed a comprehensive package to overhaul the state's water system. The plan calls for a comprehensive ecosystem restoration in the Sacramento-San Joaquin river delta, the construction of new dams, water storage projects, infrastructure improvements, aggressive water conservation goals and the monitoring of groundwater use, as well as paving the way for a new canal that would move water from the north to the south of the state.

Whereas certain segments of the water market can look forward to growth rates of 5–10% over the next 10 years, major differences will prevail when it comes to regions and sectors.

Regional differences
Regional differences are significant. Based on economic growth and the need to catch up with basic infrastructure, water sector investments in emerging markets are expected to grow faster than in developed markets (Figure 20).

Growth is likely to be sluggish in a number of European markets and sub-Saharan Africa. Other countries will however enjoy above-average growth rates, especially emerging Asia and the Middle East and North Africa (MENA). The US market is expected to grow in the coming years, driven by increased levels of investment to expand and upgrade ageing water infrastructure as well as to meet the growing water demand in water-scarce areas where the population continues to grow, particularly in Southern California. This market continues to be heavily influenced by public budgets and water-related policies.

Economic performance in the Middle East is closely linked to the provision of additional water through desalination, leading to strong growth rates for related technologies and services.

Areas of more acute water stress have seen greater investment. China and Australia are two such examples. In Australia, problems are concentrated in the south. According to the Murray-Darling Basin Authority (MDBA), water flow into the Murray river and its main tributary, the Darling, is now at a 117-year low. The MDBA has warned that there may not be sufficient water flow to meet the "basic human needs" of the 1 million population of Adelaide from as early as 2011, as Adelaide has had to rely on the Murray-Darling basin for 85% of its water supply. Total

Figure 20. Regional forecast for water and wastewater capital expenditure

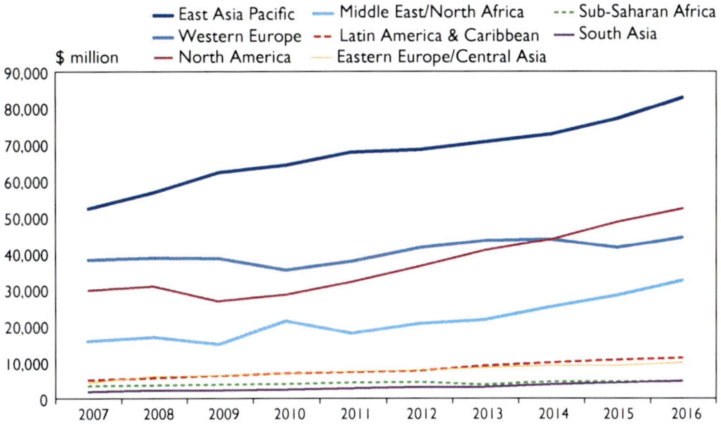

Source: GWI (2010), Global Water Market 2011

annual water and sewage capital expenditures by the Australian water utilities have increased by 220% since 2002.[37] Driven by a government-led programme, total water and sewerage capital expenditure is projected to increase by a further 60% over the next nine years.

Consolidation of the water industry
The water industry is heavily fragmented at the moment. In Switzerland, for example, there are still about 3,000 water utilities and 1,000 organisations operating sewage treatment plants, while in Germany there are 4,833 water utilities and 6,900 wastewater companies. Globally there are an estimated 250,000 plants in service, all of them operating under very different economic and legal conditions.[38] The supplier industry is also heavily fragmented. This is because no individual technology dominates the market and local providers often have to be catered for. Nevertheless, a number of global players have established themselves by building up their water business in the past 10 years, especially through the acquisition of smaller, specialised companies.

Bigger companies are trying to generate additional growth by developing a global distribution network. This will inevitably speed up the consolidation of the market. This trend will be fuelled by the fact that local authorities are increasingly opting for integrated solutions along the lines of public-private partnership (PPP) models. Looking at the different options available for establishing water purification and wastewater treatment plants, the picture that emerges is quite varied: market

---
37 Water Services Association of Australia (2009), *WSAA Report Card 2008–2009*.
38 GWI (2007), *Global Water Market 2008*.

growth rates are lowest for those projects where the local authorities commission specialist firms to handle only the planning aspects. By contrast, the build-operate-transfer (BOT) segment of the market is enjoying more than double the rate of annual growth, at 13.6%.[39] With the BOT model, local authorities commission all-inclusive solutions – ie, a single contractor handles the financing, planning, construction and operation of the plant. Companies able to offer the entire range of services therefore enjoy a competitive advantage.

New openings for private providers
In most countries, public authorities or state-owned organisations are responsible for the drinking water supply and wastewater treatment. Only in a few countries have these sensitive areas been privatised or organised as PPPs. In recent years, however, the number of people whose drinking water and wastewater services are provided by private companies has increased significantly. In Europe, 44% of the population is served by the private sector, about 21% in North America and 12% in Southeast Asia.[40]

Globally active private operators currently account for roughly 19% of all investments in facilities for drinking water supply and wastewater treatment. The remaining 81% is invested by public authorities or state-owned organisations. The same percentage applies when it comes to running costs.

The proportion of private companies is expected to rise to almost 30% by 2016.[41]

In many countries, however, there is an underlying scepticism towards private water utilities for a wide variety of reasons. Both positive and negative examples can be produced to support or challenge their case. International organisations, such as the World Bank's Public-Private Infrastructure Advisory Facility (PPIAF), offer comprehensive support in the preparation and definition of agreements with private operators, in order to avoid subsequent conflicts.

Opportunities do exist for companies to establish themselves as private operators, particularly in the Middle East and East Asia. The strongest growth in private investment is therefore expected in these regions.

Water tariffs increasing
Whereas most utilities encounter problems in raising cost-covering water tariffs, the price of water has increased significantly in many places around the globe in recent years. In the US and UK, water tariffs have outstripped headline inflation by 18% and 27% respectively over the past five years.[42]

There is considerable disparity in water prices between countries (Figure 21).

---

39 GWI (2007), *Global Water Market 2008*.
40 Credit Suisse Research (2009), *Water, the pressure is rising*.
41 GWI (2007), *Global Water Market 2008*.
42 Credit Suisse Research (2009), *Water, the pressure is rising*.

Figure 21. Global water and wastewater tariffs (combined)

City	$/m³
Barcelona (Spain)	2.30
Beijing (China)	0.54
Copenhagen (Denmark)	9.07
Dublin (Ireland)	0
Ho Chi Minh City (Vietnam)	0.36
Hong Kong (China)	0.54
Jeddah (Saudi Arabia)	0.05
Kiev (Ukraine)	0.58
Kuala Lumpur (Malaysia)	0.25
London (UK)	3.46
Luxembourg (Luxembourg)	5.50
New Delhi (India)	0.08
New York City (US)	2.11
Paris (France)	4.08
Riyadh (Saudi Arabia)	0.03
Singapore (Singapore)	3.56
Sydney (Australia)	4.26
Tripoli (Libya)	0
Zurich (Switzerland)	5.52

Source: GWI (2010), Global Water Market 2011

The price of a cubic metre of water in France, which is relatively water-rich, is about 50% higher than the price of a cubic metre of water in Spain, which is considered to be water-poor. Also, countries such as the UK, Denmark and Germany set tariffs not only covering operating costs, but also covering the capital financing costs to a large degree. On the other hand, in countries such as Libya, Ireland and Turkmenistan, which barely charge for water services at all, the taxpayers bear the entire financing burden. In China and India, water is very cheap as a percentage of disposable income, but this fosters over-extraction of water resources, a situation that will prove to be unsustainable in the long term.

In the case of China, in 2009 the integrated water price of 36 large and medium-sized cities went up 5.5% year on year to CNY2.88/m³. Larger increases can be expected in the years ahead, given that many hike requests have been lodged with the local pricing agency but have yet to be implemented.[43] The latest tariff announcement highlights the government's strong commitment to raise tariffs, and is an important factor for the future development of the Chinese water market.

The need to upgrade or build installations is intensifying and at the same time the pressure for higher water standards has also intensified. Significant capital requirements, in conjunction with fiscal constraints limiting central government expenditure, imply higher prices. Higher tariffs may also reduce water consumption and inefficiencies in the use of water. The Australian Water Association predicts that prices will double in Australia over the next five years to meet the rising costs of production and to fund investment. This follows a 38% increase in average water prices over the past two years. A number of other utilities, like Phnom Pehn Water

---

[43] Nomura Research (2010), *Water & Environment Asia*.

Supply Authority, Manila Water and Senegalaise des Eaux have also raised their tariffs in recent years.[44]

Where poverty and affordability is an issue, water tariffs can take the form of a tiered pricing system. This enables water provision at very low prices to cover 'basic household needs', typically 30–50 litres per person per day, but acts as a deterrent to overuse. Tiered pricing schemes have been successfully implemented in Israel, Australia, Hong Kong, Japan, Korea and parts of the US.

DISTRIBUTION AND MANAGEMENT

Exploration
To meet soaring demand for drinking water, the ability to locate and exploit new water reserves is becoming far more important. In some cases this means tapping into aquifers under very challenging geological conditions. A number of modern drilling technologies capable of reaching very low depths are used for this task.

The highest quality standards must be adhered to, particularly when tapping into new sources of water. To ensure that a new source is capable of delivering water of sufficiently high quality over the long term, boreholes are now equipped with devices capable of providing operators with information about the hydrological situation beneath the ground. Specialist companies are now able to use state-of-the-art monitoring techniques to inspect existing water sources and related infrastructure, and carry out the required maintenance work where necessary.

Expansion of distribution networks per year
Worldwide, current annual capital expenditure by utilities on water infrastructure is estimated at $90 billion and spending on wastewater infrastructure is estimated at $82 billion. Capital spending per annum on water and wastewater infrastructure by 2016 is projected to grow at a CAGR of 6.5% and 5.6%, respectively.[45] In the case of both drinking water and wastewater, more than half of the investments will be directed to new water and wastewater networks and network rehabilitations. Current capital investment of about $85 billion is directed to new water and wastewater networks, and network rehabilitations. This amount is expected to reach more than $120 billion over the next six years. In addition, current operating expenditures amount to $135 billion and $87 billion for water and wastewater, respectively. Providers of services and equipment such as pipes, pumps, valves, building materials as well as engineering and construction firms specialising in the water business all stand to benefit from this trend.

The bulk of this growth is attributable to the burgeoning global population. Since the population is growing fastest in developing countries, economical as well as effi-

---
44 GWI (2010), *Global Water Market 2011.*
45 GWI (2010), *Global Water Market 2011.*

Figure 22. Growth of private investments

Expected annual investments made by private water and wastewater suppliers in different market regions.

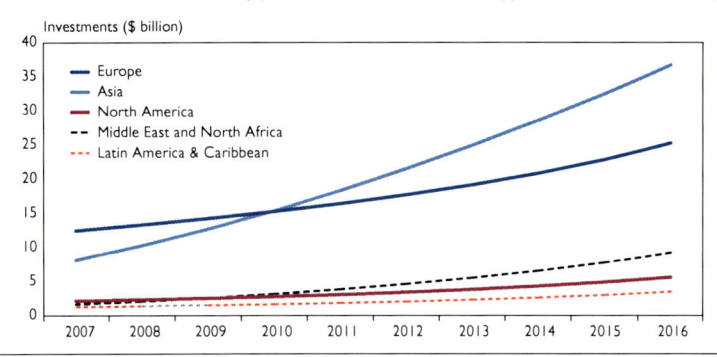

Source: GWI (2007), Global Water Market 2008

cient technologies are needed to cater for these countries' requirements. Decentralised water supply and wastewater treatment systems also play an important role here, since the provision of new infrastructure cannot keep pace with rapid urbanisation.

Nowadays a number of different techniques are used for pipework construction and maintenance: These include laying pipes by excavation or using trenchless technology, cement mortar linings, slip-linings and long pipe relining. Particularly in built-up areas, where most of the systems in need of renovation are located, alternative pipelaying technologies are in greater demand in order to minimise the disruption on the surface. New approaches are also being developed for maintaining pipework. In particular, these include monitoring and early detection of damage using remote-controlled cameras.

Figure 23. Distribution and management

Overview of selected segments of the global market

	Market volume 2010 ($bn)	Expected annual growth (2010–16 CAGR)
Pumps	20.7	6%
Valves	5.9	5%
Pipes	36.2	6%
Pipes rehabilitation services	28.6	5%
Engineering, planning and construction	49.7	6%
Water operating expenditures	134.9	2%
Wastewater operating expenditures	87.3	3%

Source: GWI (2010), Global Water Market 2011

Management

In a number of regions there has recently been a move towards an integrated approach to the management of limited water resources. The European Union has adopted common guidelines for this, in the form of the EU Water Framework Directive. Intelligent approaches that promote sustainable management of water resources are required. Individual companies have specialized in the management of entire river basin areas and ecosystems. To this end, they use sophisticated remote control and geoinformation systems, besides more traditional assessment methods. Management services of this type will become increasingly important, as climate change will have a dramatic impact on the water supply in many regions. Because of this, it is likely that the distribution of water in various river basins will need to be reviewed, as part of a proactive risk management policy.

ADVANCED WATER TREATMENT

Wastewater treatment

Demand for wastewater treatment is set to rise sharply in the coming years. This is particularly true for Asia: in India and China, untreated industrial and communal effluents are posing a serious threat to the population's health. In these two countries especially, enormous investments are required to bring wastewater treatment up to a standard that is commensurate with these countries' economic standing.

Currently, global utilities invest more than $165 billion in wastewater capital expenditure and operating expenditure each year and this figure is expected to reach $220 billion by 2016. The challenge is not simply to channel the water back into the waterways once it has been treated, but to process it so that it can be reused for other applications – for example, landscape irrigation such as watering golf courses, groundwater recharge or even reuse for potable water supply and other recreational uses. There has been an increasing trend for water reuse projects such as the Singapore NEWater, Australia's Western Corridor and the Orange County New Blue Water programme in California to deliver high-quality treated water that can be used to augment potable water supply, through blending in reservoirs, storing in aquifers or selling directly to industrial users.

Worldwide, the total volume of wastewater produced per day is estimated to be about 684 million m^3 and the total capacity of tertiary and advanced reused water produced per day is about 28 million m^3. Capital expenditure for water reuse is projected to rise from $4.9 billion in 2010 to $8.4 billion in 2016.[46]

Lately, the industrial wastewater treatment market has received much attention as environmental regulations on effluent discharge are getting stricter and tougher. The potential for water reuse and industrial wastewater treatment in the industrial

---
46 GWI (2010), *Global Water Market 2011*.

Figure 24. Advanced water treatment

Overview of selected segments of the global market

	Market volume 2010 ($bn)	Expected annual growth (2010–16 CAGR)
Primary intakes/screens	2.9	7%
Standard process equipment: aeration/flocculation/clarifiers/sedimentation/mixers	10.9	5%
Ultrafiltration/microfiltration membranes	0.7	18%
Reverse osmosis/nanofiltration	0.6	18%
Membrane bioreactor	0.1	17%
Ion exchange/electrodionisation	0.3	15%
Disinfection	3.0	6%
Zero liquid discharge	0.4	26%
Sludge management	7.1	9%
Media filtration	3.7	6%
Monitoring control/analytics/chemical feed	2.3	7%
Other specialist systems	2.6	2%
Industrial water treatment services	2.9	5%
Desalination plants	11.0	9%

Source: GWI (2010), Global Water Market 2011

markets is becoming an attractive source of growth for water technology companies. For example, the oil and gas sector requires increasing amounts of water and wastewater treatment technology. The total expenditure for the oil and gas industry on water and wastewater treatment equipment, including chemicals, is projected to grow at a CAGR of about 17% over the next six years, the fastest growth rate among all other industries. Current investment in water and wastewater equipment for industrial markets is estimated at $14 billion in 2010 and is projected to reach $23 billion in 2016, representing a CAGR of 7.5%.[47]

Among the industrial wastewater treatment technologies, the reverse osmosis market is expected to be one of the fast-growing areas. The industrial reverse osmosis membrane market is expected to grow from $238.5 million in 2010 to $647.9 million in 2016, representing a CAGR of 18%.[48] The ultra-filtration/microfiltration market will also experience a high growth rate of CAGR of 17%, while standard process equipment such as aerators, and sedimentation systems is likely to achieve only a CAGR of 1.6%. As the regulatory barriers to discharging effluents for many industries have been raised, the market for zero liquid discharge systems, including brine concentrators, crystallisers and evaporators, is expected to enjoy an above-average growth rate in the coming years.

---
47 GWI (2010), *Global Water Market 2011*.
48 GWI (2010), *Global Water Market 2011*.

Figure 25. Industrial end user: water and wastewater equipment and chemical market

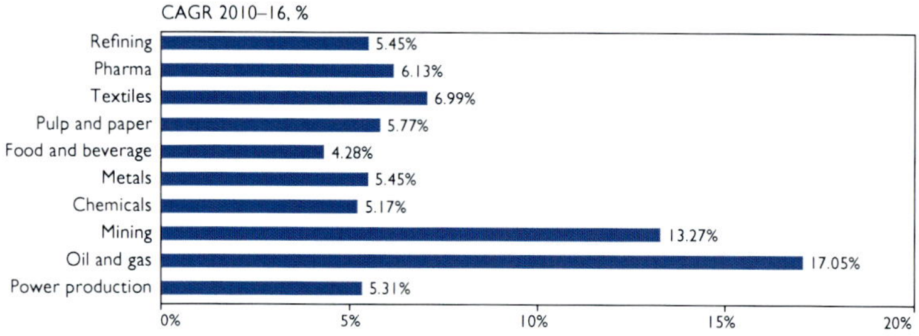

CAGR 2010–16, %

Sector	CAGR
Refining	5.45%
Pharma	6.13%
Textiles	6.99%
Pulp and paper	5.77%
Food and beverage	4.28%
Metals	5.45%
Chemicals	5.17%
Mining	13.27%
Oil and gas	17.05%
Power production	5.31%

Source: GWI (2010), Global Water Market 2011

At the same time, new challenges are constantly arising. For example, the contamination of wastewater with endocrine-active substances presents a serious problem that urgently needs to be solved, as conventional sewage treatment plants are generally not up to the task. The entire chain – from the polluter through to release into the waterways – needs to be rethought. If attempts to remove the problematic substances at source are unsuccessful, more sophisticated wastewater treatment techniques, such as ozonation or advanced oxidation might be necessary.[49]

Drinking water disinfection
Providing clean drinking water is one of the main missions of the water industry. The task here is to provide water not simply in sufficient quantity, but also of sufficient purity. There are a number of ways to treat water to make it fit to drink, including disinfection with ozone, chlorine or chlorine dioxide, ultraviolet radiation or purification using membrane filters. Ozone and UV treatment both have significant growth potential. The market for membrane technology is particularly attractive, with sales in the drinking water segment expected to expand by a factor of three within six years.

Desalination
Over the past five years, total global desalination capacity has grown by 55%. In 2010 the installed capacity should reach 66 million m^3 per day and is forecast to reach 120 million m^3 per day by 2016. This implies a CAGR of 10.5%. The capital expenditure on desalination plants will rise from $11 billion in 2010 to $18 billion in 2016.

Interestingly, in 2009, approximately $4 billion was invested in membrane systems desalination plants compared to $1 billion in thermal desalination plants. These figures are expected to reach $13 billion and $5 billion respectively by 2016.

Growth in desalination using membrane technology is expected to outpace thermal desalination. The MENA region is expected to invest $30 billion in desali-

---
[49] Buffle M-O, *et al* (2007), The Use of UV and Hydrogen Peroxide in Wastewater Reuse to Accomplish Multiple Treatment Objectives. IWA Wastewater Reclamation and Reuse Conference, Antwerp, Belgium.

Figure 26. Desalination versus reuse additional capacity

Source: GWI (2010), Global Water Market 2011

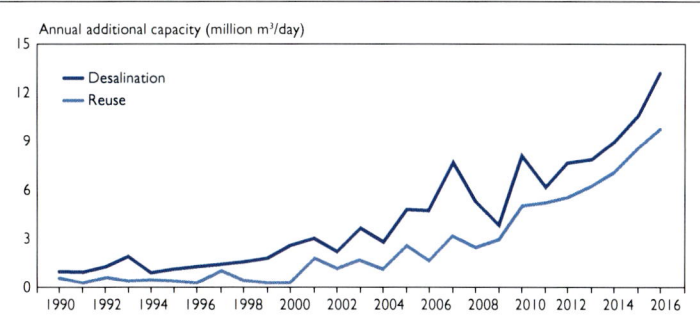

Figure 27. Membrane system versus thermal desalination

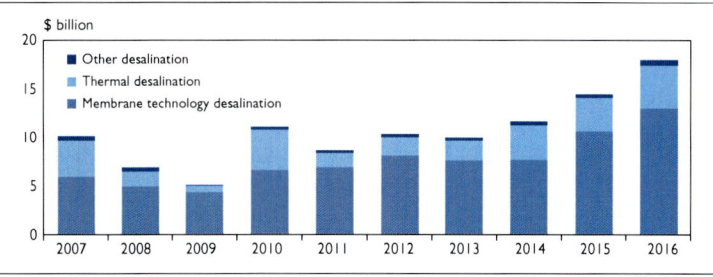

Source: GWI (2010), Global Water Market 2011

nation projects by 2015, having more than 60% of the world's desalination plants.[50]

The cost of desalination has come down significantly. Forty years ago it cost as much as $10 to produce a cubic metre of water. Newer desalination plants have brought costs down to well below $1/m^3$. For example, the Ashkelon plant in Israel reportedly desalinises seawater for $0.53/m^3$ and Singapore is desalinising for $0.49/m^3$.

DEMAND-SIDE EFFICIENCY

In many regions of the world, water has now become a precious good. The most efficient way to prevent overexploitation of available water resources is to invest in technologies that promote more efficient water usage. The aim here is to achieve the same level of service with less water, without compromising on convenience and performance.

Industry
Industrial water consumption has stabilised in industrialised nations over the past 20 years. Per capita usage of industrial water fell from 927 litres in 1950 to 450 litres

---
50 DBS Vickers Securities Research.

Figure 28. Demand-side efficiency

Overview of selected segments of the global market

	Market volume 2010 ($bn)	Expected annual growth (2010–16 CAGR)
Water meters	2.1	7%
Domestic installations	14.9	15%
Chemicals/additives	19.5	4%

Source: GWI (2010), Global Water Market 2011

in 2000. This proves that efficient water use can be achieved together with solid economic growth. Despite massive efforts, industry is still the biggest consumer of water in Europe and North America. As water reserves continue to dwindle, additional initiatives will be necessary to reduce industrial water consumption further.

The situation is particularly critical in Asia: Industrial water consumption continues to rise in this region. In addition, in countries such as China many companies have discharged their industrial effluents into rivers without prior treatment. This has led to a massive deterioration in water quality in many cities.

Industrial water efficiencies can be achieved by water recycling as well as by cutting down water input into industrial processes through the use of chemicals/additives as well as metering to monitor and regulate the flow of water.

Today the market for industrial water treatment is worth roughly $27 billion and is forecast to grow to about $45 billion by 2016. This market also includes the manufacture of technical equipment, the provision of chemicals and additives for water treatment, and the development of integrated solutions.

Domestic consumption
Compared with the industrial sector, where water consumption has stabilised in Europe and North America at least, domestic water consumption continues to rise in most countries. Household water consumption varies enormously from one country to the next. This implies that large quantities of water could possibly be saved if appropriate technologies were installed.

Switzerland is a good example to illustrate how much potential there is: in the past 25 years, per capita consumption has steadily declined. Today each Swiss resident consumes 160 litres of water a day on average to cover their personal requirements – roughly 20 litres less than 20 years ago. Almost 70% of the water consumed goes on flushing toilets, taking baths and showers and washing clothes – a similar pattern to the rest of Europe (Figure 29).

Household water-efficient devices like low-flush toilets, point-of-use devices that reduce tap flows and efficient plumbing systems offer significant water-saving potential.

Figure 29. Breakdown of water use in Swiss households

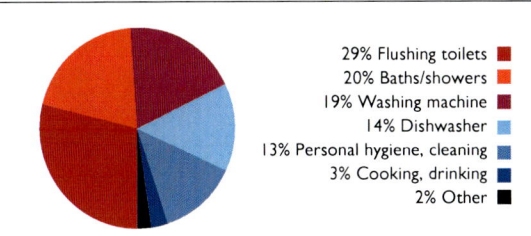

29% Flushing toilets
20% Baths/showers
19% Washing machine
14% Dishwasher
13% Personal hygiene, cleaning
3% Cooking, drinking
2% Other

Source: European Environment Agency, www.eea.europa.eu/themes/climate/ (accessed 5 October 2007)

Water efficiency can also be achieved through limiting water losses in the distribution network or through reducing non-revenue water (NRW). NRW includes water not billed due to leakage, illegal use and inadequate measurement. NRW water stands in the range of 4% to 65% in Asian cities.[51] For improvements to be made, consumers need to be billed on the basis of water use, which is good news for companies that manufacture water meters. Modern water meters now have components to record and/or transmit electronic data on water use automatically.

WATER AND FOOD

Irrigation
Agriculture is by far the biggest consumer of water worldwide, accounting for about 70% of water use. Approximately 28% of cropland is now under irrigation, with half of this located in Asia. Many countries are starting to experience severe water shortages. There will be mounting pressure in these regions for fields to be irrigated more efficiently.

Nowadays most fields are irrigated using a system of ditches or sprinkler equipment. Although both of these methods are relatively economical, they are also highly inefficient, because most of the water is wasted. Modern micro-irrigation systems could cut water consumption by as much as 30–70%. The positive side effects of this technology include the prevention of soil salination and a decrease in the use of pesticides.

Figure 30. Irrigated agricultural area

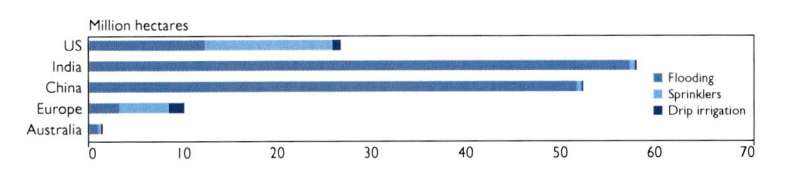

Million hectares — US, India, China, Europe, Australia

Flooding
Sprinklers
Drip irrigation

Source: FAO; ICID; SAM

---

51 ADB (2008), *Asian Water Supplies, Reaching the Urban Poor.*

Figure 31. Irrigation efficiency

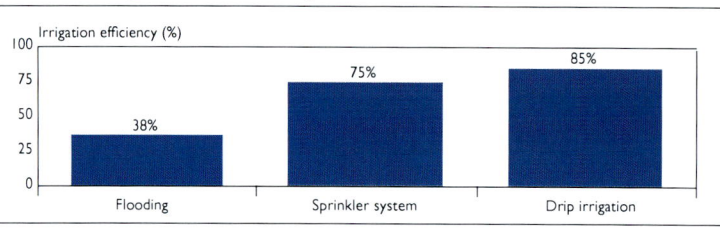

Irrigation method	Efficiency (%)
Flooding	38%
Sprinkler system	75%
Drip irrigation	85%

Source: Citigroup (2009), Water Worries

While these new irrigation technologies are economically viable, the speed at which they actually establish themselves ultimately depends to a large extent on the available financing. It is usually the farmers themselves who have to make the investments in irrigation systems, and the amount available for investment depends largely on the farmer's income. One of the decisive factors is still the price that farmers have to pay for the water and the extent to which the authorities are prepared to clamp down on illegal water extraction. One interesting point worth noting in this context is that the current amount invested globally in irrigation systems amounts to about $10 billion, which is a surprisingly low figure given the importance of the agricultural sector for water consumption.

Sustainable agriculture
The global organic products market has seen sustained growth over the past decade, reaching an estimated size of $51 billion in 2008.[52]

In the US, sales of organic food grew from $3.5 billion in 1997 to an estimated $23 billion in 2008.[53] The most important markets for the import of organic products continue to be the EU, the US and Japan.

In Asia, demand for organic food has been growing at 15–20% every year over the last decade – a remarkable growth rate in a region where agriculture competes intensively for land and other resources with the industrial and construction sectors. However, the market share of organic food products in Asia-Pacific remains small compared to leading organic food markets like the US.

Organic or sustainably produced foods are not only becoming increasingly popular with consumers, but also have a very positive impact on water resources. The use of more environmentally friendly fertilisers and crop protection agents also protects the groundwater and reduces topsoil run-off. Slow-release fertilisers act selectively and increase yields. This is key for sustainable agriculture practices, particularly in developing nations with burgeoning populations. Fortunately, specialist firms now exist, which stand to benefit from strong growth in this area.

India – also a country facing a major water crisis – has the world's largest rice

---
[52] FiBL and IFOAM (2010), *The World of Organic Agriculture – Statistics and Emerging Trends.*
[53] The Organic Trade Association's 2009 Organic Industry Survey.

Figure 32. Water and food

Overview of selected segments of the global market

	Market volume 2010 ($bn)	Expected annual growth (2010–16 CAGR)
Bottled water	59	8%
Organic food	51*	10–12%
Irrigation	10	10–12%

Market volume 2008

Source: GWI (2010), Global Water Market 2011

cultivated area. With organic farming techniques, the system of rice intensification has helped increase yields by over 30% while using 40% less water than conventional methods. This will not only massively reduce the use of water but also help ensure food security. Moreover, unlike more conventional farming techniques, such organic farming techniques do not emit methane (a powerful greenhouse gas).

Case studies

CHINA – THE DOWNSIDE OF MINING

Various trends combine to make China's water situation one of its greatest challenges as the country moves further into the 21st century. Urbanisation, industrialisation, historically weak environmental regulations, a per capita water consumption approaching that of the West and a population increasingly aware of the health impact of pollution are trends that have set the scene for what will be one of the largest governmental and private capital outlays in history, reaching $1.2 trillion over the next 20 years.

The village of Shangba[54] in Guangdong Province, while an extreme example, illustrates the challenge faced by regions undergoing rapid industrialisation. The Dabaoshan mine, a major zinc mine that also produces up to 6,000 tons of copper and 850,000 tons of iron ore annually, has over the years been the source of contamination of more than 500 hectares of agricultural land irrigated by the Hengshui river. Surface water and groundwater have been highly contaminated by heavy metals such as lead and cadmium. The water to irrigate crops exhibited concentrations of heavy metals well above international standards. This significant intake of heavy metals resulted in a very high incidence of cancer among the 3,000 residents of Shangba.

While the situation may seem hopeless at first sight, a positive development has taken place. With the help of a major water technology provider and the determination of local government officials, a drinking water treatment plant applying coagula-

---

54 Chen, A, C Lin, W Lu, Y Wu, Y Ma, J Li and L Zhu (2007), Chemosphere, well water contaminated by acidic mine water from the Dabaoshan Mine, South China. *Chemistry and toxicity*.

tion and multi-media filter treatment processes was installed in October 2008. The system now reduces contaminant concentrations to international standards.

In recent years, China has significantly ramped up its efforts to increase wastewater treatment coverage. It had become clear that poor surface water quality (due to untreated municipal and industrial wastewater discharges) had had a negative impact on economic growth (annual GDP loss of 1.5–2.8%). This incentivised the central government to focus on increasing China's wastewater coverage, which translated into a $60 billion investment in wastewater infrastructure. The impact on the water sector has been significant, with many private companies taking advantage of this new market opportunity. Western visitors at Shanghai's Aquatech (an international water industry trade show) in June 2009 were impressed by the number of local water companies participating (more than 300) and the variety of products displayed. In particular the large number of home treatment systems (point-of-use) was evidence that the Chinese population is becoming increasingly aware of water quality issues; this represents a key driver for future growth in the Chinese water sector.

INDIA'S WATER AVAILABILITY COST CURVE

By 2030, India will face a large gap between current water supply and projected demand, amounting to 50% of demand or 754 billion m^3 of water. The agriculture sector is the biggest user of water, followed by the domestic sector and the industrial sector. The imbalance is driven by a burgeoning population and rapid economic growth, putting significant pressures on water resources. The over-extraction of groundwater in about two-thirds of the country has also caused depleting water tables and seawater intrusion in coastal regions. Furthermore, the demand and supply condition is made worse by the lack of water infrastructure in the country.

India's water demand

Water demand in India will grow to about 1.5 trillion m^3 in 20 years' time. Currently, agriculture is responsible for 80% of India's water demand and this will still be the dominant sector in 2030.

As more than 95% of India's agricultural production is and will continue to be for domestic consumption, the rapid population growth, coupled with rising income supporting the increasing caloric intake and meat consumption, are both key drivers underlying the water resource challenge. Agricultural demand for the precious liquid is estimated to double during this period. Projected municipal and domestic water demand will also double in 2030, to 108 billion m^3, accounting for approximately 7% of total water demand. Demand from industry will also double to 196 billion m^3, accounting for 13% of water demand. This demand, weighed against today's accessible water supply, would create severe projected deficits for most of India's river basins.[55]

---

55 2030 Water Resources Group (2009). *Charting our Water Future*.

Water Technologies | 139

Figure 33. India: gap between existing supply and projected demand in 2030

The unconstrained projection of water requirements under a static policy regime and at existing levels of productivity and efficiency

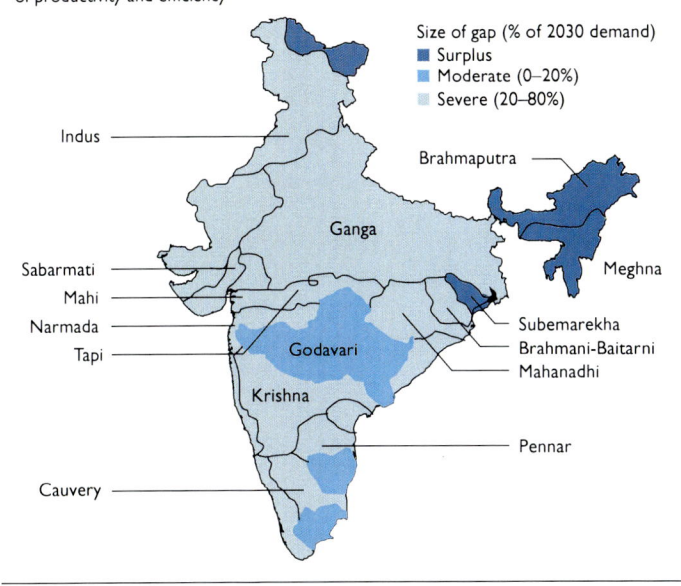

Size of gap (% of 2030 demand)
- Surplus
- Moderate (0–20%)
- Severe (20–80%)

Indus
Brahmaputra
Ganga
Sabarmati
Mahi
Narmada
Tapi
Godavari
Krishna
Meghna
Subemarekha
Brahmani-Baitarni
Mahanadhi
Pennar
Cauvery

Source: 2030 Water Resources Group (2009): Charting our Water Future

India's water supply

India's water supply is expected to reach approximately 740 billion m³ in 2030, significantly short of aggregate demand of approximately 1.5 trillion m³. India is a vast country with many river basins, including two of the world's largest rivers, the Ganges and the Brahmaputra.

Average annual precipitation received by the country is about 4,000km³ and, of this, exploitable water resources amount to about 1,900km³. According to the FAO Aquastat 2010, the current surface and groundwater water resource base is estimated to be about 1,880 billion m³ per year, of which 418.5km³ is groundwater and about 1,842km³ is surface water. This number is highly variable because of the monsoon season, which brings roughly 80% of the annual precipitation. With increasing climate variability, Indian monsoons are becoming less predictable and the frequency of extreme events like droughts and floods has increased over the past decades.

Due to poor government policies and insufficient infrastructure, surface water is unable to meet India's total water requirement. Groundwater is virtually free (pumping costs only, with electricity being highly subsidised by the government). This inefficiency results in overextraction of the groundwater. Groundwater supply differs substantially by region. In the western rivers, the truly renewable groundwater supply is much less than what is actually pumped, leading to massive overdraft, declining water tables and elevated pumping costs, while in basins such as the Eastern Ganges additional groundwater supply could be increased sustainably. The availability of groundwater is compounded by rapidly deteriorating water quality in many areas of the country by agriculture and industrial pollution.

India has only 200m^3 of water storage capacity per person, compared to 2,200m^3 per person in China and 6,000m^3 per person in the US. The ability of the current infrastructure to buffer that variability is low, making it difficult for accessible water supply to meet projected demand.

As the distribution of water supply is uneven across the subcontinent, a basin such as the Ganga accounts for a large portion of accessible water supply, about 311 million m^3. Yet – at the same time – the Ganga basin also has the highest water demand resulting in the largest gap of 350 million m^3, followed by the Indus basin and Krishna basin with gaps of 106 million m^3 and 90 million m^3, respectively.

Closing the gap
A 2009 study published by the 2030 Water Resources Group lists 37 levers to close the water availability gap by 2030, ranked according to the related cost. Using the cheapest solutions will result in an annual investment of $5.9 billion, much less than the

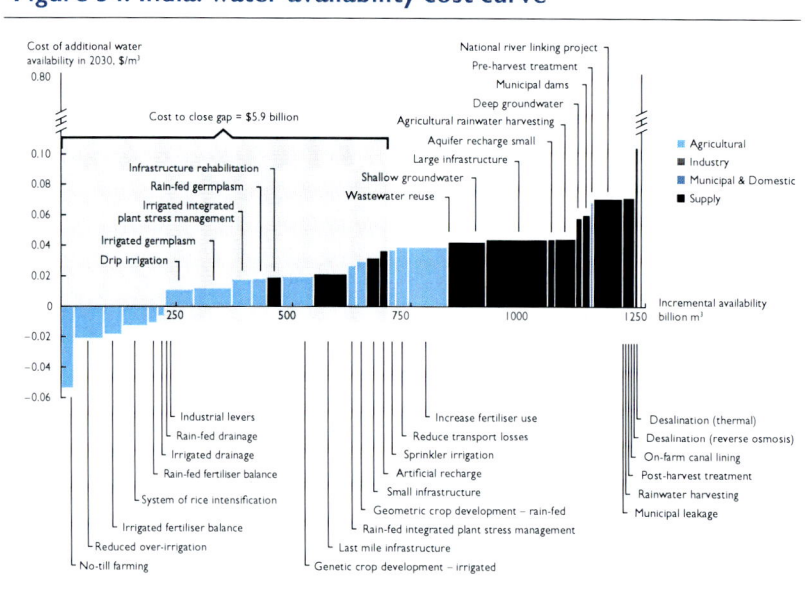

Figure 34. India: water availability cost curve

Source: 2030 Water Resources Group (2009): Charting our Water Future

estimated total annual expenditure of $12.3 billion in 2007 for the total water sector.

About 80% of the cheapest solutions to close the base case demand-supply gap lie in improving agriculture's water efficiency and productivity. The remaining 20% of solutions to close the gap lie in additional supply solutions such as desalination plants, rehabilitation of existing infrastructure and last-mile canals.

To meet the implied demand for food and feed in the country (only 4% of India's agricultural production is exported), about 31 million hectares of additional irrigated land would be needed. As such, measures that increase the yields of fields, offsetting the need for additional land and additional irrigation are necessary. Agricultural yield can also be improved by making land more productive, including no-till farming, improved drainage, optimised fertiliser use or innovative crop protection technologies. Other major agricultural opportunities are further investment in genetic crop development, improved irrigation control and drip irrigation.

To the right side of the lever bar, we note that desalination projects, the National River-Linking Project and even the repair of municipal leakage are significantly more expensive than the solutions available in agriculture. However, for political reasons they may still rank higher on the governmental agenda.

In conclusion, the cost-effective solutions to address India's water challenge will require support from the national agricultural policy as well as technological innovation.

Conclusion: new investment opportunities in the water sector

The importance of water as a life-sustaining resource will steadily increase over the next few years. As the global population continues to boom, pressure will mount on water resources that are already under enormous strain, and in many regions the traditionally careless use of water will have visible negative consequences.

Consumers are therefore becoming increasingly aware that water is a precious resource that needs to be managed in a sustainable way. Technologies that promote more efficient use of water are already available: water-saving domestic appliances, efficient industrial plants or low-cost methods for repairing pipes are just some of the practical ways of reducing water consumption. Enormous efforts are also being made in agriculture to try and improve the frequently wasteful utilisation of water.

These major challenges open up interesting opportunities for investors: Companies that grasp the increasing need for sustainable solutions as an opportunity – and respond by offering innovative solutions – can look forward to a sharp increase in demand in the years ahead.

If we are to ensure sustainable management of water resources and avert a global water crisis, water must be given a price tag that accurately reflects its vital role in our lives. It is therefore the duty of politicians and lawmakers to lay down the relevant rules and to push through measures that promote more sustainable use of water. This change of mind-set has already occurred in those countries confronted with urgent water problems, whether in terms of quality or quantity, encouraging them to adopt the necessary laws, ordinances or budget allocations. But action is still needed at the political level, combined with a greater awareness by the general public of the importance of using water resources efficiently.

To make successful investments in the water sector, investors therefore not only need to be informed about the latest technical advances and industry solutions, but must also closely follow developments and decisions on the political and legislative front. The introduction of new environmental standards, tougher demands on water quality, more public spending on infrastructure construction and maintenance as well as the fixing of tariffs and fees will have a significant impact on the growth of individual segments of the water market and, consequently, on the attractiveness of companies doing business in these segments.

In the years to come, water will develop into a dynamic market of the future. Given the global trends that are shaping the water market, demand is unlikely to drop off in the long term. While due account needs to be taken of company valuations, investors with a long-term horizon can therefore expect to find numerous worthwhile and attractive investment opportunities.

Chapter 8

Investment opportunities in renewable energy and environmental infrastructure

Dr Erich Becker, Zouk Capital LLP

Introduction

Renewable energy and environmental infrastructure (REEI) assets are attracting an increasing amount of investment capital due to the sector's strong fundamental and regulatory drivers. Risk/return profiles are to, a large degree, uncorrelated with other asset classes. Institutional investors are adding infrastructure and REEI investments to their portfolios either by investing in specialist funds or directly in projects.

Impressive REEI capacity growth has been witnessed in markets with strong regulatory support schemes, pushing more expensive, conventional capacity out of the market and allowing equipment manufacturers to improve technologies and benefit from economies of scale. This has driven installation costs down – in some markets to, or close to, grid parity. National cost benefit analyses commissioned by governments substantiate continued support for incentivising REEI investments.

Typical capital structures vary between geared and ungeared investments and different investment strategies target higher or lower returns, depending on which risks investors are capable of managing or when in a project's lifetime, between inception and operations, capital is provided.

The current market environment, especially reduced lending capacity, stretched balance sheets of strategic industry participants and governments' budget concerns, have an impact on the REEI sector while deal flow is strong and investors are presented with numerous high-quality investment opportunities.

The REEI sectors

When approaching the sectors under consideration, literature as well as regulators and practitioners use various definitions for the terms 'renewable energy' and 'environmental infrastructure'. The definitions below are intended to specify the scope of industries to be discussed.

According to the relevant EU Directive's definition[1] "energy from renewable sources" means energy from renewable non-fossil sources, namely wind, solar, aerothermal (energy stored in the form of heat in the ambient air), geothermal (energy stored in the form of heat beneath the surface of solid earth), hydrothermal (energy stored in the form of heat in surface water) and ocean energy, hydropower, biomass (the biodegradable fraction of products, waste and residues of biological origin from agriculture [including vegetal and animal substances], forestry and related industries including fisheries and aquaculture, as well as the biodegradable fraction of industrial and municipal waste), landfill gas, sewage treatment plant gas and biogases.

For the purpose of this chapter, the discussion applies a wider definition of 'renewable energy' and includes all assets that generate energy using resources which are renewable, sustainable or result in a reduced consumption of fossil fuels. This is more aligned with the 'green energy' definition used by the UK government as "energy generated from renewable or small-scale low-carbon local sources and energy efficiency measures"[2].

'Environmental infrastructure' shall be defined as hard assets that protect environmental quality as well as human health, including sustainable resource management, water processing and pollution control and reduction technologies (water treatment, waste management, recycling, biogas).

The REEI sectors are interlinked. Combining renewable energy and environmental infrastructure projects is common. Hence, both areas are targeted by the same investment strategy as long as the projects fulfil strict sustainability criteria with respect to responsible use of available natural resources.

The common features of the target area are the following facts: they are real, hard assets requiring in-depth technical, commercial, operational, financial and legal expertise to develop and operate.

Key drivers

Investment opportunities in the REEI sectors are driven by a number of strong fundamental and regulatory factors.

GLOBAL AND REGIONAL DEMAND GROWTH

Demand for all major natural resources will increase by 30–80% across all major resources over the next 20 years, according to McKinsey[3], driven by the "unprec-

---

1 Directive 2009/28/EC of the European Parliament and of the Council of 23 April 2009 on the promotion of the use of energy from renewable sources and amending and subsequently repealing Directives 2001/77/EC and 2003/30/ EC, Official Journal of the European Union, 5 June 2009.
2 Research Paper 09/41, 5 May 2009, Green Energy (Definition and Promotion) Bill, Bill 15 of 2008–09 by Donna Gore and Christopher Barclay, Science and Environment Section, Keith Parry, Parliament and Constitution Centre, House of Commons Library
3 Richard Dobbs, Jeremy Oppenheim, Fraser Thompson, Marcel Brinkman and Marc Zornes, November 2011, *Resource Revolution: Meeting the world's energy, materials, food, and water needs.* McKinsey Global Institute; McKinsey Sustainability & Resource Productivity Practice.

edented arrival of three billion additional consumers into the middle classes compared with 1.8 billion today". To satisfy this demand growth, new sources of supply have to be found while environmental factors constrain production, especially in the agricultural and energy sectors. Finding new supply sources for any resource is increasingly challenging and expensive – although a few exceptions exist, such as the discovery of and technological progress allowing economic production of shale gas in the United States or renewable energy. According to McKinsey, the average real cost of bringing a new oil well online doubled between 2000 and 2010.

Global energy demand is expected to grow by 33% between 2010 and 2030, the additional demand being equivalent to the current annual consumption of the US and the European members of the OECD combined. McKinsey's energy demand growth forecast for the next 20 years is about 1.6 times that of the 1980–2000 period. This growth is largely driven by the increasing requirements of developing economies. Developed economies such as Europe's are continuing to experience growth in energy demand, particularly as they shift to greater electrification of infrastructure. Base case forecasts see Europe experiencing an electricity demand increase of 15% from 2010–20[4].

CAPACITY REPLACEMENT AND ADDITIONS
Conventional assets, especially power generation capacity, are being retired across the sectors under consideration. Europe's existing conventional electricity generation capacity is decreasing as old coal and nuclear power assets are decommissioned.

Legislation directed at coal-fired capacity is resulting in the decommissioning of older assets. For example, the EU's Large Combustion Plant Directive 2007 imposed restrictions on pollutant emissions, requiring plants either to install emission abatement technology or face closure by the end of 2015[5]. In the UK alone, the government estimates that 27% or 20GW of electricity generation capacity requires decommissioning by 2016[6]; a significant proportion of this is coal-fired.

Nuclear power technology has inherent risks associated with large-scale disasters. As a result of Japan's earthquake and tsunami in March 2011, which led to a dramatic nuclear power crisis, many European countries have reassessed the suitability of nuclear power as a reliable and safe energy source. Germany has taken the strategic decision to decommission its entire nuclear power capacity by 2022, which represents 22% of its current electricity generation base[7]. Other countries are following suit, rethinking their future power generation mix based on rising scepticism about the long-term viability of nuclear power generation.

---

4 Energy Research Centre of the Netherlands, 1 February 2011, *Renewable Energy Projections as Published in the National Renewable Energy Action Plans of the European Member States*.
5 E.ON UK, *Large Combustion Plant Directive*.
6 *The Economist*, 6 August 2009, 'The looming electricity crunch: Dark days ahead'.
7 Floriane Bernardot, 30 May 2011 'The Energy Future of Germany will be Non-Nuclear', *Energy Cities*.

UTILITY BALANCE SHEET CONSTRAINTS

The majority of European utility companies are going through extensive rationalisation and divestiture programmes, selling non-core assets to maintain credit ratings or to refinance debt facilities. Financing solutions for new-build capacity and upgrades of existing capacity have yet to be identified.

ENERGY SECURITY

Energy security is a key driver of energy policies in all industrialised nations. Two key considerations ensure energy infrastructure operates effectively and economically:

- *Primary energy supply must be secured.* The EU currently imports 54% of its primary energy demand[8]; the region's gas deficit is largely balanced by supplies from Russia and North Africa[9]. Germany, the largest economy in the EU, imports 38% of its gas from Russia[10]. Russian restrictions on gas exports to Europe in the winter of 2009–10 had a severe impact on many countries in the EU[11].
- *Energy commodity prices must be stable.* With the exception of energy in the 1970s, the volatility of resource prices today is at an all-time high. Since the turn of the century, the average annual volatility of resource prices has been more than three times that witnessed over the course of the 20th century and more than 50% higher than in the 1980s[12]. In a world of diminishing resources and increasing demand, geopolitical disputes drive volatility in commodity prices; in the six months from 1 October 2010, spot oil prices rose 45%[13].

MITIGATING GLOBAL CLIMATE CHANGE

Industrialisation was to a large extent enabled and driven by the provision of energy using fossil fuels causing emissions of greenhouse gases. An elevated level of greenhouse gases in the world's atmosphere is the cause of rising average temperatures and, as a result, climate change. This is now considered "unequivocal" by scientists[14]. A failure to address climate change and invest in measures to reduce greenhouse gas emissions is predicted to have adverse effects on global social, biological and

---

8 Eurostat, April 2011, *Energy production and imports, Statistics Explained*.
9 EurActiv, 2007, *Geopolitics of EU energy supply*.
10 Energy Delta Institute, April 2011, *Country Gas Profile – Germany*.
11 Oxford Institute for Energy Studies, *The Russo-Ukrainian gas dispute of January 2009: a comprehensive assessment*.
12 Richard Dobbs, Jeremy Oppenheim, Fraser Thompson, Marcel Brinkman and Marc Zornes, November 2011, *Resource Revolution: Meeting the world's energy, materials, food, and water needs*. McKinsey Global Institute; McKinsey Sustainability & Resource Productivity Practice.
13 Deutsche Welle, March 2011, 'Distribution to Libyan oil supply highlights need for EU energy diversification'; International Energy Agency, 21 February 2011, *Facts on Libya: oil and gas*; Financial Times, 1 October 2010–1 April 2011, commodities and agriculture reports.
14 An Assessment of the Intergovernmental Panel on Climate Change, 2007.

Investment in renewable energy and environmental infrastructure | 147

geophysical systems[15]. The cost of mitigating the risks of climate change is estimated by the International Energy Agency (IEA) to be $45 trillion of investment by 2050[16]. Lord Stern's report, commissioned by the UK government, estimated the cost of neglecting to work towards mitigating climate change at up to 20% of global GDP every year[17].

Renewable energy infrastructure, by definition, relies on inputs which have little or no net carbon impact and enables the decarbonisation of power networks. Environmental infrastructure replaces systems which may have been environmentally damaging (eg, industrial pollution processing, water treatment and purification, waste management and recycling) and can work with energy generation technologies to provide an additional decarbonisation benefit (eg, waste-to-energy systems).

LEGAL FRAMEWORKS SUPPORTING INVESTMENT IN REEI

The EU requires 20% of all energy to be produced from renewable sources by 2020[18]. At the national level, governments across Europe have enacted legislation which implements the EU directive and supports investment in REEI via various mechanisms.

Incentive-based legislation supports investment by guaranteeing the payment of additional premiums on outputs such as electricity and heat. Two common examples are feed-in tariffs (FiTs) and tradeable certificates. Since the widespread introduction of such legislation, Europe has experienced significant investment in renewable energy assets.

In the case of compliance-based legislation, infrastructure owners are forced to comply with new legislation or face financial penalties. The continued operation of outdated assets therefore becomes illegal or the cost of remedial works is uneconomical, resulting in a requirement for new infrastructure which complies with regulations. Compliance-based legislation is often used to improve environmental infrastructure such as waste management, pollution and water treatment. For example, the UK Landfill Tax incentivises the industry to invest in new, more economical capacity which diverts waste from landfill[19]. This type of legislation is also used in the energy generation sector; an example is the above-mentioned Large Combustion Plant Directive[20].

To streamline the implementation of legislation and increase its effectiveness, governments are also undertaking reforms of key aspects of their energy infrastructures. In the UK, for example, it is expected that the electricity market reform will

---

15 Intergovernmental Panel on Climate Change, *Assessing key vulnerabilities and the risk from climate change*, IPCC Fourth Assessment Report, page 782.
16 IEA, April 2011, 'Now or Never – IEA Energy Technology Perspectives 2008 shows pathways to sustained economic growth based on clean and affordable energy technology'.
17 World Resources Institute, *Climate Change Economics*.
18 Directive 2009/28/EC of the European Parliament and of the Council of 23 April 2009 on the promotion of the use of energy from renewable sources and amending and subsequently repealing Directives 2001/77/EC and 2003/30/EC, *Official Journal of the European Union*, 5 June 2009.
19 HM Revenue and Customs, June 2011, *UK Landfill Tax*.
20 E.ON UK, *Large Combustion Plant Directive*.

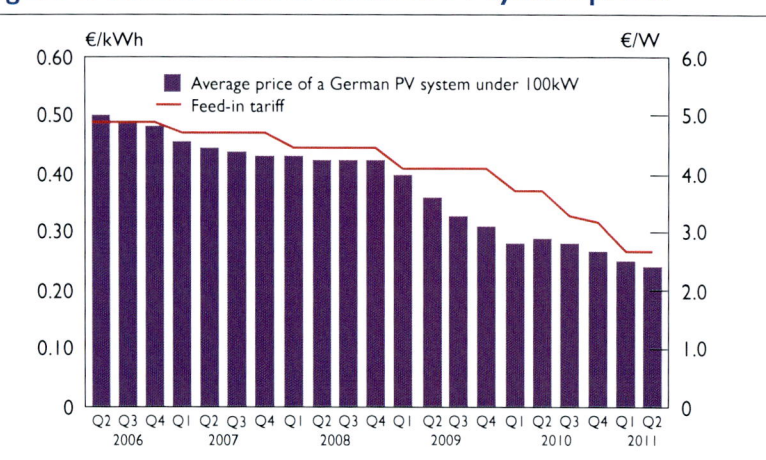

Figure 1. German feed-in tariffs vs PV system prices

■ Average price of a German PV system under 100kW
— Feed-in tariff

Source: Bundesverband Solarwirtschaft, Bloomberg New Energy Finance

deliver a "new market framework that will enable cost effective, secure supplies of low-carbon energy"[21].

IMPROVING ECONOMICS

The legislative frameworks in Europe have directed significant investment to the sector, enabling increased production capacity and reduced equipment costs. The result has been a decrease in the cost of installing many technologies used in REEI[22]. Governments have responded by reducing FiTs in response to declining equipment costs (see Figure 1).

According to McKinsey, breakthroughs in technology could lower the levellised cost of electricity (LCOE – defined as an assessment of the breakeven price of electricity production including all the costs over an asset's lifetime, such as capital expenditure, operations and maintenance, fuel, cost of capital etc) by 2030 to as low as $35/MWh for onshore wind and even $29/MWh for solar, compared with $66/MWh for coal. Average LCOE for solar, wind and other renewables would fall to $56/MWh in 2030, implying total savings of $75 billion a year. According to Bloomberg New Energy Finance (BNEF) figures[23], LCOE from onshore wind can currently be as low as $60/MWh (as seen in Brazilian tenders in August 2011, where wind priced at $62/MWh was under-bidding conventional gas-fired power projects). This makes today's most competitive wind farms comparable to state-of-the-art coal-fired and cheaper than gas-fired power plants, even before taking carbon cost into consideration.

---
21 UK Department of Energy and Climate Change, *Consultation on Electricity Market Reform*.
22 BIS, NDS, 24 May 2011, 'Vision for world's first dedicated Green Investment Bank published'.
23 *Bloomberg New Energy Finance*, September 2011, Volume V Issue 53.

Other technologies, such as landfill gas and municipal solid waste-to-energy plants can produce electricity for around $50/MWh; geothermal starts at about $80/MWh and biomass-based electricity can be generated for less than $100/MWh. Solar power generation costs have fallen by 70% since 2008, to as low as $170/MWh for photovoltaics and around $200/MWh for solar thermal. In many markets, this ensures grid parity without subsidies compared to daytime household electricity prices.

Size of the investment opportunity

Depending on the definition of REEI, the size of the investment requirement is enormous. This coincides with an era of overburdened sovereign budgets, stretched balance sheets of traditional strategic investors in the relevant sectors, fears of the current recession's impact on employment rates and social problems, and increasingly difficult lending markets.

Below are some estimates of the size of different segments of the target sectors:
- As stated above, the EU requires 20% of all energy to be produced from renewable sources by 2020. According to the European Commission, over €1 trillion of investment in Europe's renewable energy infrastructure is required by 2020[24].
- According to BNEF, a record total of $243 billion was invested in renewable energy in 2010 on a global basis. Of this figure, Europe accounted for $94 billion.
- McKinsey estimates the annual capital requirements to scale up renewable energy at between $210 billion and $305 billion over the next 20 years (including costs for hydro, wind, solar, dedicated biomass, geothermal, marine and coal-to-gas shifts as well as costs for additional transmission and distribution infrastructure).

Risk and returns

The risk/return profiles of the REEI asset class are, to a large degree, uncorrelated with other asset classes and considered attractive due to the sectors' strong fundamental drivers and regulatory support. Institutional investors are increasingly adding REEI to their investment allocation to diversify their portfolios, partly driven by high volatility in 'traditional' assets.

KEY RISKS
This section is not intended to provide an exhaustive list of risk factors but an overview of the most material risks common to REEI projects. In addition to addressing each risk factor individually, an investment fund can achieve portfolio diversification by spreading its investments across countries, technologies, and pricing regimes.

---
24 European Commission, 2011, *Energy infrastructure priorities for 2020 and beyond – A blueprint for an integrated European energy network*.

150 | Investment Opportunities for a Low-Carbon World

Regulatory risk
Since the REEI markets are supported by legal and regulatory frameworks, any unexpected or even scheduled regulatory change poses a risk to the underlying projects' viability and economic returns. This requires a pro-active risk management approach when developing, constructing or operating REEI assets. Key activities to prepare for any regulatory changes are observations of, and discussions with, regulators to understand developments early on. Scenario analyses to understand a project's performance without subsidies are an important tool to determine the downside. Investors should generally focus on quality assets, which are cost leaders in

---

Case study: Quantifying the costs and benefits of renewable energy in Germany

Germany implemented the first feed-in tariff (FiT) regime in the 1990s, setting fixed prices for every kilowatt-hour generated by qualifying renewable energy assets guaranteed for 20 years from the year of commissioning. Under the German Renewable Energy Act (REA), qualifying renewable energy plants also have the right to deliver their energy production into the local transmission grid whenever they are producing and as long as there are no physical limitations on balancing the grid. Hence, whenever weather conditions allow for electricity generation from wind and solar plants, their electricity production will be fed into the German electricity market (assuming grid operators face no stability issues). In 2011, renewable energy assets produced around a quarter of German electricity, setting them on an equal footing with the country's nuclear power generation.

In 2008, the German Federal Ministry for the Environment, Nature Conservation and Nuclear Safety (BMU) assigned a multi-year scientific project to improve the methodological basis for an integrated, economically sound analysis of the costs and benefits of renewable energy sources.

The analysis commissioned by the BMU reveals total system costs in the renewable heat and power sectors of around €10.3 billion for 2010 and €7.5 billion for 2009 (including the difference between production costs of renewable energy technologies compared with available fossil options, grid expansion, transaction costs and basic/balancing energy). This compares with quantified gross benefits (defined as avoided cost of environmental damage by using renewable energy only) for the same years of about €8.4 billion and €7.8 billion respectively.

Analysing the distribution aspects of renewable energy (ie, which economic actors or groups enjoy benefits or suffer burdens), electricity consumers paid a renewable energy surcharge (ie, the total 'FiT bill') of around €9.4 billion in 2010 and €5.3 billion in 2009. The published benefits include: a reduction in the market's overall electricity prices by €3.1 billion in both years; avoided net energy imports due to renewable energy of €5.8 billion in 2010 and €5.7 billion in 2009; and a positive macroeconomic impact of the en-

their respective subsectors, have higher efficiency than comparable assets and would operate below the merit order's marginal cost of production in a merchant world.

When addressing regulatory risk concerns, critics of REEI subsidies highlight the sector's dependence on government support. Most such arguments ignore the fact that even fossil energy sources benefit from large subsidies. New or cleaner forms of energy would not be on a level playing field without subsidies as the economics in nearly all commodities are increasingly interdependent and distorted due to national or regional subsidies. The IEA estimates that fossil fuels benefited from $312 billion of production and consumption subsidies in 2009, against a fig-

---

ergy price effect on GDP amounting to around €100 million–200 million a year[1].

Due to the scale of the German renewable energy market, wholesale electricity prices have developed in a way that took some market observers by surprise. For a sustained period, and at times of increasing gas prices, base and peak load electricity prices have fallen to levels that make gas-fired power plants uneconomic to run – despite Germany's decision to phase out its nuclear capacity over the next decade. The primary causes are the production characteristics and economics of predominantly wind and solar photovoltaic plants – the above-mentioned feed-in rights based on the REA as well as the low cost of production.

Wind and solar plants have close to zero short-term marginal electricity generation costs because their fuel (wind or irradiation) is free. Gas-fired power plants, on the other hand, have to pay for natural gas and emission costs. Other operational costs of wind and solar plants are also extremely low compared to conventional power assets as they are normally unmanned and require comparatively less maintenance. From an economic perspective, and assuming there is demand for electricity, it always makes sense to dispatch wind and solar assets, as their production cost is close to zero, while gas-fired plants have to cover costs for fuel and emissions plus other operating costs before they generate positive operating cash flows. This has led to the most expensive plants to operate being ramped down when wind or solar assets are producing.

In addition, the production pattern of solar plants is correlated to German peak electricity demand hours. Therefore, the difference between peak and base pricing has also narrowed as during peak demand times a source of electricity with close to zero short-term marginal cost was producing.

Since significant fossil-fired power plant capacities were ramped down during peak demand hours and when wind and solar plants were producing, the German market has witnessed substantial savings in the nation's fossil fuel and emissions bill.

---

1 Michael van Mark, June 2010, *Cost and benefit effects of renewable energy expansion in the power and heat sectors*, German Federal Ministry for the Environment, Nature Conservation and Nuclear Safety; Dieter Böhme, Wolfhart Dürrschmidt and Michael van Mark, July 2011, *Entwicklung Erneuerbare Energien in Zahlen. Nationale und internationale Entwicklung*. German Federal Ministry for the Environment, Nature Conservation and Nuclear Safety.

ure of just $57 billion for clean energy. This estimate does not include externalities such as emission costs, health costs associated with fossil fuels, defence costs for securing oil, coal or nuclear supply chains, subsidies to energy-intensive industries etc[25]. McKinsey cites more than $1 trillion of subsidies on resources, including energy and water, which are keeping prices for these products artificially low. Many countries are subsidising energy by 5% or more of their GDP. Some governments in developing countries introduced consumption subsidies for energy, the value ranging from $300 billion to $550 billion depending on the oil price. In subsidised economies, consumers pay only 81% of the oil products' reference price and 49% of the natural gas reference price when compared to competitive markets, according to the McKinsey report.

Permitting risk
Developing, constructing and operating REEI projects requires a number of consents, including permits, authorisations, licences, land rights and approvals. Securing the necessary rights cannot be guaranteed. In a worst-case scenario, a project might have to be aborted if a permit is severely delayed or not granted at all; otherwise costs might increase or the asset might not be approved to operate according to expectations.

A disciplined development, construction and operations approach, detailed understanding of relevant regulations, and engineering, construction and operating know-how allow investors in this asset class to mitigate permitting risk to a large degree.

Operational risk
REEI investors are investing in hard assets with associated operational risks. A detailed understanding of the underlying operations is essential to identify potential risks and mitigate them in the context of development, construction and operations. This is one of the reasons why financial investors tend to invest in specialist funds with sector expertise rather than directly in infrastructure assets.

Financing risk
Infrastructure investors have the choice to fund investment either entirely by equity or to gear their investment by attracting project finance. If target returns are based on the assumption of levered returns, failure to secure debt for a project will lead to underperformance compared to investment base cases.

Counterparty risk
The key counterparties in infrastructure projects include engineering, procurement and construction (EPC) contractors, operations and maintenance (O&M) contrac-

---
25 *Bloomberg New Energy Finance*, September 2011, Volume V Issue 53.

tors, suppliers, fuel providers, offtakers, tollers and insurance providers. Apart from equity investors, project financiers will do careful due diligence on the experience and creditworthiness of a project's key counterparties before providing firm financing commitments. Traditional ways of mitigating counterparty risks include guarantees from financially stronger parties, letters of credit and bonds.

Return drivers

Returns of REEI assets are driven by the underlying project's cash flow patterns, which are typically secured by long-term contracts and may be linked to inflation. Consequently, infrastructure cashflows are usually uncorrelated with other asset classes such as equities, bonds, commodities or currencies.

The REEI assets' risk/return profile depends on the timing of investment with respect to a project's stage in its lifetime: the greenfield, late-stage development, construction or operational phases. Any asset in the sectors under consideration is cash flow negative until commissioned and operational.

Quantifying return expectations across all asset classes and stages is difficult as they depend on the certainty and stability of future cash flows, the country a project is based in, the relevant legislation and regulation for a specific asset class in this country, the technology applied, and feedstock supply and offtake, among many other factors. The highest prices (resulting in lowest returns to investors) are being paid for projects with transparent, stable cash flows with low volatility in countries with stable regulatory environments and a reliable track record.

Figure 2 on page 154 illustrates the returns investors in renewable generation assets should expect as a function of an asset's development stage.

OFFTAKE PRICING REGIMES

Once an asset is commissioned, one of the most significant return drivers is the pricing regime for the project's product. Common structures grant long-term, fixed prices under the above-mentioned FiT regimes, a combination of merchant power pricing and green certificates, capacity or availability payments, tolling or processing fees similar to conventional energy and infrastructure projects.

Offtake pricing regimes are typically dynamic and evolve over time. As technologies become more established and cost-competitive, regulators tend to lower the offtake pricing to avoid excessive subsidised returns to developers and owners of operational capacity (see above). In addition to adjusting the applicable FiTs, Germany has created an incentive for qualifying renewable energy producers to opt out of the FiT and sell electricity directly to consumers. In Turkey, FiTs for renewable energy projects have been below wholesale prices for electricity – in such a scenario renewable generation assets would be dispatched into the wholesale market and the FiT could be considered as a floor price protecting an asset's debt.

Figure 2. Returns to investors at different stages of project development

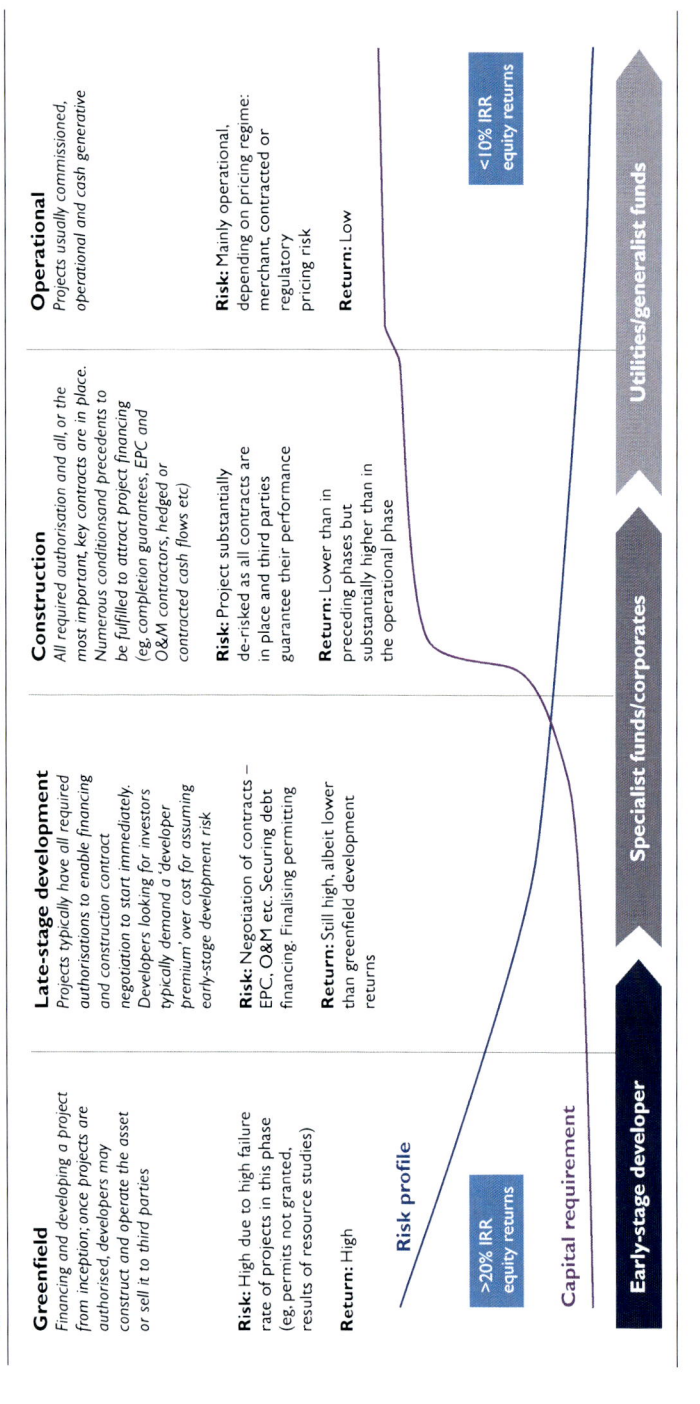

Greenfield
Financing and developing a project from inception; once projects are authorised, developers may construct and operate the asset or sell it to third parties

Risk: High due to high failure rate of projects in this phase (eg, permits not granted, results of resource studies)

Return: High

Late-stage development
Projects typically have all required authorisations to enable financing and construction contract negotiation to start immediately. Developers looking for investors typically demand a 'developer premium' over cost for assuming early-stage development risk

Risk: Negotiation of contracts – EPC, O&M etc. Securing debt financing. Finalising permitting

Return: Still high, albeit lower than in greenfield development returns

Construction
All required authorisation and all, or the most important, key contracts are in place. Numerous conditions and precedents to be fulfilled to attract project financing (eg, completion guarantees, EPC and O&M contractors, hedged or contracted cash flows etc)

Risk: Project substantially de-risked as all contracts are in place and third parties guarantee their performance

Return: Lower than in preceding phases but substantially higher than in the operational phase

Operational
Projects usually commissioned, operational and cash generative

Risk: Mainly operational, depending on pricing regime: merchant, contracted or regulatory pricing risk

Return: Low

Risk profile

Capital requirement

>20% IRR equity returns

<10% IRR equity returns

Early-stage developer → Specialist funds/corporates → Utilities/generalist funds

Typical investment structures

GEARED VERSUS UNGEARED

Project finance loans
Assets generating long-term, stable and certain cash flows can normally attract project financing with no or limited recourse to the projects' equity sponsors. Non-recourse project finance loans are secured by a project's assets and its cash flows rather than by recourse to its sponsors.

Loan amounts and tenors are sized on the basis of cash flow forecasts and, in the case of REEI assets, depend heavily on the predictable duration of cash flows (ie, the robustness and term of the pricing regime in which they are operating).

Financial leverage is key to securing optimised returns in infrastructure investment and has been common practice for decades. Depending on the asset class and region we focus on, gearing ratios achieved for long-term contracted or tolled projects have been from 70% to 95%.

A project's development stage is one of the factors determining availability of debt. Early development is typically financed using equity, while project finance debt can be drawn down once an asset has been de-risked to a large extent – ie, at the start of construction, once all authorisations have been received and key contracts are in place.

Bankable projects also use proven technologies with appropriate performance guarantees and warranties from suppliers and contractors – ideally turnkey, price- and date-certain EPC contracts with experienced engineering firms and O&M contracts with operators that have sufficient relevant track records. Appropriate credit quality or credit support instruments are a requirement for most, if not all of the contractors involved.

Ungeared investments
Strategic investors, such as utilities, or recently a number of financial investors (such as insurance companies investing directly in assets) have been funding infrastructure assets on-balance sheet or ungeared. While the financial returns on their capital invested might not be as high as geared returns in project finance structures, ungeared investments might perform better in downside scenarios due to the senior ranking of loans when cash flows are paid out (senior loans take the first cash available until they are serviced). For example, in years with bad wind conditions, cash flows of wind power assets might be 20% lower than the base case. Aggressively geared projects might not see any equity dividends or even breach the loan's covenants under these conditions, while an ungeared project's cash flows might still yield a positive return (depending on the investment base case).

LONG-TERM INVESTMENTS VERSUS BUILD-AND-SELL STRATEGIES

Infrastructure investments are mostly associated with long-term strategies targeting stable and safe yields. Typical infrastructure investors include mainly strategic industry participants, which build or acquire assets to own and operate as their core business, or financial investors looking for long-term investment opportunities that offer a low risk and stable return profile. This, however, is not the only approach to seeking attractive, risk-adjusted returns in this asset class.

As indicated above, return requirements for operating assets with long-term, stable cash flows are lower than for greenfield projects. Another, arguably higher-risk and higher-return, approach to investing in infrastructure assets is the asset development approach targeting greenfield or late-stage development assets, de-risking the projects by managing permitting and construction and, once commissioned, selling them to long-term investors as operational assets. Operational assets normally trade at a net present value that assumes a lower discount rate than a greenfield project (due to the lower return requirements for lower-risk assets). Hence, this strategy achieves capital gains rather than yield income due to the yield compression between the higher-return development project and the de-risked, lower-return operational asset.

CURRENT MARKET

The current market environment is impacted by a number of factors, most significantly by reduced capacity in lending markets due to the financial and economic crisis; a surprising availability of equity seeking long-term, low-risk investment opportunities; a good deal flow of high-quality assets that are up for sale; and significant capital expenditure requirements in the REEI sectors.

Debt is still available but a 'flight to quality' can be observed. To attract project finance loans, robust project structuring is key. During the boom phase preceding the current financial crisis a number of renewable assets were developed like real estate assets, ignoring operational risks and taking shortcuts during the planning, design, engineering and construction stages. Lenders now carry out careful due diligence on the experience of sponsors and contractors involved, with a clear preference for established players and proven technologies. Individual lending lines tend to be smaller and larger projects have to approach lending clubs or syndicates. Europe has yet to benefit from the establishment of institutional project finance or an increased presence of infrastructure debt funds rather than bank debt. The former is more common in the US, where a number of financial institutions, such as insurance companies, are providing long-term project finance loans to match their own liabilities with long-term cash flows.

Funding projects at the development stage is certainly more challenging than selling or financing operational assets, as most infrastructure investors cannot invest at or before the construction phase. This is where Zouk sees an attractive opportunity to provide development capital with a focus on late-stage development projects.

Similarly to financial institutions, although for other reasons, a number of sizeable European strategic industry participants are under financial and regulatory pressure. Their credit ratings are at risk due to pre-crisis addition of financial leverage, changing risk profiles of utilities' core business and significant refinancing requirements, leading to strategic reviews and divestitures of assets that have been labelled as non-core. From a regulatory perspective, unbundling requirements are forcing utilities to sell high-quality infrastructure assets (eg, gas and electricity grids).

As mentioned previously, massive new capacity additions have to be financed and new and innovative structures are being applied. Where companies and institutions had previously been competing against each other, they now form joint ventures, syndicates or clubs to fund REEI assets together. Strategic industry participants are teaming up, financial investors form consortia and 'hybrid' structures see utilities involving financial investors to make more efficient use of their own balance sheets.

In 2009, the British utility Centrica sold half of a 220MW portfolio of operational wind farms to an alternative investment firm; it then sold half of the 270MW Lincs offshore wind development project to engineering conglomerate Siemens and Danish utility Dong Energy. To fund the £1 billion debt package the consortium is trying to raise, the sponsors have been proposing to use commercial loans together with £500 million of their own funds to construct the Lincs project, effectively involving the sponsors as quasi-lenders. This leaves bank debt at only about 40% of project cost, well below the 65% seen on some other offshore wind projects[26].

Another international consortium, Abu Dhabi renewable energy firm Masdar, German utility E.ON and Dong Energy, is developing the 1GW London Array offshore wind project. Dong Energy and E.ON are financing their shares on-balance sheet (Dong Energy with the help of a loan from the European Investment Bank) and Masdar is targeting a project finance deal with a club of banks[27].

This is occuring at a time when not only are industry participants deleveraging their balance sheets but also governments have to attract private investors to fund core infrastructure, leading to privatisations, various incentive programmes to stimulate investment and numerous public-private partnerships. Some of the regulatory incentive mechanisms have already been elaborated on; key for investors is to rely on protection mechanisms for existing law as, unfortunately, not all governments have adhered to laws or regulations investors relied on when funding renewable energy projects (eg, retroactive changes to the Spanish FiT and in the Czech Republic and the recent announcement of changes to the UK FiT for solar photovoltaic plants earlier than previously planned). This also leads to geographical differences in return expectations, driven not only by sovereign credit considerations but increasingly their regulatory track record.

---

26 *Bloomberg New Energy Finance*, September 2011, Volume V Issue 53.
27 *Bloomberg New Energy Finance*, October 2011, Volume V Issue 54.

Conclusion

REEI assets deliver attractive risk-adjusted returns which are to a large degree uncorrelated with traditional asset classes. The sector represents an interesting way of diversifying an investment portfolio, especially when compared to equities, bonds, currencies, commodities, general private equity strategies and hedge funds.

Even without subsidies, some of the technologies under consideration are competitive today and equipment costs are continuing to come down. According to selected analyses commissioned by governments, the benefits of supporting renewable energy projects exceed the cost in various areas.

The scale of investment requirement in REEI to meet new capacity targets is too large for governments alone. A significant amount of private capital needs to be mobilised to finance the required capacity additions and upgrades. Increasingly, pension and sovereign wealth funds are investing in REEI, often drawing expertise from specialist and corporate investors.

Investors have the choice of when in an REEI project's lifetime to invest and which returns to target. Due to the unique risk profile and operational risks involved, sector expertise is a precondition to managing risks. Consequently, most institutional investors prefer to invest in specialist funds rather than directly in REEI projects.

Chapter 9

Heat pumps

Philip Wolfe, Ownergy Plc

Investors will wish to track a growing range of technologies, as renewable energies continue to expand their share of the overall energy mix. Historically, most of the focus has been on electricity generation sources like solar photovoltaic (PV), wind and more recently wave and tidal power.

The more demanding penetration targets now being adopted are extending attention to biofuels and renewable heat. Europe's renewable energy targets, in particular, have been broadened from electricity alone to be based on total energy consumption. Energy consumption in Europe is divided roughly equally between electricity, heat (and cooling) and transport. The heat sector should, therefore, show dynamic growth over the next decade, since it has historically been overlooked and offers a comparatively low-cost path to increasing the contribution of renewables in total energy.

The main sources of renewable heat are solar thermal, bioenergy, geothermal and heat pumps. This chapter will deal with the latter.

What are heat pumps?

Heat pumps can provide hot water and also space heating or cooling for buildings. As the name suggests, they operate by transferring heat from an external source to the hot water or air system of the building.

There are three main types depending on the source of heat used. Ground-source heat pumps use ambient heat from the surrounding ground. This is rather different from geothermal energy, which tends to use much higher temperature sources from deeper in the earth's crust. The two other types are air-source heat pumps, which use the ambient air, and water-source heat pumps, which use water from a nearby lake, pond or river. While none of these sources are very hot, the heat pump can work with a comparatively small temperature difference and effectively amplify it to produce the heat energy required.

The heat pump itself is in many ways similar to a domestic refrigerator operating in reverse. It is powered by electricity, but each kilowatt (kW) of power used draws several kilowatts from the heat source. The ratio between the electricity used and the heat delivered is called the 'coefficient of performance', and is typically up to 4:1 for modern devices.

Why are heat pumps renewable if they use standard electricity? The reason, of course, is the coefficient of performance multiplier. If a ground-source heat pump delivers 8kW of heat to a building and uses 2kW of electricity, then 6kW come from the surrounding ground and are renewable. Of course, if the 2kW come from a solar panel or wind turbine, they are renewable too.

Heat pumps are now available in many different sizes and configurations. They are already widely used internationally, especially in continental Europe, and more widely adopted in the UK. Today, the most common are ground-source heat pumps.

Domestic systems look very similar to a large refrigerator, with pipes connected to so-called ground loops buried underground. These may be coils or arrays of (usually plastic) piping buried 1–2 metres below ground level or one or more boreholes going straight down.

Air-source heat pumps are becoming increasingly efficient and, therefore, widely used. These have the benefit of not needing ground loops, because they use fans that pass ambient air over the heat collector elements. Water-source heat pumps are similar to ground-source but with the heat collection loops immersed in water, where a suitable source is available.

Where is the technology going?

Heat pump technology is well established, with most production based in Scandinavia, the Far East and continental Europe. Developments are focused mainly on improving efficiency – the coefficient of performance. Recently this has particularly benefited the air-source heat pumps that were used mainly for heating swimming pools, but are now increasingly used for buildings due to their improving winter performance. Combining this trend with the advantage of easier installation, many observers expect air-source heat pumps to take over from ground-source as the volume leader in the medium-term future.

Control technology is also advancing with most systems now capable of fully automatic operation with no demands on the user. System integration capabilities are also evolving to enable heat pumps to be combined with solar thermal panels and other renewable heat sources. Heat pumps can also, in most cases, be run in reverse cycle to provide cooling, by transferring heat from the building back into the ground, air or water.

Larger devices are also being developed, and industrial-scale heating systems are becoming common, usually incorporating a number of pumps working in tandem.

What are the main market drivers?

The market for heat pumps is expected to grow as part of a general expansion of the proportion of renewable heating generally within the built environment.

Considering first the drivers for renewable heating in general (and these apply equally to solar thermal, biomass and other heat technologies covered in other chap-

Heat Pumps | 161

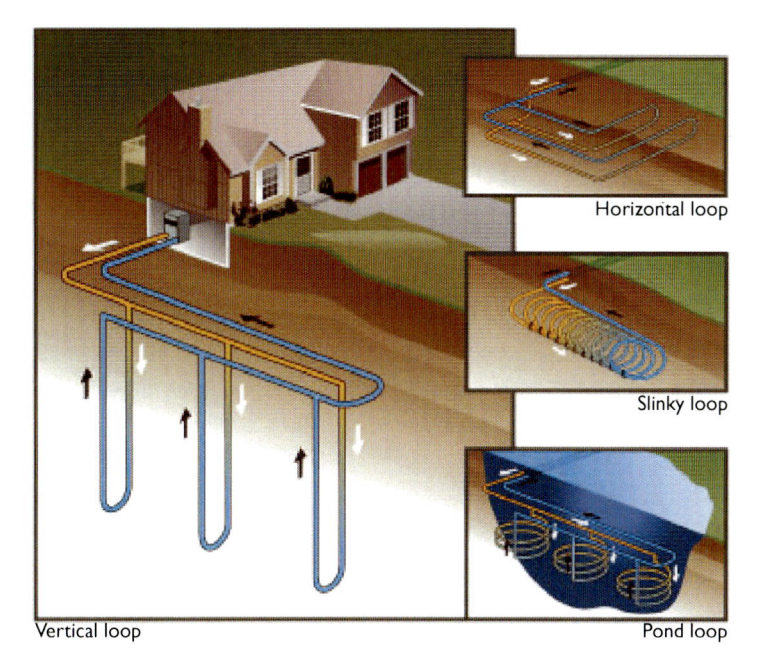

Ground- and water-source heat pumps for the home

ters), these derive mainly from trends that impact all renewable energies. The main underlying positive drivers for growth in renewables are reducing costs and customer preference – both consumer choice and corporate social responsibility – caused by rising awareness of climate change and resource depletion.

This is strongly enhanced by a rapidly accelerating international and national policy framework. Most OECD countries and many others have, or are designing, policies to increase the level of renewable energy use and in particular seeking to reduce emissions from buildings and businesses. Renewable heat can make a significant contribution to the policies and should enjoy exceptional growth, especially as it has historically not been addressed within energy policies. The Renewable Heat Incentive measure to be introduced in the UK in 2011 is being designed to mirror the feed-in tariffs now adopted for electricity in many countries and will be a pioneering measure to support a wide range of technologies.

The comparative position of heat pumps, alongside other renewable heat options, will vary substantially, depending on the individual buildings in which they will be used. Some options are also suitable for use in a combined system – solar thermal, for example.

The primary issue will be the access to the heat source. Heat pumps have the comparative benefit over fuel-consuming renewable resources, such as biomass, in that there is no need to procure or store fuel.

What does the market look like?

The market extends to both residential and non-residential properties for water heating, space heating and cooling. Broadly speaking, the route to market follows that for traditional heating and air-conditioning equipment.

Many mainstream boiler suppliers now offer the core heat pump units, some from their own manufacture, but most using contracted sub-manufacturers.

Heat pumps tend to operate at lower temperatures than fossil fuel boilers, and when used in conjunction with a traditional hot water heating systems, they are best adapted to under-floor heating, though they can operate with radiator systems.

In the consumer market, an increasing proportion of the installer base for domestic boilers now offers heat pumps (and other renewable heat sources). Installers need additional training, of course, to be able to offer these systems, but the integration with traditional heating circuits is relatively straightforward. For ground-source heat pumps the installation of the ground loop is an additional requirement, which some installers offer and others sub-contract to ground workers or specialist borehole drilling companies.

Larger commercial systems are usually engineered by specialist system integration companies to ensure that the overall design is optimised. These organisations will, generally, procure the individual components from the manufacturers and supply the finished system as a turnkey project.

They will also handle any customised integration aspects. For example, in office or industrial buildings, some of the ground loops can be incorporated into pilings and building foundations.

What are the investment opportunities?

The supply chain described above gives opportunities for investment at several levels. In addition to companies already producing heat pump units, there may periodically be new designs ready to be released in the market. In either case, the keys to success will be the robustness and efficiency of the unit itself, and the access to market which, except for specialist units, probably requires a distribution agreement with a major volume heating equipment supplier.

Heat pump system engineering companies will be able to establish substantial niche positions especially in the market for larger and more specialised systems for commercial, industrial and public sector customers, and for new residential developments and blocks of flats, for example. The unique selling point in this sector is likely to be in terms of engineering expertise, systems technology (eg, control interfaces) and customer relationships.

There is major growth potential for installers in the domestic market, especially in European markets, particularly those starting from a low base, like the UK. While many players will be small and regionalised, more broadly based installation companies with critical mass, good organisation and a complementary offering in other renewable energy technologies will enjoy substantial market growth.

Chapter 10

Sustainable timberland investing

Simon Fox, Mercer

Introduction
Investing in timberland (or forests to you and me) may seem a slightly archaic choice in this world of technological innovation, shiny skyscrapers and white goods. Yet for investors, the ability to profit from the stable biological growth of trees, rather than rely on turbulent financial markets and changing consumer appetites, presents a particular appeal. Investments in sustainable timberland can also provide investors with something of a hedge against the impact of both climate change and the technology and policy responses that may be introduced to deal with it.

The world of timber is by no means outmoded. The UN Food and Agriculture Organization (FAO) estimates that the global trade in timber is now worth more than $200 billion, contributing around 1% of world GDP. Moreover, as with other commodities, the seemingly insatiable appetite for timber from China and other emerging markets continues to grow.

But owning timberland isn't just about owning the eventual commodity. Timberland investors earn the majority of the return from actually funding the production of the wood, rather than from changing commodity prices. Timberland therefore provides investors with some key attributes in the current economic environment: it is a diversifying asset (trees continue to grow through a recession), it should provide inflation sensitivity over the long run (buoyed by relatively attractive market conditions at the moment) and it can provide exposure to emerging market growth. That it is also one of the few investments with a direct impact on greenhouse gas emissions only increases its appeal in a low-carbon world.

Uses for industrial timber
The FAO estimates that timber and forest products "contribute about one percent of world gross domestic product and ... account[s] for three percent of international merchandise trade". Annual consumption of industrial roundwood has averaged over 1.6 billion m^3 over the past 10 years and is estimated to grow by almost 50% over the next 20 years, as illustrated in Figure 1.

So what is all this timber used for? Around two thirds of the industrial timber produced is sawtimber (large logs that can be sawn into lumber), while just under

Figure 1. Global consumption of industrial roundwood, 1965–2030
Million cubic metres

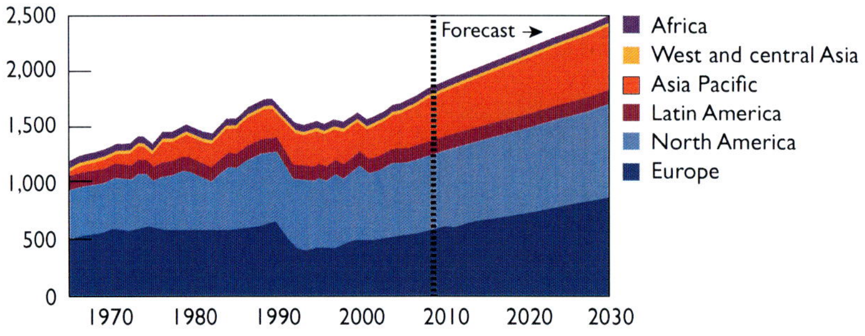

Source: Dasos and FAO 2009, unpublished data

one third is pulpwood (timber that is broken down into wood fibres, either mechanically or with chemicals). From these two main forest products, timber is used in a variety of ways. This includes using sawtimber in building construction (particularly in the US, but increasingly elsewhere), using a mix of sawtimber and pulpwood for wood-based panels (eg, chipboard and plywood – used in furniture, construction and housing repair) and using pulpwood for cardboard and paper[1].

Timber is also used in some more niche areas, such as for decking and, increasingly, wood chips and pellets for bioenergy.

While timber demand has dipped in the past few years on the back of global economic weakness, there is a long-term trend of increasing demand.

Characteristics of timberland investments

As trees grow they increase in volume and go through 'step changes' in what they can be used for. The timber moves from being suitable only for pulpwood, to chip 'n' saw and then to sawtimber – each commanding a higher price per tonne (Figure 2).

This growth is independent of economic cycles and timber can be left growing 'on the stump' during market weakness. This helps drive some of the diversification benefit of timberland. It also introduces different risks to a portfolio – for example, from climate, fire or disease. To deal with these risks, diversification across different tree species and regions, as well as active forestry management, are key issues for investors. The investment will also be particularly illiquid.

However, while the biological growth drives the harvest value of an area of tim-

---

[1] While global demand for paper for newsprint is decreasing, packaging and tissue paper has been growing strongly, according to data from FAOSTAT. The data illustrates that there has been a particular demand increase from countries such as China, reflecting population growth, a growing middle class and the expansion of export industries (for example, increasing the demand for packaging). Forest products industry information provider RISI has noted that, for example, around 1 billion people have never touched toilet paper.

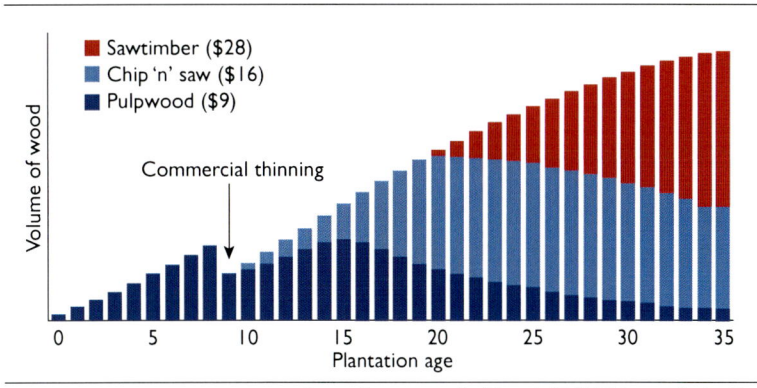

Figure 2. Volume growth and value

- Sawtimber ($28)
- Chip 'n' saw ($16)
- Pulpwood ($9)

Commercial thinning

Volume of wood vs Plantation age (0–35)

Source: Mercer; prices for US south Q3 2010 (source: Timber Mart South)

berland, the ultimate return from a timberland investment is heavily influenced by the purchase price. Indeed, 'buying right' will be a key driver of future expected returns.

The expected return from timberland can broadly be separated into the following three components:

Expected return = strategic (real) risk premium +
expected change in timber prices +
active management contribution

- The *strategic risk premium* is equivalent to the real discount rate built into the purchase price of a piece of timberland. Investors that purchase timberland are in effect funding the production of the timber – timber growth is relatively predictable and it is possible to estimate the future cash flows that you could earn from the growing trees. Discounting these cash flows can give a price for the timberland – and this in turn provides an expected return on capital over time[2].
- *Changes in timber prices* affect both the value of wood harvested and the ultimate resale value of the land. The predicted change in timber prices can broadly be added to (or subtracted from) the strategic risk premium in estimating expected return. Prices will be driven by the supply and demand dynamics in the market, although over the long term timber is seen by many as a 'real asset' and is therefore expected to rise in line with inflation.

---

2 The discount rate is chosen to compensate investors for the risk of the investment. In timberland this includes the illiquidity of the investment (the value of timberland will only be realised over many years – Eucalyptus is one of the quickest growing trees, at six to 16 years to maturity when grown in places such as Brazil, but the Western hemlock and Douglas fir that dominate the northwest of the US typically have 45–60-year rotations); physical risks from climate, fire and disease (in the region of 0.5% a year, based on industry estimates); price risks (mitigated by the ability to leave timber 'on the stump'); biological growth rate risks (the risk that the trees don't grow as quickly as you had expected); and political, legal and tax risks.

- The *active management* of the assets can add additional value in a number of ways – including trying to identify value in distressed and unrecognised investments, the timing of timber sales and the day-to-day management of the assets.

Overall these three components can provide a strong rationale for investing in timberland on purely investment grounds. Indeed, timberland assets have been among the best performing investments in recent years; the US NCREIF[3] Timberland index, for example, has delivered a 13.5% annual return since its inception in 1987.

As with all asset classes, however, it is important to understand the pattern of past returns and to recognise that the future will not necessarily reflect the past. In fact, biological and political risks have so far worked in favour of the commercial industry in the US. Moreover, the maturing ('institutionalising') industry has seen significant yield compression over the past few years, boosting returns until recently. Nevertheless, strategically this is an asset class that is worthy of consideration by institutional investors with a long time horizon (10 years-plus). The particular attractiveness of the opportunity set is also heavily influenced by the prevailing market environment – conditions that at the moment look attractive for new investments (see below).

As well as a good return potential, there should also be attractive diversification benefits from investing in this asset class: we note that the value of the underlying asset continues to be dominated by biological growth and should therefore be lowly correlated to other investments in a typical institutional portfolio (trees continue to grow through economic downturns)[4]. Furthermore, while there will be volatility in the timber markets, the ability to leave timber 'on the stump' where it will continue to accrue value (as it matures and gets bigger) means that returns do not need to be crystallised in weak timber markets.

Timberland, though, doesn't just deserve consideration for its investment credentials; it also deserves recognition for its potential role as a 'low-carbon' asset that can help mitigate the risk of climate change in investment portfolios. The sustainability of timberland management practices is a key element for this.

From sustainability to REDD

The opportunities from commercial timberland investment are closely aligned with the interests of sustainability investors. Indeed it is fundamental to their success that timberland managers are aware of the environmental and social implications of their investments. This is particularly true as new timberland opportunities emerge in less developed countries, where regulations, standards and social conditions lag those of more established marketplaces. The emergence of internationally supported certifi-

---

[3] National Council of Real Estate Investment Fiduciaries.
[4] Harvested timber prices are also a component of underlying cash flows and are likely to show some sensitivity to broader economic health – as such it would be wrong to assume that the components of a timberland return are completely uncorrelated to equities etc.

cation schemes, such as the Forest Stewardship Council, provides a welcome level of transparency for potential investors and consumers.

While a sustainable approach to timberland management should, in and of itself, contribute to reduced carbon emissions relative to traditional logging[5], emissions trading schemes are also introducing an alternative way to reduce carbon emissions through forestry.

The Kyoto Protocol, in 1997, led to the development of a number of emissions trading schemes in different parts of the world. A common theme is to try and create a price for carbon – or, more precisely, a price for emitting carbon dioxide. Companies that emit excess amounts of carbon are required to purchase additional 'carbon credits', either from other companies that have 'spare credits', or from projects that have generated 'new credits' by preventing the emission of carbon that would otherwise have occurred. The process for approving new credits was initially set out in the Kyoto Protocol. In theory, forestry has the potential to reduce significantly the amount of carbon being emitted globally (deforestation currently accounts for 18% of global carbon emissions[6]). Projects that help reduce emissions from deforestation and forest degradation (known as 'REDD' projects) are therefore being developed as a way of generating new carbon credits.

The idea of using REDD projects to create carbon credits has, however, taken a long time to formalise. When it was initially considered at Kyoto it was deferred as a solution as being too administratively complex. Indeed today REDD projects that are being developed are having to sell the credits they create into the voluntary market rather than having them qualify as 'official trading credits'. (The voluntary market caters to companies that want to reduce their carbon footprint for, for example, ethical reasons, but that are not part of a formal emissions trading system.)

REDD can therefore be seen an emerging opportunity for investors, but it does remain a niche investment with, in particular, significant regulatory risks.

Whether investors are looking at traditional sustainable timberland or at the emerging opportunities in REDD, timberland's 'low-carbon' credentials give it a clear role within portfolios that are looking to hedge against the impact of climate change and the technology and policy responses that may be introduced to deal with it[7].

Current market environment for sustainable timberland

We believe that, overall, the characteristics of timberland, and the sources of return that underpin the investment, provide a strong case for investing. However, we also note that the attraction of timberland will be very dependent on the prevailing market environment. Timing the entry point is important.

---

5 See Rainforest Alliance, 'FSC Certification Keeps Trees Standing and Forests Intact – Responsible Forestry Reduces Emissions'.
6 *The Stern Review: The Economics of Climate Change*, 2006.
7 See www.mercer.com/climatechange for more details.

Figure 3. Established investible timberland: relative sizes

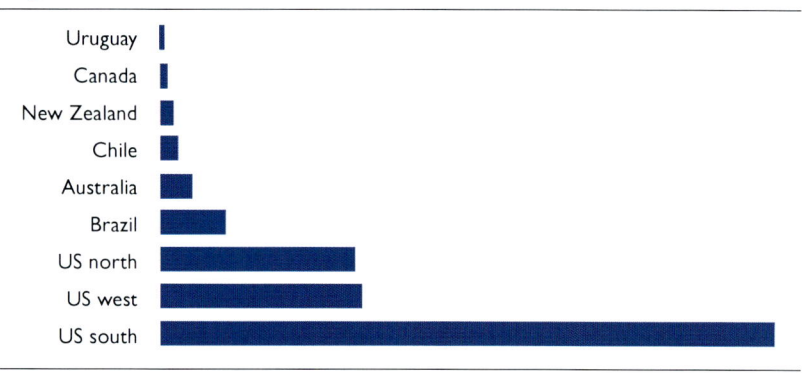

Source: Timberland Investment Resources

Figure 4. Components of expected market return

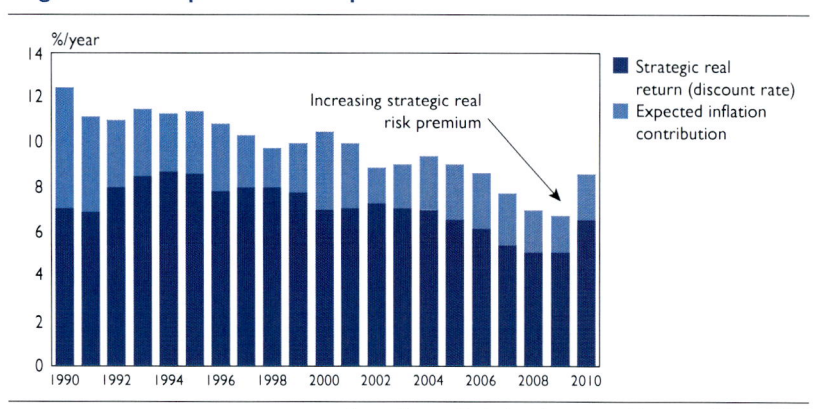

Source: Mercer, Timberland Investment white paper, February 2011

In practice, very little of the world's forest cover is usable for commercial timber production. It is inaccessible, protected or commercially unviable. Indeed, although the US accounts for just 8% of the world's forest cover[8], it is the world's largest timber producer and has the most mature timberland investment market. Figure 3 illustrates the relative size of the world's most established timberland markets[9]. The US has been the main focus for most timberland investors, but the market has also been globalising – a substantial share of the world's forests are in developing countries house and increasing numbers of timberland projects are emerging in these countries.

---
8 FAO Global Forest Resources Assessment 2005.
9 The analysis shown here relates to estimates from Timberland Investment Resources, which estimates that the investible universe in established timberland markets is about $250 billion globally.

Figure 5. Louisiana Department of Agriculture and Forestry sawtimber stumpage prices
1955–2009, $/MBF (real prices, based on 2009 prices)

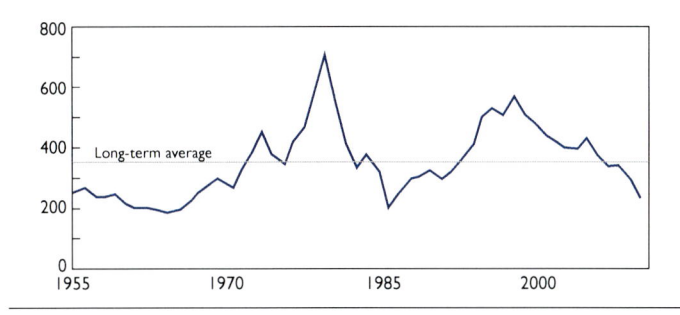

In the US, the strategic risk premiums available in the market have been increasing back to an attractive 7% per annum, having hit lamentably low levels in 2008 (Figure 4). Timber prices also now look low in a long-term context (Figure 5).

The discount rates used to value non-US timberland are typically bigger – reflecting the greater political risks of the countries and the less mature nature of the markets. This provides additional return opportunities for investors, with compelling opportunities emerging in South America and Asia Pacific.

The emerging nature of a number of these markets does provide opportunities for investors. This could be in terms of identifying unrecognised value in areas of timberland, capturing a narrowing risk premium as the markets (in particular Brazil and the more emerging countries) mature or in greenfield developments (recognising the increased risks associated with these projects). We believe that these countries present some interesting opportunities to sophisticated investors as part of a global timberland portfolio.

Conclusion

Judging by the performance of the US NCREIF Timberland index, timberland assets have been one of the best performing investments over the past 24 years. In addition to these strong historic returns, timberland would also have provided the additional benefit to investment portfolios of having a low correlation to financial assets – in particular equities – over this period.

While we believe that the future returns are likely to be lower, not least because the market has matured over this period, strategically we believe that this is an asset class that is worthy of consideration by institutional investors with a long time horizon (10 years-plus) and our current market outlook suggests that this may be a beneficial time to enter the asset class. Recently, forests have become cheaper and the return available simply for the production of the wood is now a healthy 6–8% per year in the established US market. It is higher in developing regions, where the markets are still maturing and an additional risk premium can be commanded. The long-term outlook for timber prices is also positive and may increase overall returns from the investment.

Timberland also has many positive sustainability characteristics including some more explicit opportunities: as a climate change 'hedge' by mitigation and carbon sequestration, as a bioenergy source and for conservation, including the provision of ecosystem services – eg, protecting hydrological cycles and preventing erosion.

Overall, timberland investments look compelling, warranting serious consideration for investors' portfolios as we look to create a low-carbon world.

Bibliography

Binkley, C, International Forestry Investment Advisors: *The sensitivity of the value of timberland assets to changes in the discount rate*, February 2009.

Brookfield Asset Management, Various publications including (1) *Introduction to timberland investing*, March 2010, and (2) *Quarterly letter – Higher and better use lands within timberland portfolios*, Q2 2009.

Caulfield, J, *Real Estate Finance: Timberland Return Drivers and Investing Styles*, Winter 1998.

Dasos Capital, *Inherent features of timberland investment*, October 2010.

Flynn, B, RISI: *Market Projections for Wood Fiber and Wood Products: Understanding the key drivers of timberland values*, October 2010.

Forest Investment Associates, Various publications including *Timberland Investing – what you need to know now*, Summer 2010.

Forest Research Group, *Forest Research Notes*, Q2 2009.

Forum for the Future, *Forest Investment Review*, July 2009.

GMO Renewable Resources, Various publications including *Timber Investment Overview*, 2005.

Hancock Timber Resource Group, Various publications including *Developing a diversified global timberland portfolio to mitigate risks and enhance returns*, October 2010.

Healey, Corriero and Rozenor, *Timber as an institutional investment*, Winter 2005.

IWC, *Timberland investments in an institutional portfolio*, March 2009.

James W Sewall Company, *Timberland Report – discount rates and timberland investments*.

Lutz, J, James W Sewall Company: *Trends in Timberland Investment*, 2001.

Pepke, E, UNECE/FAO: *Global Wood Markets – Consumption, Production and Trade*, May 2010.

Resource Management Service, Various publications, including *Timberland Investment Opportunities*, October 2010.

Rinehart, J, R&A Investment Forestry: *US timberland post-recession*, April 2010.

SAM and Indufor, *Sustainable investing in forestry*, 2010.

Stafford Timberland, *The Stafford Diaries*, April 2010.
Timberland Investment Resources, Various publications, including (1) *Timberland Investment Styles*, June 2010, (2) *Estimating the global market size of investible timberland*, November 2008, (3) *Addressing the European perspective: US timberland in a global timberland allocation*, June 2009, and (3) *Looking back and ahead*, 2011.

Chapter 11

Climate change: key issues for institutional investors

Mark Fulton and Bruce Kahn, Deutsche Bank Climate Change Advisors[1]

The megatrend persists: managing risk and return for investors

Climate change is a long-term trend that will affect the value of assets in the real economy and will produce long-term investment opportunities. We define the climate change investment universe as those companies that mitigate climate change by developing low-carbon emissions technologies or that adapt to climate change – for example, companies that foster energy efficiency and cleaner energy, or respond to new pressures on society and the economy from climatic changes, such as food production and water management. The transition to a lower-carbon economy creates opportunities for active asset managers, but also requires understanding of the supply and demand dynamics of traditional energy commodities such as natural gas, coal and oil, as well as agricultural commodities. Total capital deployed continues to rise, although on a global basis it needs to rise significantly to support climate stability.

According to Bloomberg New Energy Finance (BNEF), investment in clean energy asset classes has increased since 2004, and was the largest on record in 2010 (Figure 1). Asset finance (investment in large-scale clean energy projects) is the largest single area of investment. This is an infrastructure play. Small-scale renewable energy investment – much of which is solar photovoltaic (PV) in Germany – is captured in the small distributed capacity category. This figure is only reported by BNEF once a year, so it is not always recorded in intra-year investment totals.

BP recently concluded that world primary energy consumption grew by 45% over the past 20 years and is expected to grow by a further 39% over the next 20 years. Non-OECD energy consumption will comprise the lion's share of global energy growth by 2030, expected to be 68% higher by 2030 than today. BP also finds that the fuel mix will change, with renewable energy gaining share at the expense of

---

1 DBCCA's White Paper: *Investing in Climate Change 2011* looked at the key investment drivers in climate change strategies and how they play out at the asset level in terms of risk and return. In this chapter the key points of that paper are presented in terms of key themes. The full paper is available at: www.dbcca.com/dbcca/EN/investment-research/investment_research_2361.jsp

174 | Investment Opportunities for a Low-Carbon World

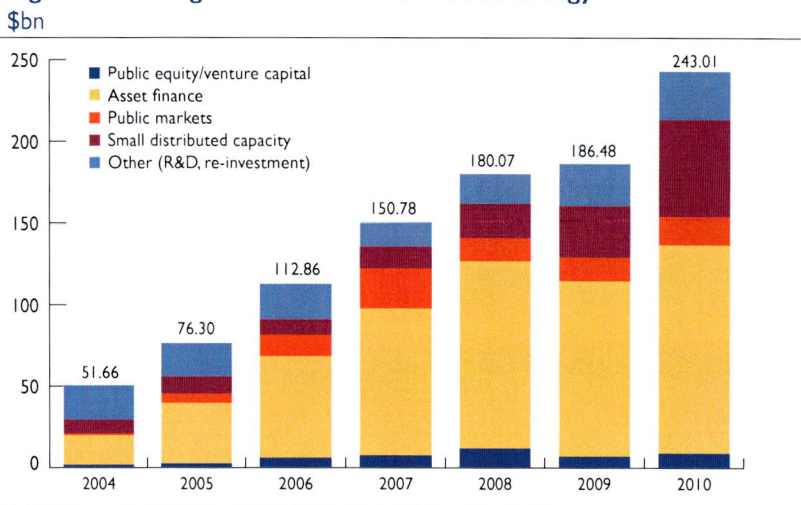

Figure 1. Total global investment in clean energy
$bn

- Public equity/venture capital
- Asset finance
- Public markets
- Small distributed capacity
- Other (R&D, re-investment)

Year	Total
2004	51.66
2005	76.30
2006	112.86
2007	150.78
2008	180.07
2009	186.48
2010	243.01

Source: Bloomberg New Energy Finance

coal and oil. BP estimates that renewables will represent the fastest-growing sector, projected to grow at 8.2% a year between 2010 and 2030.

Exploring risk for investors

Our investment thesis rests on this longer-term megatrend of climate change which creates opportunities across asset classes. However, markets, economies and policy support for climate change industries can be volatile and generate asset class-specific risks that require in-depth understanding and active management. Markets, such as the public equity markets, are volatile. Movements in prices can be dramatic. Economic cycles are also volatile, and the recent recession is evidence that systemic risk can impact all asset values. Many renewable energy technologies are in different maturity stages, and therefore require different levels of funding, coming from different sources of capital. Often, financing of renewable energy will be subject to the variable rate of adoption and commercialisation of new technologies. And, finally, government policy volatility, or more obviously lack of policy, can result in short-term asset mispricing and a reluctance to deploy capital. Policy and incentives are key drivers in many of the markets because many climate change investments, such as wind and solar, are not yet commercially viable on their own. This does vary by sector, however, and in some sectors large incentive support is not needed, even though market adoption is only just beginning.

In our 2010 report[2], we focused on quantitative returns and risks rather than

---
2 *Investing in Climate Change 2010 – A Strategic Asset Allocation Perspective.* Available at: www.dbcca.com/dbcca/EN/investment-research/investment_research_2253.jsp.

unpacking the constituents of risk by asset class. 2010 exhibited significant uncertainty in markets and climate change-related policies. Investor focus thus turned to looking at risk. This reflected a shift in institutional asset allocation trends towards a portfolio-level consideration of climate change[3]. The portfolio-level and investment process seeks to hedge climate 'impact' risk. A CIO or other investor can focus on how various climate change strategies can be added to a portfolio, its impact on hedging the climate impact risk as well as the portfolio-level risks such as diversification/correlation. In this section, we seek to evaluate the risks associated with climate change investing across the different asset classes and provide frameworks for investors to understand how asset managers manage those risks.

And while the above-mentioned risks certainly require management, the returns investors look for partly reflect the nature of the asset classes and are commensurate with the risks inherent in each. Despite recent volatility, the return potential for public equities can be significant and, since the end of 2006, clean-tech equities have outperformed the MSCI World, where investors are looking for secular movements in a variety of industries across the climate change universe. The private equity and venture capital asset class also continues to show opportunity for capital deployment and exit opportunities to strategic buyers and into the IPO market. More measured returns, yet with lower risk, will come from the infrastructure markets, where returns are in the low double digits, but have a more secure yield embedded into the return. Investors can seek out strong risk-adjusted returns from the climate change-tilted fixed income asset class, which can act as a hedge against further expansion of carbon markets. And, finally, investors can deploy a carbon overlay strategy using carbon offset credits to hedge their carbon price risk at a portfolio level.

In our recent paper, we analyse risk by climate change asset class and map it across three primary categories – economic/market risk, technology risk and climate policy risk. These pillars aggregate to produce a composite/price risk (Figure 2). The asset class's risk is then viewed quantitatively in conjunction with return potential at an asset class proxy or climate change public equity sub-sector level. Investors pursue asset allocation as a function of these two measures and seek to meet their individual investment goals at a portfolio level. Summaries of the asset class level findings are listed below.

BONDS
In the context of a climate change asset class, we view bonds as the application of a climate or carbon 'tilt' to a traditional fixed-income strategy. In this context, climate change bonds offer a relatively low-risk hedge on future carbon risk. The tilt seeks to identify either long or short opportunities that are positioned to be most impacted by future climate and carbon impacts on markets and companies. As a strategy, fixed income is inherently a risk-hedge approach.

---
3 See the recent report from Mercer Responsible Investment Consulting, *Climate Change Scenarios – Implications for Strategic Asset Allocation*, www.mercer.com/climatechange.

Figure 2. Overview of risk analysis by asset class for climate change strategies

	Market/ economic risk	Technology risk	Climate policy risk	Composite risk	Return potential
Fixed income: corporate	High	N/A	High	Low (Carbon tilt)	Low
Fixed income: government	High	N/A	Medium	Low (Carbon tilt)	Low
Public equities	High	Low/Medium/High	Low/Medium/High	High	Medium/High/Very High
Private equity/ venture capital	High/Medium	Low/High/Very High	Low/Medium/High	Very High	High/Very High
Infrastructure	Medium	Low	Low/High	Medium	Low/High

● Low ● Medium ● High ● Very High

*Source: DBCCA analysis, 2011

PUBLIC MARKETS

Climate change public equities are companies engaged in the mitigation of, or adaptation to, climate change and its effects, including cleaner energy, energy efficiency, agriculture and water. Climate change public equities are relatively high risk and are strongly exposed to economic/market risks. Investors can allocate to relatively higher or lower technology and policy risk positions, with renewable energy operators potentially representing less technology risk than a photovoltaic module manufacturer. Returns in the asset class have recently been affected by increased policy uncertainty and the scaling back of some incentives, although energy efficiency and agriculture have outperformed. Risks can be managed via policy knowledge and sector selection.

PRIVATE EQUITY/VENTURE CAPITAL

Climate change private equity/venture capital (PE/VC) investors seek to invest through the early-stage development of private companies. As such, the asset class is typically exposed to higher technology and business model risks at the earlier stage, which are somewhat moderated as companies move into the expansion stage of capital requirements. PE/VC offers potentially high returns, and as an asset class it has varying degrees of policy risk exposure. Investors can mitigate risk through sector selection and policy knowledge.

INFRASTRUCTURE

Climate change infrastructure strategies seek to invest at a project level in operating assets such as renewable energy or cleaner energy power plants. As an asset class, infrastructure has relatively low technology risk and offers investors the ability to 'lock in' policy after the financial close of an investment. The return profile of the asset class is based on steady long-term contracted cash flows (see Chapter 8).

Policy: key driver for cleaner energy

Investments in the renewable energy sector are frequently driven by government policy and so are subject to government policy risk. Transparent, long-lived and certain (TLC) policies provide the investor with the framework to mobilise capital (Figure 3). However, when policies lack TLC, increased risk to these investments ranges across asset classes.

In terms of policy momentum, we have tracked binding and accountable announcements from the Major Economies Forum (MEF) countries in a rigorous approach. This shows continued strong momentum on a global scale, with Europe overall a core backbone, China strong, the US federal level lagging, but key US states moving forward (Figure 4).

Figure 3. DBCCA's concept of TLC
Investors essentially look for three key drivers in policy

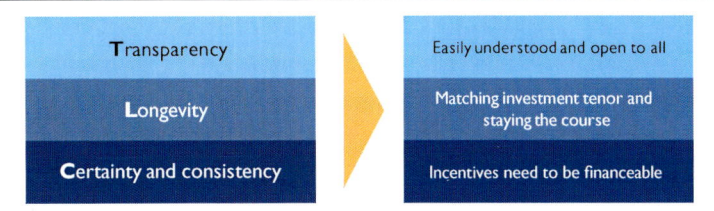

Transparency	Easily understood and open to all
Longevity	Matching investment tenor and staying the course
Certainty and consistency	Incentives need to be financeable

Source: DBCCA, Paying for Renewable Energy: TLC at the Right Price: Achieving Scale through Efficient Policy Design, 2009; DBCCA analysis

Figure 4. Cumulative policy momentum
Policy momentum is evident in many countries other than at US federal level

Net total binding and accountable climate policies tracked (December 2008–December 2010): 293

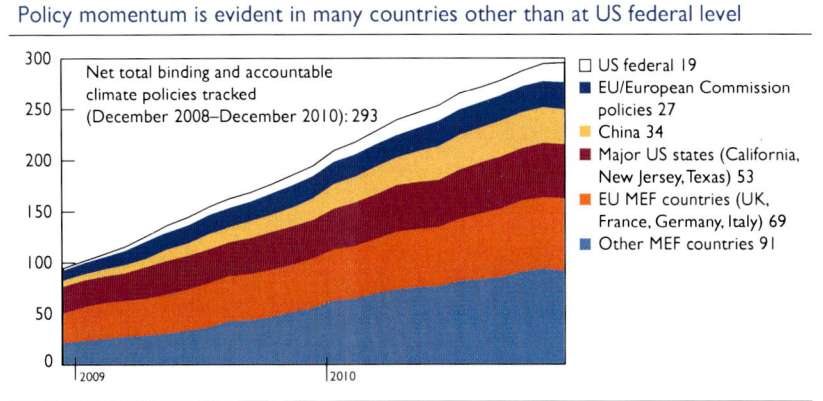

- US federal 19
- EU/European Commission policies 27
- China 34
- Major US states (California, New Jersey, Texas) 53
- EU MEF countries (UK, France, Germany, Italy) 69
- Other MEF countries 91

MEF = Major Economies Forum. Source: DBCCA, 2011

Chinese leadership: scale, scope and commitment

The number of national climate policies in China is twice as large as that of the US at the federal level. While China is a strong emerging policy leader in mitigating policy, it is the magnitude of its policies, especially its incentives and mandates, which are supported by investment and enabling legislation that are intended to drive changes to the Chinese power system (Figure 5). Some significant examples of China's ambitious policies are set out below:

THREE NATIONAL TARGETS ON NON-FOSSIL FUEL USE
- 15% renewables in primary energy consumption by 2020;
- 35–40% energy intensity reduction by 2015 from 2005 levels; and
- 40–45% carbon intensity reduction by 2020 from 2005 levels.

STRINGENT CAPACITY TARGETS BY SECTOR FOR 2020
- 27GW of biomass power, from 3GW today;
- 3GW of waste-to-energy power, from 1.5GW today;
- 20GW of solar PV power, from 300MW today; and
- 150GW of wind power, from 25.5GW today.

In 2009, China installed more wind capacity than any other country. Additionally, China is planning for substantial growth in nuclear generation resources, growing from about 11GW in place at the end of 2010 to an estimated 70–80GW by 2020. This significant increase, accounting for 5% of 2020 generation capacity, is contained within the 15% non-fossil fuel by 2020 target.

On the transportation front, China's Ministry of Science and Technology has

Figure 5. China's renewable energy policies

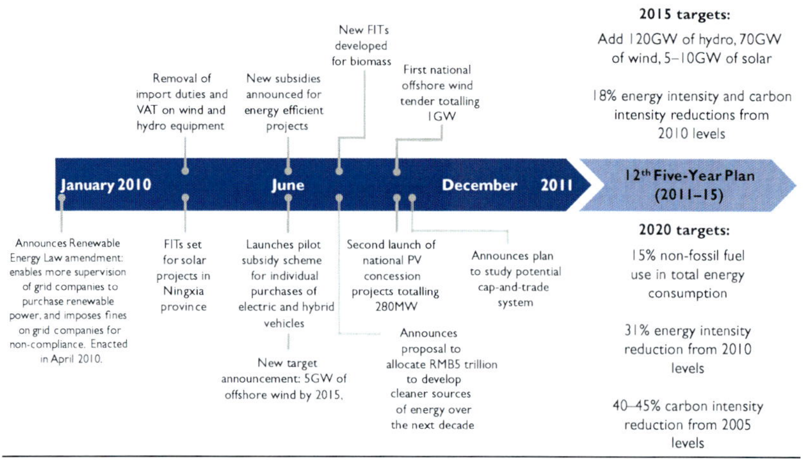

January 2010
- Announces Renewable Energy Law amendment: enables more supervision of grid companies to purchase renewable power, and imposes fines on grid companies for non-compliance. Enacted in April 2010.
- Removal of import duties and VAT on wind and hydro equipment
- FITs set for solar projects in Ningxia province
- New subsidies announced for energy efficient projects

June
- Launches pilot subsidy scheme for individual purchases of electric and hybrid vehicles
- New FITs developed for biomass
- New target announcement: 5GW of offshore wind by 2015.

December 2011
- Second launch of national PV concession projects totalling 280MW
- First national offshore wind tender totalling 1GW
- Announces plan to study potential cap-and-trade system
- Announces proposal to allocate RMB5 trillion to develop cleaner sources of energy over the next decade

12th Five-Year Plan (2011–15)

2015 targets:
- Add 120GW of hydro, 70GW of wind, 5–10GW of solar
- 18% energy intensity and carbon intensity reductions from 2010 levels

2020 targets:
- 15% non-fossil fuel use in total energy consumption
- 31% energy intensity reduction from 2010 levels
- 40–45% carbon intensity reduction from 2005 levels

Source: DBCCA analysis, 2011

suggested that approximately 1 million electric vehicles could be sold by 2020, out of an estimated 40 million new vehicles. To accommodate this, China is planning to have in place 10 million charging stations by 2020.

With the majority of the 1979–99 vintage housing stock in China deemed unsuitable for the future by the Ministry of Housing and Urban-Rural Development, China plans to demolish and rebuild that capacity over the next 20 years. This is in addition to the annual 2 million square metres of construction that is tied to basic economic expansion. With an emphasis on energy efficiency, many of the newly constructed buildings are likely to be proving grounds for all manner of green construction (and reclamation) techniques.

China's National Development and Reform Committee implemented a new feed-in tariff (FiT) programme for wind energy in 2009. Chinese wind energy FiTs are differentiated based on four wind energy zones (see Chapter 21). China is the first jurisdiction outside Europe to implement wind energy tariffs differentiated by geographic location.

In July 2010, the government announced a plan to allocate approximately RMB5 trillion ($738 billion) over the next decade to developing cleaner sources of energy, including nuclear and gas, to reduce emissions. China's 12th Five Year Plan, approved in March 2011, includes plans for multiple pilot implementations of carbon and emissions/pollutant market trading schemes and consideration of carbon taxes. Additionally, we expect to see a range of resource taxes and fees levied on industries that consume natural resources as primary inputs to their businesses. China expects to use the proceeds from the prospective taxes and fees to address environmental damage mitigation in certain provinces. The upshot of this will be higher costs for both energy and primary industry output, which could serve to narrow adverse cost differentials between traditional and cleaner energy sources.

The 12th Five Year Plan, introduced on 5 March 2011, includes many new and expanding strong policy initiatives and green targets – clear evidence that China's low-carbon policies remain global best-in-class. Some 33% of the targets in the 12th Five Year Plan address resource or environmental objectives.

US federal policy disappoints; investors rely on key states

The US exhibits less TLC than other countries in its policy framework at a federal level, as it still has a long way to go to demonstrate a comprehensive and stable regulatory framework (see our white paper for more details – see footnote 1). Nonetheless, policy action is being developed at the state level. California, Texas and New Jersey continue to lead the expansion and adoption of clean technologies within the US. These three states have the highest installed capacity in wind and solar. Policy development, particularly in California, has been a key driver of these markets.

We have tracked 54 net binding and accountable climate policies for California, New Jersey and Texas, almost three times greater than the number of policies

Figure 6. Annual installation of wind energy capacity in US
MW

Uncertainty over short-term policy frameworks has caused repeated fall-offs in growth of renewable energy capacity as support measures approach expiry

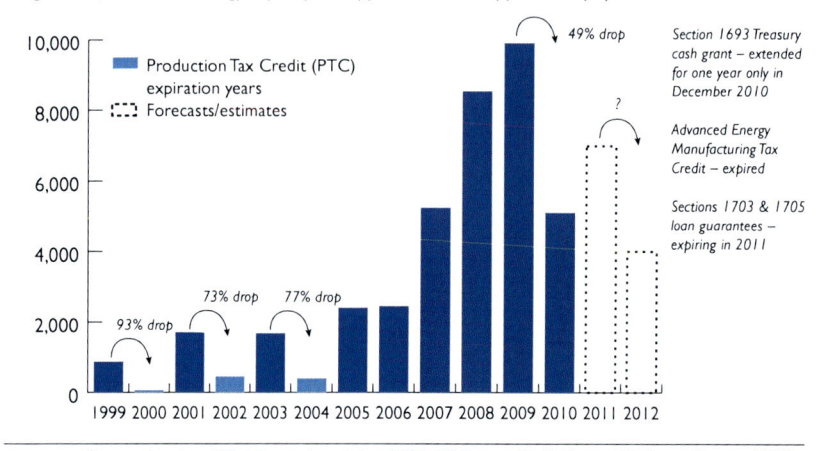

[Bar chart showing annual wind installations 1999-2012, with Production Tax Credit (PTC) expiration years highlighted. Drops noted: 93% drop (2000), 73% drop (2002), 77% drop (2004), 49% drop (2010). Annotations: Section 1693 Treasury cash grant – extended for one year only in December 2010; Advanced Energy Manufacturing Tax Credit – expired; Sections 1703 & 1705 loan guarantees – expiring in 2011]

Sources: American Wind Energy Association, 2009; US Partnership for Renewable Energy Finance, 2010; DBCCA Analysis, 2011

Figure 7. US market annual solar PV installations
MW

	2007	2008	2009	2010*	2011*	2012*	2013*
California	91.8	176.0	220.0	550.0	1,200.0	1,750.0	2,500.0
New Jersey	20.4	22.5	57.0	125.0	250.0	350.0	400.0
Florida	–	–	36.0	35.0	60.0	50.0	60.0
Colorado	12.0	22.0	23.0	30.0	60.0	75.0	100.0
Arizona	3.0	6.0	23.0	35.0	60.0	70.0	100.0
Hawaii	3.0	9.0	14.0	23.0	60.0	99.0	150.0
New York	4.0	7.0	12.0	19.0	31.0	52.0	86.0
Massachusetts	2.0	5.0	10.0	15.0	55.0	80.0	100.0
Connecticut	3.0	5.0	9.0	14.0	15.0	25.0	41.0
North Carolina	–	4.0	8.0	10.0	25.0	50.0	60.0
Nevada	16.0	15.0	2.0	6.0	15.0	20.0	50.0
Oregon	1.0	5.0	3.0	8.0	15.0	15.0	25.0
Texas	–	–	2.0	10.0	55.0	70.0	75.0
Pennsylvania	–	–	2.0	15.0	30.0	55.0	70.0
Others	7.0	16.0	25.0	54.0	254.0	349.0	237.0
Non-grid	60.0	64.0	40.0	50.0	40.0	40.0	40.0
Total	222.0	356.0	485.0	1,000.0	2,225.0	3,150.0	4,094.0

*Estimates. Numbers may not sum due to rounding. Source: Barclays Capital Research, Solar Energy Industries Association.

tracked for the US at the federal level. Some recent significant policies for these three states include:
- *California:* On 23 September 2010, the California Air Resources Board (ARB) unanimously adopted a Renewable Electricity Standard of 33% by 2020. In December, the ARB approved rules for a carbon market, which will limit greenhouse gas (GHG) emissions and set up a cap-and-trade scheme.
- *New Jersey:* The state has set a target to reduce GHG emissions by 80% from 2006 levels by 2050. In August 2010, New Jersey's governor signed into law the Offshore Wind Economic Development Act, which will create a programme that requires utilities to generate a percentage (still to be determined) of the power they sell in the state from offshore wind. The bill also created tax incentives for certain businesses engaged in manufacturing wind energy equipment.
- *Texas:* The state has enacted a mandate to produce 5,880MW of renewables by 2015 and 10,000MW by 2025. Texas's renewable energy is heavily dominated by wind installations – and thus not reflected in the data for solar PV installations shown in Figure 7.

Investment data shows that project investment in clean energy in the US is not as large and is not growing as fast as in other regions. It has rebounded from lows seen in 2009, but is outpaced by China and Europe (Figure 8). However, the US remains the primary area of focus for venture capital and expansion-stage private equity investors. Venture capital firms often invest in the US but seek to deploy clean technology globally to locations with policy regimes embodying stronger TLC.

Gas as a lower-emission transition fuel in the US

Given the start-stop nature of renewable energy deployment, a coal-to-natural gas fuel switch in the US would help to ensure a reliable electricity system that is not only much cleaner but also more environmentally sustainable. A significant switch by the US electricity sector from coal to natural gas-fired generation would be the most secure, least-cost approach to lower emissions. (On the basis of publicly available data, burning natural gas creates approximately half the amount of CO_2 compared with coal.) These reductions would be realised by using domestically abundant and secure sources of energy based on known technology that can easily be deployed at reasonable cost.

In a recent paper[4], we set out a pathway where coal's share of power generation decreases to 22% by 2030 compared to 47% in 2009, while the share of natural gas generation increases from 23% in 2009 to 35% (Figure 9). Wind and solar increase from 2% in 2009 to 14% in 2030. Renewables, natural gas and nuclear energy contribute 41%, 35% and 16%, respectively, to the reduction in power sector CO_2 emissions by 2030. Total electricity sector natural gas demand increases to 9.7 trillion cu-

---
4 DBCCA (November 2010), *Natural Gas and Renewables: A Secure Low-Carbon Future Energy Plan for the United States.* Available at: www.dbcca.com/dbcca/EN/investment-research/investment_research_2358.jsp.

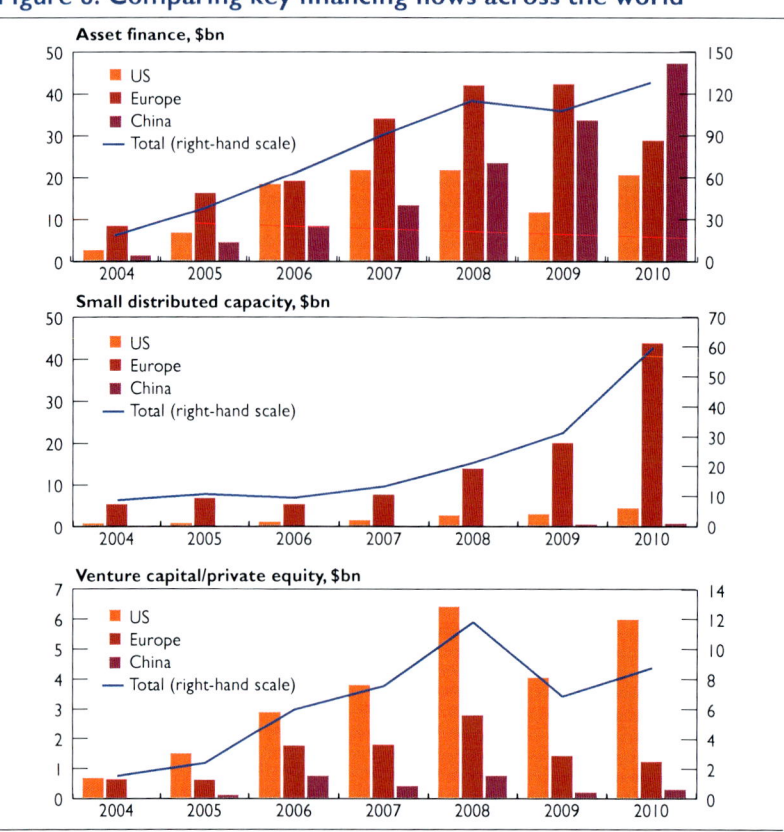

Figure 8. Comparing key financing flows across the world

Asset finance, $bn

Small distributed capacity, $bn

Venture capital/private equity, $bn

Source: Bloomberg New Energy Finance, 2011

bic feet (Tcf) per year in 2030 versus 6.9Tcf in 2009, a 2.8Tcf increase. US aggregate natural gas consumption increases to 27Tcf in 2030 compared to 22.6Tcf in 2009. Total electricity sector coal demand decreases from 930 million tons per year in 2009 to 460 million tons in 2030. We forecast total installed US renewable capacity to increase from 34.7GW in 2009 to 126GW in 2020 and 219GW in 2030. Transmission grid improvements need building out to accommodate renewables and are expected to total $41 billion through 2020 and will reach $158 billion by 2030. We expect that at least 32,000 miles of transmission lines will be built by 2020.

Capital investment in new gas-fired generation to replace the retiring coal fleet totals $39 billion between 2010 and 2030, resulting in 13,000MW of cumulative natural gas additions in the period 2010–20 and 20,500MW of cumulative additions over 2020–30.

Figure 9. DBCCA's US electricity supply mix forecast
% total kWh (except where otherwise stated)

	2005	2009	2020*	2030*	Comments
Coal (traditional)	50	47	34	21	Reduced to meet emissions target and comply with EPA regulation
Coal (CCS)	0	0	0	1	Limited deployment 2020–30 with government R&D support
Natural gas	19	23	30	35	Coal to gas fuel switch, underutilised assets, strong new build
Natural gas (CCS)	0	0	0	0	No deployment, assume that gas CCS is viable post 2030 and cheaper than coal
Petroleum	3	0	0	0	No additions; existing capital stock remains for reliability but hardly used
Nuclear	19	20	21	23	Modest gains from nuclear steam generation 'uprates', limited new builds
Wind and solar (intermittent)	0	2	9	14	Large capacity additions; transmission & dispatchability limit growth vs potential
Baseload renewables (geothermal & hydro)	7	8	6	6	Share decreases modestly as only very limited new builds
Total	100	100	100	100	
Renewables share (intermittent & baseload)	9	10	15	20	Doubling of share 2010–30 due to wind and solar additions to meet RPS
Electricity demand (kWh)	4,055	3,784	3,978	4,181	0.5% CAGR growth due to energy efficiency and operational improvements
CO_2 emissions (million tonnes)	2,397	2,200	1,691	1,347	Emissions reduced substantially due to coal–gas fuel switch and renewables build-up
% CO_2 emissions reduction vs 2005	–	–8	–29	–44	

*Estimates. Sources: EIA, DBCCA analysis, 2010.

Climate markets offer varied performance

Returns have varied significantly across asset class proxies, sectors and timeframes. Recent returns have been driven by policy headwinds and strong cross-asset correlation in the financial crisis. Private equity, venture capital and infrastructure represent proxies for the climate change asset classes, with expectations that actual climate asset returns have been and will be stronger, as seen in part by relevant IPOs, acquisitions and project-level internal rates of return. Clean energy has faced significant policy challenges, leading to recent underperformance in particular and high historical volatility. Energy efficiency has performed well in the public equity markets. It is a future area for project-level investment, and it requires less policy support than other climate sectors. Agriculture has performed strongly in public equity markets with the recent run-up in commodity pricing, and the long-term investment theme[5] persists (Figure 10).

---
5 Presented in DBCCA's 2009 paper, *Investing in Agriculture*. Available at: www.dbcca.com/dbcca/EN/investment-research/investment_research_1735.jsp.

184 | Investment Opportunities for a Low-Carbon World

Figure 10. Performance of climate-related markets

%	1 yr	2 yr	3 yr (annualised)	4 yr	4-yr volatility
Asset class proxies					
MSCI ACWI (Global Public Equities)	10.4	20.5	−6.4	−2.6	25
Infrastructure proxy	9.1	17.2	−5.2	0.2	23
Bonds proxy (Lehman Aggregate)	9.9	15.3	13.6	13.1	8
Private equity proxy (Cambridge Research)	6.0	−2.9	−0.4	7.2	13
Venture capital proxy (Cambridge Research)	1.1	−6.0	−2.5	3.1	9
Energy					
Crude oil (West Texas Intermediate)	15.1	43.1	−1.6	10.6	46
Natural gas (National Balancing Point)	75.9	2.1	6.7	24.6	63
Natural Gas (Henry Hub)	−27.4	−13.3	−16.1	−6.4	65
Climate public equity sectors					
DBCC (clean-tech public equities)	−8.3	17.2	−13.9	−0.1	36
Clean energy (public)	−24.3	3.6	−25.2	−4.1	47
Energy efficiency (public)	10.4	54.2	1.8	9.3	38
Waste management and water (public)	−3.1	11.8	−8.6	−2.3	25
Public agribusiness (DXAG Index)	22.2	41.4	−0.9	16.6	38

Sources: Bloomberg, 2011; DBCCA Analysis, 2011. Note: Four-year volatility refers to annualized standard deviation returns; performance is 31 Dec 2010; past performance is not a guarantee of future result

Clean energy public equities have a small-cap bias, and many feature capital intensive and cyclically exposed business models. The DB NASDAQ OMX Clean Tech Index (DBCC), a collaboration between DBCCA and NASDAQ OMX, is an accurate representation of the global clean-tech industry, covering clean energy, energy efficiency, transport, waste management and water. The price return clean-tech index has outperformed the MSCI World Index between the end of 2006 and the end of 2010 by 9.8% on an absolute basis; on an annualised basis, the DBCC returned −0.1% and the MSCI World returned −2.6%. There has been strong recent performance from the energy efficiency sector through the end of 2010. The water theme has returned a less volatile but more consistent and stable return, and clean energy has seen periods of strong outperformance and higher volatility (Figure 11).

Figure 11. The DB NASDAQ OMX Clean Tech Index (DBCC)
DBCC vs MSCI World, rebased to 31 December 2006

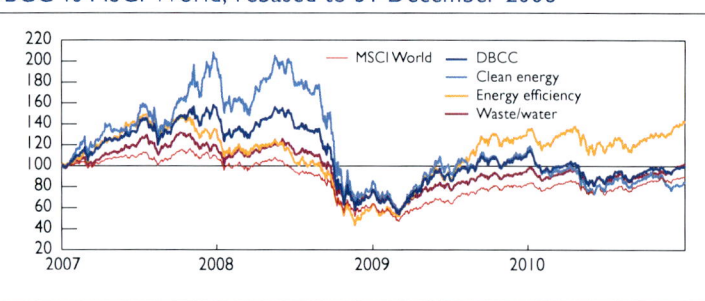

Source: DBCCA analysis 2011, Bloomberg 2011, NASDAQ OMX

Since the start of 2009, the relative bounce-back in some commodity and energy prices also contributed to the rebound off the bottom of the market, although natural gas prices remain depressed. During 2010 political uncertainty over government incentive programmes such as FiT revisions and sovereign credit fears initially placed negative downward pressure on the clean-tech theme. Policy uncertainty remains a key risk factor for the sector, but as our policy tracker work shows, there is still broad support globally.

Growth outlook for climate change sectors

AGRICULTURE
In addition to low-carbon technologies, the agriculture sector also requires additional support and investment. Agricultural production is growing much faster in developing countries, and key factors reinforce higher food demand and higher long-term prices for commodities.

The agriculture sector has experienced a number of shocks in recent years, with record high oil and commodity prices, food security fears and resultant trade restrictions, and the global economic downturn. While world net production of commodities will have grown 22% over the period to 2019, production in the OECD countries is projected to grow by only 10%.

For virtually all commodities, the projected growth to 2019 in imports and exports of developing countries exceeds that of the OECD countries. Only exports of processed protein meals increase faster in the OECD area by 2019. The UN Food and Agriculture Organization (FAO) estimates that an additional $67 billion of investment will be needed each year due to a lack of infrastructure for efficient farming.

WATER
Water demand remains one of the key sustainability challenges facing the world today. Key water investment opportunities fall into six main categories: clean water; conservation: reuse/recycle; waste management; energy mitigation; next-generation desalination; and storm water management.

Water stress can contribute to local or regional conflict. Also, there are huge water basins where large populations rely on a single watershed for their livelihood, such as the 1 billion-plus people living directly along the Ganges river watershed. This makes the water issue a unique potential tipping point.

China is expected to increase its water demand by 178 billion m^3 in industry, 300 billion m^3 in agriculture and 54 billion m^3 in the domestic sector by 2030, the highest projected demand growth globally.

As 71% of global water consumption, 3,100 billion m^3, is related to agriculture, the direct link between food and water is incredibly important and impacts almost all points of the economic value chain for both developing and developed societies.

Figure 12. Emerging investment opportunities in climate change sectors

Sector	Statistics/opportunities
AGRICULTURE	● World net production of commodities will grow 22% over the period to 2019. However production in the OECD is projected to grow only 10% over this period. ● The projected growth to 2019 in imports and exports of developing countries exceeds that of the OECD. *Source: OECD and FAO secretariats*
WATER	● China has the greatest increase in annual water demand between 2005 and 2030 at 532 billion m^3. This is followed by India (467 billion m^3), sub-Saharan Africa (440 billion m^3) and rest of Asia (440 billion m^3). Oceania has the lowest increase in annual water demand at 28 billion m^3. ● Agriculture continues to be the most water-intensive sector in seven of the nine primary world regions to 2030. For China and Europe the most intensive water-using sector is industry, with increases of 300 billion m^3 and 100 billion m^3 respectively. ● A total of $22.6 trillion of infrastructure development in the water sector is needed between 2005 and 2030 to modernise systems. Geographically, Asia/Oceania needs the most investment, comprising 40% of the total projected cumulative infrastructure investment needed. Europe and South America/Latin America will need 20% and 22% of infrastructure investment respectively. The lowest investment in water infrastructure spending between 2005 and 2030 will be in the Middle East and Africa (both 1%). *Sources: McKinsey & Company, Booz Allen Hamilton, Global Infrastructure Partners, WEO, OECD, Boeing, Drewry Shipping Consultants, US Department of Transportation*
ENERGY EFFICIENCY	● 53% of cumulative carbon abatement in the IEA's 450 Scenario between 2010 and 2035 comes from energy efficiency. This compares to 21% of abatement from renewables, 15% from carbon capture and storage technologies, 9% from nuclear and 3% from biofuels. *Source: International Energy Agency, World Energy Outlook, 2010*
WASTE-TO-ENERGY	● There are around 780 waste-to-energy facilities processing approximately 140 million tons a year worldwide. Around 50% of these plants are in operation in Western Europe (388), with 39% in Asia (301) and 11% in the US (87). *Source: Jefferies, March 2010*

Without efficiency gains, the level of water demand in the agricultural sector will increase to 4,500 billion m³ by 2030. The impacts of global climate change on local water availability are likely to exacerbate the problem in many countries. DB Research has estimated that the global investment required for the global water market is likely to total €400 billion–500 billion a year.[6] In addition to the challenge of an increasing physical demand for water, over the next 25 years, modernising and expanding water infrastructure systems of major cities of the world will require investments of around $22.6 trillion.

ENERGY EFFICIENCY

Energy efficiency is both the largest and least expensive energy resource. Demand-side energy efficiency measures offer the best near-term solution for carbon emissions reduction.

Energy efficiency measures could account for 53% of world energy-related CO_2 emission savings according to the International Energy Agency's 450 Scenario relative to the Current Policies Scenario.

According to a PNAS[7] study, direct energy use by households accounts for around 38% of overall US CO_2 emissions and is larger than the emissions of any entire country except China. An astounding 34% of the energy consumed in buildings is lost directly through building envelopes.

With the majority of the 1979–99 vintage housing stock in China deemed unsuitable for the future by the Ministry of Housing and Urban-Rural Development, China plans to demolish and rebuild that capacity over the next 20 years.

Energy efficiency in the US has the potential to reduce annual non-transport energy consumption by approximately 23% by 2020, according to McKinsey & Company's analysis. Cumulatively, the total investment in the new energy efficiency technology infrastructure would reach $7 trillion over the period 2008–30, according to the IEA's *World Economic Outlook*, 2009. The IEA believes that $2 trillion could be spent globally between 2010 and 2020 on end-use energy efficiency and power plant efficiency measures.

The challenge for policy-makers, business leaders and nations is to implement energy policies and fashion new financing mechanisms to unlock this underutilised energy efficiency opportunity. Energy efficiency retrofits in commercial buildings represent a $400 billion market opportunity in the US.

WASTE-TO-ENERGY

Waste-to-energy sectors are poised for strong growth internationally. Global de-

---

6 DB Research (1 June 2010), *World Water Markets*. Available at: www.dbresearch.com/PROD/DBR_INTERNET_EN-PROD/PROD0000000000258353.pdf.
7 PNAS (2009), 'Household actions can provide a behavioral wedge to rapidly reduce US carbon emissions', Available at: www.pnas.org/content/106/44/18452.full.pdf.

Figure 12. Technologies by sector to increase energy efficiency

Sector	Technologies	Potential barriers
RESIDENTIAL	Efficient HVAC, water heating, lighting and appliances; building/pipe insulation; smart meters; programmable thermostats; efficient windows.	● Low awareness of cost benefit ● Ownership issues ● Information deficiency ● Irrational decision-making ● Lack of long-term policy development
COMMERCIAL	Efficient HVAC, water heating and refrigeration; lighting controls; water temperature reset; energy management systems: CHP	● Low awareness of cost benefi ● Ownership issues ● Changing corporate strategies ● Lack of fiscal incentives ● Lack of long-term policy development
INDUSTRIAL	Process improvements; high-efficiency motors; insulation; efficient HVAC, water heating and lighting; variable-speed drives	● System inertia ● Capital stock turnover ● Inflexible labour market
TRANSPORT	Improved aerodynamics; advanced low resistance tyres; advanced combustion engines; lithium-ion batteries, hybrid vehicles	● Habit ● Irrational decision-making ● Lack of fiscal incentives

Source: DBCCA analysis, 2011

mand for waste-to-energy is expected to increase as solid waste generation continues to increase, landfill capacity decreases and energy costs rise. Strong growth will be seen internationally, specifically in Europe and Asia, with moderate growth in the US.

The waste-to-energy sector is driven by global population expansion, which leads to increased landfill use. The growth of landfill use is garnering awareness and support over alternatives such as waste-to-energy, especially in heavily populated areas.

The GET FiT programme

In the run-up to and following the Cancún climate change summit in December 2010, global policy-makers recognised the need for a more in-depth dialogue to explore how public and private sector funds could most effectively deliver support to renewable energy scale-up and energy access in developing countries.

Direct financial support and risk mitigation strategies can create the financial conditions necessary to attract domestic and international capital. In developing countries, however, renewable energy projects can also face an array of non-financial challenges.

The Global Energy Transfer Feed-in Tariffs (GET FiT) programme seeks to address the challenges by coordinating existing resources in the energy sector and directly involving domestic players in the development of renewable energy expertise and capacity.

GET FiT is a concept to support both renewable energy scale-up and energy access in the developing world through the creation of new international public-private partnerships, with the public partner implementing a strong and transparent regulatory environment and funding for the renewable premium while the private sector deploys capital to fund the projects, as well as using concessional and loan guarantee financing, particularly in hybrid structures:

- GET FiT identifies the key public sector financing instruments, outlines their potential impacts both quantitatively and qualitatively, discusses their constraints and availability, and considers the potential for hybrid public sector approaches.
- GET FiT recognises the need to establish an enabling environment for renewable energy technologies and the key role that technical assistance plays in supporting developing country governments' efforts to create such an environment.
- GET FiT ensures a maximum incentive capture at least cost to the funding partners. Importantly, it provides what is crucial for private investors – transparency, longevity and certainty (TLC).

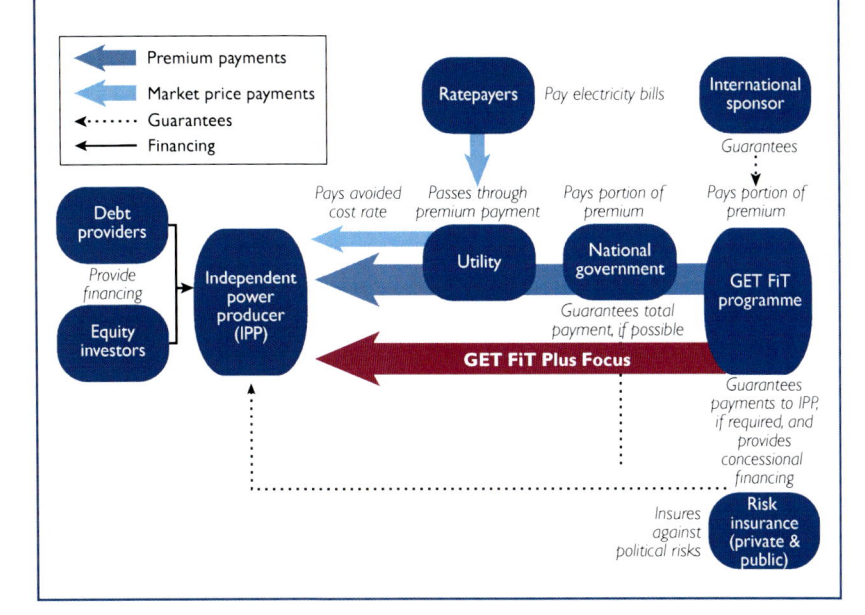

Section 2

Investment Approaches, Products and Markets

Chapter 12

Environmental technologies within strategic asset allocation

Dr Danyelle Guyatt, Catholic Super; Laureen Bird, Mercer

Introduction
Climate change was described by Nicholas Stern as 'the greatest market failure the world has seen'.[1] Despite this, relatively little research to date has focused on the investment implications of climate change at the total portfolio level, and how institutional investors might respond.

Uncertainty is a key stumbling block in climate change research. Every link in the chain of man-made greenhouse gas emissions, physical changes in the climate system and their socio-economic impacts is highly uncertain. Therefore, investors cannot simply rely on a best guess as to how the future will unfold when planning their investments.

In this context, deep uncertainty implies that probabilities cannot be assigned to future states with high confidence. This calls into question the appropriateness of relying too heavily on quantitative modelling tools, for which investors must specify probability distributions to underpin the parameters of investment models.

Institutional investors must develop new tools to model systemic risks such as climate change more effectively. These tools require an expansion of the way portfolio risk is thought about to extend beyond mere volatility. Describing probable scenarios, identifying the potential sources of risks, measuring and monitoring them over time are the components of an improved risk management strategy that seeks to protect the long-term assets that institutional investors oversee on behalf of their stakeholders.

This chapter looks at the implications of climate change for strategic asset allocation (SAA) and the potential impact on investment in low-carbon technologies and services. The box on the next page summarises the role of SAA in the institutional investment management process.

Asset allocation methodologies and climate risks
Traditional modelling approaches do not adequately capture the nature of the economic transformation process and the potential source of risks associated with cli-

---
1 Nicholas Stern (2007), *The Economic of Climate Change. The Stern Review*. Cambridge University Press.

mate change. To address this inadequacy, the tools to integrate climate risk into the way we think about SAA must be expanded to reflect the following:

- *Embed climate risk into asset allocation processes:* Climate change can have a significant impact on the performance of a portfolio mix over the long term, with the primary source of risk resulting from uncertainty about climate policy and its associated adjustment costs. Mercer's research shows that for most asset classes the impact of climate change varies significantly across its four proposed

Systemic risk and the role of strategic asset allocation

Strategic asset allocation (SAA) can be broadly defined as the use of optimisation tools by asset owners to determine asset allocation benchmarks to achieve their long-term risk and return objectives. The objectives vary depending on the type of asset owner and its obligations to beneficiaries or other stakeholders. For example, the objective may be to generate sufficient returns to hedge liabilities, to protect a reserve pool of assets while minimising risk and maximising return, to minimise variations in contribution for sponsors, or to target a certain funding level.

SAA involves making decisions around allocation to high-level asset classes – ie, equity/fixed income split, domestic/international/emerging equity split, duration of fixed income, and the split between nominal and inflation-adjusted fixed income, allocation to unlisted assets and sustainability themed assets. This is distinct from other considerations such as portfolio structuring (including allocation to capital weightings, styles, sectors, and includes active/passive analysis) and manager selection (the evaluation of manager performance in order to select one suitable for a client's requirements).

Visually, the distinction between SAA decisions and other investment decisions is shown below.

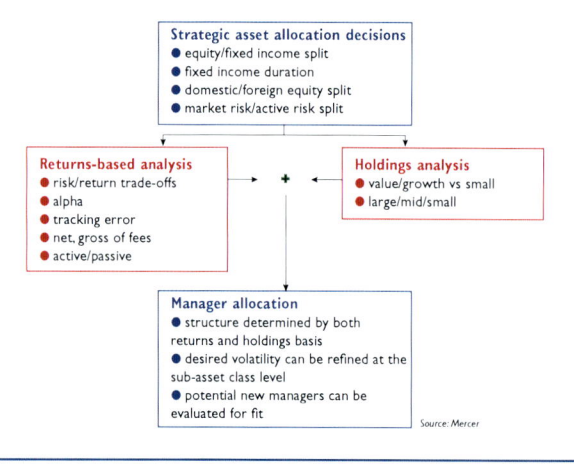

Strategic asset allocation decisions
- equity/fixed income split
- fixed income duration
- domestic/foreign equity split
- market risk/active risk split

Returns-based analysis
- risk/return trade-offs
- alpha
- tracking error
- net, gross of fees
- active/passive

Holdings analysis
- value/growth vs small
- large/mid/small

Manager allocation
- structure determined by both returns and holdings basis
- desired volatility can be refined at the sub-asset class level
- potential new managers can be evaluated for fit

Source: Mercer

scenarios, contributing as much as 10% to portfolio risk for a representative asset mix. This highlights the need for a clear climate policy framework as well as ongoing analysis to build these risks into asset allocation models.
- *Look beyond macroeconomic impacts:* Analysis by Grantham LSE/Vivid Economics demonstrates that the potential impact of climate change on GDP, interest rates and inflation magnifies beyond 2050. However, until that time, climate change will not be the driving force behind investment risks. Additional analysis

---

SAA is a key component of the portfolio management process, with academic research estimating SAA attributes more than 90% of the variation in portfolio returns over time.[1] When considered just in terms of contribution to returns, SAA dominates other factors such as market timing and security selection.

However, it is also important to consider the risks that may impact on an institutional investor's ability to meet its long-term objectives. Potential sources of risk may come from changing macroeconomic conditions such as interest rates, inflation or GDP growth, or changing market conditions such as volatility or illiquidity. Both sides of the risk and return coin are therefore essential for building a robust approach to SAA.

Despite the seeming importance of SAA decisions and the need to encompass the potential source of risks and return, in reality, many institutional investors allocate a much larger component of their resources, time and risk budget to bottom-up considerations (market timing and security selection) than to SAA decisions.

An additional consideration is what climate change might mean for the underlying determinants of asset class risk, return and overall market risk. Bottom up analysis may not in itself be sufficient to reveal market shortcomings in the pricing of systemic risks ahead of time, which potentially leaves institutional investors exposed to unexpected adjustment costs from large-scale events, as the global financial crisis has reminded us.

It is therefore prudent for institutional investors to work towards building in potentially large scale systemic risks, such as climate change, into risk management and SAA decision-making processes ahead of time to the extent possible.[2] This requires the development of a framework to unravel the uncertainties around climate change, combining both top-down and bottom-up tools and processes.

---

[1] See, for example, Brinson *et al* (1986); Grinblatt and Titman (1989); Brinson *et al* (1991); Blake *et al* (1999); and Ibbotson and Kaplan (2000).
[2] See 'Beyond the credit crisis: The role of pension funds in moving to a more sustainable capital market' (2009). www.mercer.com/referencecontent.htm?idContent=1332305.

was undertaken by Mercer to determine the source of investment risk in the interim – ie, over the next 20–30 years – and concluded that the material investment risks associated with climate change will result from increased uncertainty around new technology, physical impacts and climate policy.

- *Think about diversification across sources of risk:* To varying degrees, traditional asset allocation techniques optimise portfolio exposure based on assumptions about the risk, return and correlation between asset classes where diversification across assets is sought. An additional tool for this analytic approach is to think of SAA in terms of diversifying across sources of risk, rather than via asset classes *per se*. This means utilising a factor risk approach to supplement asset allocation decision-making.
- *Be more forward-looking:* Climate change requires forward-looking analysis and cannot rely on the traditional technique of modelling historical asset class relationships. This means utilising tools such as scenario analysis.
- *Go beyond quantitative analysis:* Qualitative factors need to be embedded into the decision-making process. SAA decision-making processes rely heavily on quantitative analysis, whereas much of the investment risk around climate change requires the exercise of judgement about how things might develop in terms of the science of climate change, the policy-makers' response and the types of technologies that may or may not prosper.
- *Review assumptions regarding market risk:* Past periods of economic transformation have been associated with a significant change in the realised equity risk premium (ERP)[2] over time, ranging from destructive wartime periods to positive periods of substantial efficiency improvements arising from a growing service sector and innovations in IT. Assumptions regarding the ERP should therefore be reviewed in light of the potential impacts of climate change on the process of economic transformation that may occur in the transition to a low-carbon global economy.

Low-carbon technology, policy and impacts as a SAA tool

The lack of cohesion between SAA and current traditional modelling frameworks led Mercer to develop an assessment framework to analyse the contributing risk factors associated with climate change. Climate change factors have thus far been ignored in part due to the extended time horizon of its implications; typical strategic investment decisions tend to be set with a 10-year-plus horizon in mind. To capture the economic implications associated with climate change, investors must address the following key questions:

- What are the investment risks and climate change issues that must be taken into account as part of the strategic decision-making processes?

---

2 Broadly defined, the ERP represents the compensation for taking on equity risk versus a risk-free rate.

- What impact could climate change have on different asset classes and regions?
- What actions can be taken?
- What are the messages for climate policy-makers?

CLIMATE RISK FRAMEWORK

To establish an assessment model incorporating climate risk into SAA, a framework was built on the following three elements:

- Determination of factors to represent the investment impacts of climate change and the consequent linking of these factors to the key drivers of different asset returns.
- Developing different scenarios and an understanding of how climate change and asset classes may respond in each hypothetical scenario.
- Building a simple quantitative framework to test the relationships established in the factor analysis and to decide whether any action is appropriate.
- The framework is intended to help investors gain additional insight into the risks within their current investment policy and decide how best to manage the added risks arising from climate change.

DETERMINATION OF INVESTMENT IMPACTS

Mercer's analysis determined that the three highest contributors of climate risk over the next 20–30 years result from uncertainty about new low-carbon technology, physical climate impacts and climate policy. Specifically, the three areas refer to the following:

- *Technology (T):* broadly defined as the rate of progress and investment flows into technology related to low carbon and efficiency which are expected to provide investment gains;
- *Impacts (I):* the extent to which changes to the physical environment will impact (negatively) on investments; and
- *Policy (P):* the cost of climate policy in terms of the change in the cost of carbon and emissions levels that result from policy depending on the extent to which it is coordinated, transparent and timely.

DEVELOPING DIFFERENT CLIMATE SCENARIOS

In considering how climate change might have an impact on a portfolio's asset mix in the specified time horizon, four scenarios were developed. The scenarios do not represent a forecast of the future and should not be interpreted in a probabilistic way, but rather they provide a framework for considering the key climate change drivers from an investment perspective over the coming decades.

Regional divergence

Some regions demonstrate strong leadership in responding to the need to reduce emissions and act locally with policy mechanisms ranging from market-based to regulatory solutions (EU and China/East Asia). Other regions fail to respond and continue to emit high levels of carbon (Russia), while others fall somewhere in the middle, with local initiatives and measures associated with high policy implementation risk (US, India/South Asia and Japan). Overall, this scenario involves a high degree of economic transformation and investment in some regions, but the level of uncertainty increases for investors due to the disparate nature of the policy response across the different regions, increasing market volatility.

Delayed action
Business as usual continues until 2020, when rapid policy measures are introduced that lead to significant shifts in behaviour resulting in the dramatic increase in cost of fossil fuel usage (such as a global carbon tax) resulting in a rapid reduction of emissions. There is a high degree of economic transformation led by public sector regulation rather than private sector innovation; this will necessitate relatively high levels of adjustment costs to comply with the new regulations. After the introduction of regulatory changes, the level of uncertainty regarding climate policy will decline, creating a stronger investment backdrop.

Stern action
This scenario has been named to reflect the policy response advocated by Nicholas Stern, author of the Stern Review. It is the most aggressive scenario in terms of policy response and private sector innovation. Under this scenario there will be swift agreement to a global framework and a very high level of coordination in policy efforts internationally, resulting in a high degree of economic transformation globally with new investment opportunities arising as well as risks. The uncertainties are lower than for the other scenarios, due to the ability to predict the development of policy with a reasonable degree of confidence as policies are implemented in a transparent and orderly manner internationally. There will be a higher economic cost associated with this scenario to achieve the level of abatement in emissions; however, the GDP impact is expected to be secondary in driving asset class returns within the 20–30-year time horizon. Less uncertainty for investors about climate policy and new technology investments will be the major drivers of positive transformation.

Climate breakdown
The *status quo* prevails in terms of policy, business and consumer behaviour. With continued reliance on fossil fuels, carbon emissions remain high and there is little economic transformation. The investment impacts are hard to predict, although the risk of catastrophic climate-related events increases significantly over time, reaching critical levels toward the end of this century. This scenario brings very high potential risks for investors over the long term, particularly for regions, assets and sectors that are most sensitive to the physical impacts of climate change.

Figure 1. Key features and potential outcomes of the climate scenarios to 2030

Scenario	Global policy response	Carbon cost (in 2030)	Emissions levels (now to 2030)
Regional divergence *Most likely*	Divergent and unpredictable Framework agreed to succeed Kyoto Protocol Targets announced of medium ambition	$110/t CO_2e in all countries studied (EU, US, China/East Asia and Japan), except India/South Asia and Russia	50Gt CO_2e/year in 2030 (equivalent to –20% from BAU)
Delayed action *Close second in likelihood*	Late and led by hard policy measures Strong mitigation, but only after 2020 when sudden drive by major emitting nations results in hasty agreement Very little support for vulnerable regions on adaptation	$15/t CO_2e to 2020 then dramatic rise to $220 globally (not unanticipated by the market)	40Gt CO_2e/year in 2030 (equivalent to –40% from BAU)
Stern action *Much less likely*	Strong, transparent and internationally coordinated action Generous support to vulnerable regions for adaptation	$110/t CO_2e globally (anticipated by the market)	30Gt CO_2e/year in 2030 (equivalent to –50% from BAU)
Climate breakdown *Least likely*	Business as usual No mitigation beyond current efforts Very little support to vulnerable regions for adaptation	$15/t CO_2e limited to the EU ETS, regional schemes and implicit cost of carbon estimates	63Gt CO_2e/year in 2030 (equivalent to BAU)

BAU = business as usual. Source: Grantham Research Institute LSE/Vivid Economics

Building a simple quantitative framework

Following the identification of the main contributing factors of investment impacts caused by climate change and the creation of the varying climate change scenarios, a simple quantitative framework was constructed. The consequent 'TIP' risk factor framework (see Figure 2) allows the examination of the factors driving asset class returns within the three identified areas.

The model reflects that the factors are interdependent, and that each factor needs to be considered to reflect future asset performance accurately.

Sensitivity of assets to investment risks

Research was undertaken to assess the sensitivity of each asset class to climate change under each of the four climate scenarios. The sensitivity of each asset class to the different sources of investment risk is presented in Figure 3, where the asset classes are located according to whether they have a high or very high sensitivity to each source of risk. Some of these risks can be quantified, such as the equity risk premium and volatility. However, some risks cannot be quantified but are still important to consider as part of the risks associated with an investment strategy[3].

Highlights from Figure 3:
- Listed equities, government bonds and investment grade credit all have a high sensitivity to fundamental risk factors but not to climate change factors.

Figure 2. TIP framework

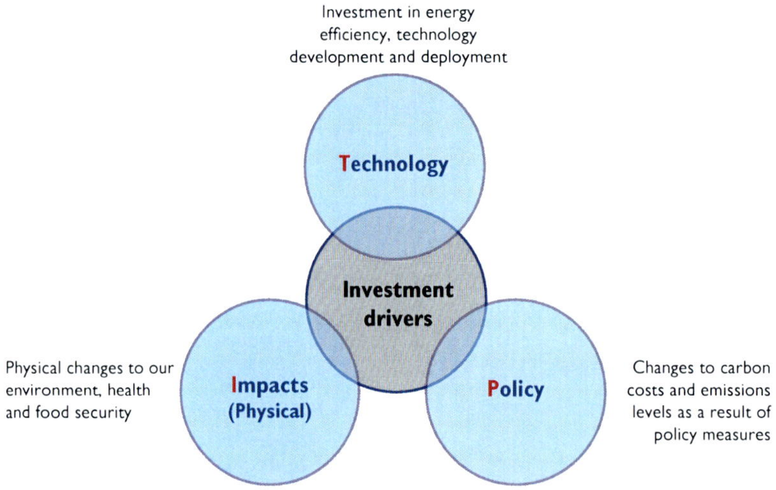

Source: Mercer

---

3 See 'Diversification: A look at factor risks', www.mercer.com/summary.htm?idContent=1378620.

Figure 3. Assets with 'high' or 'very high' sensitivity to investment risks

Fundamental factors	Market factors	Climate change factors
Economic cycle	*Equity risk premium*	*Technology*
Inflation	*Volatility*	*Impact*
		Policy
Listed equities	Listed equities	Real estate
Emerging equities	Private equity	Infrastructure
Government bonds	Infrastructure	Private equity
Emerging debt	Real estate	Sustainable equities
Investment grade credit		Efficiency/renewables
Commodities		Commodities

Source: Mercer

- In contrast, real estate, infrastructure, private equity, sustainable equities, efficiency/renewables and commodities are highly sensitive to climate change factors.

To put it simply, this means that portfolios that are dominated by listed equities and bonds may not be as sensitive to climate change, which may be a positive outcome under a 'no mitigation' scenario such as climate breakdown (which is also the least likely scenario). For all other scenarios where some degree of mitigation will occur, portfolios with a low allocation to assets that are sensitive to climate change may be less resilient in terms of both the risks and opportunities.

A broad overview of the investment impact based on the scenario deemed most likely, regional divergence, is provided in Figure 4.

Figure 4. Sensitivities of asset classes to TIP factor risks (regional divergence scenario)

Asset class	Sensitivity
EQUITY	
Global equities	Low

Risk of increased uncertainty and volatility due to regional disparity on climate policy. Regional differences within major sectors will become exaggerated, where carbon-intensive industries in countries with carbon constraints will become less competitive relative to companies in countries without carbon constraints. Multinational companies may find the cost of operating across borders increasing due to a higher cost of complying with different national policies.

Emerging market equities	*Moderate*

Higher volatility in emerging market equities is likely. A gap will open between emerging market countries that have the capacity and willingness to grow as low-carbon economies versus those not as able or willing to adapt. Current evidence suggests emerging economies positioned to lead in this scenario include China/East Asia, South Korea, Brazil, Mexico, South Africa and India/South Asia.

Figure 4 (continued)

Asset class	Sensitivity
EQUITY *(continued)*	
Broad sustainability-themed	*High*

A broadly positive environment, with sporadic policy encouraging some industries in some regions to grow strongly. Sustainability-themed investments stand to benefit in the leading regions, but those in the 'wrong' regions or sectors will suffer more than traditional equity portfolios. Policy and technology will be the dominant driver of new opportunities, driven by cost/efficiency savings as well as expectation of further policy advances.

Renewables	*Very high*

Similar to broad sustainability-themed equities. Very high sensitivity to the climate risk factors means that supportive climate policy will attract investment in renewable energy to leading regions. The most supportive policies for renewable energy currently include parts of Europe – particularly Scandinavia, France, Germany, Spain and the UK – and Brazil.

FIXED INCOME	
Global fixed income	*Low*

Governments with a proactive approach to climate policy could issue more debt to finance spending on programmes to shift to a low-carbon economy. These may be hypothecated financing instruments (such as green bonds). Countries (eg, Russia, Canada, the US, Australia) heavily dependent on high-emitting sectors that lag in terms of climate change policy may attract a higher country risk premium.

Emerging market debt	*Moderate*

The market and/or credit rating agencies may attach a higher risk premium to some emerging debt issuers that are lagging in terms of climate policy response (eg, Russia) and/or are more vulnerable to the physical impacts of climate change (such as India/South Asia, Africa and parts of China/East Asia).

Investment grade debt	*Low*

Credit rating agencies may begin to factor in future climate risks, which would exaggerate the differences between leading and laggard companies in terms of the sectors they operate in, including fossil-fuel industries (coal mining, crude oil and gas extraction, petroleum refining, gas utilities) and carbon-intensive primary and manufacturing industries, including mining and chemicals.

PRIVATE EQUITY	
Leveraged buyout	*Moderate*

The transformation that will take place in some regions that implement climate policy and invest in technology will be significant, with LBO activity expected to increase as the economies in those regions shift from high- to low-carbon industries. The economies likely to experience the greatest shift in this transformation are high-emitting nations that implement policy measures; at present this could include the EU, China/East Asia, the UK, states within the US and Japan.

Venture capital	*High*

As for LBO, with the key difference being a very high opportunity related to technology in some regions. Countries with highest expenditure on low-carbon solutions and deepest VC markets include the EU, the US, China/East Asia, Japan, the UK and parts of Latin America (Brazil and Mexico).

VC renewable energy	*Very high*

Renewable investments may be highly sensitive to the climate policy variability by countries. The regions with the most supportive policies for renewable energy and the deepest investment markets based on the current policy environment and clean energy markets include parts of Europe – particularly Scandinavia, France, Germany, Spain and the UK – China/East Asia, and states within the US, Brazil, India/South Asia and Japan.

INFRASTRUCTURE	
Core – unlisted	*High*
This scenario produces some new opportunities for infrastructure but it increases volatility due to political and regulatory uncertainty over which regions will lead and lag. Replacement of existing infrastructure will generally be highest in developed economies where stock is old, unsuitable for climate change and unsustainable from an energy efficiency perspective. Investment in new infrastructure that is geared towards low carbon and adaptation to climate change will be stronger in the fast-growing developing economies, including China/East Asia, Brazil, Mexico and South Korea.	
Renewable – unlisted	*High*
The high sensitivity to the climate factors means that investments may be highly sensitive to climate policy variation by countries. The North American market is focusing on smart grid and technology solutions to improve efficiency of delivery rather than adaptation of infrastructure assets. Electrification of vehicles and recharge solutions may also attract investments. The UK and Europe are leading on the development and deployment of many renewables and decentralisation of electricity generation. The regions with greatest need for water storage and desalination include those facing water shortages as population growth and changing climate conditions reduce availability. The studies suggest this will be in the Middle East and North Africa, central America, southern US, southern Africa and southern Australia.	

REAL ESTATE	
Core – unlisted	*High*
It will be important to consider climate change preparedness and vulnerability at the regional level when considering real estate investments. Those regions that are most at risk from the physical impact of climate change will attract a higher risk premium under the less internationally coordinated emission reduction outcome as it increases future impact risks. Efficiency in buildings and appliances will be where most opportunities exist. In China/East Asia, measures to promote the uptake of more efficient air conditioning may present opportunities. Within the OECD, opportunities will be primarily in more efficient heating and cooling systems and appliances from retro-fitting rather than new build (in particular installing better insulation to reduce heating and cooling needs).	

COMMODITIES	
Agricultural land	*High*
This scenario is neutral overall for timberland assets, although some regions are leading in promoting sustainable forestry and alignment with the REDD and REDD+ frameworks. Some examples of adaptation finance include the Forest Carbon Management programme in Canada, the California Climate Action registry in the US, Brazil's Amazon Fund, the Congo Basin Forest Fund and funds under the International Climate and Forest Initiative supported by countries such as Australia and Norway.[1]	
Timberland	*High*
Agricultural prices are expected to rise by around 30% under this scenario due to climate change[2], which is not dissimilar to the other scenarios out to 2030. The regional differences become magnified beyond 2050 with an increase in global unrest and geopolitical risk due to food shortages. There are substantial increases in the risk of hunger among the poorest countries,[3] especially in Sub-Saharan Africa and South Asia, where a large portion of the population depends on agriculture, and where capacities at the national and farm levels to adapt to climate change are lowest.	
Carbon	*Very high*
This scenario is neutral overall for carbon, with the participating regions leading to a rise in the price of carbon to as high as $110/t CO_2e (for participating regions and industries only). By 2020, there will still be different carbon prices in different trading schemes and other non-market mechanisms that are utilised. In most cases, the carbon emission permits are allocated free to emitters; by 2030, there will be linked trading schemes with increasing coverage of global emissions.	

Source: Mercer, drawing from various sources as referenced:
1 For further details, see www.forumforthefuture.org/files/Appendix_FIR.pdf;
2 Grantham LSE/Vivid Economics estimates; 3 Parry et al (2004).

Figure 5. Impact of scenarios on source of investment risks

Scenario	Fundamental factors — Economic cycle / Inflation	Market factors — Equity risk premium / Volatility	Climate change factors — Technology	Impact	Policy
Regional divergence	Unchanged	Higher volatility	High dispersion of capital inflow into low-carbon investments. Leading countries include the EU and China	Higher risk of future impact costs due to slower reduction in emissions	Higher uncertainty and potentially higher reward for some assets due to regional disparity in climate policy
Delayed action	Higher inflation / Higher interest rates	Higher volatility / Lower realised ERP	Business-as-usual investment in low carbon until 2020 when policy measures stimulate flows	Higher risk of future impact costs due to delay in policy response	Higher uncertainty around policy until 2020, then dramatic u-turn reduces policy uncertainty
Stern action	Unchanged	Lower volatility / Higher realised ERP	Clarity on climate policy stimulates strong capital flows into low-carbon solutions	Lower risk of future impact costs due to reduction in emissions	Policy clarity at the global level reduces investment uncertainty
Climate breakdown	Unchanged	Unchanged, risk of higher volatility	Higher risk attached to low-carbon technology investments due to policy inaction	Higher impact risks due to lack of policy action, rising future costs and market pricing in future policy shift	Business-as-usual climate policy (unchanged from today's measures)

Source: Mercer

Impacts on low-carbon technology investments

A representative portfolio mix was analysed using the framework against each of the four climate scenarios. The key highlights of the research are detailed below:

- *Climate change increases investment risk:* Climate change increases the uncertainty and event risk that could impact on the realised returns for risky assets across the scenarios, with higher risk resulting from inefficient policy (see Figure 5).
- *Low-carbon technology investments could accumulate to $5 trillion by 2030:* The private sector response to changing environmental conditions, new technology and policy measures may produce a substantial number of new investment opportunities. Figure 6 shows the shift in energy demand and supply under Stern action. About two-thirds of the shift is attributable to lower overall energy demand, primarily due to improvements in energy efficiency, while the remaining third results from supply-side changes. Mercer estimates based on International Energy Agency (IEA) data suggest that additional cumulative investment in efficiency improvements, renewable energy, biofuels, nuclear and carbon capture and storage could expand in the range of $3 trillion to $5 trillion by 2030. This presents meaningful opportunities to investors in these investment areas that are still in their infant stages.
- *Infrastructure, private equity, real estate and some commodities are highly sensitive to climate change:* The results of the asset-class impacts are summarised in Figure 7, where the overall sensitivity of each asset class to the climate-change

Figure 6. Renewables and nuclear overtake fossil fuels in Stern Action scenario by 2050
Energy supply (EJ)

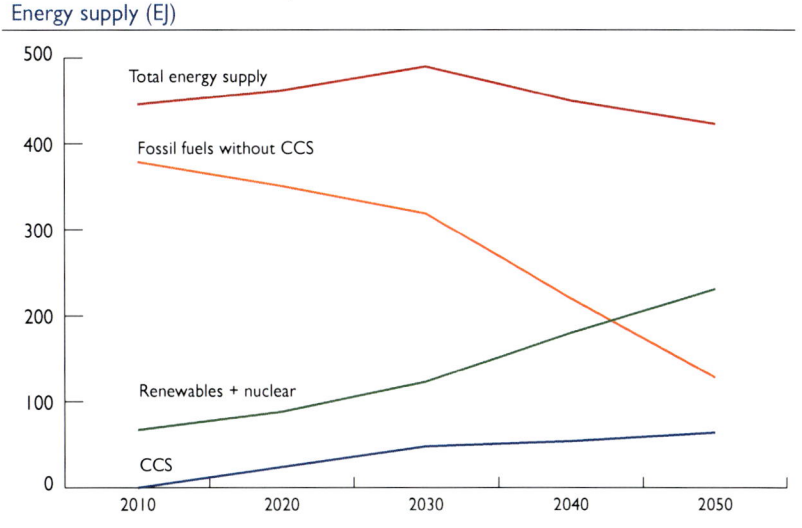

Source: Grantham LSE/Vivid Economics, based on Edenhofer et al (2009)

Figure 7. TIP factor risk sensitivity and direction of impact: asset classes

	\multicolumn{4}{c	}{Listed equities}	\multicolumn{3}{c	}{Fixed income}	Commod		RE	\multicolumn{3}{c	}{Private equity}	\multicolumn{2}{c	}{Infra}
	Global equity	Emerging markets equity	Sustainability equity	Efficiency/renewables	Global fixed income	Emerging market debt	Investment grade credit	Agricultural land	Timberland	Unlisted real estate	Leveraged buy-out	Venture capital	Efficiency/renewables	Core/unlisted	Efficiency/renewables
Sensitivity	L	M	H	VH	L	M	L	H	H	H	M	H	VH	H	VH
Regional divergence															
Delayed action															
Stern action															
Climate breakdown															

Sensitivity of impact to combined climate change factors: L = low; M = moderate; H = high; VH = very high
Direction of impact: ■ = positive; ■ = neutral; ■ = negative.
RE = real estate; infra = infrastructure.
Sustainable equity = broad multi-themed listed equity companies that generate a substantial proportion (typically more than 25%) of their earnings through sustainable activities.
Efficiency/renewables assets = both listed/unlisted sustainability themed assets whose core activities are theme-specific and more concentrated in terms of exposure than broad sustainability equity. This includes (but is not limited to) energy efficiency, low energy transport, renewable energy, bioenergy, carbon capture and storage, smart grid, water supply, usage and management, waste management, hydro energy and geothermal, to name but a few.

Source: Mercer

TIP risk factors is presented in the highlighted section at the top of the table, with the direction of the impact (positive, negative or neutral) denoted by the colour.

- *Sustainable assets could act as a hedge:* Sustainable assets perform comparatively well across the mitigation scenarios compared to core assets as highlighted in the previous table[4]. The exception to this is climate breakdown, which is not surprising as this scenario assumes no further progress on policy from current governance. Exposure to sustainable-themed equities, efficiency/renewables in listed and unlisted assets, timberland and agricultural land could therefore improve the resilience of a portfolio mix across the climate scenarios.
- *The EU and China set to lead the low-carbon transformation:* The regions that

---

4 Sustainable assets refer to investments that generate a substantial proportion (typically more than 25%) of their earnings through sustainable activities. At its broadest level, sustainable investment seeks to support sustainable economic development, enhance quality of life and safeguard the environment. This includes sustainable themes such as energy efficiency, low-energy transport, renewable energy, bioenergy, carbon capture and storage, smart grid, water supply, usage and management, waste management, hydro energy, geothermal and biofuels, to name but a few.

Figure 8. TIP factor risk sensitivity and direction of impact: regions

	EU	US	Japan	China/East Asia	Russia	India/South Asia
Sensitivity	Moderate	High	Moderate	High	Moderate	Moderate
Regional divergence	🟩	🟧	🟧	🟩	🟥	🟧
Delayed action	🟥	🟥	🟥	🟥	🟥	🟥
Stern action	🟩	🟩	🟩	🟩	🟧	🟩
Climate breakdown	🟧	🟧	🟧	🟧	🟥	🟥

Mercer assessment as per aggregate estimates, using T, I and P data available at the regional level.
Direction of impact derived through a qualitative process: ■ = positive; ■ = neutral; ■ = negative in terms of the direction of the impact for investments for each region.

Source: Mercer

are best placed to lead the climate change transformation are those that preemptively find alternative sources of energy, improve efficiency, reduce carbon emissions and invest in new technology. Indicators of current and future investment flows and policy measures out to 2030 suggest that the 'leaders' are likely to be the EU and China/East Asia (see Figure 8, with sensitivity at the top and direction denoted by colour). The potential for low-carbon transformation in the US is also significant in the best case scenario of Stern Action, but political impasse on climate change suggests it may lag in the other mitigation scenarios, with 'improver' countries coming through including Japan and India/South Asia.

While the climate breakdown scenario may appear to have lower risk than the delayed action scenario across the regions, this is because the investment impacts were examined over the next 20 years, when the policy costs will need to be absorbed. Grantham LSE/Vivid Economics points out that the physical impact costs, as well as policy adjustment costs, will rise substantially in the climate breakdown scenario beyond 2050 in the absence of any action.

Actions for institutional investors to consider

The most important step for institutional investors to undertake is to consider climate change in strategic discussions of long-term investment risks and opportunities. The framework is not intended to provide a simplistic 'tick box' solution for investors to apply in a mechanistic way but to help provide a better understanding of the driving forces behind climate change, the sensitivity of asset classes and regions to these drivers and the uncertainties that remain, opening the way to further debate and discussion amongst investment decision-makers.

Given the high level of uncertainty associated with climate change, caution should be exercised against optimising portfolio holdings to any one scenario. Rather, it is encouraged to incorporate climate change risk factors into strategic discussions and risk management processes to diversify across the different sources of investment risk. This will help ensure that a process is in place, and that a portfolio will be more resilient to the different future possibilities.

Actions to consider for institutional investors include:

- *Allocate to sustainable assets:* An additional response might be an allocation to sustainable investments across both listed and unlisted assets. This could be viewed as a hedge against some of the risks around climate change, particularly climate policy. The risks and opportunities within each asset class could be used as an initial guide for the selection of the type of investments that might feature in a well-diversified portfolio.
- *Evolve and transform portfolio mix:* Rather than optimising to any one scenario, investors should consider a gradual rebalancing of a portfolio toward climate-sensitive assets that are also tilted toward the sustainability theme across infrastructure, private equity, real estate, timberland and agricultural land. The adoption of this approach will diversify the portfolio across the sources of investment risk (including climate change) and improve resilience across the mitigation scenarios.
- *Understand the risks associated with climate change and embed these into asset allocation policies:* Monitor the evidence related to climate change in terms of technology, impacts and policy, and discuss what features of the climate scenarios are emerging, and what this means for investments. This could be built into annual strategic review and risk management assessments.
- *Consider a wider pool of passive options:* Where portfolios are passively managed, consider investing in a wider pool of products against different (environmental) indices to better capture the potential upside and/or help mitigate the risks of climate change. Passive equity investors should consider the index constituents and the weighting attached to sustainability issues when considering benchmarks for investments. Ownership rights through voting and engagement can be exercised on climate change issues, either directly, through third-party agencies or via the provider of the passive index product where appropriate.
- *Engage with active fund managers:* This will help to ensure that a portfolio is better positioned for responding to the uncertainties in a way that helps reduce the risk of being too late, reactive and costly. Fund managers should be questioned on the key criteria and pressure points that will be measured and integrated into investment processes. This could include an ongoing assessment of climate policy developments, cost of carbon scenario analysis, the impact of technology flows on risks and opportunities and an evaluation of any possible risks from climate damage, including assumptions regarding expected returns such as the equity risk premium.
- *Engage with companies:* Institutional investors should engage with companies in which they are invested on climate risk management issues to proactively man-

age the risks. Requests should focus on improved disclosure of emissions levels and environmental impact assessments, as well as full disclosure and reporting of sustainability management policies and practices. This can be undertaken collaboratively, through initiatives such as the Carbon Disclosure Project, the Water Disclosure Project, the UN Principles for Responsible Investment or investor groups such as the Institutional Investors Group on Climate Change (in Europe), the Investor Network on Climate Risk (in the US) and the Investor Group on Climate Change (Australia/New Zealand), to name but a few. Engagement can also be undertaken through third-party engagement agencies, via fund managers that are delegated with the management responsibility or, where the assets are managed internally, asset owners can engage directly with investee companies on these issues.

- *Engage with policy-makers:* Climate policy uncertainty is a notable source of risk for investors over the coming 20 years, contributing as much as 10% to risk for a representative portfolio. Stretching further into the future, the longer the policy delay, the higher the impact costs will be for investors. It is therefore crucial for institutional investors to engage with policy-makers on the specific details of policy plans and measures as part of the risk management process to help protect and enhance the long-term value of the assets they oversee. This should go beyond high-level motherhood statements, and should be appropriately resourced and focused on targeting specific policy measures at the local and global level, to actively manage the policy risk that climate change produces.
- *Support ongoing research:* Consider areas for further research and look for collaborative opportunities to support this with academics, policy-makers and relevant experts.

Summary

The private sector response to changing environmental conditions, new technology and policy measures may produce a substantial number of new investment opportunities. Cumulative investment in efficiency improvements, renewable energy, biofuels, nuclear and carbon capture and storage could expand in the range of $3 trillion to $5 trillion by 2030. This presents meaningful opportunities to investors in these investment areas that are still in their infant stages.

Bibliography

Blake D, B Lehmann and A Timmermann (1999), 'Asset Allocation Dynamics and Pension Fund Performance', *The Journal of Business*, vol 72, no 4, pp 429–461.

Brinson G, R Hood and G Beebower (1986), 'Determinants of Portfolio Performance', *Financial Analysts Journal* (July/August), pp 39–44.

Brinson G, B Singer and G Beebower (1991), 'Determinants of Portfolio Perfor-

mance II: An Update', *Financial Analysts Journal*, vol 47, no 3, pp 40–48.
Edenhofer O, *et al* (2009), *The Economics of Decarbonization*, Report of the RECIPE Project, Potsdam Institute for Climate Impact Research.
Grinblatt M and S Titman (1989), 'Mutual Fund Performance: An Analysis of Quarterly Portfolio Holdings', *The Journal of Business*, vol 62, no 3, pp 393–416.
Ibbotson R and P Kaplan (2000), 'Does Asset Allocation Policy Explain 40%, 90%, or 100% of Performance?', *Financial Analysts Journal*, January/February.
Parry M, *et al* (2004), 'Effects of Climate Change on Global Food Production under SRES Emissions and Socio-economic Scenarios', *Global Environmental Change*, vol 14, pp 53–67.

Chapter 13

Investment approaches to environmental markets

Ian Simm, Impax Asset Management

Two decades ago, at the time of the last recession, alternative energy, water treatment and waste management stocks were typically viewed as niche investments that were unacceptably exposed to regulatory risk. Today, however, environmental markets (EM) are diversified and well populated with robust, profitable companies, and are increasingly viewed by investors as mainstream.

At a time when risk-adjusted pension fund liabilities are growing inexorably, uncertainties in the global economy are undermining confidence in traditional asset allocation and many institutional investors are returning to the drawing board. In this context, evidence that EM portfolios have attractive investment characteristics that can enhance expected growth, diversify risk and, in some instances, improve projected cash flow, is strengthening the case that investors should pro-actively allocate capital to them.

Investment characteristics of environmental markets

The vast majority of institutional investors have a responsibility to seek out the best risk-adjusted returns from their underlying investments. Most typically use asset allocation models with a framework that includes equities, fixed income and alternatives (which can include real estate, hedge funds, private equity, commodities and/or other real assets such as infrastructure). To justify an investment in a distinct investment area such as EM, they must be convinced that the area offers risk-adjusted returns that are competitive with other opportunities in the same asset class.

With this perspective, environmental markets offer three attractive characteristics for institutional investors:

SUPERIOR GROWTH IN A DISTINCT, INVESTIBLE SECTOR
As described in Chapter 20, environmental markets should continue to benefit from a predictable long-term trend in which national governments implement and enforce legislation to limit and reduce pollution from rising, more affluent populations, build/renew infrastructure to support further economic growth and raise the efficiency of the consumption of natural resources. Over the five years to 31 Decem-

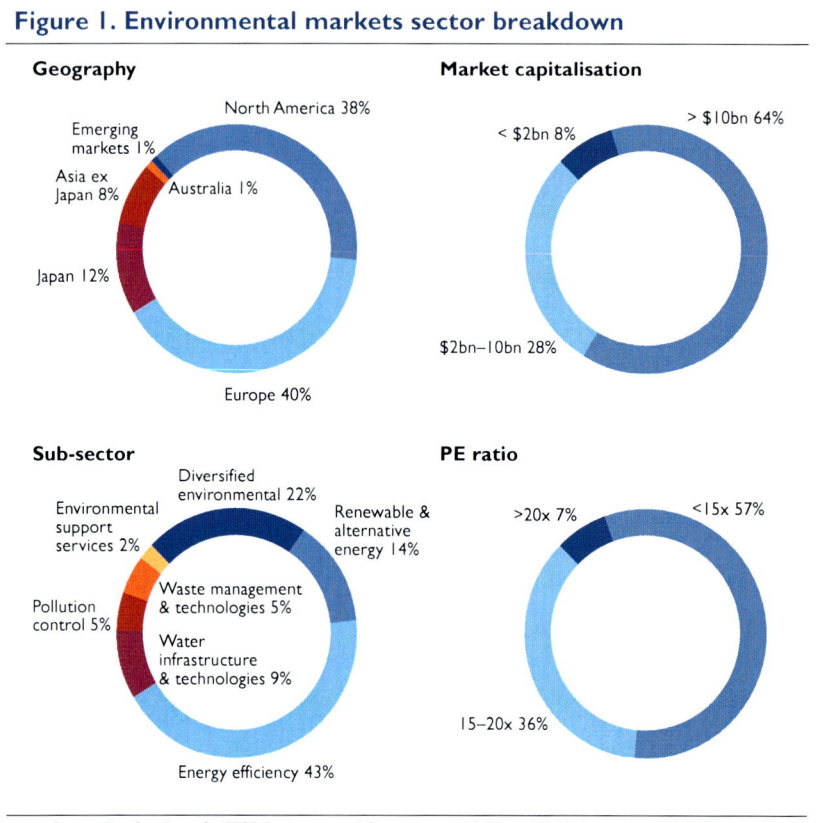

212 | Investment Opportunities for a Low-Carbon World

Figure 1. Environmental markets sector breakdown

Geography
- North America 38%
- Emerging markets 1%
- Asia ex Japan 8%
- Australia 1%
- Japan 12%
- Europe 40%

Market capitalisation
- > $10bn 64%
- < $2bn 8%
- $2bn–10bn 28%

Sub-sector
- Diversified environmental 22%
- Environmental support services 2%
- Renewable & alternative energy 14%
- Pollution control 5%
- Waste management & technologies 5%
- Water infrastructure & technologies 9%
- Energy efficiency 43%

PE ratio
- >20x 7%
- <15x 57%
- 15–20x 36%

Source: FactSet. Data for FTSE Environmental Opportunities All Share (EOAS) Index as at 31 December 2010. PE ratios forward 12 months

ber 2010, the 21 EM sub-sectors have produced compound annual earnings growth of 8.5%, while the FTSE World Index has grown at an equivalent rate of 7.5%. Looking ahead, as of August 2011, anticipated EM growth is 14.9% per annum, which is comfortably ahead of expected market growth of 13.1%.

During the past decade, this superior growth has propelled the EM sector to being a significant component of global stock markets. As described in Chapter 14, at 30 June 2011 the EM sector comprised 1,387 quoted companies representing 6% of recognised investment exchanges world-wide (by market capitalisation), and generating 6% of the revenues of all companies on recognised investment exchanges worldwide.

ATTRACTIVE RISK PROFILE

Investors attracted by the EM sector's superior growth prospects should also be interested in two additional characteristics of baskets of stocks in the EM sector. First, a basket of EM stocks tends to have a significant tracking error against a generic index – ie, EM investments can provide diversification for investors seeking generic equity exposure. For example, the tracking error of the FTSE Environmental Opportunities All Share (EOAS) Index versus the FTSE World Index over the five years to 30 June 2011 was 6%.

Second, the volatility of such baskets is typically similar to the volatility of a generic index, implying that there is no appreciable risk penalty for investing in the EM sector: over the three years to 30 June 2011, the daily volatility of the FTSE EOAS Index was 1.4% while the volatility of the FTSE World Index was 1.3%. Over the same period, the EOAS returned 39.2% in sterling, a significant outperformance against the FTSE World Index, which grew by 30.1%.

Intuitively, the low volatility (and hence the low risk) and the notable tracking error arise because the EM sub-sectors have drivers that have low correlation both with each other and with the mainstream economy. For example, the development of policy driving the adoption of clean energy in the United States is unconnected with the roll-out of legislation mandating investment in water supply infrastructure in China, which, again, is not linked to strengthening of the European waste management framework.

Investors concerned about risk should also be wary about baskets giving exposure to one EM sub-sector. For example, over the year to 30 June 2011, the monthly volatility of the FTSE EO Renewable and Alternative Energy Index was 14.6% – ie, significantly higher than the volatility of the EOAS (12.2% over the same period).

POTENTIAL FOR INFLATION-LINKED CASH FLOW
With a bias towards new asset creation or asset replacement, the EM sector has a strong infrastructure component. From an investment perspective, this means that many EM businesses benefit from the relatively stable, inflation-linked cash flow inherent in infrastructure projects, which is particularly attractive to institutional investors that have inflation-linked, cash-based liabilities such as pension payments.

Typical EM projects that may have such a profile include renewable power generation stations, waste management plants and water supply/treatment facilities.

Environmental markets investment strategies

Mainstream investors, assessing the opportunities from an asset allocation perspective, have several attractive options for securing EM exposure to environmental markets.

GLOBAL EQUITIES
With an attractive return-risk profile, portfolios of listed EM stocks can fit well within a conventional global equities portfolio. EM portfolios can be expected to have moderate to high tracking error versus global equity indices and thereby provide a

degree of diversification. Investors using a 'core-satellite' approach to constructing a global equities portfolio may therefore find that an EM portfolio provides a useful 'satellite' position.

To gain low-cost exposure to the superior growth potential of the EM sector, investors can select among a small number of relatively new exchange traded funds (ETFs – see Chapter 15). However, in a sector that is inherently mis-priced as a consequence of rapidly evolving regulation and technology, high-quality active management may create significant alpha. At August 2011, there were about 30 actively managed funds targeting listed EM stocks.

Analysis of actively managed EM funds indicates that they have a wide dispersion of performance. For example, during 2007 returns ranged from +3% to +70%, while 2008 saw reported falls in performance of between −55% and −12%. Prospective investors should therefore conduct careful due diligence on individual funds and managers' investment processes.

HEDGE FUNDS

Most specialist hedge funds investing in environmental markets or related sectors are relatively new; however, after the stock market shocks of recent years, investors are increasingly interested in asset classes that offer a low correlation to equities with active risk management, and so this type of product has significant potential.

There is an established universe of long-short equity funds in the EM sector. As a rapidly evolving, inefficiently priced sector, EM provides investment managers with the scope to make money from short ideas. These ideas may focus on the stocks of poorly positioned and/or managed companies or from sectors that have become over-valued or have flawed structures; for example, between 30 June 2006 and 30 June 2008, the basket of five quoted US and UK biofuels stocks fell 92% in US dollars, with three of the five quoted companies filing for bankruptcy.

By combining long and short positions in a manner that takes account of market sentiment, a long-short equity fund should be able to generate more stable returns with limited downside. At the time of writing, funds with this type of strategy have only a limited track record.

Hedge funds trading electricity contracts or weather derivatives may also be of interest to investors seeking exposure to the EM sector, broadly defined.

REAL ASSETS/INFRASTRUCTURE

Driven in part by demand for 'cleaner', more efficient infrastructure, the EM sector offers considerable opportunity for investment in real assets, particularly in the power generation/transmission, water supply/treatment and waste processing/disposal areas.

In common with many other infrastructure sectors, 'environmental infrastructure' typically enjoys long-term contracts for the supply of services (such as clean water) and financial returns that are partially or fully linked to inflation. In certain sub-sectors, the price for services stipulated in public sector contracts or in government legislation is not directly linked to the economic cycle. For renewable power generation in many European countries, government-mandated feed-in tariffs are often set for 20 years or more and may be fully inflation-linked, ensuring that investors can enjoy particularly stable cash flows. In the water sector, prices may be determined through a 'return on investment' formula.

A key issue for environmental infrastructure is the degree to which prices (and thereby revenues) are vulnerable to political decisions. In principle, governments should be very reluctant to renege on promises made to infrastructure investors, for fear of permanently undermining their ability to attract private sector capital in future. However, the Spanish government's retrospective change (in late 2010) to tariffs for solar PV projects that had been built in 2007 and 2008 unnerved European investors, and prompted legal challenge. Given the obligations on all EU member states and Spain's unique position in funding tariff subsidies directly from the national budget rather than adding them to utility bills (where they are outside the direct influence of politicians), many in the investment community doubt that other countries will follow suit.

Many investors identify forestry as an environmental asset class. Although not currently included within the definition of EM used by FTSE, forestry is increasingly seen as key component of policy designed to reduce net emissions of greenhouse gases, and the sector should therefore be a beneficiary of environmental regulation. Properly developed and managed, forestry assets grow in a predictable manner and produce a steady 'biological growth'. However, under 'fair-value' accounting rules, the value of forestry assets will typically reflect the market price of wood products, hence claims that forestry has a low correlation with other asset classes, particularly equities, should be treated with caution.

FIXED INCOME

Although companies in several EM sub-sectors, such as waste infrastructure, water utilities and some industrial energy efficiency companies, utilise bond financing, equity finance is still predominant: for example, of the 1,387 stocks in the FTSE Environmental Markets universe, only 220 have issued corporate bonds.

Recently, there has been significant discussion over the market appetite for Green Bonds issued by government entities with the purpose of funding environmental infrastructure or similar investments. In 2008, the World Bank issued the first tranche of green bonds to finance projects that tackle the causes and consequences of climate change in the developing world, such as renewable energy installations, reforestation, watershed management and flood protection schemes. To date, the bank has raised more than $2 billion of green bonds, raising capital from public sector and private sector investors, with a particular focus on the US, Japan and Scandinavia (see Chapter 16).

PRIVATE EQUITY

As a relatively young sector, the flow of capital into private businesses active in environmental markets has typically been in growth capital. However, with increasing maturity, there is likely to be increased scope for buy-outs.

The EM sector is characterised by relatively high levels of innovation and business creation, and has therefore become a target for both specialist and generalist venture capital. Early stage businesses may emerge from university commercialisation programmes or corporate spin-outs, and, with appropriate business plans, management teams and funding, have the potential to scale significantly. Larger, well established corporates in the technology, industrial or related sectors are typically interested in acquiring businesses that have compelling intellectual property, strong business models and growth potential, and are an attractive exit route for early-stage financial investors.

Investors considering allocations to EM venture capital funds must take into account the usual range of diligence issues, though, as set out in the section on risk below, should focus in particular on the market potential for an underlying business, the risk of adverse changes to regulation, exposure to the capital expenditure cycle and commodities pricing risk.

To date, investors seeking funds that are dedicated to providing buyout or equivalent capital to larger businesses in the EM sector have limited options. This situation is likely to change as the sector matures.

OTHER STRATEGIES

As the EM investment arena develops, it is likely that new asset classes will emerge. The past five years has seen the emergence of several funds trading assets linked to regulatory frameworks designed to limit carbon dioxide emissions (carbon trading). Investors have also allocated capital to traders of water extraction permits, and there are also signs of markets being created in biodiversity. It is too early to predict the success of these strategies.

Risks of investment

Investing in the environmental markets sector entails both generic and sector specific risks. Generically, EM stocks are exposed to stock market risk, and many are likely to be negatively affected by high interest rates.

With a relatively high exposure to industrial and utility markets, portfolios of EM stocks are typically partially correlated to the industrial capital expenditure cycle. Similarly, many EM companies are dependent on revenue streams linked directly or indirectly to commodities, for example metals prices (affecting recycling businesses) and electricity prices (affecting renewable power generators and equipment suppliers).

The most obvious sector-specific risk is regulation. Many environmental markets are shaped by government policy that limits pollution, mandates minimum market sizes and/or stipulates rates of return on investment. A policy change can materially affect the prospects of an individual company. However, today's environmental markets are sufficiently diverse that investment managers usually have little difficulty in limiting the risk of a specific regulatory change in their EM portfolios, while the probability of simultaneous changes to multiple regulations is low.

Looking ahead

As the world population expands from around 7 billion today to more than 9 billion by 2050, it appears inevitable that environmental markets will continue to grow at a faster rate than the global economy, and that the attractive investment characteristics described in this chapter will be sustained. Over the past decade, the EM sector has emerged as an investment sector that is robust enough to withstand mainstream quantitative analysis. It is therefore likely that investor interest in the sector will continue to build and that allocations will grow.

Chapter 14

Capturing the performance of environmental technology companies

David Harris, FTSE Group

Introduction

Disruptions to the world economy brought about by climate change and other environmental drivers present a range of opportunities and threats for investors. A broad spectrum of public policy interventions at national and international levels is providing incentives for cleaner technologies while increasing the costs associated with carbon and other pollutants. Over the next two decades a new 'clean technology revolution' is predicted to take place. This mega trend provides investors with a great opportunity, but the technologies and companies that will drive this change are, as yet, unknown and unpredictable.

Environmental market indices are used to provide investors with low-cost exposure to this important sector, while offering efficient diversification and hence lower-risk investment opportunities. Indices are also playing an important role in defining and measuring the environmental technology market.

Investing in environmental markets

Environmental markets are likely to offer exceptional growth due to the critical environmental challenges facing human societies globally. As outlined in other chapters, the transformation in global economies required to deliver a 50%[1] global cut in greenhouse gas emissions by 2050 is leading to a redeployment of capital into environmental markets. Climate change, although the most pressing of environmental concerns, is one of a number of interrelated environmental and resource challenges that face the world today, which also include water scarcity, resource shortages and wider forms of pollution.

The FTSE Environmental Opportunities All-share Index recorded a growth of 57.3%, over the five years between 2005 and the start of 2011, more than double the returns of the FTSE Global All-Cap index over the period[2]. If environmental

---
1 G8 Statement, July 2008, also reflected in Nicholas Stern, *Key Elements of a Global Deal on Climate Change*, London School of Economics, April 2008. This would require developed countries to make an 80–90% cut in emissions by 2050.
2 FTSE Global All-Cap Index returned 25.4%, against 57.3% for the FTSE Environmental Opportunities All-share over the five-year period to 30 December 2010 (US$, total returns). Data table available at www.ftse.com/Indices/FTSE_Environmental_Markets_Index_Series/Downloads/FTSE_Environmental_Markets_Research_Report_Q410.pdf.

technologies are to grow quickly enough to combat the environmental constraints and challenges confronting society then this market can be expected to continue the trend of growing more rapidly than the broader equity markets.

Although the prospects for international carbon markets look weak due to the difficulties in agreeing an international binding deal for delivering emission reductions, the national policy frameworks that incentivise growth in cleaner technologies continue to strengthen in most countries. This is particularly the case in emerging markets and in Europe. Policy incentives range from enhanced environmental standards for buildings, increasing carbon taxes, setting floors for carbon prices, renewable energy generation obligations and feed-in tariffs, car fuel efficiency standards and investments in more efficient infrastructure such as high-speed rail. Brazil, China, India, South Africa and South Korea are introducing an array of policies both to reduce emissions and to support the growth of their domestic clean technology industries. In Europe the 2020 emissions reduction target of 20% is likely to be maintained rather than being increased to 30%, but there is likely to be an increased focus on energy efficiency requirements.

Managing investment risk in environmental markets

The growth of the environmental technology sector not only provides opportunities for investors but also represents risk. It is unclear how important different technologies will be in combating climate change, providing solutions to water scarcity and managing waste and resource use. For example, there was much excitement over solar technology, but because the wider renewables sector is also evolving so rapidly, it is hard to predict how important solar will be, relative to other renewable energies such as wind, wave, tidal and geothermal energy.

An investor focusing purely on one specific environmental technology sub-sector faces high investment risks. Solar power investors experienced huge gains in 2007; however, this was followed by huge losses at the end of 2008, as the value of solar companies fell by over 60%, and this has not recovered since, with a further 40% fall over 2010. There is also now a wide array of different solar technologies, some relatively new but with great potential, such as solar dye concentrator technology[3]. Over the long term, even if solar does becomes a significant component of global electricity generation, it could be newer companies with more recent and novel solar technologies that become successful. On the other hand, larger, established environmental technology companies may be better equipped to bring innovative products to market.

Active managers claim they can identify those companies with above-market average growth potential, but at this stage in the sector's evolution it is impossible to know which environmental technology companies will be the winners. Therefore, to

---

[3] Currie, M J et al (July 2008), 'High-efficiency organic solar concentrators for photovoltaics', *Science*.

> **Figure 1. Example of a structured product**
>
> **EIB Climate Awareness Bond**
>
> The largest-ever syndicated equity index-linked structured product was the Climate Awareness Bond, which was issued by the European Investment Bank. It took the form of a five-year certificate that would deliver 90% of the performance of the FTSE4Good Environmental Leaders Europe 40 Index.
>
> The value of each bond was €100 and more than €600 million was raised in sales through a syndicate of banks across all 27 EU countries. There was also a capital guarantee aspect of the certificate. This meant that, if the index was below its starting value at the end of the five-year period, the certificate holders would not suffer any loss, regaining their original capital. Investors had the option to use part of their returns to buy and destroy carbon allowances from the European Emissions Trading System.

reduce risk, while maximising growth, an investment strategy should be as diversified as possible across the whole environmental technology market. There will be many losers, but these will be offset by numerous winners and vast growth from certain well-positioned companies.

Role of indices in investment strategies

Indices offer the most efficient and accurate method to measure the performance of a market as a whole. An investment strategy that aims to follow an entire market is known as passive investing, and this requires the use of indices to capture accurately the market's performance. There are a range of passive investment mechanisms available to investors including tracker funds, structured products and exchange-traded funds (ETFs – see Chapter 15).

A tracker fund is an open-ended[4] fund that tracks a particular index. The investment manager simply buys the stocks that are included in the index according to the weights specified and re-balances their portfolio at index reviews. Examples of fund managers well known for running tracker funds are Legal and General in the UK, and State Street Global Advisors and Vanguard in the US.

The term structured product covers a range of investment products that are closed-ended[4] and expire, delivering the returns, at the end of a fixed period. This covers notes, certificates and derivative products. These products can have complex structures but can provide useful investment characteristics such as capital protection. See Figure 1 for an interesting example of an environmental structured product.

---

4 Open-ended refers to when the total volume of investment in the fund or investment vehicle is unrestricted. Closed-ended is when the total investment volume is fixed, so for a new investor to access the investment vehicle, there has to be a transfer (sale) from an existing investor.

Environmental/clean technology indices

There are now a very large number of clean-tech indices available, of varying sophistication, that take a variety of approaches in defining clean technology, covering different regions and with different investability requirements and methodologies. These indices were first produced by small boutique fund managers, brokers and research organisations, but more recently investment banks and three of the major index specialists have also launched clean-tech indices.

The original global clean technology index was the ET50 (Environmental Technology 50 Index) launched by Impax Asset Management in 1999. It includes the largest 50 companies globally that had over half their business in the development and deployment of environmental technologies. Impax defined these as falling into three areas: alternative energy and energy efficiency; water technologies and pollution control; and waste technologies and resource management. Definitions for environmental or clean technology, almost invariably, are based on these core categories. Figure 2 shows more details on how these areas are defined by the independent FTSE Environmental Markets Committee, which has taken these categories as a starting point to create a much more detailed taxonomy system. In the US, the first domestic clean energy index was the WilderHill Clean Energy Index (ECO) launched in 2004. These two indices, the ET50 and WilderHill, were ahead of their time, with most other significant clean technology indices being launched more recently, since 2006.

In 2007 and 2008, two of the major global index providers, FTSE Group and Standard & Poor's, also entered this market and were able to build on the work of those that came before. The employment of international index calculation standards by independent index specialists marked an important next stage in the quality and reliability of clean technology indices.

FTSE Group took over the calculation and management of the ET50 Index, with Impax continuing to provide research for the index. FTSE improved the investability of the index by adding liquidity screens and introducing free-float adjustments to constituent weights. Now, there is also an independent committee to direct the ongoing management of the index, chaired by Winston Hickox, the architect of CalPERS 'Green-Wave' investment strategy (see Chapter 23).

Standard & Poor's independently developed its own methodology and research to create a suite of Global Thematic Indices, including a Global Eco Index and Global Clean Energy Index. It also created a Global Alternative Energy Index that combines the Clean Energy and Nuclear Energy indices. S&P's approach is similar to FTSE's in terms of liquidity screens and free-float adjustments and is governed by an internal index committee. In 2010 MSCI also joined the market through its acquisition of RiskMetrics, which had itself acquired KLD, a US-based social research provider, and took over calculation of the KLD environmental thematic indices. See Figure 3 on pages 228–230 for an overview of the different index approaches.

There are also an increasing number of environmental technology indices pro-

Figure 2. Environmental markets definitions used for the selection of constituents for the FTSE environmental market indices

Environmental markets definition: Companies that provide products and services offering value-added solutions to environmental problems, or that improve the efficiency of natural resource use.

These are categorised by the independent FTSE Environmental Technology Committee into the following sectors:

SECTOR	
E1.0	**RENEWABLE AND ALTERNATIVE ENERGY**
	Companies that provide products and services along the renewable and alternative energy value chain.
Sub-sectors	
E1.1	**Wind power generation equipment**
	Companies that design, develop, manufacture, distribute or install wind turbine equipment and components (including bearings, gearboxes, blades and towers); and companies that supply specialist materials into the wind value chain.
E1.2	**Solar energy generation equipment**
	Companies that design, develop, manufacture, distribute or install solar photovoltaic or solar thermal equipment and components (including wafers, cells and modules); and companies that supply specialist materials into the solar value-chain.
E1.3	**Other renewables equipment**
	Companies that design, develop, manufacture, distribute and/or install other renewable energy technologies (other than wind and solar power), including equipment for hydro, wave, tidal, fuel-cell and geothermal energy generation.
E1.4	**Renewable energy developers and independent power producers (IPPs)**
	Companies involved in the development and operation of renewable energy power generation including the provision of power from sources such as wind, solar, geothermal, hydro, biomass, landfill gas and waste incineration.
E1.5	**Biofuels**
	Companies involved in the development, processing, production and distribution of bio-derived fuels for transport, heat and electrical power generation. Bio-derived fuels include bioethanol, biodiesel and 'advanced' biofuels such as cellulosic ethanol.
E1.6	**Diversified renewable and alternative energy**
	Diversified renewable and alternative energy companies with less than the business threshold derived from any one of the subsectors, but over the threshold when combined.
SECTOR	
E2.0	**ENERGY EFFICIENCY**
	Companies that provide products and services enabling more efficient methods of energy usage.
Sub-sectors	
E2.1	**Power network efficiency**
	Companies that design, develop, manufacture, distribute or install equipment and

Figure 2 continued

	services which enhance the efficiency of operation of the electrical power network. This includes advanced meters, distributed generation, 'smart grid' technologies, high-efficiency power generation, transmission and distribution technologies, and technologies for advanced energy storage and back-up power.
E2.2	**Industrial energy efficiency**
	Companies that design, develop, manufacture, distribute or install energy efficient products and services for use in varied industrial markets. These include products and core components which improve energy profiles, and products or systems which reduce energy usage within processes.
E2.3	**Buildings energy efficiency**
	Companies that design, develop, manufacture, distribute or install energy efficient products and services for use in residential, commercial and municipal buildings. Products include integrated buildings control systems, insulation materials, energy efficient lighting, efficient heating, ventilation and air-conditioning equipment.
E2.4	**Transport energy efficiency**
	Companies that design, develop, manufacture, distribute or apply technology to deliver improved efficiency in the transport sector (including automotive, heavy duty, rail and aerospace). This includes higher efficiency conventional engine and power-train technologies, and new vehicle technology (such as natural gas engines, hybrids and electric vehicles, including specialist batteries).
E2.5	**General energy efficiency**
	Diversified energy efficiency companies with less than the business threshold derived from any one of these subsectors, but over the threshold when combined.
SECTOR	
E3.0	**WATER INFRASTRUCTURE & TECHNOLOGIES**
	Companies that provide or operate technologies, infrastructure and services for the supply, management and treatment of water for industrial, residential, utility and agricultural users.
Sub-sectors	
E3.1	**Water infrastructure companies**
	Companies that supply products (including specialty pipes, pumps, valves, actuators, hydrants and meters) and services that enhance water infrastructure systems. This includes companies engaged in the development and construction of water infrastructure or coastal defense projects.
E3.2	**Water treatment equipment**
	Companies that design, develop, manufacture, distribute and/or install technologies or facilities for the separation and purification of water to meet environmental standards. This includes membranes, ultra-violet, desalination, filtration, ion exchange and biological treatment.
E3.3	**Water utilities**
	Companies that operate water treatment and supply infrastructure, providing potable water or wastewater and sewage services.
E3.4	**General water infrastructure and technology**
	Diversified water infrastructure and technology companies with less than the business threshold derived from any one of these subsectors, but over the threshold when combined.

Figure 2 continued

SECTOR	
E4.0	**POLLUTION CONTROL**
	Companies that provide technologies to reduce and monitor the contamination of air and soil to address global, regional and local environmental problems.
Sub-sectors	
E4.1	**Pollution control solutions**
	Companies that design, develop, manufacture, distribute or install equipment and services for reduction, prevention or clean-up of air or soil pollution. Pollutants include sulphur dioxide, nitrous oxide, mercury, particulates, carbon monoxide and carbon dioxide. Principal areas are the industrial and power generation sectors (such as smokestack-scrubbing technologies) and the transportation sector (such as particulate filters and catalytic converters). This also includes companies facilitating the substitution of more polluting fuels by cleaner-burning fuels in areas of chronic air pollution.
E4.2	**Environmental testing and gas sensing**
	Companies that provide environmental testing, sensing, measuring and monitoring technologies and services, such as chromatography and mass spectrometry.
SECTOR	
E5.0	**WASTE MANAGEMENT & TECHNOLOGIES**
	Companies that provide and/or operate technologies, systems and services for waste management, reuse and recycling.
Sub-sectors	
E5.1	**Waste technology equipment**
	Companies that design, develop, manufacture, distribute and/or install waste technology equipment and system services that create value from the waste stream. Equipment includes sorters, reverse-vending machines, composters, anaerobic digesters, waste-to-energy systems, collection, registration and logistics systems and other materials processors.
E5.2	**Value added waste processing**
	Companies that are involved in the processing of waste to derive value. Operations include recycling (in particular metals, plastics, oils, paper and aggregates), composting, mechanical biological treatment and energy recovery.
E5.3	**Hazardous waste management**
	Companies that are involved in the processing and treatment of hazardous waste such as clinical waste, batteries, end-of-life vehicles, electronic equipment (e-waste) and radioactive waste.
E5.4	**General waste management**
	Companies that are involved in general residential and commercial waste management operations, typically including collection, processing and disposal (including landfill).
E5.5	**General waste & technology**
	Diversified water infrastructure and technology companies with less than the business threshold derived from any one of these subsectors, but over the threshold when combined.

Figure 2 continued	
SECTOR	
E6.0	**ENVIRONMENTAL SUPPORT SERVICES**
	Companies that provide environmental support services through consultancy, or trading services in environmental assets and securities. Diversified environmental companies are also included in this sector.
Sub-sectors	
E6.1	Carbon and other environmental assets trading
	Companies that derive investment returns from sourcing, creating and trading carbon credits and other environmental assets such as sulphur dioxide pollution permits.
E6.2	Environmental consultancies
	Companies that provide advice and/or support regarding environmental issues and strategies, and in the development of projects and infrastructure (eg, the building of renewable energy projects). Companies that manage and certify environmental performance and planning issues for new and existing construction, and engineering projects are included.
E6.3	General environmental
	Diversified environmental companies with less than the 20% threshold derived from any one environmental sector, but over 20% when combined.

Using these sector definitions in FTSE indices
There are two FTSE environmental market index series that use the definitions above:
Environmental Opportunities. This series uses the definitions above and requires companies to derive at least 20% of their business from these sectors.
Environmental Technology. This series uses the sector definitions above, with the following exceptions, which are not considered eligible: water utilities, general waste management, general environmental and hydro power. There is the requirement for this series that companies derive at least 50% of their business from the eligible sectors.

vided by investment banks, most notably HSBC, Bank of America Merrill Lynch and Deutsche Bank. These increase the variety of clean-tech indices to the market, providing more options for investment products. However, investment bank indices can have limited market appeal as some investors are wary of indices that are not calculated by independent providers.

Targeted 'pure play' versus broader diversified investments
Some of these indices, such as the FTSE ET50, are considered 'pure play'; this simply means that the constituents are companies that have a majority of their businesses in environmental technology. An example would be Vestas, a company that is only involved in the wind power technology business. A restricting factor is that there is only a limited pool of these companies and there is a lot of investment going into them. This means that some may become over-valued, with extremely high price-to-earnings (P/E) ratios. In 2008 Vestas, for example, had a P/E ratio of over 100. An alternative approach to gaining exposure to the sector is to invest in companies that

have a lower, but still significant, environmental technology involvement. This also brings many larger companies into the investment universe. An example is Alstom, a global energy and transport infrastructure company. Approximately 27% of its revenues are from environmental markets, with 17% from power network efficiency, 8% from hydro, wind and solar energy, and 2% from pollution control.

The market does not appear always to fully value the environmental technology portion of companies with a partial involvement in the sector. This has led some companies, including Iberdrola, the Spanish electricity utility, and EDF, to spin off a portion of their renewable businesses to gain market recognition of their value. Investing in these large and more diversified companies, such as Alstom, represents the basis of a lower risk strategy for investors. Some indices, including the Wilder-Hill New Energy Global Innovation Index (NEX) and HSBC's Climate Change index use a 10% environmental involvement threshold; the FTSE Environmental Opportunities Series uses a higher 20% level (see Figure 3). This means that over 20% of a company's business, measured by revenues, invested capital or EBITDA must be from environmental markets (as defined in Figure 2) to be eligible for the FTSE Environmental Opportunities Series.

Thematic indices are also available, focusing on a smaller proportion of companies involved in a particular type of environmental technology. For example, there are indices that focus only on clean energy, such as the S&P Global Clean Energy or the FTSE EO Renewable & Alternative Energy index. Others focus purely on water technology, energy efficiency or waste technologies. Investment in these particular thematic components of the environmental technology market can provide different risk/return profiles. For example, renewable energy would be higher risk, with higher potential returns, due to the early stage of this sector's development, while the energy efficiency or waste management sector would represent lower-risk, lower-return investments.

The case for passive environmental technology investment

In tough conditions for public equity markets, the case for indices becomes even stronger, as passive investment avoids the higher management fees charged by active managers. Indices, therefore, can provide a cost-effective but also low-risk method for investment in a defined market and are particularly suited for clean-tech investments. This is because the environmental technology market offers attractive growth opportunities but, as explained above, can also represent significant investment risk. Indices provide a vehicle for gaining exposure to this exciting and important market, while reducing investment risk through diversification. Indices are also playing an important role in helping to define, classify and facilitate investment in the environmental technology market.

As outlined in Figure 3, there is a growing range of indices covering the clean-tech sector. The definitions, transparency and approaches of these indices vary con-

Figure 3. Comparing leading clean technology indices

(Investment bank indices have not been included)

Index provider	Index	Launch date	ETFs available	Regional/ global	No of constituents	Approach
FTSE (with Impax Asset Management)	ET50 Index (Environmental Technology 50)	Sept 1999[1]	Pax World (sShares FTSE Environmental Technologies Index ETF)	Global	50	*Universe*: All publicly listed companies are eligible. *Sector/criteria definitions*: Six environmental technology sector definitions, and 23 sub-sectors. The broader sectors are: Alternative Energy & Renewable Energy; Energy Efficiency; Water Infrastructure & Technologies; Pollution Control; Waste Management & Technologies; and Environmental Resource Management & Trading. Full details at www.ftse.com. *Approach*: Constituents must have over 50% of their business in the sectors above. Reviewed twice a year in March and September by an independent committee, largest 50 companies by market cap are selected. Full ground rules on web site. *Capping and weights*: Free float-adjusted weights, constituents capped at 10%.
FTSE (with Impax Asset Management)	Environmental Opportunity All-Share (EOAS) and sub-indices: ● Water Technology ● Energy Efficiency; ● Renewable & Alternative Energy; ● Waste and Pollution Control ● EO100 (largest 100 stocks) ● regional indices.	June 2008	Easy ETF on the EO100	Global	469[2]	*Universe*: FTSE Global Equity Index Series (8,000 companies) *Sector/criteria definitions*: Uses equivalent definitions as above, although slightly expanded definitions to cover water utilities, waste management companies and hydropower with two extra related sub-sectors (25 rather than 23). Again full details available at www.ftse.com. *Approach*: Constituents must have over 20% of their business in the sectors identified above. Reviewed twice a year in March and September by an independent committee, all companies in the universe that exceed the 20% threshold are included. Full ground rules on web site. Later in 2008, FTSE launched eight EO sub-indices. For each of the following sectors a wider benchmark index and smaller (30 or 50) tradable index was created: Water Technology; Energy Efficiency; Renewable & Alternative Energy; and Waste and Pollution Control. In 2009 further indices were added; a global 100 index (EO100) and additional regional indices for the US, Europe, Asia Pacific and the UK (both main market and an AIM index). *Capping and weights*: Free float-adjusted weights

Index provider	Index	Launch date	ETFs available	Regional/ global	No of constituents	Approach
MSCI (former KLD indices[3])	Global Climate Select Global Environment	2005 2010	No	Global	100	*Universe*: For the GCS index, companies drawn from the MSCI Global Investable Market Indices and for the GE indices companies drawn from the MSCI All Country World Investable Market Index. *Sector/criteria definitions*: For the GCS, companies are from a large mix of sectors that have some level of climate change involvement (or offsetting). There is a focus on renewable energy, future fuels, and clean technology and efficiency, but it also includes companies from oil, automotive, consumer products, utilities and financial services sectors. The GE indices cover companies with a majority of revenues from alternative energy, clean technology, sustainable water, green building or pollution prevention. *Approach*: Little detail is available for the GCS index. More is available with respect to the GE indices, with further details of the five themes above on the MSCI website. *Capping and weights*: The GCS is an equal-weighted index; each constituent represents 1% and is re-weighted at reviews. The GE indices are free float-adjusted, market-capitalisation weighted.
Standard & Poor's	Global Eco Index	Jan 2008	No	Global	30	*Universe*: Stocks must have a developed market listing, a market capitalisation of at least $1 billion, and a three-month daily value traded of more than $2 million. *Sector/criteria definitions*: S&P defines the following six 'clusters': Clean Energy Producers; Clean Energy Technology & Equipment Suppliers; Timber; Water Equipment; Instruments and Material; and Water Utilities and Infrastructure. Five constituents from each industry are selected. *Approach*: Companies are assigned a score of 1 or 0.5 based on their exposure to the sector. In each cluster, stocks are sorted first by exposure score and then by float-adjusted market cap. For each cluster, the five largest stocks with an exposure score of 1 are chosen. If there are no five stocks with an exposure score of 1, the largest stocks with an exposure score of 0.5 are chosen until the count reaches five. Full methodology available on S&P web site. *Capping and weights*: Constituent weights are relative to market cap. Constituents are capped at 10% and those with an exposure score of 0.5 are awarded only half their market-cap weight.

Index provider	Index	Launch date	ETFs available	Regional/ global	No of constituents	Approach
Standard & Poor's	Global Clean Energy Index	Feb 2008	iShares ETF (Barclays)	Global	30	*Universe*: Stocks must have a developed market listing, a minimum market cap of $250 million and a three-month average daily volume of at least $2 million. *Sector/criteria definitions*: Clean energy production and clean energy equipment and technology companies. *Approach*: The largest 30 stocks are selected, using the approach outlined above. *Capping and weights*: Constituent weights are relative to market cap. Constituents are capped at 5% and those with an exposure score of 0.5 are only awarded half their market-cap weight.
WilderHill (with New Energy Finance, calculated by Dow Jones)	New Energy Global Innovation Index (NEX)	Jan 2006	PowerShares (Invesco)	Global	89	*Universe*: Global, a three-month average market cap of at least $100 million and significant daily trading volume; at least 50% of the stocks outside of the US. *Sector/criteria definitions*: wind, solar, biofuels, hydro, wave and tidal, geothermal and other renewable energy businesses, energy conversion, storage, conservation, efficiency, materials, pollution control, emerging hydrogen and fuel cells. *Approach*: A bias towards companies with over 50% involvement in the sectors above, but may include stocks with over a 10% involvement. Ground rules available at www.nexindex.com. *Capping and weights*: The methodology is based on an equal-weighting approach but with weights modified by sector and two different market-cap bands. Constituents are capped at 5%.
WilderHill (with New Energy Finance, calculated by Dow Jones)	Clean Energy Index (ECO)	Aug 2004	PowerShares (Invesco)	US	54	*Universe*: US, a three-month average market cap of at least $50 million, a three-month average closing price above $1, and a significant daily trading volume. *Sector/criteria definitions*: A stock must have 'significant exposure' to clean energy, contribute to the advancement of clean energy or be important to the development of clean energy. *Approach*: No specific company clean energy involvement threshold given. Basic rules at www.wildershares.com. *Capping and weights*: The methodology is based on an equal-weighting approach but with weights modified by sector and two different market-cap bands. Constituents are capped at 4%.

1 Started in 1999 as the Impax ET50, re-launched with an enhanced methodology in January 2008 as the FTSE ET50. 2 As on 8 April 2011. 3 Previously calculated by S&P and then FTSE and most recently by MSCI, which has led to some methodology changes.

siderably. There is a risk that this diversity of choice becomes bewildering, but for canny investors it provides the capacity to target an index approach that most closely fits their investment requirements – including, if relevant, their social and environmental objectives.

Many large institutional investors have recently been making astute index-based investments into this sector, and there is now a growing range of options for retail investors to follow them into the rewarding world of clean-tech structured products, index tracker funds and ETFs.

Chapter 15

Exchange traded funds as an investment option

Lillian Goldthwaite, Friends Provident

Introduction

Exchange traded funds (ETFs) have grown tremendously over recent years, yet somehow they have been a bit misunderstood since birth by most retail investors. Although they are still predominantly used by institutional investors, this is rapidly changing as knowledge grows.

In simple terms, ETFs are exactly what it says on the tin: exchange traded funds. They are baskets of stocks that are passively managed to track a specific benchmark index and, like a stock (but unlike a typical fund), they are listed and traded throughout the day on a stock exchange, can be sold short, bought on margin and are lendable. They can be bought and sold using market, limit or stop orders. As with index funds, they give investors easy access to a broad range of markets, asset classes and sectors. The vast majority are structured as open-ended funds.

To price the funds continuously, the ETF holdings must also be disclosed on a real-time basis. This is why all ETFs must be based on a published index with a rules-driven methodology. What is held in the portfolio is transparent at all times, unlike with a fund where managers are reluctant to disclose positions except as required by regulators – semi-annually. As with any index fund, investors have the opportunity to learn how the index is constructed from its methodology document, should they choose to. In addition, they have the comfort of knowing that security selection and weighting is strictly controlled by a fixed process. It is worth identifying the index used in an ETF's prospectus and learning more about it before investing.

The uniqueness of the funds is that they are buoyed by two aspects of liquidity: the first is the trading between investors on the secondary market; the second is their unique method of allowing institutional investors to exchange stock for units in the ETF to create new, or redeem, ETF shares. This process causes the liquidity in the ETF shares to be driven by the liquidity of the underlying stocks, preventing any risk of sizable discounts developing between the net asset value (NAV) and the portfolio's value.

ETFs exist for almost any asset class or market segment, ranging from broad swathes of the market (global, region or country) or slices based on industry sectors, investment style or themes to more sophisticated indexes that seek to create performance through different methods of stock selection and weighting.

Typical costs relative to funds

While ETFs are bought and sold on commission like any other common share, they also have an annual expense fee, as with other funds, but no sales load. Overall, ETFs are known for their lower costs relative to other index and, certainly, active funds. The annual management fee cost with the additional annual expense is called the total expense ratio (TER). Broad market ETFs, such as a UK All-Share ETF, have a TER of approximately 0.3–0.4%. 'Specialist' ETFs, such as those referred to in this chapter, have TERs generally of 0.65%.

If they are so simple, why have they been confusing?

Initial understanding and acceptance of ETFs in the market evolved slowly because of a number of factors. Many early ETFs were given names – 'SPDRs', 'Qubes' or 'HOLDRs' – that tended to create the perception that these were complicated and, perhaps, slightly 'crafty' instruments meant only for sophisticated investors. Although meant simply to promote an issuer's brand of ETFs, the names unintentionally gave the impression that ETFs were vastly different from and more complicated than buying a stock – which they are not.

Also, too much emphasis has often been given to describing in detail the 'behind-the-scenes' process of maintaining the ETF's NAV as close to 'par' as possible with the value of the underlying assets. Investors need not be overly concerned with the mechanics, as they simply buy and sell their shares on the secondary market, as with any other stock. Although we will describe how this 'primary' creation and redemption process works, the discussion of 'arbitrage' by ETF promoters has possibly had the unintended effect of confusing many investors.

The evolution of ETFs

The ETF vehicle was launched in 1993, with the State Street Global Advisors SPDR ETF on the S&P 500, which remains the largest and most heavily traded ETF and stock globally. This came about when the American Stock Exchange used the US Securities and Exchange Commission's (SEC's) 'SuperTrust Order' to request authorisation for the first index-based ETF. Trends on two sides of the fund business had been leading up to this. The trend of index investing through open-ended funds had grown since its beginnings in 1973, spurred on with the launch of Vanguard's S&P 500 fund. Yet the closed-end fund institutions were offering basket securities with maturity dates, which could be traded on the secondary market and continuously priced. The best of both vehicles was brought together in the ETF, providing the trading frequency of the closed-end fund and the liquidity and stability of the NAV to underlying assets of the open-ended fund.

Size of ETF market relative to mutual funds
As of the first-quarter 2011, there were 3,649 ETFs with $1.5 trillion in assets under management globally. This compares with some 68,863 mutual funds globally, representing about $23.07 trillion in assets at the end of the third quarter of 2010.

Although still comparatively small, the ETF industry is remarkable in how quickly it has grown relative to the growth of the traditional fund industry. The first mutual fund was launched in 1924. It took approximately 60 years for assets to reach the level ETFs have achieved in the 15 years since the first was launched in 1993. However, since much of the growth in funds can be attributed to their use in defined contribution plans – which have become the retirement vehicle of choice – we can expect that as ETFs gain greater currency with the administration in Washington, a similar demographic engine will propel their acceleration.

Different legal structures
Most ETFs are structured as open-ended funds because this provides the greatest flexibility. They are allowed to reinvest dividends and to use options and futures, which in turn sample the index rather than fully replicate it.

As ETFs have evolved from the parentage of exchange traded unit trusts (UITs), some of the first ETFs were structured as unit trusts or closed-end funds instead of the more commonly used open-ended structure preferred today.

The most well known of these are the SPDRs, but not the more recent Select Sector SPDRs, and Qubes (QQQ). Although unit trusts also trade on an exchange, their structure does not allow the reinvestment of dividends daily as open-ended funds do. They must hold dividends until they are distributed to shareholders quarterly or annually. This results in higher levels of cash being carried, higher tracking error to the index and a potential drag on performance. They are actually set with an expiration date – at which time the trust may close – but most simply extend this on a rolling basis. UITs must use full replication of an index and cannot receive income from stock lending.

The Merrill Lynch HOLDRs were also created in the early days of ETFs and they too use a guarantor trust structure, another form of closed-end unit trust. An important point here is that the HOLDRs are a fixed basket of stocks that are not re-balanced to an index following a merger or an acquisition of a company. As a result, the funds become less representative of a sector over time and become more concentrated with fewer holdings. They can only be bought and sold in 100-share lots.

More recently, we have seen the development of additional exchange traded products that are not funds: exchange traded notes (ETNs) and exchange traded commodities (ETCs).

ETNs are registered debt instruments that offer a return linked to the performance of an index plus principal at maturity. Their tax treatment is different from that of funds, but this generally means that as prepaid contracts the taxable event occurs only upon sale, redemption or at maturity.

ETCs are open-ended securities but not funds. They can be traded throughout the day on an exchange by investors and created and redeemed by market makers, ensuring matching liquidity of the underlying securities.

Figure 1. ETFs made simple – how they compare with mutual funds

	ETFs	Mutual funds
How traded	Bought through a broker, traded on an exchange throughout the day on the secondary market between investors	Bought and sold from the fund company, which values the portfolio and prices the fund daily
Trading flexibility	Throughout a trading session	Once daily
Short selling/stock lending	Yes	None
Bought or sold on margin	Yes	No
Types of orders	Market, limit and stop orders	Only market orders
Passive or active	Always passive, tied to a specific index (even if the index includes elements of more active security selection and weighting); may change with fund company's willingness to disclose holdings continuously	Passive or active
Frequency of reporting fund holdings	Transparent continuously throughout the day	Semi-annually or as required by regulator
When priced	Continuously throughout the trading session	At end of each day
Fees/costs	Commission and annual expense fee (typically lower than average active funds)	Annual expense fee; may have sales load
Tax implications	In-kind creation and redemption process, generally, shields the fund from having to sell underlying holdings to fund redemptions. This bypasses a trigger of taxable gains for shareholders	Taxable events are triggered when fund redemptions cause the fund to sell holdings. These sales are passed through to the investor as a taxable gain
Fund type	Mostly open-ended	Open-ended, closed-ended
Risk of NAV trading at discount to underlying portfolio	Very little – designed to keep NAV close to value of underlying holdings. But may vary from time to time	None with open-ended, as the value of each share is a portion of the portfolio priced each day. Closed-ended shares can often trade at a discount or premium to the underlying portfolio

Applications in an investment strategy

ETFs are so flexible and cost effective that they can be used to execute many portfolio strategies ranging from core equity to accessing specialist sectors. They are uniquely suited to implementing asset allocation or sector rotation strategies, offering diversification and cash equitisation at a stroke. Since they can be sold short, and many have options and futures traded on the ETF, they can equally be used by institutions to effectively hedge exposures to countries or sectors.

The mechanism that keeps ETFs trading at 'par'

ETFs were designed with a unique feature to ensure that the share price trades roughly at 'par' to the value of the underlying holdings. In simple terms, the fund company allows large institutional investors (called authorised participants) to buy or redeem shares by exchanging the equal value of underlying stocks in kind. Should there be a time when an ETF begins to trade at a discount to the true underlying portfolio value, institutions can take advantage of this opportunity to make money by buying 50,000-share blocks of the ETF in the open market. These can then be redeemed through the fund company for the underlying stocks – which can then be sold in the open market for a profit.

In theory, this arbitrage opportunity will drive up demand for the shares in the ETF, thereby closing the gap between the NAV and the value of the portfolio. This arbitrage opportunity is the much-described creation and redemption process that keeps the ETF price roughly at equilibrium. Figure 2 illustrates this process:

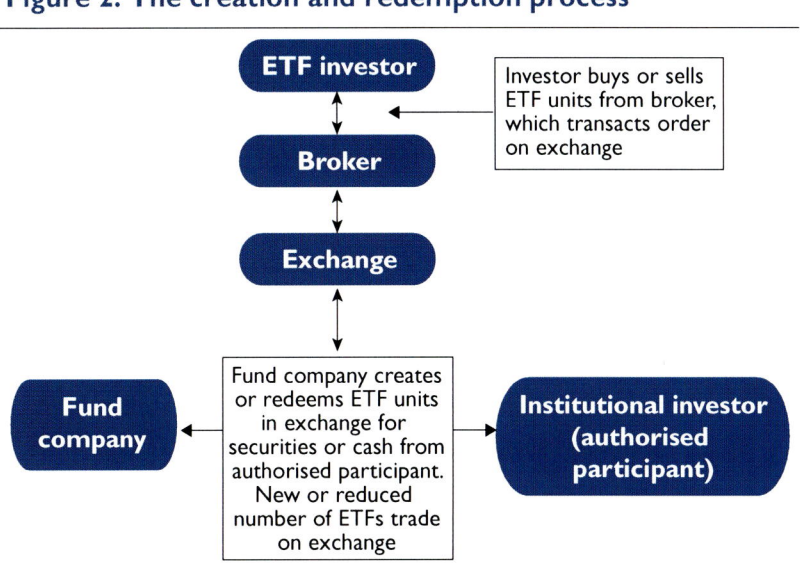

Figure 2. The creation and redemption process

```
         ETF investor
              ↕              Investor buys or sells
                             ETF units from broker,
           Broker            which transacts order
              ↕              on exchange
          Exchange
              ↕
Fund      Fund company creates    Institutional investor
company ← or redeems ETF units →  (authorised
          in exchange for          participant)
          securities or cash from
          authorised participant.
          New or reduced
          number of ETFs trade
          on exchange
```

Evaluating an ETF means understanding its underlying index

Evaluating an ETF is like evaluating any other security. It requires a good understanding of its place in the portfolio, match to the investment objectives, assessment of fees and structure, and comparison to comparable offerings.

Index funds and ETFs have the advantage that they are based upon a published 'rule book' that documents the method of security selection, weighting and maintenance of the index. This is probably the most important element of ETF selection that most investors skip because it enables the investor to predict the types of securities that will be held over time in the index – not just those in the 'top 10' list of the factsheet today. This is of utmost importance when seeking to invest in very specific sectors or strategies, such as clean technology. Under close inspection, one may find that some clean-tech indexes 'dilute' the objective of the fund, investing in utility companies that may receive only a small portion of their revenues from new environmentally beneficial technologies. However, it means taking the time to discover from the ETF prospectus the index that is to be used, and then going to that index provider's website to download the methodology description.

ETFs in clean technology and limited resources

The list of new ETFs in the areas of environmentally sound technology and practices is growing daily. Figure 3 lists those ETFs available today covering companies that provide clean energy and access to scarce resources.

Figure 3. Examples of ETFs on clean energy and other resources

ETF	Bloomberg price ticker	Annual TER, basis points
BROAD MARKET ENVIRONMENTAL SOLUTIONS		
EasyETF FTSE Environmental Opportunities 100	EEVEUR FP	45
Osmosis Climate Solutions ETF	OCS LN	70
iShares Jantzi Social Index Fund	XEN CN	50*
iShares MSCI USA ESG Select Social Index Fund	KLD US	50
iShares MSCI KLD 400 Social Index Fund	DSI US	50
KTB GREAT SRI ETF	120210 KS	na
Listed Index Fund FTSE Japan Green Chip 35	1347 JP	40
CLEAN/ALTERNATIVE ENERGY		
CS ETF IE on Credit Suisse Global Alternative Energy	CSAE SW	65
Elements Linked to the Credit Suisse Global Warming Index (ETN)	GWO US	75
ETFX DAXglobal Alternative Energy Fund	ETLG ID	65
First Trust NASDAQ Clean Edge Green Energy Index Fund	QCLN US	60
iShares S&P Global Clean Energy Index Fund	ICLN US	48
iShares S&P Global Clean Energy	INRG LN	65
KSM Cleartech	KSMCLNT	na

ETF	Bloomberg price ticker	Annual TER, basis points
CLEAN/ALTERNATIVE ENERGY *continued*		
Lyxor ETF New Energy	NRJ FP	60
Market Vectors Global Alternative Energy ETF	GEX US	62
PowerShares Cleantech Portfolio	PZD US	67
PowerShares Global Clean Energy Fund	PSBW LN	75
PowerShares Global Clean Energy Portfolio	PBD US	75
PowerShares Wilder Hill Clean Energy Portfolio	PBW US	70
PowerShares Wilder Hill Progressive Energy Portfolio	PUW US	70
WIND POWER		
First Trust ISE Global Wind Energy	FAN US	60
PowerShares Global Wind Energy Portfolio	PWND US	75
SOLAR POWER		
Guggenheim Solar ETF	TAN US	65
Market Vectors Solar Energy ETF	KWT US	65
NUCLEAR ENERGY		
ETFX WNA Global Nuclear Energy Fund	ETLA ID	65
iShares S&P Global Nuclear Energy Index Fund	NUCL US	48
Market Vectors Uranium+Nuclear Energy ETF	NLR US	62
PowerShares Global Nuclear Energy Portfolio	PKN US	75
CARBON EMISSIONS		
db x-trackers S&P US Carbon Efficient	XGRD LN	50
EasyETF Low Carbon 100 Europe	ECN FP	60
iPath Global Carbon ETN	GRN	75
WATER		
Claymore S&P Global Water ETF	CWW CN	60*
ETFX S-Network Global Water Fund	ETLF ID	65
First Trust ISE Water Index Fund	FIW US	60
Guggenheim S&P Global Water Index ETF	CGW US	65
iShares S&P Global Water	IH2O LN	65
KSM Water	KSMDJWA IT	na
Lyxor ETF World Water	WAT FP	60
Power Shares Global Water Portfolio	PIO US	75
PowerShares Palisades Global Water Fund	PSHO LN	75
PowerShares Water Resources Portfolio	PHO US	64
TIMBER/FORESTRY		
Guggenheim Timber ETF	CUT US	65
iShares S&P Global Timber & Forestry Index Fund	WOOD US	48
iShares S&P Global Timber & Forestry	WOOD LN	65
WASTE DISPOSAL/ENVIRONMENTAL CLEAN-UP		
Market Vectors Environment Service ETF	EVX US	55

*Management fee only   Source: BlackRock ETF Landscape Global Handbook Q1 2011

Due diligence checklist

To ensure that you know what you are buying, it is worth considering the following as a checklist prior to placing an order:

- **Benchmark used as basis for ETF:** Understand not only what securities will be held in the index, but also on what basis they may be changed. The key is to understand the methodology. It should be transparent enough in its description to enable the methodology to be replicated easily.
- **Turnover:** How much turnover should be expected? What is the frequency of re-balancing?
- **Concentration limits:** For the investor's domicile, does the index and prospectus identify regulations the fund will follow for limits on concentration of single securities or sectors? Is the fund UCITS III compliant?
- **Method of index replication:** Will the fund buy and sell every stock in the index using the full replication method? Or can the fund sample and optimise the index, creating a portfolio that is similar in performance and characteristics but with different securities and weights? Can the fund potentially use a different universe of stocks or derivatives through synthetic replication?
- **Costs:** What is the expense ratio? Are similar funds available on the same index at lower cost? Is the expense ratio capped in the prospectus or could it be increased in future? What might be the turnover implied by the frequency of re-balancing?
- **Track record:** How closely has the ETF tracked its benchmark? Does the difference reflect trading costs or does it seem unacceptably large? There should be at least three years of back-tested history for the index if the fund is new. How has it performed relative to similar sectors and does it provide the correlation or diversification the investor is seeking?
- **Liquidity:** If the ETF has been in existence for some time, look at the average daily volume and the bid/offer spread versus comparable ETFs and ensure that it is the most frequently traded fund. The first fund to market often takes the lion's share of the market. Subsequent funds at apparently lower expense ratios may still have lower assets under management, be more thinly traded and not offer the liquidity or derivative exposure that is available on larger funds. Likewise, the investor should enquire to what degree the fund has ever traded at a discount to its underlying portfolio.

Chapter 16

Climate bonds – the investment case

*Sean Kidney, Stuart Clenaghan and Padraig Oliver,
The Climate Bonds Initiative*

Introduction

There is now a broad international consensus among governments, corporations and the public that urgent action is required to cut greenhouse gas emissions. This consensus is built upon a widespread acknowledgement that climate change will impact the livelihoods of a majority of the world's population and leave few areas of the economy unaffected. The challenge now is to mobilise the capital required to invest in alternatives to fossil fuels, and to make the infrastructural investments that are necessary for adaptation to climate change.

This capital is required urgently as greenhouse gas levels continue to rise, causing changes in climate patterns that are resulting in economic disruption. According to the International Energy Agency (IEA), each year of delay adds a further $1 trillion to the bill for the transition to a global low-carbon economy.

Reducing dependence on fossil fuels and adopting a low-carbon economy is of global importance, and is a priority for policy-makers in both developed and developing economies.

However, many governments are severely constrained in their ability to invest in greening their economies, given already extended public balance sheets and fragile global economic conditions. It is clear the vast majority of the required investment must come from mobilising private sector capital, in particular from the institutional investors that manage the bulk of the world's private wealth.

The largest portion of funds managed by institutions is allocated to the bond market. It is estimated that more than $95 trillion of bonds were outstanding in 2010.[1] Of this amount, 72% is held by long-term investors such as pension funds, mutual funds, insurance companies and sovereign wealth funds.

The challenge is not to create new capital, but to shift a portion of existing investment into low-carbon development.

There is evidence that a growing number of fund managers and advisers are now seeking to align their investments with the low-carbon agenda. This is not just

---
1 *Bond Markets*, CityUK Financial Market Series (July 2011), www.thecityuk.co.uk.

in response to public opinion, but also because they see new opportunities arising from green technologies, as well as threats to conventional investments from climate change. Although some investors are calling for greater policy certainty before making investments, others are already demonstrating their commitment by investing in bonds and other instruments that are specifically targeted at financing low-carbon projects.

It is in this context that a market has developed for 'climate' and 'green' bonds, which are defined as asset-backed or ring-fenced bonds designed to raise finance for climate change mitigation projects that deliver genuine reductions in emissions, or for climate change adaptation measures.

Although the market is relatively small in size, at about $12 billion (July 2011), climate bond investors have a growing appetite for products that can be independently verified as contributing to the financing of a low-carbon economy.

The development of a market for climate bonds (used interchangeably with the term green bonds) is supported by the Climate Bonds Initiative, an international network comprising a group of more than 50 leading finance and climate experts, together with some of the world's largest institutional investors. One of the Climate Bond Initiative's key projects is the creation of an International Standards and Certification Scheme that will promote the integrity and liquidity of this important market.

The immediate low-carbon financing need

Climate change presents one of the greatest challenges ever faced by the global community. Practically every economic activity, including production, transport and construction, is founded upon the use of fossil fuels that produce high carbon emissions. As more countries make the transition towards industrialisation, so the world faces greater risks as energy consumption rises.

A structural shift in key sectors of the global economy is required to ensure that future development is placed on a sustainable footing. This will encompass investment in many sectors, including clean energy, and also in the infrastructure and technology required for delivery. As an example, the successful adoption of electric vehicles needs the installation of charging points or battery exchange stations as well as the development of vehicles that meet consumer expectations. Reducing energy consumption in the construction sector requires retrofitting existing stock as well as the construction of efficient new buildings.

At the same time, more and more countries face the expense of investing in new infrastructure to adapt to the effects of climate change that are already being experienced. For example, municipal, coastal and agricultural areas require climate-proofing infrastructural investment to ensure that clean water and food supply is secured.

The investment required to achieve transitions to low-carbon transport, low-carbon energy and low-carbon buildings is estimated by the IEA to be $1 trillion a year above business as usual.[2] If the sustainable management of natural resources such as forests, fisheries, agricultural land, water and tourism is included, an average investment of $1.3 trillion per year is required out to 2050, according to the UN Environment Programme's Green Economy Initiative.[3]

In the EU alone, the consulting group Accenture has calculated that €2.9 trillion of investment is required by 2020 to support the deployment of 15 low-carbon technologies in electricity generation and transmission, transport and buildings.[4]

However, the capital deployed to date is a small fraction of what is required to effect the necessary transition to a low-carbon economy. Investment in clean energy reached $243 billion in 2010, with asset finance comprising the largest component of this at $127.8 billion.[5]

Many people believe that the key to unlocking the required investment lies in wholesale capital markets, and especially the $95 trillion bond market. To achieve this, bond issuers need to deliver products that meet defined low-carbon objectives while offering acceptable risks and returns for investors.

Policy perspective

Although there has been no international agreement on climate change following the UN Framework Convention on Climate Change meeting at Copenhagen in 2009, governments around the world are unilaterally introducing climate-friendly policies and regulations.

The EU has long championed low-carbon economic development and is now considering strategies that would deliver 80–95% reductions in emissions by 2050.

China has committed to carbon intensity-based reduction targets and is actively promoting policy support for low-carbon industry sectors. China recently announced its 12th Five-Year Plan for 2011–15, which sets out specific targets to reduce carbon intensity by 17% and increase non-fossil fuel energy to 11.4% of primary energy consumption, together with ambitious investment budgets for clean energy and environmental protection.

And the US, which lacks a federal framework for climate change mitigation, has kick-started low-carbon industries and has a target of producing 80% of its electricity from clean technology by 2035.[6]

However, austerity measures in many industrialised countries have severely limited the scope with which governments can use tax revenues to support low-carbon projects. This is particularly relevant to energy and infrastructure projects, which

---
2 International Energy Agency, *World Energy Outlook 2010*, www.iea.org.
3 UNEP (2011), *Towards a Green Economy: Pathways to Sustainable Development and Poverty Eradication*, www.unep.org/greeneconomy.
4 Barclays (2011), *Carbon Capital: Financing the low carbon economy* – a report prepared by Accenture. London, UK.
5 www.bnef.com/PressReleases/view/134.
6 www.reuters.com/article/2011/01/26/us-obama-speech-energy-idUSTRE70O50V20110126.

often require secure long-term revenue streams to enable up-front finance to be put in place. As a result the cost of capital for these projects has increased significantly.

This is exacerbated in countries with developing economies which face higher financing costs because of country risk ratings. The capital-heavy nature of renewable energy investment often makes it much more expensive than traditional energy generation and as a result capital has been largely flowing into fossil fuel-based technologies.

Policy-makers have responded to calls for certainty by introducing carbon pricing through emissions trading systems, or carbon taxes in the form of price floors. While carbon markets are important for the long-term sustainability of a low-carbon economy, poor market design and low prices have meant that insufficient investment has flowed to low-carbon projects to date.

Clean energy technologies require more targeted support, particularly for long-term revenue streams. Feed-in tariff (FiT) regimes have been introduced across Europe spurring a scaling up of global manufacturing in the solar photovoltaic and wind industries. However, the risk for prospective long-term investors, such as bondholders, is that successor governments may undermine such revenue support. Poor investment sentiment has been exacerbated by recent discussions aimed at amending existing subsidy schemes, notably in Spain, the Czech Republic and the UK.

Investment perspective

The unfortunate reality is that government policy responses have yet to deliver an adequate framework for meeting the risk/return requirements of long-term institutional investors. From a fund manager's perspective, climate change presents both a potential risk to conventional investments, but also an opportunity to participate in a huge and dynamic new low-carbon economy. What is certain is that no investor can afford to ignore the issue, as climate change will undoubtedly alter macroeconomic conditions as well as the business environment for most corporations around the world.

With these considerations in mind many of the world's largest fund managers are already factoring the impact of climate change into their investment decisions. This has led to institutions making investment allocations based upon criteria that take account of the projected effects of a rise in mean global temperatures. For example, Denmark's ATP pension fund has set up a $1 billion climate change investment fund and, last year, the California State Teachers' Retirement System (CalSTRS) instructed managers to incorporate climate risk into their investment analysis and corporate governance voting practices.[7] The Norwegian Global Fund, one of the largest in the world, has been active in shifting funds away from investments regarded as harmful to the environment.

---

[7] www.pionline.com/article/20100111/PRINTSUB/301119988.

Climate bonds – the investment case | 245

In February 2011, leading investment consultant Mercer released a major report looking at how institutional investors could begin to mitigate climate risks in their portfolios. It concluded that allocating investment to climate-sensitive assets – such as infrastructure, agriculture, timberland and real estate – can help to de-risk portfolios from the impacts of climate change compared to a business-as-usual scenario.[8]

It is not only institutions that are factoring climate change into investment decision-making. Many individual savers are now taking a greater interest in ensuring that their investments are managed responsibly and towards stated objectives. This has led to a rapid growth in socially responsible investment funds – almost doubling from $2.7 trillion of assets under management in 2008 to approximately $5 trillion in 2010[9] – as well as the nascent green bond market, where bond issuers use proceeds for low-carbon projects. To date around $12 billion equivalent of green or climate bonds have been issued, with investors targeted in specific markets ranging from Japan to Scandinavia.[10]

However, if such deal-flow is to scale up rapidly to meet investment requirements under climate change scenarios, climate bonds will need to compete in a mainstream investment environment that prioritises commercial returns above any social or environmental considerations. Specifically, the underlying characteristics of bonds will need to align with investors' needs in terms of price, credit risk and liquidity to match existing asset allocation strategies.[11]

Tapping bond markets to combat climate change

The emergence of a climate bond market presents an opportunity to stimulate private investment into the low-carbon economy, aligning investor appetite to projects with stated climate objectives.

Climate bonds are themed, asset-backed or ring-fenced bonds specifically issued to finance climate mitigation and adaptation measures. They are designed to fit the portfolio requirements of investors while meeting rigorous low-carbon financing criteria. The market for climate bonds is only a few years old but is growing strongly, with $4 billion–8 billion slated for release in 2012. As more and more investors seek to engage with the low-carbon economy, so climate bonds could become the key to unlocking the vast potential of the international bond market to bridge the financing gap.

The emergence of a climate bond market presents governments with a range of policy instruments to stimulate private investment into low-carbon projects. They could support the market directly through preferential tax treatment, or through the provision of partial guarantees. Alternatively, governments could support the

---
8 Mercer (2011), *Climate Change Scenarios: Implications for strategic asset allocation*. London, UK.
9 Eurosif (2010), *European SRI Study 2010*. Paris, France.
10 www.climatebonds.net.
11 Institutional Investors Group on Climate Change (2011), *Positioning Paper on Green Bonds*.

Figure 1. Breakdown of climate bonds market

Total climate bonds issued: $12 billion

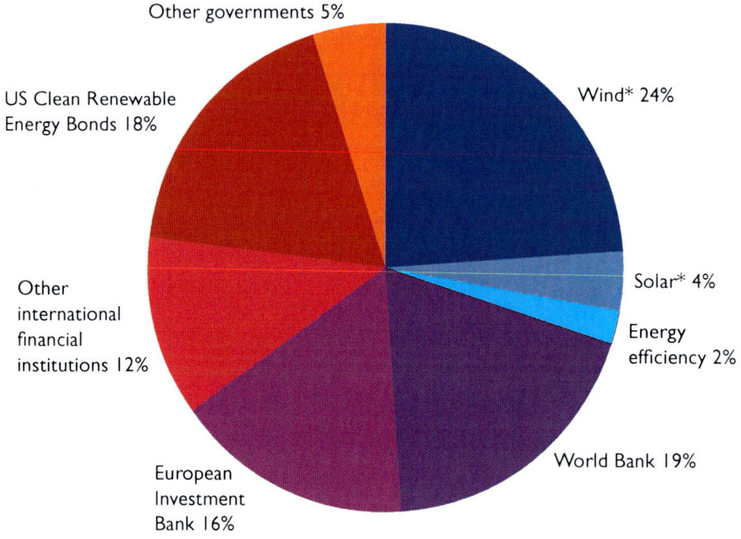

- Other governments 5%
- US Clean Renewable Energy Bonds 18%
- Other international financial institutions 12%
- European Investment Bank 16%
- World Bank 19%
- Energy efficiency 2%
- Solar* 4%
- Wind* 24%

*asset backed or corporate.   As at March 2011. Source: Climate Bonds Initiative

market indirectly through stable climate-related policy and regulatory frameworks, such as FiT regimes with locked-in, long-term characteristics, which would support the financial strength of bond issuers. In these respects governments could replicate the policy environment previously enjoyed by the fossil fuel industry.

To date, a number of bond issuers have used thematic bonds to raise finance for targeted low-carbon projects.

The first climate bond was issued by the European Investment Bank (EIB) in 2007: €600 million with a maturity of five years and an index-linked coupon with a minimum 5% pay-out. The EIB's programme of Climate Awareness Bonds[12] totalled $1.98 billion equivalent in fixed- and floating-rate formats at August 2011.

The first 'vanilla' green bond, a Skr2.85 billion issue with six-year maturity and 3.5% fixed-rate coupon and proceeds ring-fenced for climate change projects, was issued by the World Bank in November 2008 and was placed mainly with institutional investors. Since then the World Bank has followed through with 41 individual bond issues denominated in various currencies, and each targeted at specific investor segments. By January 2011 an equivalent of $2.2 billion had been issued.[13] Other international finance institutions that have issued green labelled bonds include the

12 www.eib.org/investor_relations/documents/eib-cab-newsletter-2010.htm.
13 http://treasury.worldbank.org/cmd/htm/WorldBankGreenBonds.html.

International Finance Corporation (IFC), the Asian Development Bank (ADB), the African Development Bank (AfDB) and the European Bank for Reconstruction and Development (EBRD).

The US government has taken a lead in supporting the issuance of clean renewable energy bonds (CREBs) by providing tax incentives for investors, and is promoting legislation to support energy conservation efforts through Property-Assessed Clean Energy (PACE) programmes.

Asset-backed bond issuance is beginning to attract investors. Early financings, such as the 2006 and 2007 Breeze bonds portfolio issuances totalling $1.6 billion and the 2006 $129 million Alte Liebe issue, were downgraded by credit rating agencies as a result of lower than expected wind strength and thus lower cash flows than expected.

However, market conditions in the wake of the financial crisis have led to more innovative bond financing structures developing for project finance. Examples include Alta Wind Energy Centre, a 3GW wind farm project funded in part by a $580 million bond in 2010 and the first major solar project bond, launched in 2010, when Sunpower/Andromeda Finance raised $260 million. In an example of conducive government support, the Sunpower bond was partially supported by a credit enhancement facility from SACE, the export credit agency of Italy, where the 44MW solar farm is located.

There is considerable scope to scale up the supply of climate bonds. Barclays and Accenture estimate that €1.4 trillion could be unlocked by 2020 through the securitisation of long-term low-carbon project loans and lease financing in the EU alone.[14]

Tools to grow the climate bond market

The Climate Bonds Initiative (CBI) was set up to bring together key participants including investors, industry and governments to help crystallise the rapid emergence of bond finance for the low-carbon economy. The CBI comprises some 50 finance and climate experts from around the world, together with organisation partners including some of the world's largest institutional investors.

The CBI is developing a series of models and financial architecture designed to provide supporting infrastructure to facilitate bond investments that credibly contribute to transitioning to a low-carbon economy. This includes an International Standards and Certification Scheme for climate bonds.

Standardisation of climate bonds

Currently there is little in the way of standard terms and definitions that investors can use to verify that the proceeds of climate bonds are specifically applied to fund low-carbon projects. Without standardised terms the growth of the market is likely

---

14 Barclays (2011), *Carbon Capital: Financing the low carbon economy* – a report prepared by Accenture. London, UK.

to falter, as investors need confidence that bond issuers are actually using funds in a way that contributes to building the low-carbon economy. Indeed, some issuers such as the World Bank have already found it necessary to obtain independent verification of their 'green' claims to re-assure investors.

The CBI has established a standards and certification scheme for climate bonds, backed by a broad-based coalition of asset-owners, NGOs and key stakeholders from the financial and low-carbon industry. A working prototype of the standard was released in late August 2011, after a lengthy, transparent process of stakeholder consultation and participation.[15]

The scheme aims to reduce the cost of labelling and verification for issuers and for investors through the development of agreed standards for thematic climate bonds. It is expected that their adoption will help enhance liquidity and build critical mass for climate bonds.

Within the standards and certification work stream there are expert committees, comprising market, industry and legal professionals, which are developing industry-specific criteria. The creation of acceptable standards is by no means straightforward. For example, although it is relatively easy to define the contribution to climate change mitigation of renewable energy bonds backed by wind and solar power assets, it is more challenging to create standards for bond issues which support ethanol plants with debatable emission profiles. What level of emission reductions should qualify?

The standards and certification committees must take account of secondary impacts – for example, supporting an electric vehicle infrastructure roll-out without the parallel decarbonisation of the electricity grid. Can enabling technologies such as broadband infrastructure result in the desired emission reduction impact? While the complex nature of these issues suggests that absolute definitions could remain elusive, agreeing transparent standards will be essential to supporting climate bonds as a mainstream asset class.

Investors in green bond issuance to date have largely been attracted by the prestige and trust engendered by major supranational institutions such as the World Bank and the EIB. However, even with these issuers, transparency and standardisation has been sub-optimal. When SEB Bank was mandated to underwrite and place World Bank green bonds, an independent audit of the product's environmental claims was commissioned as part of its labelling due diligence. The findings of this review, conducted by Oslo-based research centre CICERO, drove the ring-fencing of specific capital expenditure programmes that gave the underwriter the confidence to label the bonds as 'green'. The EIB argues that it does the same for funds raised through Climate Awareness Bonds and allows for public monitoring of disbursements through its financial statements.

---

15 www.climatebonds.net

As private sector players and other stakeholders enter the market, the questions of agreed and credible definitions become more urgent. climate bonds have progressed from plain vanilla bonds solely issued by supranational institutions, to corporate bonds for projects supported by feed-in tariffs, and to hybrid structures such as index-linked bonds based on a basket of green companies' performance or the achievement of certified emission reductions.

To support the growth of climate finance, standardised definitions will need to be formulated down to the sub-classes of climate bonds including those issued by governments, corporations and infrastructure projects.

A financing bridge to a low-carbon economy

Climate bonds offer the ability for investors and policy-makers rapidly to scale up finance and action for the transition to a low carbon economy. There is growing appetite from the investment community for bonds that are specifically targeted at financing the low-carbon economy. However, for the market to grow and for liquidity to develop, investors need tools to help them monitor and verify the climate effectiveness of their investments.

It is clear that the private sector will shoulder a large part of responsibility for delivering low-carbon economic transition, especially given the tight fiscal conditions that many governments are experiencing. A large and liquid climate bond market will stimulate innovation from banks, issuers and policy-makers alike and will make an important contribution to bridging the financing gap that currently exists.

The incentives to create this environment are strong for the key stakeholders. Governments need to be able to signal encouragement for and track private capital financial flows in investment-poor areas of the economy. Investors need to be able to signal particular investment areas which they are interested in and assure the public that institutional capital is being invested in their interest. The public needs to know that a vehicle for catalysing large-scale financial flows to ensure future environmental stability is available and that the financial sector is supporting this future.

Chapter 17

Carbon risk and carbon trading: considerations for institutional investors

Xinting Jia, Mercer

Introduction

There is now near-universal agreement that climate change, if left unchecked, will have a catastrophic impact on the environment and consequently the global economy. The financial crisis has diverted attention from the issue in the short term and created additional uncertainty surrounding the way in which the climate change policy framework will develop over the coming years. Nevertheless, it seems likely that the practice of placing a price on carbon emissions will still be on the political agenda across regions and industries over the long run. Investors need to understand the carbon risk in their current portfolio to ensure that it is effectively managed and give due consideration to emerging carbon-related investment opportunities.

To address climate change, reducing greenhouse gas emissions has become a major policy objective. Thus far, most of the attention has been on carbon dioxide (CO_2), the main greenhouse gas. To achieve reductions in carbon emissions in a cost-effective manner, a number of emission trading schemes have been established following the adoption of the Kyoto Protocol in 1997. Most emission trading systems employ a cap-and-trade system and so far the vast majority of carbon emission permits have been allocated free of charge to companies coming within the scope of the schemes. Emitters must either limit carbon emissions to the level of their allocation, or purchase additional carbon emission permits in the market.

This has effectively created a new commodity – carbon (or, more accurately, carbon emission permits). And, whereas limitless carbon emissions were previously free, each tonne of carbon emitted now carries a clear cost to emitters covered by a carbon trading scheme – a direct cost if permits must be bought or an opportunity cost if the chance to generate revenue from sale of permits is forgone.

The pricing of carbon can have a substantial short- to medium-term impact on companies' cashflows, earnings, valuations and risk profiles. The effectiveness with which companies respond to the carbon challenge will also affect their competitive positioning over the longer term. Furthermore, the number of companies which are covered by the various carbon trading systems around the world looks set to increase considerably over coming years.

Companies are evaluating the impact of carbon pricing on their operations, risk management plans and broader corporate strategies. Nevertheless, institutional investors also need to review the carbon risk in their investment portfolios, both at an individual asset level and in aggregate. At the same time, new investment opportunities are arising related to carbon.

This chapter provides an overview of carbon trading markets and the investment considerations facing institutional investors.

Background to carbon trading – the Kyoto Protocol

The Kyoto Protocol was established in 1997 and came into effect in 2005 to help address climate change and reduce greenhouse gas emissions. So far, about 180 countries have signed up to the protocol and about 40 Annex I countries are committed to meeting their emissions targets. Annex I countries include Organisation for Economic Co-operation and Development countries and economies in transition.[1] Countries such as China and India are non-Annex I countries; they have ratified the protocol but are not yet required to meet any emission reduction targets.

Countries that have agreed to reduce their emissions can achieve the target either by curtailing domestic emissions or by purchasing permits from other countries – through emission trading schemes. Carbon emission permits can be categorised into two major types, allowance-based and project-based.

ALLOWANCE-BASED PERMITS

Allowance-based permits are allocated by the regulators under cap-and-trade schemes. A cap-and-trade scheme limits the total emissions by issuing emission permits. Emission permits are allocated or auctioned up to the set cap. Emitters can either sell their excess permits or buy extra in the market to meet their cap.[2]

PROJECT-BASED PERMITS

Project-based permits are generated by participation in certified projects under arrangements such as the Clean Development Mechanism (CDM) and Joint Implementation (JI). Permits issued under these schemes are called certified emission reductions (CERs) and emission reduction units (ERUs) respectively.

Figure 1 illustrates how market-based mechanisms work.

---
[1] Most economies in transition are Eastern European countries.
[2] Definition of cap and trade was sourced from EPA Australia, available at: www.epa.vic.gov.au/climate-change/glossary.asp#CTIM, accessed 6 February 2009.

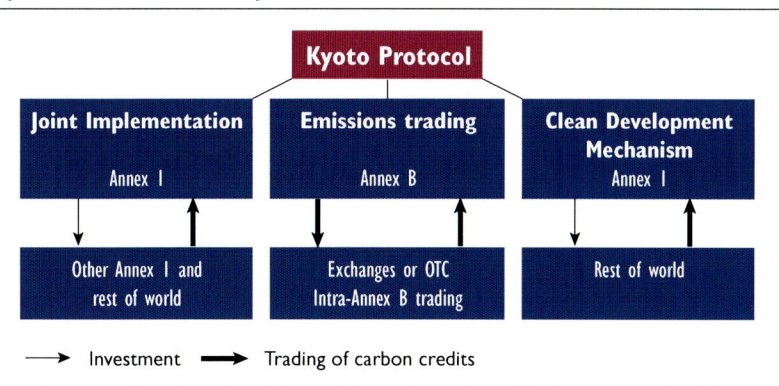

Figure 1. The Kyoto Protocol: three market-driven 'pillars' (flexible mechanisms)

```
                         Kyoto Protocol
            ┌─────────────────┼─────────────────┐
    Joint Implementation  Emissions trading  Clean Development
                                                 Mechanism
          Annex I           Annex B              Annex I
            ↓↑                ↓↑                   ↓↑
    Other Annex I and    Exchanges or OTC      Rest of world
     rest of world       Intra-Annex B trading
```

→ Investment ⇒ Trading of carbon credits

Source: Michael See (2001), Greenhouse gas emissions: global business aspects, page 12

The CDM allows an Annex I country to use carbon credits[3] (CERs) generated from projects in non-Annex I countries to achieve part of its emission reduction target. JI refers to carbon credits (ERUs) achieved from emission reduction projects in Annex I countries that can be used by other Annex I countries to achieve targets. These project-based mechanisms encourage transfer of environmentally friendly technology to economies in transition and non-Annex I countries[4] as well as facilitating collaboration among Annex I and non-Annex I parties.

To qualify for permits, CDM and JI projects must undergo a rigorous certification process. China and India are currently major sources of carbon credits generated from projects that have been certified under the CDM. In contrast, JI projects are mainly based in economies in transition countries (mostly in Eastern Europe).

Permits generated via the CDM and JI are expressed in the same units as European Union Emission Trading System (EU ETS) permits – EU allowances (EUAs) – and can be traded. They are not exchangeable one-for-one with EU ETS permits or with each other.

Most Eastern European countries have ratified the protocol. Due to economic downturn since the baseline year of 1990, some of these countries appear to have been allocated emission targets well in excess of their anticipated emissions in the first commitment period. Examples are Russia and Ukraine. This has created concern that these so called 'hot air credits' could undermine the effort to reduce emissions.

---
3 Carbon credits and permits mean the same and are used interchangeably.
4 Source: United Nations Framework Convention on Climate Change (UNFCCC).

Emission trading schemes – an overview

TRENDS IN TURNOVER AND PRICES

The EU ETS, launched in 2005, is by far the largest carbon trading scheme in the world. The volume and value of transactions have grown strongly over the relatively short period during which the EU ETS has been in operation. Nevertheless, the value of transactions remains very modest relative to transactions in major world markets relevant to institutional investors (stocks, bonds, real estate etc).

Trading of certificates issued under project-based mechanisms, CDM and JI, has also grown and represents a significant share of total transactions.

THE COMING EXTENSION OF CARBON TRADING SCHEMES

Carbon trading schemes are being extended into both emerging and developed markets. China, for example, plans to reduce carbon pollution and establish emission trading. As stated in its 12th Five-Year Plan (which was released in March 2011), China will set up an emission trading scheme within the next five years. The timeline is shown in Figure 2.

Australia, to give an example of a developed market, has released its plan on introducing a carbon pricing mechanism from 1 July 2012. It will be rolled out in two stages as shown in Figure 3.

To mitigate the likely adverse impact of a carbon price on households, the government will increase the tax-free threshold and tax-cuts to families from 1 July 2012.[5]

Figure 2. China's emission trading scheme: timeline

April 2008	Binhai new area development plan sows the seeds for a carbon market mechanism
June 2008	People's Bank of China and China Investment Corporation, among others, start drafting outlines of an emission trading scheme for the country
August 2008	Environmental exchanges are set up in Beijing, Shanghai and Tianjin
February 2010	The first carbon trades are executed in Beijing and Tianjin
October 2010	The National Development and Reform Commission affirms the prospect of environmental taxes in the forthcoming 12th Five-Year Plan (FYP) and notes that carbon taxes are also being explored
November 2010	A Panda standard is formulated to provide transparency and credibility to carbon offset projects in China
January 2011	The city of Wuxi announces a plan to map out a low-carbon strategy consistent with the concepts being formulated in the 12th FYP
March 2011	A summary draft of the 12th FYP includes cap and trade for the first time as a policy to be implemented on a pilot basis during 2011–15

[5] For further information, see Australian government, 2011, *Securing a clean energy future: the Australian government's climate change plan*, available at: www.cleanenergyfuture.gov.au/wp-content/uploads/2011/07/Consolidated-Final.pdf, accessed 18 July 2011.

Figure 3. Australia's two-stage approach to carbon pricing

1 July 2012–30 June 2015	The price for each tonne of carbon pollution will be fixed – like a tax
From 1 July 2015 onwards	The carbon pricing mechanism will transition to a cap-and-trade emissions trading scheme – the price of each tonne of carbon pollution will be set by the market

Source: *Australian government, 2011, Securing a clean energy future: the Australian government's climate change plan, page 25*

CARBON TRADING SCHEMES – KEY FEATURES

Any carbon trading scheme will provide an incentive for companies within its scope to reduce carbon emissions, and will favour those that are effective in doing so. However, the specific design features are critical to the way in which winners and losers are determined and to the scale of the impacts on companies. The key aspects are:

- *The level of emission allowances set.* All other things being equal, a lower level of allowances, consistent with a more aggressive approach to cutting emissions, will put upward pressure on the carbon price. Companies needing to buy additional allowances will face greater costs and those with a surplus will generate additional revenue.
- *The basis on which allowances are allocated.* If allowances are allocated free of charge to emitters, as has been the case with the vast majority of allowances under the EU ETS to date, the direct up-front financial impact is limited. However, if allowances are auctioned, then heavy emitters face large up-front costs. Under the EU proposal mentioned above, 60% of allowances would be auctioned by 2013 and this proportion will increase over time.
- *The industries and installations covered.* Currently, around 11,000 heavy energy-consuming installations in power generation and manufacturing are covered under the EU ETS. From 2012, emissions from air flights to and from European airports are also likely to be covered.[6]
- *The gases covered.* Carbon dioxide is the major greenhouse gas and therefore the obvious place to start when introducing a new scheme designed to combat climate change. There are, however, other significant greenhouse gases. As this chapter is focused on carbon trading, we will not comment further except to say that many of the principles that apply to carbon will apply to other greenhouse gases when they are included within trading schemes. Other gases, like methane, can be characterised by a 'CO_2 equivalent' and be incorporated in CO_2 trading schemes.
- *Banking.* Under the EU ETS, three phases have been designed: Phase I (2005–

---

[6] For further information, refer to European Commission 2009, *EU action against climate change: the EU emissions trading scheme*, available at: http://ec.europa.eu/clima/publications/docs/ets_en.pdf, accessed 18 July 2011.

07), Phase II (2008–12) and Phase III (2013–20). Banking of credits within Phase I was allowed but not between Phase I and other phases. This was part of the reason for the high fluctuation in the price of carbon permits during Phase I. The banking of credits is allowed between Phase II and Phase III and this may help to reduce the price volatility during the period 2008–20 (Phase II and III).

Carbon risk and investment portfolios

INTRODUCTION

The impact of carbon pricing on business cash-flows can be direct (costs incurred in buying permits or investing in technology to bring emissions within allocations and which cannot be passed on to customers, or revenue generated by selling surplus permits) and indirect (flow-on effects from suppliers, customers etc). Major polluters, such as energy generators and the transport sector, could be materially affected if they need either to reduce their emissions or to purchase emission permits to comply with their emission targets.

In many industries, the approach to managing carbon risk looks set to become an important element of corporate strategy over the longer term.[7] Proactively managing carbon will help to build a robust business framework. It will also help to improve corporate image, as more consumers are now aware of the importance of reducing carbon pollution.

Institutional investment portfolios already have a direct exposure to carbon risk through their underlying investments and this exposure is likely to spread over coming periods. The first task facing trustees is to ensure that analysis of the carbon risks and opportunities is appropriately integrated into decisions in respect of these existing exposures.

In addition, the position of carbon as a (priced) commodity is raising new and interesting investment opportunities. These can be classified as:
- Firstly, taking a long-term strategic (beta) exposure to carbon.
- Secondly, using carbon trading as an opportunity to add 'pure' alpha to portfolios.
- Thirdly, and the category which is likely to be most widely adopted over the short to medium term, investing in projects which can be seen as offering various combinations of alpha and beta exposures to opportunities arising from carbon trading.

Each of these areas is highlighted below.

INTEGRATION INTO DECISION-MAKING RELATING TO EXISTING INVESTMENTS

At least until recently, carbon risk has not generally been adequately considered in investment decision-making. This is because carbon risk will have its most signifi-

[7] PricewaterhouseCoopers, 2008, *Carbon value: robust carbon management- a framework to protect and enhance shareholder value in response to climate change.*

cant impact on company financials over the medium to long term, whereas markets focus on shorter-term outcomes and less on uncertain longer-term outcomes. A further factor is that standards of information disclosure are weaker in this area and analytical techniques and experience are less well developed.

In this regard, the first task for asset owners is to ensure that carbon risks and opportunities are being adequately considered in existing portfolios, most of which will be managed by external parties. Relevant questions to consider include:
- Are our existing managers on top of the issues related to carbon (and broader climate change implications)?
- Does their reporting provide us with comfort?
- Are we giving the right weight to capability in these areas when considering new manager appointments?
- Are we as a trustee group sufficiently well-informed to ask the right questions and to make the right decisions?

In most cases, the bulk of the carbon exposure will reside in equity and commodities portfolios. However, fixed income, private equity, real estate and infrastructure portfolios are potentially also affected.

CARBON AS PART OF STRATEGIC ASSET ALLOCATIONS
Over recent years, a number of institutional investors have made a strategic asset allocation to commodities. Most commonly, this allocation has been invested by taking a long position in a diversified basket of commodity futures.

As discussed above, carbon can be characterised as similar to a commodity. Furthermore, it is possible to gain exposure to carbon through futures markets in much the same way that investors are now investing in commodities. The issue arises as to whether carbon should be given a place within strategic asset allocations.

The justification for establishing a strategic allocation to a new asset class will depend on the investor's overall circumstances (such as investment objectives, risk appetite and need for liquidity) and the particular role that the asset class is expected to play (for instance, risk reduction relative to a particular set of liabilities, return generation). In general terms, however, to warrant a place in strategic asset allocations, asset classes require some combination of:
- The likelihood of generating an attractive return over the medium to long term, ideally due to some underlying fundamental return driver in which investors can have a high degree of confidence.
- Returns that display a low correlation with other key asset classes included in investment allocations, typically equities and bonds.
- Ability to protect against unanticipated inflation – ie, returns that have a relatively high correlation with inflation.
- Returns which are low risk, either relative to liabilities or in an absolute sense.

In terms of returns, the future trend of carbon prices will depend on the interaction of a number of complex factors[8]:
- Government/regulatory policy within and across regions in relation to:
  - the level to which carbon emissions should fall over the long term and the path taken to the long-term position.
  - the balance between carbon pricing and other methods of reducing emissions – eg, policy towards innovation, research and development and encouragement for various mitigation strategies.
- The rate of breakthrough in a wide range of technologies, including in the clean energy/clean-tech areas.
- The rate at which industry and society more generally adopts carbon-saving technology, including that which already exists.
- Cost curves and hence prices for oil, gas and coal.
- The rate of economic growth in key countries.

It is not possible to be certain about any of these elements, let alone the way in which they will interact. Regardless, it is likely to be some years before the arrangements surrounding carbon trading globally are sufficiently settled and before reliable guidance is available on the other important factors mentioned above. All this indicates that carbon prices could remain volatile over a relatively long period of time.

Returns from a passive investment in carbon will be heavily dependent on the liquidity of the market and the mix of participants. In particular, if a large number of investors seek to establish passive long positions in carbon futures the futures price will be bid up, thereby reducing returns as the positions are rolled over.

In terms of correlations, economic growth can be expected to boost returns to carbon in the same way that it will underpin returns to other asset classes (equities, real estate, infrastructure, commodities) over the medium to long term. Nevertheless, over the shorter term, the interplay between the various relevant policy and technological factors should impart a dynamic to the carbon price which is reasonably independent of the cycles experienced by these other asset classes.

Prices of other commodities (energy, agricultural commodities and metals) have a material and direct impact on the cost of living. This provides a fundamental rationale for the observed correlation between commodity prices and inflation. Although the price of carbon will also feed through into industry-wide cost structures, its impact on inflation is unlikely to be as substantial or as direct. Accordingly, the inflation-hedging characteristics of carbon can be expected to be weaker than those of other commodities. That being said, the returns to most asset classes display a negative correlation with inflation and we would expect that carbon would perform better than most asset classes in this regard (although not as well as either other commodities or inflation-linked bonds).

---

8 For an excellent summary of the key issues, see DB Advisors, *Investing in Climate Change 2009*, especially Chapter VI, Part I and Chapters I–III, Part II.

A further possible rationale for inclusion of carbon in strategic asset allocations is to provide protection against climate change itself. To the extent that the negative consequences of climate change become more obvious and/or the progress in cutting emissions is slower than is required, policy-makers are likely to be more prepared to impose tighter restrictions on carbon emissions, putting upward pressure on the carbon price. Accordingly, a strategic allocation to carbon via carbon futures could be seen as a long-term hedge against climate change, and one which avoids many of the difficulties associated with investing in projects with private equity-like characteristics (see below).

In summary, there may, at some stage in the future, be merit in considering a strategic allocation to carbon in order to position for a long-term rise in the price and as a hedge against the negative effects of climate change. In the end, however, there is a cap provided by the level of fines to companies that have emissions above their quota.

At present, however, the carbon market is still in its infancy. As discussed above, the existing markets have experienced certain difficulties in their initial periods of operation. The future regarding carbon trading infrastructure and the broader regulatory environment is unclear. Consequently, a pure beta exposure to carbon has not been recommended by investment advisers at this point. This is an area which investors and investment consultants will continue to follow closely.

CARBON TRADING AS AN ALPHA STRATEGY
A small number of funds have been established with a view to generating returns specifically from trading in carbon emission permits – ie, taking long and short positions in carbon with a view to profiting from price movements. Such funds typically have a cash-plus investment objective and therefore represent potential sources of 'pure' alpha.

Returns will depend on the skill of the manager in assessing shorter-term price trends. Funds of this sort could be considered for inclusion as part of a diversified hedge fund portfolio. Because the carbon market is still relatively immature, there is some logic in expecting that it should prove to be relatively fertile ground for alpha. In addition, the uncertainty regarding the current policy outlook, as discussed in the previous section, might be better captured through an active, rather than a passive, investment exposure to carbon.

INVESTING IN CARBON-RELATED PROJECTS – A COMBINATION OF ALPHA AND BETA
A number of vehicles are available which provide returns at least partly derived from generation and sale of emission credits – either carbon removal units (mainly generated from reforestation) or CERs and ERUs from CDM and JI projects. These vehicles have private equity-like features and can be seen as possessing both beta and alpha characteristics:

- Like an investment in carbon futures, they can be expected to perform better in an environment where the carbon price is strong over the medium to long term.
- However, the carbon price at which the investment becomes loss-making lies in general at a much lower level than with carbon futures. For carbon futures this is the price at which the future was bought. In these investments it is the cost of creating/generating a carbon credit.
- Returns will also depend on the skill of the manager in selecting, developing and operating the projects concerned.

Underlying projects vary widely in terms of underlying risks and in terms of the proportion which the emission credits represent of total revenue.

For funds focused on carbon credits generated from reforestation, major risks in addition to political/regulatory risk include the price of credits and sequestration risk – ie, the amount of carbon credits that can be accredited. In addition, general operational risks arise, such as drought (reduced forestry growth, reduced sequestration) and fire (destroying yield totally).

A second type of carbon fund focuses on carbon credits generated from projects under the CDM and JI.

The CDM and JI deliberately provide the possibility to 'create' carbon credits (by technological projects that result in lower emissions) in developing and emerging market countries, to encourage technology transfer. In this way carbon reductions are realised where they are the cheapest to achieve. The rationale for the long-term investor is to invest in projects that will generate carbon credits for €6–10 each and to sell them in the EU ETS at a much higher trading level.

The major return drivers for this type of product are the ability of the managers to source projects that could generate CERs (from CDM) and/or ERUs (from JI), and to finance, develop and manage these projects successfully. Projects that can qualify to generate CERs and ERUs need to go through rigorous certification processes. Projects that deliver primary CERs and ERUs (ie, potential CERs and ERUs that have yet to be qualified) carry high project delivery risk. For this reason, primary CERs are usually also traded at a considerable discount (about 20–50%) to secondary CERs (which have been certified).

This type of investment product also carries regulatory risk in terms of government policies and the changing policy landscape as to the eligibility of managers to use flexible mechanisms such as CDM and JI to reduce emissions. There is also a 'publicity' risk involved: there have been newspaper articles that characterise these investments as "subsidising pollution in China". Although this is easy to disprove, investors should be aware of this issue.

Besides having experience in private equity, emerging markets and project management, managers of these kinds of investment strategies should also have access to political and environmental networks, be able to lobby and to navigate the bureaucracy surrounding the verification process.

Carbon credit generating investment is likely to be of interest to investors, as will be broadly diversified clean-tech funds that generate a percentage of total revenues and returns from sale of emission credits.

Summary

Carbon risk may affect investment portfolios over the short, medium and long terms. It is important that these risks embedded in portfolios are analysed and well understood, and that the opportunity to add carbon funds to portfolios for diversification and potential return enhancement is considered.

To monitor and manage these risks, institutional investors could take the following steps:

- Form a view on climate change and carbon risk and reflect it in the investment policy and risk management plan. The investment policy needs to provide an overarching framework to integrate carbon risk into strategies and action plans.
- Quantify carbon risk and opportunity, via carbon risk assessments and analysis of portfolios to engage fund managers and monitor carbon in relation to selected benchmarks.
- Undertake financial modelling to determine strategic asset allocation to carbon assets.[9]
- Consider carbon funds, which can provide an additional source of investment performance or portfolio hedging.
- Integrate climate change and carbon risk into the way fund managers are monitored, reviewed and selected.
- Develop a system to track public policy developments regarding carbon pricing and emissions.

---

9 As mentioned above, carbon-related funds are worthy of consideration.

Chapter 18

The European carbon emissions market

David Peniket, ICE Futures Europe

Introduction

Despite being only six years old, carbon markets have established a solid place in the broader energy markets. Carbon is an asset class, a commodity and a derivatives market. Price discovery and risk transfer take place on regulated markets and there is broad involvement from industry, traders and fund managers in a market that has an annual underlying value of approximately $140 billion.[1]

Carbon is a complex market, and one that is still evolving, creating opportunities to derive economic value from improved environmental performance.

Cap and trade

The carbon markets are built around the concept of cap and trade. The cap, which is set by governments, guided by climate scientists, puts a limit on the amount of harmful greenhouse gases that certain industries in a region can emit into the atmosphere. The Kyoto Protocol aims to cap greenhouse gas emissions from industrialised countries at a level that is 5.2% below the 1990 baseline by the period 2008–12. Within the European Union, the EU Emissions Trading System (EU ETS) applies a cap on annual carbon dioxide (CO_2) emissions from power generation and heavy industry in 30 countries (the 27 EU member states plus Iceland, Liechtenstein and Norway).

The mechanism for imposing the cap is through the issuance of allowances, with each allowance giving the holder the legal right to emit greenhouse gases equivalent to one tonne of carbon dioxide. The number of allowances issued is equivalent to the cap. Entities that overshoot their individual caps are required to buy more allowances, whereas those that reduce their output of emissions have a surplus of allowances to sell. This constitutes the 'trade' component of 'cap and trade' whereby polluters are penalised and entities that reduce emissions are rewarded.

The carbon market and the trading of emissions allowances have developed to allow the transfer of allowances between different entities based on supply and demand and the management of price risk.

---
1 World Bank, *State and Trends of the Carbon Market 2011*

The carbon markets today

From the 'cap-and-trade' structure has grown a sophisticated range of activities. The EU ETS is the world's largest carbon market, accounting for some 86% of total market value in 2010.[2] It caps emissions from over 10,000 facilities across Europe which are allocated EU allowances (EUAs). On average, just over 27,000 EUA contracts are traded on ICE Futures Europe each day (as at August 2011), primarily futures but also options contracts. European emissions trading on ICE Futures Europe accounts for approximately 92% of the market, as at August 2011.

The EU ETS caps sectors that account for over half of Europe's CO_2 emissions: power and heat generation, iron and steel, mineral oil refineries, mineral industry (which includes cement, glass and ceramics), and pulp and paper. New sectors and gases will be added to the scheme from 2012, which will be discussed in more detail later in this chapter.

The EU ETS has been categorised into three phases. The first phase ran from 2005 to 2007 with a cap of 2.3 billion tonnes per annum. This cap proved to be in excess of requirements and so, for Phase II (2008–12) the cap was reduced to 2.1 billion tonnes in 2008, falling to 1.9 billion tonnes by 2012. The cap in Phase III (2013–20) will drop by 1.4% each year until it reaches 1.7 billion tonnes by 2020.

The second most significant carbon market is the Clean Development Mechanism (CDM), which accounts for a further 14% of the market, the majority of which is driven by demand from EU ETS participants. The CDM is an 'offset' mechanism through which the UN issues tradable permits called certified emission reductions (CERs) to certified projects in developing countries that reduce carbon emissions. Examples of such projects include wind farms or projects that capture and destroy methane produced from urban waste dumps.

EU ETS participants can use CERs in addition to EUAs for a proportion of their compliance – for example, 22% in Germany and 8% in the UK. However, their use is limited because policy-makers believe offsets should be supplementary to the primary goal of reducing emissions within the EU itself.

There are two other carbon markets: Joint Implementation (JI), an offset mechanism primarily for projects in former Communist countries which receive emission reduction units (ERUs); and the mostly inter-governmental market for assigned amount units (AAUs), which are allowances issued directly to governments under the Kyoto Protocol. ICE Futures Europe lists futures and options contracts on all these instruments with the exception of AAUs, which do not have the required liquidity for establishing a derivatives market.

Operationally, the carbon market comprises two main elements – one trading on formalised exchanges and one trading on the off-exchange, over-the-counter market via brokers or other intermediaries. The underlying products traded are the

---

2 Bloomberg New Energy Finance.

Figure 1. Growth of the carbon markets
Volume traded, million tonnes CO_2

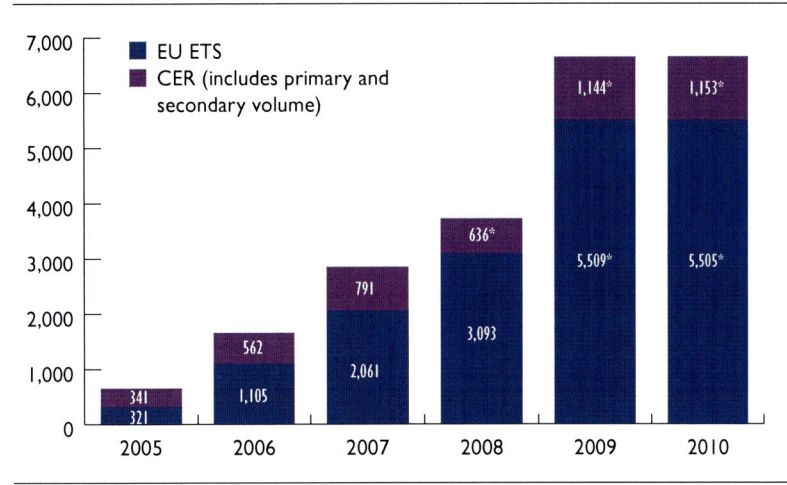

- EU ETS
- CER (includes primary and secondary volume)

Year	EU ETS	CER
2005	321	341
2006	1,105	562
2007	2,061	791
2008	3,093	636*
2009	5,509*	1,144*
2010	5,505*	1,153*

*Source: World Bank, except * Bloomberg New Energy Finance*

same – primarily EUAs and CERs, which are the two most liquid carbon permits. The broker market trades these as forward contracts while the exchanges trade them as futures contracts. Forwards and futures make up approximately 89% of the overall market volumes, with spot and options accounting for the remainder (according to ICE Futures Europe volumes during the first half of 2011).

In terms of pricing there is little difference between OTC and exchange-based trading. However, an exchange offers several other benefits, as it is a transparent, regulated market with trading in standardised contract specifications, which links directly into a clearing structure. Clearing provides a level of guarantee, credit risk mitigation and settlement services which the bilateral OTC market does not offer.

In practice, however, there is an overlap between the broker and exchange markets. Brokers, for example, can establish contract terms and prices with clients and then link into an exchange in order to clear and settle the contract. In that way, OTC forwards are transferred into exchange-held futures contracts. This element is particularly important at a time of increased counterparty credit risk. Similarly, the transparency offered by the exchange, screen-based model means that it also provides the reference price for carbon, even for OTC transactions.

ICE Futures Europe

ICE Futures Europe is the largest marketplace for trading CO_2, accounting for approximately 85% of the exchange-traded market as at July 2011, and a leading provider of services to the give-up broker market in terms of providing clearing and settlement services.

Figure 2. Market shares: EUA and CER futures

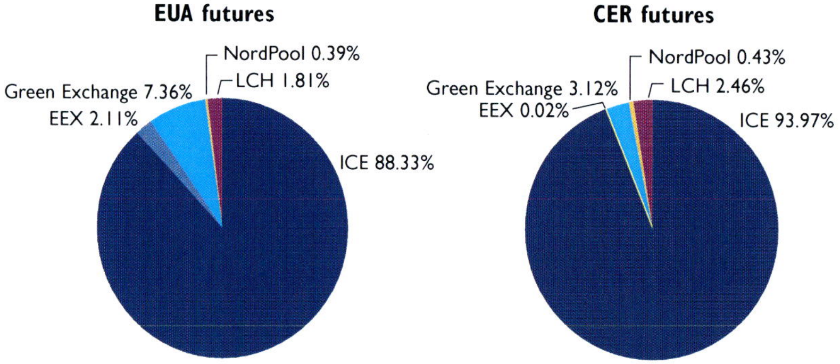

EUA futures
- NordPool 0.39%
- LCH 1.81%
- Green Exchange 7.36%
- EEX 2.11%
- ICE 88.33%

CER futures
- NordPool 0.43%
- LCH 2.46%
- Green Exchange 3.12%
- EEX 0.02%
- ICE 93.97%

As at July 2011. Source: ICE

ICE Futures Europe lists futures and options contracts. Each contract represents standardised volumes of 1,000 EUAs, CERs or ERUs, which give the holder the legal right to emit 1,000 tonnes of CO_2.

Futures contracts are standardised, exchange-traded contracts that provide buyers and sellers with the opportunity to deliver or take delivery of a certain amount of an underlying product (for instance 10,000 EUAs) at a certain time in the future (for instance December 2012) at a price agreed by both counterparties at the time of trading. Most liquidity is concentrated in contracts with a December expiry since EU ETS participants have to manage their compliance position on an annual basis. The futures contract that expires in the coming December is the benchmark contract, attracting the largest trading volumes and acting as a reference for pricing other contracts.

Carbon, like many other markets, has encountered its own share of issues related to electronic security. In 2011, various national registries in Europe were closed for a time while steps were taken to upgrade security, following the theft of EUAs.

Prices for EUAs have a clear forward curve on ICE Futures Europe, with trading out to 2020, although there is less activity beyond 2014. The market has almost always maintained a forward premium – ie, contracts expiring in later years trade at a higher price than contracts with an earlier expiry date.

Forward liquidity and a forward pricing curve allow market participants to take decisions today about investments that will create future surplus allowances. A company planning to invest in clean technology for a factory for example, can incorporate into the investment case the value of future allowances that can be sold due to a reduction in future emissions. Then, closing the circle, the company can sell a futures contract, locking in the future revenues required to justify the investment.

Since 2008, CER contracts have traded on ICE alongside EUAs and account for approximately 20% of total market activity (ERU contracts were also added in 2010). The motivation for EU ETS participants to use CERs is that CERs have generally traded at a 10–30% discount to EUAs – about €3 as at the end of July 2011. The discount reflects the fact that a CER faces limitations on its use for compliance and its bankability from one trading period to another which are not encountered with EUAs. In terms of supply and demand, the projected CER supply is increasing, especially prior to 2012, despite reduced emissions in Europe due to the economic slowdown. By mid-2011, some 660 million CERs had been issued by the UN and there is a further pipeline of over 1 billion tonnes up to 2012.

The spread between EUAs and CERs is an actively traded differential. ICE Futures Europe has created an EUA-CER spread trading facility to enable companies to take advantage of this differential in a single trade without the risk that relative prices of EUAs and CERs will change when traders have only executed one half of the transaction. Historically, ERUs trade at a discount to both EUAs and CERs.

Market participants

The largest category of regulated entities in the EU ETS is generators of power and heat, which account for 52% of allowances allocated in Phase II. Most power generators across Europe forward-sell a significant proportion of their power generation up to three years in the future. Generators will normally try to lock in fuel and carbon prices at the same time so that they can be sure of the margin they will be earning and hedge against adverse movements in power, fuel or carbon prices. The EUA futures contract is the predominant tool for this hedging activity.

Power companies that have the option of generating electricity from coal or gas are also taking the price of EUAs into account when determining which fuel to burn. Coal produces about twice the amount of CO_2 for every unit of power generated, so the coal versus gas decision must take into account the price of carbon as well as fuel prices.

As the market has grown, it has expanded beyond the particular requirements of compliance users. Several general commodity funds are already including carbon in their funds.

In this context, carbon credits are being viewed as a commodity. Some banks and investment managers have established carbon market indices that are subsequently used as the reference for structured products or exchange traded funds.

Major investment banks are also increasingly incorporating these markets in their project finance planning. Project finance decisions in industries and countries running ETSs will routinely factor in carbon pricing expectations.

EU Emissions Trading System Phase III

Phase III of the EU ETS will start on 1 January 2013. The European Commission is amending the scheme to take account of lessons learned in previous phases. The

major trends emerging are as follows:
- The expansion of the scheme to new sectors;
- Increasing harmonisation across Europe of the way EUAs are issued;
- Increasing use of auctions to distribute EUAs;
- Limits on the type of CER eligible for compliance; and
- A more demanding target.

From 2013, emissions from petrochemicals, ammonia and aluminium production will be included for the first time. Furthermore, emissions of nitrous oxide and perflourocarbons from certain sectors will be included as well as CO_2.

Emissions from all flights that either depart or land in the EU will be included in the EU ETS from 2012. The aviation sector will trade aviation allowances (EUAAs), but shortfalls can be made up by buying EUAs as well as CERs or ERUs (up to 15%).

Phase III will also see the introduction of a simple EU-wide cap instead of the previous independent arrangement whereby each country decided its own cap via National Allocation Plans. EUAs will be held in accounts within a single EU Registry as opposed to registries in each of the 27 member states.

Another significant development of the market in Phase III will be the increase in auctioning of allowances. All allowances allocated to the power sector and an increasing proportion of allowances allocated to other sectors will be auctioned rather than being allocated with no charge. Increased auctioning will create greater requirements for hedging and cash management for power companies and others, enhancing the contribution that derivatives markets can play in delivering an efficient and effective EU ETS.

It is important to note that several types of CERs will not be permitted in Phase III of the EU ETS, including CERs from 'industrial gas' projects – which have produced the majority of CERs to date – and CERs from projects registered after 2012 in countries such as India and China. ICE Futures Europe has integrated these restrictions into its CER contract and, as a result, the forward curve now reflects a premium for CERs that are acceptable for use in Phase III.

Conclusion

In 2011, four 'cap-and-trade' schemes for greenhouse gas emissions are in existence – the EU ETS, the Kyoto Protocol caps on national emissions and two smaller schemes in New Zealand and the north-eastern United States.

From an international perspective, there are considerable grounds for optimism. California and Australia are launching economy-wide schemes in 2012. There are increasingly strong signs that China will embrace cap and trade, initially on a regional basis before a national roll-out, and South Korea continues to develop its plans. In the offset markets, Japan is creating new forms of bilateral collaboration with developing countries and a new asset class relating to rainforest protection is being pioneered on a voluntary but significant scale.

Despite the European carbon market facing some challenges in the wake of recent bearish macroeconomic news, the European Commission has underlined its commitment to the EU ETS, and there is confidence in the market that cap and trade is the most viable and economical path to managing the worldwide growth in emissions.

Chapter 19

Measuring carbon intensity and risk

Simon Thomas, Liesel van Ast, Trucost

This chapter looks at ways to identify corporate greenhouse gas (GHG) emissions and exposure to carbon costs. It examines how investors are using data on company carbon intensity to manage fund carbon risk and create investment opportunities.

Carbon is an investment risk

GHGs emitted by the world's largest 3,000 companies cost more than $1.4 trillion each year, according to a report by the UN Principles for Responsible Investment (PRI) and UN Environment Programme Finance Initiative (UNEP FI).[1] The study explains how costs from business activities that damage the environment and human health can ultimately undermine the value of diversified portfolios held by large institutional investors. For instance, the costs of climate change impacts caused by emissions from oil and gas companies in a fund can increase insurance premiums, taxes and input prices, damaging the profitability of other companies held.

The PRI calls for investors to reduce these risks by engaging with portfolio companies and encouraging policy-makers to address the failure of markets to account for carbon costs. In 2010, 259 asset owners and asset managers representing over $15 trillion in assets wrote to negotiators at the UN international climate change talks in Cancún, Mexico. They called for better national policy frameworks for renewable energy, energy efficiency and low carbon infrastructure, and progress in areas such as the financial architecture of climate funding and expanding carbon markets.[2]

Asset allocations to low-carbon opportunities are growing, with $243 billion invested in clean energy in 2010.[3] However, most mainstream investors have paid little attention to financial risks from carbon-intensive companies under the emerging regulations and carbon markets needed to drive uptake of carbon-efficient tech-

---

1 UN PRI/UNEP FI (October 2010), *Universal Ownership, Why environmental externalities matter to institutional investors.*
2 www.iigcc.org/__data/assets/pdf_file/0015/15153/Global-Investor-Statement.pdf (accessed 21 January 2011).
3 Bloomberg New Energy Finance (11 January 2011), Clean energy investment storms to new record in 2010.

nologies. This myopia leaves most funds exposed to companies that will face higher costs to reduce emissions, purchase carbon allowances or use carbon-intensive fossil fuels (see below).

Carbon costs will have effects on the cash flows of every industry. Research by Goldman Sachs shows that, as the cost of carbon emissions rise, as it inevitably will to incentivise faster diffusion of low carbon technologies, value will be redistributed towards carbon-efficient companies. GS Sustain found that at a carbon cost of $60 per tonne of GHG emissions, measured in carbon dioxide equivalent (CO_2e), "10% of the total cash flow of listed companies could be transferred from companies with below-average carbon efficiency to those with above-average efficiency".[4] Carbon costs could change cost structures most in the oil and gas, utilities, transport, chemicals, mining and metals industries.

Carbon embedded in raw materials could also be important to investors, according to a UN Environment Programme overview of key investment reports on climate change. The report concludes, "There is now sufficient evidence on the materiality of climate change that all investors should routinely include climate change as a factor in asset management practice."[5]

One perceived barrier to investors addressing carbon risks is a lack of information provided by companies.[6] Following lobbying by several institutional investors and investor groups, such as the Investor Network on Climate Risk, the US Securities and Exchange Commission (SEC) issued guidance on climate risk disclosure in January 2010. It clarifies how publicly listed companies should report on climate-related issues that could be material and therefore alter a reasonable investor's view of their businesses, covering the impacts of legislation, international accords, the indirect effects of regulation or business trends and the physical impacts of climate change.

Company reporting on climate change issues has improved over the 11 years that Trucost has collected and analysed data on corporate GHG emissions. Drivers include the development of carbon reporting standards (see below) and the Carbon Disclosure Project (CDP), which asks companies for information on climate change on behalf of over 530 investors. Of the world's 500 largest companies that responded to the CDP survey in 2010, almost 80% reported at least one significant climate-related risk.[7]

Recognising that corporate carbon emissions will become a growing source of financial risk and opportunity, credit rating agency Standard & Poor's has started to integrate information on carbon risks into the credit ratings of companies in carbon-intensive sectors in Europe. For instance, S&P downgraded UK coal power utility Drax Group to 'junk' status in 2009, partly because of rising exposure to carbon

---

4 GS Sustain (21 May 2009), *Change is coming: A framework for climate change – A defining issue for the 21st century.*
5 UNEP FI (October 2009), *The materiality of climate change, How finance copes with the ticking clock.*
6 WWF/Trucost/Mercer (July 2009), *Carbon Risks in UK Equity Funds.*
7 Carbon Disclosure Project (2010), *Global 500 Report.*

costs. S&P warned in early 2011 that climate-related legislation in the US is likely to affect the credit quality of oil refiners and electric utilities.[8]

Despite mounting evidence that carbon can be financially material to earnings and valuations, there is a risk that asset managers will continue to downplay exposure to carbon costs until the value of carbon-entrenched assets falls, with knock-on effects on investment returns.

Government policies to reduce emissions

"We cannot be certain (until it is too late) that continuing to emit carbon at our current pace will lead to disaster; but we do know that the chance of a catastrophic outcome is high enough to make insuring against worst-case scenarios the rational response. Surely the financial crisis has taught us that a low-probability tail risk is still a risk."

The deal we need from Copenhagen, *Financial Times*, 3 November 2009

The costs of addressing damages from climate change impacts would be significantly higher than the costs of reducing GHG emissions that contribute to climate change.[9] The science that informs policies in 193 countries and the European Union[10] shows that global GHG emissions must peak by 2020 and be cut by 50–85% from 1990 levels by 2050 to have a chance of stabilising emissions in the atmosphere at a level that reduces the risk of climate change impacts such as water scarcity, coastal flooding and falls in food productivity becoming more severe.

Most governments are working towards a binding international agreement to cut emissions from 2013 onwards, when the first target period of the UN Kyoto Protocol expires. Under the protocol, industrialised countries agreed to cut GHG emissions by an average of 5% from 1990 levels between 2008 and 2012. More than 80 countries covering 80% of global GHG emissions and 90% of the global economy pledged targets to cut emissions by 2020 under the Copenhagen Accord of December 2009.[11] Their plans were officially recognised under the Cancún Agreements one year later, when countries agreed to work towards a goal to substantially reduce global emissions by 2050 to help limit the average rise in global temperature to 2°C above pre-industrial levels.[12,13]

Investors blaming global policy uncertainties for inaction may be overlooking

---

8 www.standardandpoors.com/prot/ratings/articles/en/us/?assetID=1245285573781, www.standardandpoors.com/prot/ratings/articles/en/us/?assetID=1245282597606 (accessed 24 January 2011).
9 Summary of Conclusions, *Stern Review: The Economics of Climate Change*, 2006, Page viii.
10 Signatories to the United Nations Framework Convention on Climate Change.
11 www.climatechange.gov.au/government/initiatives/~/media/publications/committee/international-climate-change-policies-pdf.ashx (accessed 24 January 2011).
12 http://ec.europa.eu/clima/policies/international/negotiations_en.htm; http://unfccc.int/resource/docs/2007/tp/01.pdf (accessed 21 January 2011).
13 www.ipcc.ch/pdf/assessment-report/ar4/wg2/ar4-wg2-spm.pdf (accessed 24 January 2011).

the fact that policy delays actually increase, rather than reduce, financial risks from GHG emissions. The longer action is delayed, the higher the costs of cutting global GHG emissions, with the International Energy Agency estimating a $1 trillion rise in costs in just one year because stronger, more costly action will be needed from 2020 onwards to meet climate goals.[14]

Meanwhile, national and regional climate change policies are taking shape. Cap-and-trade programmes are in place or planned in the European Union (EU), New Zealand, South Korea, Japan, Taiwan and parts of China and the US. The EU Emission Trading System (EU ETS) will require steeper emission reductions during its third phase from 2013–20, when more sectors will be covered and fewer allowances will be available. More than half of the allowances will be auctioned, up from less than 4% during the programme's second phase from 2008–12.[15] Most European power utilities will have to pay for 100% of allowances. Point Carbon forecasts that EU allowance prices could rise from around $19 in January 2011 to $49 in 2020.[16] The UK government is leading efforts to create a price floor to strengthen carbon prices under the EU ETS.

In California, a cap-and-trade programme starting in 2012 will cover 360 businesses responsible for 80% of the state's GHG emissions. Major industrial sources will need to submit an allowance for each tonne of CO_2e emitted, and Point Carbon forecasts that allowances in the California carbon market will trade at $10 in 2012 and rise to $18 by 2016.[17] The programme is designed to link to carbon trading in six US states and four Canadian provinces under the Western Climate Initiative. It could also link to the Regional Greenhouse Gas Initiative, which covers power utilities in 10 northeastern states.[18]

Carbon trading can keep the costs of reducing emissions relatively low by providing flexibility in how and where emissions are cut. However, business lobbying against cap and trade could increase economy-wide carbon costs as governments turn to other regulatory measures to cut emissions. For instance, achieving a US target to cut GHG emissions by 17% from 2005 levels by 2020 could largely depend on Environmental Protection Agency rules requiring large industrial facilities to obtain Clean Air Act permits for GHG emissions from 2011. Permits will eventually require plants to apply best available technology to control emissions. Technical measures costing below $108 per tonne of CO_2e could achieve more than half of potential global abatement.[19] Abatement costs – and potential cost savings from resource efficiency – would vary significantly by industry.

14 www.worldenergyoutlook.org/docs/weo2010/factsheets.pdf (accessed 21 January 2011).
15 http://ec.europa.eu/environment/climat/pdf/brochures/post_2012_en.pdf (accessed 23 September 2010).
16 €36/tonne in 2010; www.pointcarbon.com/aboutus/pressroom/pressreleases/1.1496970 (accessed 25 January 2011).
17 www.pointcarbon.com/polopoly_fs/1.1493644!CMNA20101217.pdf (accessed 25 January 2011).
18 www.arb.ca.gov/newsrel/newsrelease.php?id=170 (accessed 25 January 2011).
19 McKinsey & Company (2010), *Impact of the financial crisis on carbon economics*, Version 2.1 of the Global Greenhouse Gas Abatement Cost Curve.

Building codes, carbon performance and energy efficiency standards, renewable energy obligations and feed-in tariffs, and changes in subsidies and taxation to shift energy use away from fossil fuels are among further policy measures in most economies that are making company GHG emissions relevant to asset owners and fund managers.

Data to measure company carbon performance

The growing materiality of GHG emissions is fuelling demand for comparable carbon reporting by companies, so that investors can see how they are positioned for related risks and opportunities. Trucost data show that the quality and quantity of company disclosures on GHG emissions vary across sectors and geographies. Many voluntary reporting guidelines are being strengthened to improve public information on company carbon performance. The most widely-used carbon reporting standard is the GHG Protocol, developed by the World Resources Institute and World Business Council for Sustainable Development. The protocol underpins most other GHG accounting standards and provides a framework for companies to measure the six gases covered by the UN Kyoto Protocol. It breaks down emissions into three scopes – (1) direct from fuel combustion and industrial processes that are owned or controlled, (2) indirect from electricity purchases and (3) upstream from the production and transportation of goods purchased by the company, as well as downstream from the use and disposal of products sold.

Measuring and reporting emissions from operations, supply chains and investments is the first step towards managing and reducing them. During 2010, companies reporting on Scope 1 and 2 emissions began to look more closely at opportunities to reduce emissions from suppliers and address risks from carbon costs passed on in higher prices. Suppliers account for 44% of emissions from the 3,000 largest public companies in Trucost's database of environmental disclosures. For most companies, emissions from supply chains are higher than direct emissions.[20] The GHG Protocol Initiative therefore launched voluntary standards in October 2011 to help companies measure and report emissions from corporate value chains (Scope 3) and products in use. The value chain standard breaks down emissions into 15 categories, including equity and debt investments. It says that financial services companies could account for emissions from investments managed on behalf of clients.[21]

Analysing exposure to carbon costs

Most asset prices do not fully reflect company exposure to direct carbon costs or those passed through value chains. However, investors are increasingly benchmarking the carbon performance of portfolio companies against peers by measuring

---
20 UN PRI/UNEP FI (October 2010), *Universal Ownership, Why environmental externalities matter to institutional investors.*
21 www.ghgprotocol.org/standards/scope-3-standard.

emissions relative to financial metrics. Revenue provides the most stable measure of carbon intensity – measured as CO_2e emitted per $1 million – across all sectors in an index or portfolio. Carbon intensity can vary dramatically within sectors. For instance, the carbon intensity of basic resources firms in the S&P/IFCI LargeMid-Cap Index ranges from 285 to over 18,000 tonnes of CO_2e per $1 million. Companies that are more carbon-intensive than sector peers could be more exposed to carbon costs, while companies with more carbon-efficient operations and supply chains could benefit from lower carbon risks and greater market share. Resource-efficient businesses that emit fewer GHGs to generate sales are well placed for the shift to a low-carbon economy.

Investors can use data on carbon intensity, to:
- compare companies of all sizes and industries on carbon performance;
- track changes in carbon performance over time; and
- identify and reduce exposure to carbon costs.

Investors can integrate emissions data into financial analysis to examine risks to investment returns. Analysts can apply abatement costs or market carbon prices to company emissions data to model exposure to carbon costs from operations and supply chains. Modelling can assess how company earnings might be exposed under different carbon price scenarios. For instance, different projected carbon prices for 2013 and 2030 were used in a study funded by the International Finance Corporation to analyse carbon risks and opportunities in emerging markets.[22] Trucost modelled carbon costs for a share of the projected annual emissions of companies in the S&P/IFCI LargeMidCap Index. The 2030 scenario shows that, at $108 per tonne of CO_2e, carbon costs could equate to up to 20% of company revenues.

Carbon costs can be deducted from earnings before interest, tax, depreciation and amortisation (EBITDA) to identify potential profit risk. This analysis was used in a study of carbon risks in 118 UK-based institutional equity funds commissioned by WWF (2009). Findings showed that if the five companies that contributed most to the funds' carbon footprints had to pay $19 per tonne of CO_2e, their earnings could fall by between 9% and 99%.[23]

The financial implications of carbon emissions can also be measured by analysing emissions or potential carbon costs relative to value added (EBITDA plus wage costs) or market capitalisation. However, these metrics could produce variable results across sectors and over time due to factors unrelated to corporate carbon emissions.

Company exposure to carbon costs may vary due to factors including early reductions in GHG emissions, sector-specific abatement costs, future earnings, national policy mixes and access to carbon markets. Carbon-intensive companies in

---

[22] Trucost (October 2010), *Carbon Risks & Opportunities in Emerging Markets, Trucost study on the exposure of different regional equity strategies to carbon costs.*
[23] WWF/Trucost/Mercer (July 2009), *Carbon Risks in UK Equity Funds.*

sectors producing goods traded on world markets could find it particularly difficult to pass on carbon costs without losing market share.

Portfolio carbon risk audits

Many institutional investors and fund managers are using carbon footprints to quantify fund carbon risk. Trucost has measured the carbon footprints of over 1,000 equity portfolios with a total of some $1 trillion in assets under management for pension funds, investment banks, asset managers and public sector organisations. Investors such as the Australian superannuation fund VicSuper annually measure the carbon intensity and exposures of companies held using Trucost carbon footprints. The Second Swedish National Pension Fund (AP2) has used a carbon footprint of its portfolio to assess the potential effects of carbon prices on its investments. The UK Environment Agency Pension Fund (EAPF) uses footprints to monitor the environmental performance of fund managers, who use data on company impacts and disclosures to inform engagement programmes.

Carbon footprints are based on standardised GHG emissions data covering companies' operations and first tier of suppliers, such as electricity and air travel providers. The equity fund carbon footprint is calculated by allocating emissions and revenues from each company to the portfolio in proportion to ownership. The carbon emissions and revenues allocated to a fund are summed to calculate the carbon footprint, expressed as tonnes of CO_2e per $1 million. Funds with smaller carbon footprints than their benchmarks and other funds are less exposed to financial risk from carbon costs. Investors can use footprints to help identify how stock selections and sector allocations contribute to fund carbon risk.

Disclosure and management of fund carbon footprints is becoming more widespread geographically. Among ground-breaking developments in 2009–10 was the Green Century Balanced Fund becoming the first US-based mutual fund to disclose its carbon footprint. VicSuper became the first to publish fund carbon footprints on members' benefit statements. And the EAPF demonstrated that pension funds can reduce the environmental impacts of investments over five years with no loss to financial performance.

Interest in measuring the carbon footprints of other assets such as property, private equity and bond portfolios is growing. This is partly driven by more asset owners and managers signing up to responsible investor initiatives such as the UN PRI and Institutional Investors Group on Climate Change (IIGCC). GHG emissions are among metrics included in a UNEP FI toolkit on measuring the performance of property portfolios.[24] The IIGCC recommends that private equity fund managers use carbon footprints to help manage climate change risks.[25] IIGCC also advises

---

24 UNEP FI/RPIC (March 2010), *Responsible Property Investing: Metrics for Performance Measurement, Second in a Series of Toolkits on Responsible Property Investing*.
25 IIGCC (26 January 2011), *A Guide on Climate Change for Private Equity Investors*.

trustees to use company-level research to explore corporate bond exposure to climate change risks.[26]

Integrating carbon data into investment strategies

Demand is growing for financial analysts and asset managers to monitor and manage fund carbon exposure. In response, carbon data has become more widely available through financial data and analysis providers such as FactSet and Style Research. A partnership between Trucost and investment consultancy Mercer also supports the integration of carbon data into traditional investment analysis.

Investors are starting to use carbon data to manage exposure to carbon risks and create new investment products. For instance, asset managers BayernInvest Luxembourg and ELAN Capital-Partners launched the first carbon-efficient bond in 2010 – BILKU 1 Carbon Efficient Bond Fonds. The fund offers investors the opportunity to invest in bonds of companies that are carbon-efficient for their sectors. Its carbon footprint is 50–70% smaller than traditional portfolios or indices.

VicSuper invested in a low carbon equity fund launched by Vanguard in 2009. The Carbon Aware International Shares Fund is designed to reduce carbon emissions by 50% relative to the benchmark MSCI World ex-Australia Index while having investment returns similar to a broad-based passive index fund. This strategy to 'carbon-optimise' portfolios maintains diversification of stocks and overall sector weights of benchmark indices but rebalances holdings within each sector based on carbon intensity. The fund overweights companies that are carbon-efficient relative to industry peers in the underlying index and underweights carbon-intensive companies.

This approach can be used for any passive or active investment strategy, while typically reducing a fund's carbon footprint by 25–50%. Portfolios that reduce exposure to carbon costs through stock effects could be less exposed to margin risk from rising energy costs. Carbon optimisation allows for a broad market strategy with diversification for institutional investors that have a fiduciary responsibility to achieve market returns and are therefore unable to screen out carbon-intensive sectors across equity funds.

Portfolios can be carbon optimised while maintaining benchmark financial performance, and evidence shows small but emerging financial outperformance. For instance, the S&P/IFCI Carbon Efficient Index closely tracks the performance of its parent Index, the S&P/IFCI LargeMidCap.

S&P conducted a back-test from 1 November 2006 until the index launch in December 2009. Using daily returns, the S&P/IFCI Carbon Efficient Index has an annualised tracking error of 1.38% versus the S&P/IFCI LargeMidCap Index from the beginning of the back-test period through to 31 December 2010. On a price return basis, the S&P/IFCI Carbon Efficient Index has risen 21.8% from the index launch

---

26 IIGCC/Mercer Investment Consulting/The Carbon Trust (2005), *A climate for change, A trustee's guide to understanding and addressing climate risk.*

Figure 1. Daily price return levels of S&P/IFCI Carbon Efficient Index vs underlying index
Historical performance, 1 November 2006–31 December 2010 (1 Nov 2006 = 100)

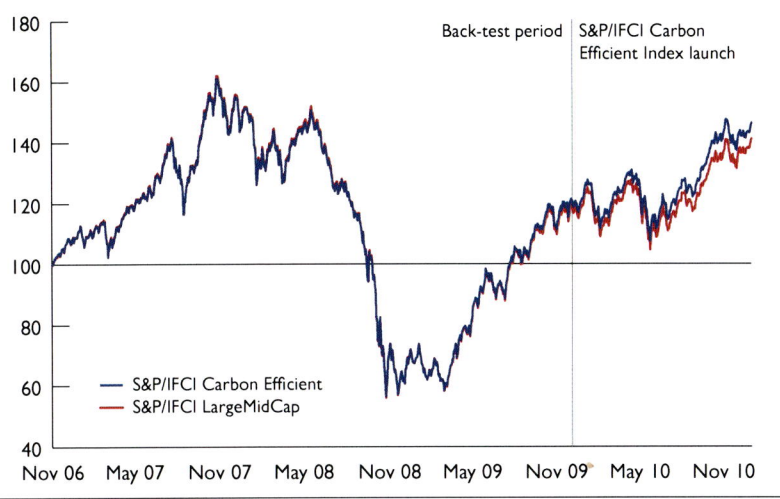

Source: Standard & Poor's

on 11 December 2009 to 31 December 2010, outperforming the S&P/IFCI LargeMidCap Index by 226 basis points. Likewise, during the back-test period, the S&P/IFCI Carbon Efficient Index returned a cumulative 20.2%, beating the 18.1% return of the S&P/IFCI LargeMidCap Index (Figure 1).[27]

Carbon-optimised investment products include the NYSE Euronext Low Carbon 100 Europe Index and S&P US Carbon Efficient Index. These indices provide market benchmarks to stimulate investment flows to carbon-efficient companies. Investors could allocate assets according to index weightings to position their investments for the transition to a low-carbon economy. The first low-carbon fund launched in 2011 is based on the UK FTSE 350 Index. Carbon Footprint Investments developed the IFSL Carbon Footprint UK 350 Equity Index Tracker Fund with a carbon footprint 22% smaller than that of the underlying Index.

Long-term shifts in assets

The PRI/UNEP FI study recommends that institutional investors ask investment managers how they are addressing fund exposure to risks from environmental costs. Opportunities to invest in companies with minimal exposure to carbon risks are highlighted as a way of balancing portfolio exposure to high-risk companies and sectors in guidance on how pension funds can address climate risk.[28] Assets are likely

---
27 Performance data provided by S&P, 27 January 2011.
28 Local Authority Pension Fund Forum (January 2011), *Investing in Climate Change*.

to flow towards funds that favour carbon-efficient companies and are well placed for growing financial risk from corporate emissions over the next decade. For now, there is a window of opportunity for asset owners and managers to use the available carbon data to prepare for investment risks in the coming carbon crunch – before it takes hold.

Section 3

Regulation, Incentives, Investors and Company Case Studies

Chapter 20

Policy regulation: a risk and an opportunity

Kirsty Hamilton, Chatham House

Introduction

Policy-driven markets, such as renewable energy, offer both risk and opportunity for investors. The risk is of policy changing in such a way that the investment case is undermined, yet at the same time creating the opportunity of commercially attractive conditions to unlock new investment linked to public policy goals. To get a better visibility on both the risk and the opportunity, it is useful to see how policies are evolving in the low-carbon space. Policy can be categorised into tiers, each performing a different role in shaping or catalysing low-carbon economic activity: international regulation driven through the UN (the Framework Convention on Climate Change and its Kyoto Protocol); national or regional policy aimed at implementing emissions goals, including within sectors that have multiple public policy objectives such as energy, transport and, increasingly, infrastructure more broadly.

This chapter first examines the international tier of policy and what factors help to understand its future evolution. Second, it looks at national or regional policy. These tiers are dynamic and interact – greater progress at national level will bolster confidence in taking greater steps internationally, and international action can spur greater domestic attention to climate where this is flagging or under pressure. At domestic level, policy developments in the renewable energy (RE) space – as systematically documented by the Renewable Energy Policy Network in its *Renewables Global Status Report* (and by Bloomberg New Energy Finance on the investment side) – are an important component of delivering climate goals, given the importance of energy-related emissions. In many countries, climate change may not be a primary driver, with more politically immediate issues such as energy security or shortages leading in the same direction.

As the RE sector grows in scale there is also an increasing focus on infrastructure and interconnection. This trend towards cross-border bilateral or regional policy and regulation will arguably be an increasing one in RE and energy policy this decade, although it is not covered in detail here.

International policy drivers: climate change and the UN process

The UN Framework Convention on Climate Change (UNFCCC) might be described as creating the global 'climate driver' in energy markets, and a key to understanding this is the scale and timing of the transformation with which policy-makers are grappling. Climate science underpins this: with the first formal international science 'status' report, under the auspices of the Intergovernmental Panel on Climate Change (IPCC), indicating that to stabilise atmospheric concentration levels of carbon dioxide (CO_2) at 1990 levels, "immediate reductions" in emissions of over 60% would be required.

This IPCC report led to the UNFCCC being signed in 1992; with a global objective to "avoid dangerous climate change". The assessment of "dangerous" is ultimately a political decision between countries, with science as a guide[1]. Through the UNFCCC, countries globally also agreed important principles, including that of "common but differentiated responsibilities" between countries: industrialised countries should lead the common efforts to tackle rising emissions, as it was their industrialisation that raised concentrations of carbon dioxide to unsustainable levels. It also contains provisions around technology transfer and financing to developing countries. This framework convention gave rise to the more specific and detailed Kyoto Protocol (KP), finally negotiated in 1997, with binding emissions targets for industrialised countries, to be met in a first commitment period from 2008–12.

Under the Protocol, for example, the EU collectively has an 8% reduction target (with each EU country also adopting a separate binding target); Japan has a 6% cut and the US, prior to pulling out of the Protocol in 2001, had agreed a 7% reduction. All are absolute reductions, against a 1990 baseline, rather than cuts against a rising trajectory.

The KP also established the now well-known "flexibility mechanisms" – emissions trading (between governments) and the two project-based options, the Clean Development Mechanism (CDM), focusing on developing countries, and Joint Implementation (JI) between industrialised countries. These aimed at facilitating least-cost location of emissions reductions, and have been followed by similar efforts nationally and regionally: notably the EU and its Emissions Trading Scheme[2] that interlinks with the CDM (see Chapter 18). Regions within the US and metropolitan

---

[1] The IPCC has done periodic updates, with the Fourth Assessment Report coming out in 2007, and Fifth Assessment Report expected in 2012/13. Highly public disputes over climate science including the IPCC, and the funding and role of climate sceptics in general over the past two decades (the 2009 University of East Anglia 'climategate' e-mails, for example) have been linked to efforts to undermine international political decisions by undermining the scientific case for action.

[2] The EU ETS started its first phase in 2005, with a second phase linked to the 2008-12 commitment period and a third phase, out to 2020, negotiated in 2008. The EU ETS places a cap on the total amount of CO_2 emissions and then provides companies with emission allowances, which they can sell to or buy from one another as needed. In the third phase (starting in 2013), the ETS will also include the aviation industry, which currently contributes about 2% of the world's emissions, and will move towards auctioning of allowances.

cities such as Tokyo have also adopted legislation in this area. Other countries, such as South Korea, Japan, Australia, New Zealand and most recently China are considering or have adopted national emissions trading markets.

THE 'NEW GLOBAL DEAL' DISCUSSIONS FOR THE POST-2012 PERIOD
With the end of the Kyoto Protocol's first round of commitments looming in 2012, governments focused on a new round of commitments for post-2012, involving industrialised and developing countries. Despite intense public and political focus, the now-infamous talks in Copenhagen in 2009 failed to secure this agreement. This was due to a complex range of factors, from the sheer complexity of the decisions, the awkward politics of the final days, the opportunity and challenge of having over 100 heads of state present, right down to weather and logistics. Despite this, it did provide an important opportunity for governments to bring new national targets or action packages to the table, and commitments for 'fast-track' finance for developing countries were made by some countries, alongside the 'Copenhagen Accord' which was agreed, but not by all. Renewed momentum was injected into the process the following year at the ministerial round in Cancún, at the end of 2010, as all ministers coalesced around a 'Cancún Agreement', which provides a common basis for negotiating a final deal.

Part of the technical difficulty in Copenhagen was the fact that a new round of commitments for industrialised countries under the Kyoto Protocol was being negotiated in parallel with a 'global deal' where developing countries for the first time would agree to take on actions to limit emissions, alongside new emissions reductions from industrialised countries. This awkward formula has been necessary to ensure the involvement of the US (due to its withdrawal from the Protocol). For developing countries, 'nationally appropriate mitigation actions' (NAMAs)[3] may be policies and measures or targets, and are likely to be set against an emissions trajectory, whereas pressure remains on industrialised countries to build on binding absolute goals, under the Kyoto framework.

The Cancún Agreement sets the framework for the international approach to a new round of commitments: a 'shared vision' between all countries for scaled-up actions and a science-driven approach with a long-term goal to keep temperature rise below 2°C (above pre-industrial levels), with a review based on science and in the context of a more stringent 1.5°C limit. This establishes the drivers for scale and timing of emissions cuts and implies very substantive actions, although specifics will have to be agreed. Governments have already acknowledged that IPCC science scenarios indicate that the 2°C target is likely to require absolute emissions reductions from all industrialised countries of 25–40% by 2020.

---
3 See 'Compilation of information on nationally appropriate mitigation actions to be implemented by Parties not included in Annex I to the Convention. Note by the Secretariat', 18 March 2011, http://unfccc.int/resource/docs/2011/awglca14/eng/inf01.pdf.

Alongside the shared objective, the key elements of the global deal agreed in Cancún are:
- Enhanced action on mitigation:
  - for developed countries – "nationally appropriate mitigation actions or commitments". This could be the pledges made in Copenhagen (which included the EU's 20% target and the US's 17% goal) and others.
  - for developing countries – this will be NAMAs (no formal commitments under international regime). These will be differentiated by those requiring international financial support, linked to monitoring, reporting and verification procedures.
- Examination of new market-based mechanisms linked to mitigation actions (alongside non market-based mechanisms) to assist mitigation.
- Financing (for developing countries): the decision to establish a "Green Climate Fund", in the context of recognising the goal of mobilising $100 billion by 2020[4] – the World Bank is the interim trustee, a "transitional committee" will design the fund and a board will be appointed. It is likely that this fund will be deployed out to national governments, which may govern any national distribution through national public financial institutions.
- A "technology mechanism" and a network of technology centres aimed at facilitating the diffusion and deployment of technologies. Technology transfer remains an important part of securing any international deal, given that developed countries agreed to provide this (as well as finance) under the UNFCCC.
- An adaptation framework, including examination of risk management, and risk sharing and transfer mechanisms.

Progress on a next round of commitments under the KP has been slower, despite the range of national pledges from developed and developing countries in Copenhagen. Some countries (notably Japan and Russia) have stated they are not in favour of a second round of binding targets, whereas most developing countries say this is a necessary sign of industrialised countries' seriousness. The 2012 deadline has created time pressure and increasing concern over the future of the CDM, and governments in Cancún sought explicitly to reassure that, should the Protocol be transformed in any way, the flexibility mechanisms would continue to be available to industrialised countries to meet mitigation targets. The EU's 2009 climate and energy package carries its ETS through to 2020.

At the start of 2011, an indication of the potential for progress was that China, India and Brazil all reaffirmed goals made in Copenhagen to reduce their carbon

---
4 The $100 billion is not expected to come from public sources alone: in Cancún note was made of the report of the Advisory Group on Finance (AGF) set up by UN Secretary General Ban Ki-moon in 2010 (reporting ahead of Cancún) to enable progress to be made on finance provisions of the UNFCCC, given their importance to securing a deal. The AGF provided analysis of potential sources of public and private finance to reach the $100 billion by 2020.

intensity. China and India will endeavour respectively to achieve a 40–45% and a 20–25% cut in domestic CO_2 per unit of GDP by 2020 (compared to 2005 levels). China also intends to increase the share of non-fossil fuels in primary energy consumption to around 15% by 2020 and to increase forest cover. Brazil intends that a package of mitigation actions (including reducing deforestation and increasing alternative energy) will reduce emissions by 36.1% and 38.9% below projections by 2020[5].

Considerable political (and environmental) importance is attached to the US, and whether it will adopt rigorous domestic efforts to reduce emissions, and play a constructive role internationally, in contrast to the Bush years. The Obama administration brought a goal of a 17% reduction in emissions by 2020 (compared to 2005 levels) to Copenhagen, and domestically supports an 80% reduction by 2050. Notwithstanding actions in 2009–10 – such as those by the US Environmental Protection Agency under the Clean Air Act, and regulations on emissions from vehicles and major manufacturing and processing plants – the US Congress did not adopt a domestic cap-and-trade plan or a comprehensive climate package. A backdrop of sustained re-questioning of climate science characterised this period. Nevertheless, the Obama administration continues to support its target internationally, and a domestic approach on climate legislation alongside a range of other legislation in the energy sector (discussed below).

While this indicates the pieces may not have fallen into place yet at the international level for a new binding stage of UN climate agreements, the ingredients are there for a conclusion to be reached, with advocacy from many countries, including a growing range of developing countries that support taking action to avoid the worst impacts of climate change.

OTHER PRIMARY INTERNATIONAL TRENDS AND DRIVERS
Around the time the Kyoto Protocol entered into force in early 2005, a confluence of other trends emerged, which started a rapid acceleration of the clean energy solutions to climate change – renewable energy – up the political and investment agenda. 2004 marked the start of a steady rise in oil prices (with gas and coal prices to follow), with dramatic growth in energy demand from the emerging economies of China and India hitting the radar screen around that time. At the same time, energy security rose up the political agenda, with concern from some importing nations about reliance on unstable or unpredictable regions, such as the Middle East and Russia, for access to oil and gas. More than half a decade later those trends, although changing in nature and with the financial crisis and economic conditions as a backdrop, are still critical factors in global energy market fundamentals, particularly as oil and gas prices remain volatile. Oil prices were rising again in the first part of the

---

5 See, for example, FCCC/AWGLCA/2011/INF.1, 'Compilation of information on nationally appropriate mitigation actions to be implemented by Parties not included in Annex I to the Convention', 18 March 2011, www.unfccc.int.

new decade as political instability in the Middle East grew, alongside concern over the safety of nuclear energy in the aftermath of the intense earthquake in Japan in March 2011. The 'climate driver' in energy markets is sitting alongside these other more traditional energy market factors.

During the financial crisis of 2008–09, economic stimulus packages, introduced by many of the world's major economies, repositioned renewable energy and 'low carbon' opportunities as an important element of economic activity, rather than simply an environmental or energy issue: industrial policy linked to the RE supply chain and linked employment, together with broader infrastructure and export policies, have reinforced this. South Korea came to international attention as it devoted the majority of its fiscal stimulus to the clean economy: reviewing the 2010 RE growth statistics, the government stated that it expects this sector to become "the country's future growth engine", likened to its semiconductor and shipbuilding industries, with sales and exports expected to show further high (+70%) growth.

These trends reinforce the fact that international policy on climate change has a clear direction of travel in terms of tightening up efforts on emissions, alongside multiple energy market factors driving in the same direction. Very few expect substantive reversal in this trend – although in the near term, until new UN global agreements are finalised, it can be expected that national endeavours will be the primary focus for delivery of emissions reductions and opportunities (or liabilities) in the energy sector.

National/regional policy

International emissions targets filter down into national or regional implementation: both emissions markets to drive short-term lower-cost emissions cuts and, importantly, policies aimed at energy and transport systems and increasingly buildings, industrial policy and infrastructure. Economic, supply and political pressures linked to conventional energy markets – for example, from oil and energy price rises – are more acute at national level, strengthening multiple policy drivers towards clean energy.

Reflecting this, government policy and regulation for scaling up deployment of RE, and increasing energy efficiency (EE), are moving at a fast pace.

Mirroring policy-led improvement of the investment environment, and as a technology track record has emerged and costs been reduced, there has been substantial year-on-year growth in investment, from $52 billion in 2004 to $243 billion in 2010, according to Bloomberg New Energy Finance (BNEF). Growth was noticeably slower in 2008 and particularly in 2009, linked to the financial crisis, but picked up again in 2010.

Greater geographic diversity in RE uptake and production reinforces the international nature of the sector and reduces the risk that its growth is vulnerable to political shifts or disruptions in a few countries. Developing countries represent more

Findings on renewable energy policy from REN21's Renewables 2010 Global Status Report

- Policy targets exist in at least 85 countries worldwide, including 45 developing countries and all 27 EU countries; more than two thirds of the 85 countries existing targets are now aiming for 2020 or beyond; many states, provinces and cities have also enacted policy targets, especially in the US and Canada.
- For power generation, at least 83 countries worldwide now have some type of RE promotion policy, providing operational support, including 42 developing countries and 41 developed/transition countries; for example:
    - at least 53 countries and 25 states or provinces have adopted feed-in tariff policies (fixed payment);
    - at least 10 countries and 46 states or provinces have enacted renewable quota obligations, also called renewable portfolio standards (RPS);
    - at least 45 countries offer some type of direct capital investment subsidy, grant or rebate, especially for solar PV.
- Targets for biofuels as part of transport energy consumption exist in at least 10 countries and the EU; mandates for blending biofuels into transport fuel exist in at least 24 countries and 41 states, provinces or countries; the US Renewable Fuels Standard mandates 136 billion litres per year by 2022 (up from 28 billion litres per year in 2007);
- National, state and city level mandates for solar and other renewable hot water and heating are also growing at a rapid pace in recent years including [what?], and more than 20 countries provide capital subsides for solar hot water/heating investments.
- Pace of policy development has accelerated: the number of countries that adopted some type of policy target and/or promotion policy almost doubled from 55 countries in 2005 to more than 100 by 2010.
- Governments are opting to bring forward particular sub-sectors through policy; notable is the recent growth in new and/or revised feed-in tariff policies directed at solar PV as seen in Japan, China, France, Greece, Kenya, the Czech Republic, Italy, Austria, Portugal, South Korea and South Australia.
- Offshore wind (eg, UK and Germany), early-stage wave and tidal power, utility-scale solar thermal and solar hot water heating are other primary RE sub-sectors that governments with natural resources in those areas are seeking to promote.

Source: Renewables 2010, Global Status Report. Renewable Energy Policy Network, www.ren21.org

than half of all countries with policy targets and now host more than half of the world's RE power capacity.

Both the policy landscape and investment statistics clearly show that the geography of leadership was shifting from Europe and North America to Asia – China specifically. In its review of 2010, Bloomberg New Energy Finance (BNEF) shows investment in China was up 30% to $51.1 billion in 2010, by far the largest figure for any country. In 2009, the Asia and Oceania region overtook the Americas, and in 2010 it narrowed the gap further on Europe, the Middle East and Africa as the leading region for clean energy investment[6]. In their 2010 overview of global investment, BNEF and the UN Environment Programme (UNEP) highlight that China, India and Brazil ranked top, fifth and eighth in the world for sustainable energy investments in 2009; even outside the 'big three', developing countries totalled $6.3 billion of investment, with Mexico and Chile highlighted in Latin America; Taiwan, Pakistan, Thailand, Vietnam and the Philippines in Asia; and Egypt and South Africa of particular interest to investors in Africa[7]. The leadership countries in the Middle East are also expected to progress policy frameworks for renewables.

A brief overview of three key markets, the EU, China and the US, illustrates both efforts and challenges in long-term energy policy development for renewables.

EU – RENEWABLE ENERGY DIRECTIVE
The EU target of 20% of final energy consumption (not only electricity) from RE, with a minimum of 10% of transport fuels by 2020, was adopted in June 2009 as part of its more comprehensive climate change and energy package. It indicates significant further activity in Europe, implying significant expansion of newer sectors such as offshore wind, renewable heat technologies (to date underutilised), biomass, and – subject to sustainability criteria – biofuels.

The EU target is legally binding, with individual targets also binding on the 27 member states, which submit a National Renewable Energy Action Plan, including two-yearly targets for each sub-sector (electricity, heat and transport). In addition, there are some 'flexibility' provisions, including the ability to trade with other EU states (only under the condition that the selling member state has reached its interim two-yearly targets) and the import of RE from neighbouring countries to the EU. RE industry analysis of the first action plans (2010) indicates 25 of the 27 EU states will reach or surpass their 2020 targets domestically; with the EU share of renewable energy collectively forecast to amount to 20.7% by 2020[8]. The EU is also examining an energy strategy for 2050, linked to decarbonisation, including creating the con-

---

6 Bloomberg New Energy Finance, press release, 11 January 2011, 'Clean Energy Investment Storms to New Record in 2010: New investment in clean energy reached $243bn last year, driven by soaring activity in China, offshore wind and European rooftop photovoltaics'.
7 UNEP, Bloomberg New Energy Finance, June 2010, *Global Trends in Sustainable Energy Investment, 2010*, www.sefi.unep.org.
8 EREC press release, 5 January 2011, 'Member states to exceed 2020 targets'.

ditions for significant scale of RE in the mix, with interconnection issues between member states a key factor in this longer timeframe.

Notwithstanding this positive story, the policy landscape at the end of the decade was overshadowed by the decision of the Spanish government, facing difficult economic conditions, to introduce retrospective changes to its solar PV tariffs, putting millions of invested euros at risk. This move rippled through the investment community across the EU and further afield, undermining confidence in policy-driven markets, and underscoring the strategic importance of policy stability in attracting private investment. Underscoring the importance of this issue, EU commissioners wrote to Spain warning of the impact of retrospective policy change.

The trend for RE growth in Europe, however, has a strong track record: 2010 saw an increase of 31% of installed RE power capacity (22.6GW) compared to 2009, more than any other year, according to the European Wind Energy Association. This made 2010 the fifth consecutive year that RE accounted for more than 40% of new electricity generation installations[9].

CHINA

In 2010, investment in Chinese clean energy grew 30% over 2009 levels[10], continuing the growth trend emerging since the introduction of its National Renewable Energy Law in 2005. In that year, installed wind capacity grew more than 60%, and has doubled each year since, surpassing market forecasts to become the fastest-growing wind power market worldwide by 2009. In 2010 China overtook the US as the largest wind-installation country in the world.

Implementation of the law started on 1 January 2006. The law contains a provision for renewable portfolio standards, feed-in tariffs for some technologies and establishes grid feed-in requirements and standard procedures. It establishes cost-sharing mechanisms so the incremental cost will be shared among utility consumers. It also creates new financing mechanisms and supports rural uses of renewable energy[11].

In 2010, new proposals targeted 500GW of RE capacity by 2020 (300GW of hydro, 150GW of wind, 30GW of biomass and 20GW of solar PV), which would account for almost one-third of China's expected total power[12].

During this period of rapid growth, Chinese manufacturers have risen in global importance; three Chinese companies were in the top 10 ranking global wind turbine manufacturers in 2009. There is now an expectation that Chinese RE manufac-

---

9 ewea.org/fileadmin/ewea_documents/documents/statistics/EWEA_Annual_Statistics_2010.pdf.
10 Bloomberg New Energy Finance, press release, 11 January 2011. Clean energy includes investment in renewable energy, biofuels, energy efficiency, smart grid and other energy technologies, carbon capture and storage and infrastructure investments targeted purely at integrating clean energy.
11 www.martinot.info/china.htm#targets.
12 Eric Martinot and Li Jungfeng, July 2010, 'Renewable Energy Policy Update', *Renewable Energy World*.

turers will play an increasingly significant role in the global market, particularly as the track record of its newer technologies is built up.

However, a significant challenge for achieving China's potential is the overhaul of its outdated national grid, new transmission capacity and the implementation of effective incentives for grid companies to ensure installed capacity can get to end-users. According to the Chinese Renewable Energy Industry Association (CREIA), grid-connected capacity lags behind installed capacity by more than 30% (in contrast to the average 10% gap in industrialised countries).

US

President Barack Obama's administration has led a renewed drive towards renewable energy and tackling climate change as a federal agenda. However, challenges getting legislation through Congress mean that extensive policy leadership at state level remains a central determinant of sector growth; indeed, state-based support schemes (often Renewable Portfolio Standards) alongside the federal Production Tax Credit, discussed below, led to the US being ranked top in installed capacity globally for wind power for a number of years until 2009.

In his State of the Union address in January 2011, Obama called for a clean energy target of 80% by 2035 (including clean coal and nuclear for constituency-building). This followed calls from the White House in 2010 for Congress to phase out fossil fuel subsidies, and a strong argument to end reliance on foreign oil for energy. Indeed, in the US national recovery package (US Reinvestment and Recovery Act) around $80 billion was allocated for renewable energy, according to White House figures.

Preceding the financial crisis, the Production Tax Credit was a primary support mechanism at federal level. While it successfully mobilised billions of dollars of investment, the exposure to politics and its resultant 'on-again, off-again' nature damaged the potential for steady growth, as investors had to second-guess Congress. The collapse of the tax equity market at the time of the financial crisis meant that a raft of new or revised incentives were brought in the US economic stimulus package, including direct Treasury grants towards 30% of project costs, viewed as one of the most effective stimulus measures.

The lack of central, clear policy – through Congress – has hampered the scale of potential growth. Nevertheless, as in the first decade of the century, state-level RE targets and support packages continue to drive sector growth across the country, as outlined in the American Council for Renewable Energy's updated overview of state-level policy developments[13]. The top five states for cumulative wind energy capacity at the close of 2010 all have state targets: Texas, Iowa, California, Minnesota and Washington[14].

---
13 For a regularly updated overview of state policy see interactive report: *Renewable Energy in America, Markets, Economic Development and Policy in the 50 States*, www.acore.org/publications/50states.
14 American Wind Energy Association, press release, 24 January 2011.

Conclusion

Specific investment opportunities in RE and other 'low-carbon' sectors (although the scope of what this means needs to be carefully defined) are currently being driven by national, and in some cases regional, policy conditions. However, international climate policy driven through the UN Framework Convention on Climate Change architecture heralds profound changes, as this defines the scale and timing of the response ultimately through into national conditions. While seeming slow, the UN is the only forum that can bring about government-to-government agreement on common actions that have the capacity to be binding or accountable. Given the economic and energy consequences of climate change – both of which are long-term strategic foreign policy issues at national level – the nature of the debate is unsurprisingly sticky. That said, the direction of travel is clear.

For key 'solutions' like renewable energy, there are several long-term drivers all combining alongside climate change to produce impetus behind new and more effective policy development, in both industrialised and developing countries, at national level. This is producing strong investment growth internationally, albeit with changing regional positioning as the market internationalises.

As the policy debate increasingly turns to investment needs for 'low carbon' energy infrastructure (generally based around a plethora of estimates of the large dollar figures required), governments are becoming aware that attracting private finance is not so much a finance issue as one of underlying policy conditions, interlinked with the well-defined use of public monies, as necessary. To get investment from the world of mobile capital, policy conditions need to be 'investment grade' on the ground. This essentially means not just a target or a feed-in tariff, to level the playing field with conventional generation, but also an attractive broader package of energy policy: land has to be accessed, grid to market has to be available and affordable, power purchase agreements have to be signed, and conditions for longer-term market growth (interconnection) need to be understood. The whole package has to instill confidence.

This chapter started with policy as risk and opportunity. We are now in an arena where top-down international policy and bottom-up national policy are moving, haltingly at times, in the same direction. The importance of reducing policy and regulatory risk – particularly given the post-financial crisis economic constraints in many parts of the world – is a central message for policy-makers to understand. As more financiers and investors engage with the policy community, that message is starting to be better understood.

The 2011 update of this chapter would not have been possible without the extensive time and expertise of Lily Riahi of the REN21 team. Virginia Sonntag O'Brien, former executive director of REN21, and at the helm of UNEP's annual Global Trends in Sustainable

Energy Investment *alongside Bloomberg New Energy Finance, also provided invaluable advice. This important work is central to providing a strong factual and updated evidence base on RE sector development and growth.*

Chapter 21

Renewable energy incentive mechanisms

Louise Moore, Henry Davey, Herbert Smith LLP[1]

An incisive understanding and management of regulatory and legal risk can be the difference between a good investment and a poor one, optimising performance and minimising underperformance, winners and losers. This chapter looks at regulatory incentives and other legal drivers and barriers in the renewable energy market and how these differ from jurisdiction to jurisdiction. Although the chapter is only an overview of some of the issues, from Europe to Asia, we explore how preferential pricing support is merely part of the pre-investment analysis.

The market place and the renewable energy market

Of the regulatory mechanisms in place to promote investment in low-carbon technologies, those aimed at renewable energy, and in particular renewable electricity generation, are almost invariably the most advanced.

The financial viability of renewable energy has historically been, and in many cases remains, a major hurdle to development. In order to promote investment in renewables, most jurisdictions have introduced a variety of fiscal incentives and levy schemes, with varying degrees of success.

Despite some expectations that environmental convictions would fade from view in light of the global downturn and the lack of material progress at UN climate change talks, there remain more positive signs in the renewable energy (and wider clean technology) markets than in many others. Although the hoped-for 'Third Industrial Revolution' has not materialised, there continues to be a renewed focus on renewables and other low-carbon technologies, in terms of their role both in promoting economic recovery and in reducing climate change[2]. Properly focused public investment in green energy programmes, in addition to the obvious environmental upside, is seen as a further motivator for parallel private investment in the same or similar projects – a trend that the UK seeks to capitalise on with its proposed 'Green

---

[1] The authors would like to thank the following for their contributions to this chapter: Minoru Ota of Nagashima Ohno & Tsunematsu; Yvonne Kerth of Gleiss Lutz; and Anna Howell, Lynda Haigh, Peter Ramsden, Kevin O'Connor and Marta Sanchez-Villalta of Herbert Smith LLP.
[2] See, for example, Ottmar Edenhofer and Lord Nicholas Stern (March 2009), *Towards a Global Green Recovery*.

Investment Bank', which is expected to combine public and private funds for investment in key renewable energy projects, amongst other things.

At the European level, on which we focus first, the Renewable Energy Directive, which fixes the target for the EU to achieve 20% of its final energy consumption (including heating, transport and electricity) from renewable sources by 2020, has entered into force alongside a number of other measures directed at climate change (see below). Additional targets have been set for individual member states, many of which will have to invest significantly to come close to meeting them. Without the right financial and other regulatory incentives, these targets will not be met and new markets will not materialise.

Inevitably, there will be investors who will continue to 'wait and see', in light of limited progress with the international climate negotiations, and doubts over the future of the Kyoto Protocol after 2012. For example, in the days following the conclusion of the Cancún conference in December 2010, Huaneng Renewables Corporation, China's third largest wind energy company, pulled plans for an initial public offering of up to $1.3 billion, citing the lack of progress at the climate negotiations[3].

It was not all bad news though on the international stage, albeit certainly far from revolutionary. Negotiators at Cancún did agree to establish the Green Climate Fund to act as a repository and channel for $100 billion of climate finance per year, which is to be provided by developed nations. The fund will be able to give national institutions 'direct access' without the intervention of international implementing agencies like the World Bank or the UN. The fund could play a vital role in financing renewable energy projects, but its success will depend on meeting the challenges involved in making the fund operational, and ensuring that the commitment to provide funding is honoured by developed countries.

An introduction to certain EU incentives and their role in the UK

GREEN CERTIFICATE SCHEMES

Green certificate schemes are a widely used fiscal incentive for renewable energy generation. They operate, simply, by awarding certificates to qualifying renewable energy producers, while obliging energy suppliers to obtain and surrender a fixed amount of certificates over a given timescale. A market for the certificates is thereby created, with the additional income received from the sale of the certificate enabling higher-cost renewables projects to compete better with their fossil fuel counterparts. Adjustments to the incentive may be made to give more support to certain technologies, or to boost the scheme by increasing the obligation on energy suppliers in terms of volume or overall duration of the incentive. Green certificate schemes

---

3 'Huaneng pulls HK IPO as Cancun hurts China renewables', Reuters, 13 December 2010.

are highly dependent on market confidence in the value of the certificates. This can be difficult to establish where schemes are solely based on a regulatory framework with no underpinning contractual commitments. As such, the relative effectiveness of green certificates has varied enormously.

In the UK, a green certificate scheme for electricity generation has been operating since 2002, known as the Renewables Obligation, with Renewables Obligation Certificates (ROCs) issued under it. The scheme has had mixed success. In late 2010, the UK government began to consult on the design and implementation of a large-scale feed-in tariff regime, which will initially sit alongside, but ultimately replace, the Renewables Obligation. When the Renewables Obligation was introduced, the form of the scheme met with initial opposition, having moved away from a fixed-price contract model (under the Non-Fossil Fuel Obligation scheme) to a market-based mechanism. This, understandably, gave rise to investor concerns about exposure to power market prices and uncertainty over future certificate values. The ROC scheme features a 'buy-out' option – so that an electricity supplier that is not able, or does not wish, to satisfy its obligation by purchasing sufficient certificates can instead pay a fixed sum into a fund. The fund is then recycled to those electricity suppliers that have surrendered certificates, thereby boosting the value of a certificate. However, problems have occurred, such as when major energy supplier TXU Europe went into administration and defaulted on buy-out payments totalling £23 million, leaving a deficit in the expected value of the fund and bringing the market in ROCs to a temporary halt[4].

Addressing these kinds of issues, and introducing greater flexibility to adjust the incentive[5], has led to the arrangements becoming increasingly complex[6]. The operation of the proposed large-scale feed-in tariff regime alongside the Renewables Obligation may add further complexity and pricing concerns. Despite widespread

---

4 'UK wind power industry warns of funding crisis', Reuters, 16 October 2003.
5 By way of example, in the UK a system of 'banding' was introduced on 1 April 2009 which enables differentiated levels of support for different technologies. The bands range from 0.25 ROCs/MWh for landfill gas to 2 ROCs/MWh for wave, solar PV and some biomass plants. Onshore and offshore wind plants receive 1 ROC/MWh and 2 ROCs/MWh respectively. The bands are to be reviewed periodically or if specific criteria are met. On 31 March 2010, the Department of Energy and Climate Change launched a consultation on the grandfathering of support for biomass, anaerobic digestion and energy from waste under the Renewables Obligation. The consultation closed on 28 May 2010 and the outcome of the consultation will feed into the periodic banding review which was originally scheduled to be undertaken between 2010 and 2013, but will now be concluded by January 2012.
6 The UK's Office for Gas and Electricity Markets (OFGEM) criticised the proposed banding provisions in the modified Renewables Obligation, citing potentially high costs of administration and the difficulties stakeholders would face in trying to understand the mechanics of the scheme. The government took on board some of these criticisms and introduced a feed-in (FIT) tariff regime for small-scale producers which commenced on 1 April 2010 but is now subject to review. As part of this review, the government has already announced plans to cut by up to 72% the FIT support for new farm-scale solar projects (50kW–5MW) due to concerns that these projects could soak up funds government intended to be available for residential and community schemes. Government now proposes to introduce a FIT regime for large-scale producers as well, while maintaining the Renewables Obligation for a limited period. Projects will be able to seek accreditation under the Renewables Obligation until 2017 and will have support grandfathered for 20 years from the date of accreditation until the scheme ends in 2037. The government hopes this will protect investment in projects that have been planned or are being developed and/or financed on the basis of the level of support provided through the Renewables Obligation.

concerns about the cost-effectiveness of the Renewables Obligation as an incentive mechanism, this model has been used to create a sister scheme, the Renewable Transport Fuel Obligation, to give a boost to the UK biofuels market[7].

Single jurisdiction markets are, by their design, limited, and there has been renewed interest in expanding the market for green certificates. Despite calls from some member states to harmonise schemes, the EU has backed away from a pan-European market, instead leaving it up to individual member states to agree to co-operate and co-ordinate their schemes if they wish[8].

GREEN TAXES

While taxation measures can often provide a quick and targeted boost for project development, they generally suffer from a lack of stability and predictability, resulting in heavy discounting from any business case.

The UK has had a green tax mechanism since 2001 in the form of the Climate Change Levy (CCL), which taxes supplies of fossil fuels and brown electricity. Currently, the levy is charged on the non-domestic supply of electricity, gas, petrol and coal. Renewable source electricity[9] is exempt from the CCL, making this source of energy more attractive to non-domestic markets. Eligible generators are issued with levy exemption certificates (LECs), which exempt the supplier of the electricity from having to pay the CCL (the current rate is £0.0047/kWh and will rise from 2012 in line with inflation) in relation to those supplies.

Exemptions from CCL that apply to fuel used for power generation would be removed under proposals to introduce a floor price for carbon in the non-renewable power generating sector. The floor price is planned to start in April 2013 at £16 per tonne and follow a linear path to reach £30 per tonne in 2020. It will comprise the price to the generator of an EU Emissions Trading System (EU ETS) allowance and additional price support in the form of CCL or oil fuel duty charged on fossil fuels used to generate electricity. Relief will be introduced for carbon capture and storage and combined heat and power (CHP) producers. The carbon floor price has been welcomed for providing a degree of certainty for investors in low-carbon energy, but commentators are divided

---

7 The Renewable Transport Fuel Obligations Order 2007 introduced a certificate scheme for renewable transport fuels in April 2008 and requires suppliers of fossil fuels to ensure that a specified percentage of the road fuels they supply in the UK is made up of renewable fuels. The target for the first year of the obligation, 2008/09, was 2.5% by volume. Following public consultation, the government decided to introduce legislation setting an obligation level for 2009/10 of 3.25%. Looking forward, under the Renewable Energy Directive the UK will be required to meet a target of 10% renewable energy in transport by 2020. The Renewable Transport Fuel Obligation is the current mechanism for delivering renewable energy in this sector. Government intends to consult further on amendments to the RTFO that will take these commitments into account and is engaged in further work on the sustainability of biofuels.
8 The role of Guarantees of Origin has been limited to use for fuel mix disclosure requirements.
9 'Renewable sources' are defined as sources of energy other than peat, fossil fuel or nuclear fuel, and include biomass, waste (provided that no more than 90% of the energy content is derived from fossil fuels) and hydroelectric stations with a capacity of less than 10MW (Section 47, Climate Change Levy (General) Regulations 2001).

on whether the proposed price levels will be sufficient to drive significant investment. Some investors continue to call for the UK government to embed the carbon floor price in a contractual obligation with investors rather than by measures that may be subject to revision by the government (or its successors) in the future.

LECs take a similar form to ROCs (essentially electronic certificates evidenced by a unique reference number), but have a maximum value (based on the tax saving) and cannot generally be traded separately from the electricity to which they relate. The requirement to demonstrate a link between the production of the electricity by the generator and the supply to an end consumer creates its own issues for those wishing to claim the benefit of the exemption. Further complexities are created by the exemption of certain categories of customers and supplies, and the relationship with the related exemption scheme for CHP producers, all of which have detracted from the scheme's effectiveness in bolstering renewables.

FEED-IN TARIFFS AND OTHER FORMS OF TARIFF SUBSIDY
The most popular measure of direct financial incentive within the EU has been the use of feed-in tariffs (FITs) to support specific types of renewable energy. There are different types of FIT, such as premium FITs[10], sliding premium FITs[11] and FITs with a contract for difference[12], but the simplest is a fixed tariff that usually takes the form of a fixed price per unit of energy generated by an eligible producer, paid for by a central purchaser or by the energy supplier. The tariff may vary, depending on the fuel source or technology or by reference to a time period or the commissioning date of the facility. Like green certificates, some schemes rely purely on regulatory requirements while others may be backed by long-term contracts.

In the UK, subsidised tariffs were made available under long-term contracts as early as 1990 through the Non-Fossil Fuel Obligation (NFFO). The obligation required electricity suppliers to make arrangements to secure that certain amounts of electricity are generated from renewable sources over a defined period. Developers were invited to bid for the award of long-term contracts under which electricity suppliers would buy all electricity generated by an eligible non-fossil fuel station. The scheme was funded by the imposition of a tax on final electricity supplies (the Fossil Fuel Levy), and had the advantage of providing electricity generators with the security of long-term fixed price contracts. This fiscal stimulus proved less successful than had been hoped, as pricing advantages were outweighed by external factors such as planning controls and grid connection issues.

These issues are now being addressed through relaxations in National Grid's connection standards (the so-called 'Connect and Manage' approach) and, for larger

---

10 As used in Spain.
11 As used in the Netherlands.
12 The regime design that the UK government has stated as its preferred option in its electricity market reform proposals, with a premium FIT regime being an alternative.

schemes, through the introduction of an expedited planning and consenting process under the Planning Act 2008. The UK planning system has frequently been cited as a major obstacle to the development of renewables and other projects. The government has recently announced further plans to streamline the general planning application and consents regimes and to ensure that there is a fast-track planning process for major infrastructure projects. It also plans to introduce a new presumption in favour of sustainable development, so that the default position is that consent should be granted.

While subsidised tariffs are making a comeback in the UK, the key beneficiaries in the short term may be other forms of low-carbon generation, such as nuclear and clean fossil plant fitted with carbon capture and storage technology. At the time of writing the design and implementation of the FIT regime that will be introduced – including details of how it will interact with the Renewables Obligation and whether eligible producers will be able to choose between the two schemes in the period prior to 1 April 2017 (from which point it will no longer be possible to apply for accreditation under the Renewables Obligation) – have yet to be finalised.

COMBINED SUPPORT FOR CHP

The use of CHP offers the potential for significant increases in energy efficiency, and with the right technology and operation, can provide very favourable incentives. The CHP Quality Assurance (CHPQA) programme is a UK government initiative (driven by the EU Directive on the promotion of cogeneration) designed to provide incentives to encourage the development of the CHP sector. CHP plants that qualify as 'good quality' CHP plants[13] are currently entitled to receive: (i) LECs on power output; (ii) favourable allocations of allowances under the EU ETS; (iii) Enhanced Capital Allowances (tax deductions on capital spent on certain plant and machinery); as well as (iv) ROCs (whether or not 'good quality') in relation to renewable feedstock including energy from waste with CHP[14].

However, the government has recently announced that it will end the entitlement to LECs in respect of power generated by CHP which is supplied to consumers indirectly (ie, via grid). Further, the rules for Phase III of the EU ETS (2013–20) have yet to be finalised and it is unclear to what extent and on what basis CHP producers will continue to receive favourable allocations. With the exception of ROCs, the level of entitlement to these benefits is determined by the overall energy efficiency of the plant. While the benefits are potentially lucrative, the CHPQA programme is administratively complex. Additionally, operators need to ensure high levels of demand for both the heat and power generated in order to achieve a sufficiently high level of efficiency and entitlement as a 'good quality' CHP plant.

---

13 Note that, from 1 April 2013, as part of the UK government's plans to introduce carbon price support by reforming the CCL, all fossil fuels burnt in CHP stations will be subject to CCL or fuel duty regardless of their rating through the CHPQA programme.
14 Under the UK government's plans to introduce a FIT regime as part of its electricity market reform proposals, eligible producers will only be able to seek accreditation under the Renewables Obligation until 2017.

Incentives in other EU jurisdictions

In certain other EU member states, the incentives for renewable energy have historically been more favourable than those in the UK, resulting in greater growth and opportunity in the renewable energy sector. Some examples of the incentive regimes used in other EU states are discussed below.

GERMANY
Germany began installing renewable generation capacity on a relatively large scale in the early 1990s. As a consequence it quickly became the world leader in wind power generation. In addition to providing financial subsidies, the feed-in tariff model, in place since 1991[15], obliges grid operators to connect all facilities (including domestic producers) generating renewable electricity, and also requires public utility companies to purchase and distribute all power generated by renewable energy producers.

In 2007, the expansion of renewable generation capacity in Germany began to slow, especially in the wind sector, due to problems associated with grid connection and turbine manufacture. Moreover, much of the German coastline is reserved for nature conservation or shipping lanes, and German offshore projects had to be located further out to sea than is often the case in other countries. Such difficulties have meant that installing fewer, but larger, 5MW turbines is often the most commercially viable option for offshore wind farm developers in Germany. However, large turbines are only manufactured by a small number of companies, which has led to order backlogs.

Since 1 January 2009, the amended Renewable Energy Sources Act has provided for a higher feed-in tariff for wind energy than was previously available to try to re-stimulate the market. Conversely, the tariff for photovoltaic (PV) solar arrays has been reduced. The feed-in tariff for onshore wind farms is €0.092/kWh for the first five years of operation and €0.0502/kWh subsequently. These tariffs decrease by 1% every year for new installations. For offshore wind generation the starting tariff for new installations (*Anfangsvergütung*) is set at €0.15/kWh until the end of 2014, before decreasing to €0.1425/kWh in 2015 and €0.1173/kWh in 2016; after which point it will decrease by 5% per year. The starting tariff applies for (at least) the first 12 years after a turbine has been commissioned, but this period may be extended for some months depending on the location of the installation. After this the basic tariff (*Grundvergütung*), which is set at €0.035/kWh, applies. The total period for which the feed-in tariffs are guaranteed is 20 years plus the year in which the installation is commissioned.

The certainty and robustness provided by this kind of government incentive is credited with the vast growth of not only wind generating capacity in Germany, but also solar PV. A large number of wind projects are being planned for the future,

---

15 *Stromeinspeisungsgesetz* (Energy Feed-in Act), replaced by the Renewable Energy Sources Act (*Erneuerbare-Energien-Gesetz*) in 2000.

both offshore and onshore. Growth is also expected in the solar market despite the reduced feed-in tariffs and ongoing discussions regarding further tariff reductions.

SPAIN

In the *Spanish Renewable Energies Plan 1998 to 2010*, the Spanish government committed to producing a minimum of 12% of total energy consumption from renewable sources. The production of electricity from renewable energy sources is now regulated by a 'special regime'[16] (as opposed to the 'ordinary' regime that governs conventional energy generation).

The special regime promotes the development of renewable energy generation and gives developers of renewable installations with a generating capacity below 50MW the option either to lock in to a fixed feed-in tariff (Option A) or to opt for a floating tariff linked to the pool price in Spain (Option B). Renewable generation installations between 50MW and 100MW also receive a bonus payment for electricity produced. The feed-in tariffs are paid throughout the operational life of an installation, although the tariffs are reduced after a specified number of years: 25 years for solar PV, ocean and hydro systems, 20 years for wind and geothermal, and 15 years for biomass systems.

Once installations start generating electricity they must be registered in the Administrative Register of Generation Installations under the special regime (RIPRE), overseen and administered by the Ministry of Industry, Tourism and Commerce. Final registration of the installation in the RIPRE is necessary to secure the benefit of the feed-in tariff regime.

Installations that have chosen to lock in to a fixed tariff will sell their energy through the bid system managed by the market operator, OMEL, for the purposes of quantifying deviations in the amount of electricity generated, and if appropriate, settling any resulting costs directly or through a representative. The system operator, Red Eléctrica de España (REE), will settle the cost of the deviations. On a monthly basis, the OMEL and REE send the National Energy Commission (CNE) information relating to settlements made with these installations.

Installations that have chosen a floating tariff linked to the pool price may sell their energy either directly or indirectly through representatives both in the bidding market and by signing bilateral contracts, or by forward negotiation.

In the case of either Option A or Option B above, generators under the special regime can select a market representative, which could be a supplier of last resort (*comercializador de ultimo recurso*) or a private market representative (or 'retailer'). Alternatively, generators may sell power directly. The supplier of last resort or the retailer, as the case may be, will represent the generator in the market and 'trade' the electricity it generates on the generator's behalf, charging a fee for this service. The main difference between a supplier of last resort and a retailer is that the price

---
16 Royal Decree 661/2007.

charged by the retailer is negotiated, whereas the price charged by suppliers of last resort is determined by the applicable regulations (€10/MWh).

It should be noted that, under the special regime, generators receive part of the tariff from OMEL and REE (the part that corresponds to the market price), and the rest of the tariff (the difference between the market price and the applicable tariff) from CNE. These amounts are not paid directly to the generators but to their market representative (which is also the representative for the purposes of the CNE). For generators that elected to receive a floating tariff linked to the pool price, OMEL and REE will pay the generator the amount corresponding to the market price, and the premium to the CNE.

Implementation of Royal Decree 661/2007: PV technology
The entitlement of PV solar systems to receive feed-in tariffs was established by Royal Decree 661/2007. Royal Decree 1578/2008 established a competitive pre-registration mechanism to allocate income to new PV solar installations based on quarterly power quotas. The tariffs are adjusted every quarter for new systems completing the registration process. For the second pre-registration process of 2011 (April–June), the quotas for type I.1 installations (small rooftop installations), type I.2 installations (large rooftop installations) and type II installations (ground installations) are 7.163MW, 67.846MW and 40.450MW respectively[17].

In December 2010, new limits on the number of hours per year for which PV solar installations are entitled to receive feed-in tariffs were introduced under Royal Decree-Law 14/2010. To compensate generators, the period for which they are entitled to receive feed-in tariffs has been extended from 25 to 30 years. However, the new limits are controversial, particularly as they will apply to new and existing installations. The new limits may threaten the economic viability of many existing and planned projects, and there are reports that solar investors are in the process of bringing legal claims against the Spanish government.

Pre-allocation registry
One of the fundamental aims of Royal Decree-Law 6/2009 (RDL 6/2009), is to establish mechanisms to prevent the special regime (excluding PV installations) from increasing the tariff deficit.

For this purpose, the RDL 6/2009 creates a pre-allocation register in which every installation intending to participate in the special regime needs to be listed before being able to register for the special regime.

A generation capacity threshold has been set for each of the technologies included in the RD 661/2007. If the aggregate generation capacity of the installations registered with the pre-allocation registry is below the threshold for each technol-

---

17 As a result of the generation capacity of registered installations and the application of the formula established in the regulation, the new tariffs for the second pre-registration process in 2011 will be 28.8821 c€/kWh, 20.3726 c€/kWh and 13.4585 c€/kWh for type I.1, I.2 and II installations, respectively.

ogy type, the new installations that fulfil the requirements to be pre-allocated can continue to apply for registration with the pre-allocation registry until the threshold is reached (and will be able to benefit from the special regime).

If the aggregate generation capacity of the installations registered with the pre-allocation registry exceeds the threshold, pre-registration will only be granted to installations which, at the time the RDL 6/2009 came into force, fulfilled the relevant requirements.

Currently, wind energy and solar thermal energy have exceeded the target and no further pre-registration applications are being accepted (around 2,339.89 MW of solar thermal power and 6,389MW of wind power were pre-registered).

Implementation of Royal Decree 661/2007: Other technologies
It is expected that, during 2011 the tariffs, premiums, caps and floor will be revised in the light of reports tracking the implementation and success of the Renewable Energy Plan, the Spanish Energy Savings and Efficiency Strategy and the new objectives included in the Renewable Energy Plan for the 2011–20 period. The revisions will be based on the costs associated with each technology type, the effectiveness of the special regime in meeting renewable energy demand and the impact of the regime on the technical and economic management of the system.

ELSEWHERE IN THE EU
Feed-in tariffs remain the most popular choice of incentive in other EU countries. France employs a fixed feed-in tariff for wind power and introduced a new tariff for solar PV arrays placed on large private industrial buildings such as supermarkets, factories and agricultural buildings in January 2010. The tariff structure is complex and is a little more restrictive than the market expected. It forms part of a new set of measures designed to kick-start the French renewables economy, including the building of solar PV power plants in each French region by 2011 with a cumulative capacity of at least 300MW[18].

As can be seen in the example of Germany above, one of the major problems project developers face in the EU (and, indeed, elsewhere) when building renewable power installations concerns securing a grid connection. This is, to a large degree, related to insufficient grid capacity being available, non-objective and non-transparent procedures for the award of grid connections, high grid connection costs and long lead times to obtain authorisation for grid connections. Article 16 of the new Renewable Energy Directive seeks to combat some of these problems by requiring member states to provide priority or guaranteed access to grid connections for new installations generating electricity from renewable sources, which if successful, may enhance renewable energy development going forwards.

---

18 *Plan national de développement des énergies renouvelables de la France*, presented by Jean-Louis Borloo (Minister of Ecology, Energy, Sustainability and Territorial Development), 17 November 2008, and *Renewable energy country attractiveness indices*, published by Ernst & Young, February 2010.

Developments at the EU level

EU CLIMATE CHANGE AND ENERGY PACKAGE
The EU Climate Change and Energy Package was formally adopted in April 2009. The package includes a number of measures of significant direct and indirect relevance to the renewables sector, and is an important marker of current and future EU policy, albeit the big question in terms of future planning is what happens post-2020. The package includes the Renewable Energy Directive and the target for renewables to produce 20% of EU energy by 2020. The renewables targets for member states differ (from 10% for Malta to 49% for Sweden) based on the level of deployment of renewable technologies in their territories, and thus their ability to contribute to EU targets.

The measures also require a 20% cut in greenhouse gases by 2020 (compared with 1990 levels), increasing to 30% if other countries agree to similar cuts (unfortunately this was not achieved at the UN meeting in Copenhagen in December 2009, as had initially been hoped, nor in Cancún in 2010) and requirements on the European Commission to assess and report on progress towards an existing target to cut energy consumption by 20% by 2020 against projected 2020 levels.

Regarding the EU ETS, the proportion of allowances auctioned will now increase year on year, so that at least 70% of allowances will be auctioned by 2020 with a view to this increasing to 100% by 2027. Significantly, power companies will have to purchase all their allowances by auction from 2013, which should drive up the price of allowances and increase the competitiveness of renewable energy. Auction revenue will accrue to member states. The EU ETS Directive recommends that at least half the auction revenue, and all of the revenue from auctioning allowances in respect of aviation, should be used to fight and adapt to climate change and lists a number of purposes, mainly within the EU, but also in developing countries.

Finally, the package also includes a target for 10% of transport fuels to come from renewable sources, including biofuels, by 2020. The EU's Renewable Energy Directive stipulates that biofuels and bioliquids taken into account in the 10% target must not be produced from raw materials from land with "high biodiversity value", land that has a high carbon stock, or peatlands. The Renewable Energy Directive initially requires a 35% carbon dioxide (CO_2) saving resulting from the use of biofuels compared with fossil fuels, which will then be scaled up to at least 50% in 2017 and 60% thereafter.

STATE AID
The implementation of the EU Third Energy Package is also beginning to have an impact on the renewables market. Proposals for EU-wide 'Network Codes' that will harmonise certain aspects of energy delivery and trading are well under way, with the pilot electricity code focusing on the connection of wind generation.

In Europe, enhanced incentives to encourage investment in renewable energy came with further relaxation of state aid rules in this area. As part of the European Council's call in spring 2007 for a sustainable integrated European climate and energy policy, it invited the European Commission to review the guidelines on state aid for environmental protection, which had been in existence since 2001. The new guidelines came into force on 1 April 2008[19], and state that: "[t]he primary objective of State aid control in the field of environmental protection is to ensure that State aid measures will result in a higher level of environmental protection than would occur without the aid...". Among other measures, the guidelines highlight that: "[t]he high cost of production of some types of renewable energy does not allow undertakings to charge competitive prices on the market and thus creates a market access barrier for renewable energy". The 2001 guidelines were very effective at encouraging state aid for environmental protection purposes: between 2001 and 2006, state aid targeting environmental protection doubled in value from €7 billion to €14 billion. It is hoped that the new guidelines will encourage further increases in state aid, in particular to meet targets for a 20% reduction in greenhouse gas emissions and a 20% share of energy consumption from being sourced from renewable energy by 2020, providing further incentive in this area.

Asia

The Asian renewables market, while having some similarities with the EU market, also has some quite different characteristics which bear direct relevance to their relative performance and consequently, on investment strategy.

CLEAN DEVELOPMENT MECHANISM

Asia continues to be a key market for renewable energy projects, with Clean Development Mechanism (CDM) projects, in particular, having risen in scale significantly over the past few years. CDM-supported projects entail different considerations to equivalent renewable energy projects in the EU. The surge in CDM projects (up until recent times) has largely been driven by public and private sector entities vying for certified emission reduction (CER) credits to help meet their Kyoto Protocol and EU targets, taking advantage of the relatively lower costs associated with achieving greenhouse gas emission reductions in developing countries in contrast to home control measures as well as private equity, hedge funds, banks and other institutions looking to capitalise on opportunities in the carbon markets. A report by the International Emissions Trading Association (IETA) shows that, in 2006, CERs contributed by Asia accounted for 80% of the world's total carbon trade volume. According to the UN Framework Convention on Climate Change (UNFCCC), Asia currently accounts for almost 85% of the sell-side market

---
19 Official Journal 2008/C 82/01.

for CERs. CDM projects include small-scale hydro[20], wind, co-generation, solar, biomass and waste to energy.

CHINA

In Asian markets we focus on China, the largest supplier of CERs in the world, which has issued 54.83% of all CERs, according to the UNFCCC[21]. Analysts say China will make approximately $8 billion by 2012 from the sale of all the CERs it issues. One aspect for special consideration is the fixing of a floor price for credits by the National Development and Reform Commission (NRDC). Analysts indicate that the market for long-term Chinese CER units is in a pricing limbo, after China failed to agree on a binding deal at the Copenhagen climate change summit in December 2009. It remains to be seen how political pressure is brought to bear upon China and what impact this will have on the worth of post-2012 CERs from China. However, in the meantime the floor price is said to be fixed at €8 ($12) per CER for chemical projects and €10 ($15) for renewable energy projects[22]. This is a practice not enshrined in any published regulation and, while currently the price is fixed for each project at the authorisation stage, there is no guarantee that this practice will continue (or that the NDRC will not revise the floor price at a later stage). Also, when the market price of credits and EU allowances is near to, or lower than, the floor price, margins weaken and could become negative.

With an aim to police its greenhouse gas emissions, China will introduce a domestic emissions trading scheme with a potential domestic trading market value estimated at about £125 billion a year, nearly twice that of the entire global carbon trading market[23]. It plans to introduce pilot regional schemes before 2013 and a national scheme from 2015.

The Chinese government is also entitled to a share of the profits on the sale of credits by the CDM project company (although much less than on other projects, with renewable energy being only 2%) which, together with the share of credits taken for administrative expenses and adaptation projects deducted pursuant to the Kyoto Protocol, must be factored into expected returns. While CDM can help lower some of the financial barriers to renewables, it does not remove all obstacles, some (but not all) of which arise from developing and operating in countries like China. A CDM project therefore requires the usual risk assessment one would undertake before embarking on any project in China.

Project structure also has to be considered as China requires a domestic party to be the majority owner in any CDM project company. However, following recent

---

20 Large-scale hydro can prove difficult in terms of demonstrating additionality as required by Article 12.5 of the Kyoto Protocol.
21 http://cdm.unfccc.int (24 January 2011).
22 The floor price is not published and this figure is based on research.
23 'China's carbon-trading pledge signals new world order', *The Times*, 27 September 2009.

guidance issued by the Hong Kong government, it is possible, provided certain criteria are met, for foreign businesses to fully own and operate, through qualified Hong Kong companies, CDM projects in China, without the need for a local joint venture partner.

In April 2009 the Hong Kong director of environment announced that Hong Kong companies would be permitted to participate in Chinese CDM projects as Chinese enterprises, subject to meeting certain criteria on the establishment and control of the Hong Kong company. On 1 December 2009, the Hong Kong Environmental Protection Department issued the 'Supplementary Notes on the Implementation of Projects under the Clean Development Mechanism'[24], which provide the criteria that have to be met to obtain a letter of certification for Hong Kong enterprises from the Environmental Protection Department. The qualification criteria are:

- the company should be registered and set up in Hong Kong, and its principal location of business operation or its headquarters should be situated in Hong Kong[25];
- the executive director of the company should be a Chinese national or a holder of a Hong Kong permanent ID card, and more than half of the board members should be Chinese nationals or holders of a Hong Kong permanent ID card if a board of directors has been set up for the company[26]; and
- the ratio of non-tradable shares should be more than 50% if the company concerned is publicly listed[27].

Once a letter of certification has been obtained from the Hong Kong Environmental Protection Department, it is then submitted to the NDRC by the CDM project company, together with its application for a letter of approval. Although we can find no indication of this under Chinese legislation, according to the Supplemental Notes, the Hong Kong Environmental Protection Department grants letters of certification for Hong Kong enterprises in accordance with the 'Measures for Operation and Management of CDM Projects in China', a document issued on 12 October 2005 by central government, and which contains the eligibility requirements for enterprises. Accordingly, the Hong Kong Environmental Protection Department states on its website that enterprises that have obtained a letter of certification from it will be recognised as a Chinese enterprise for the purpose of applying to the NDRC for undertaking CDM projects.

Although the procedure under the Supplementary Notes is untested, as they stand, they open up considerable potential for foreign and Hong Kong investors to

---

24 www.epd.gov.hk/epd/english/climate_change/files/CDM_Sup_notes.pdf.
25 There is no suggestion in the Supplementary Notes that the company cannot be set up specifically to meet the requirements of the notes.
26 Foreigners can apply for Hong Kong permanent citizenship after seven years' residence in Hong Kong.
27 This criterion is met by a declaration issued by the directors of the company.

use a qualifying Hong Kong company to wholly or majority own and operate a Chinese CDM project.

Chinese renewable energy policy and incentives
Concerns over issues such as energy security, increases in conventional energy prices, a recognised over-reliance on coal-powered generation and increasing environmental awareness have resulted in new policies in China. An increased emphasis on sustainability and protection of the environment is driving support for a clean energy market.

China's growth has come at a significant cost. It is suggested that by 2010 China's consumption of coal will be around 4 billion tons. A report by Greenpeace, the Worldwide Fund for Nature and the Energy Foundation, published in January 2010, claims that 80% of China's carbon dioxide emissions come from burning coal[28]. The same report estimates that the environmental and social costs associated with the country's use of coal amounted to RMB1.7 trillion in 2007, about 7.1% of China's GDP for that year.

The Chinese government has, over the past few years, adopted a range of measures that are again affecting the market dynamics for renewable energy. In 2005, it adopted the Renewable Energy Law (which was amended in 2009), then in 2007 it issued a white paper on energy[29], and in 2008 a further white paper on climate change[30]. It also issued a draft Energy Law in December 2007 for public comment, which is yet to be formally passed. In 2010, China established the National Energy Commission which is responsible for coordinating the formulation of energy strategy and development planning. The commission announced in March 2010 that China will be seeking to produce around 15% of all the country's energy by renewable means within the next 10 years.

The Renewable Energy Law enshrines renewable energy as a "state priority". It establishes a national renewable energy target; ensures that renewable power projects are given enhanced off-take rights; and requires all power generated by a renewable project to be purchased by the grid, with feed-in tariff subsidies also applied. The 2009 amendments set specific targets for a renewable power quota and technical requirements for grid connection for generators. Moreover, the Renewable Energy Law now requires utilities to buy all renewable electricity produced by generators; failure to do this will result in fines of up to an amount double that of the economic loss to the renewable energy company[31].

---
28 Mao Yushi, Sheng Hong and Yang Fuqiang, *The True Cost of Coal*.
29 *China's Energy Conditions and Policies*, 26 December 2007, http://english.gov.cn/2007-12/26/content_844218.htm.
30 *China's Policies and Actions for Addressing Climate Change*, 29 October 2008, www.gov.cn/english/2008-10/29/content_1134544.htm.
31 DB Climate Change Advisors (March 2010), *Global Cimate Change Policy Tracker, The Green Economy: the Race is on*.

In addition, China has begun to establish feed-in tariffs for renewable energy sources. It set a feed-in tariff for wind power in August 2009, in which wind power is divided into four tiers ranging between RMB0.51 and RMB0.61/kWh. The areas with most wind resources are to receive the lowest tariff. The feed-in tariff for biomass power is RMB0.25/kWh plus the 2005 benchmark desulphurised coal price in the area where the facility is located. As yet, there is no nationwide feed-in tariff for solar power. However, specific solar projects can receive a feed-in tariff through a tender process. Solar projects in 2010 received a tariff of RMB1.15/kWh[32].

The climate change white paper provides further support for renewable energy power generation, setting out targets to raise the proportion of renewable sources (including large-scale hydropower in China) and to ensure further increases in the extraction of coal bed methane. According to China's Mid and Long-Term Plan for the Development of Renewable Energy, China will continue to promote large hydropower stations, look to grow more rapidly its wind power, ensure encouragement for marsh gas, biomass and also for solid and liquid biofuels and actively promote the continued expansion of solar power generation and technology. New incentives are also likely to be applied in other areas, such as preferential policies on taxation and investment for new nuclear, and in the field of clean coal, notably carbon capture and storage. In March 2009, the Chinese government took the step of providing subsidies for the installation of domestic PV solar arrays, with an undertaking to pay half of the installation costs. This provided a significant stimulus to boost China's already large PV manufacturing industry. In addition to environmental considerations, some say competitive forces played a hand here, with China at risk of coming second to the US PV industry following the passage of the American Recovery and Reinvestment Act 2009, which provides strong financial support for renewable energy technologies[33].

In August 2009, the National People's Congress passed an important resolution on climate change which indicated that China will accord priority to evolving new policies on carbon emissions, renewable resources, efficiency and conservation in energy use and other fields to combat global warming.

As part of China's support for renewable energy, it is also expected that tax breaks will be developed for renewable energy generation. An inter-ministerial team has been put together to research possibilities for environmental taxation and it is suggested that China is likely to levy a carbon tax – an environmental tax that is paid for carbon emissions – on its enterprises in the near future. This would mean enterprises including coal, natural gas and oil companies would have to pay the carbon tax in accordance with their CO_2 emissions, while energy saving and environmentally friendly industries are likely to be subsidised.

---

32 DB Climate Change Advisors (March 2010), *Global Cimate Change Policy Tracker, The Green Economy: the Race is on*.

33 'China solar subsidy chases cleantech jobs', Reuters, 27 March 2009.

By way of comparison of the potential effectiveness of such measures, the tax authorities in China cut tax rebates for exports of certain high energy-consumption products in June 2007, a move which it is said lowered exports of the affected products by 40%[34]. However, as recently reported by the *People's Daily*, owing to current global economic conditions, China expects to maintain the stability of its export-related policy, and it is "highly unlikely" that the country will reduce export rebates for highly polluting and energy-intensive industries "during the first half", according to a senior Ministry of Commerce official[35].

Despite the many potential fiscal upsides to doing business in China, it does present certain unique risks in terms of the development of renewable projects; for example, obtaining valid land use rights is often a critical aspect to such projects, with possible resettlement issues to address. An environmental impact assessment is required for all CDM projects and the Equator Principles[36] may also need to be followed. While these, and other specific legal issues, will need to be met, China's increasing high-level support for renewable energy, and, hopefully, continuing benefits to investors of CER credits, present ongoing investment opportunities. In terms of CERs, much clearly hangs on the post-2012 Kyoto Protocol framework: whether agreement can be reached, including as to the continued role of the CDM, as well as other aspects, such as the possible extension of CERs to carbon capture and storage projects[37]. The lifeline at the EU level[38] itself is unlikely to be enough if there is insufficient viability in terms of the approach to global emissions reductions and global emissions markets.

As the world's largest emitter of greenhouse gases, China is a key player in global climate change mitigation, with a prominent role in the United Nations climate change negotiations. Following the Copenhagen summit, China has pledged to reduce its CO_2 emissions per unit of GDP by 40–45% by 2020, compared to 2005 levels, and raise the level of non-fossil fuels in primary energy consumption to 15%. However, some have argued that these pledges do not amount to any reduction in carbon emissions, but rather a deceleration of rising emissions.

---

34 'Green tax considered to help cut emissions', *China Daily*, 13 September 2008.
35 http://english.peopledaily.com.cn/90001/90778/7271428.html, 25 January 2011.
36 The Equator Principles are a set of voluntary benchmarks for assessing and managing environmental and social issues associated with project finance and have particular relevance to developing economies. The principles have been adopted by around 70 financial institutions responsible for at least 85% of global project financing; since 2009 these include China's Industrial Bank. The Equator Principles apply to all project finance transactions of more than $10 million. A social and environmental assessment (SEA), to identify the potential environmental and social impacts of a project, and an action plan which draws on the conclusions of the SEA form the foundation of the principles.
37 Carbon pricing issues and carbon availability controls are beyond the scope of this chapter but this clearly remains an important issue for the relative viability and returns profile of energy projects and CDM projects generally.
38 The revised EU Emissions Trading Directive included in the EU Climate Change and Energy Package seeks to provide operators and investors with some certainty concerning the use after 2012 of CERs generated by projects established before 2013. It therefore requires member states to allow operators to use such CERs from 2013 onwards, but this requirement shall not extend beyond March 2015.

Environmental issues
Finally, the Chinese white paper on energy highlighted that one of China's primary policies is the strengthening of the environmental management of energy projects, including those relating to renewable energy projects. As identified later in this chapter, there are other environmental issues to consider in terms of renewable energy investments separate and distinct from carbon costs, incentives and the clean energy end-product. With environmental investment mistakes acutely highlighted in the current credit-constrained market[39], this may be a good sign for future renewable energy investments in China, perhaps reducing risks in this area in the future. In the interim, however, proper due diligence will need to be conducted to avoid environmental pitfalls and to ensuring upside only (financially and in terms of social investment) of renewable energy investments in Asia.

JAPAN
In Japan, energy from renewable resources such as sunlight, wind and biomass is not widely used for power generation for economic reasons and thus requires government support to become more widely accepted and used. Renewable energy is classified as 'new energy', and the Japanese government promotes the use of new energy under several pieces of legislation, including the Renewable Portfolio Standard (RPS), which came into force in 2003. The RPS is an obligation imposed on electricity supply companies that is intended to encourage the generation of electricity from renewable energy sources.

A draft bill, the Basic Act for Global Warming Countermeasures, was submitted to the Diet, the Japanese legislature, in 2010. It contemplates the introduction of three new schemes to promote clean and renewable energy: (a) a global warming tax; (b) feed-in tariffs for renewable energy; and (c) a domestic emissions trading system with a 'cap-and-trade' mechanism. The bill stems from policy statements by the Japanese government, first announced under the Hatoyama administration and subsequently supported by the current Kan administration, pledging that by 2020 Japan would reduce its greenhouse gas emissions by 25% compared to 1990 levels. While the draft bill has yet to be passed, the Japanese cabinet committee announced in December 2010 that it intends to establish and implement feed-in tariffs for renewable energy and a global warming tax during 2011, and that it would carefully consider the possible introduction of a domestic emissions trading system. The Ministry of Economy, Trade and Industry is to submit a draft bill establishing feed-in tariffs for renewable energy during 2011, covering all existing types of renewable energy. The tariffs will be available for 10 years for PV power generation (the tariff will be gradually reduced), and for 15 to 20 years for all other forms of renewable

---
39 Greg Larkin (March 2009), 'An environmental sub-prime crisis?', *Environmental Finance*.

energy (for which the tariffs will remain fixed). When this new bill comes into force, the RPS will be abolished.

The PV market is rapidly expanding as countries seek to expand the use of solar power. The world's solar power market is expected to grow to ¥10 trillion by 2015. Until 2004, Japan was a world leader in solar power generation, but since 2005, when a policy decision was taken to remove subsidies for this technology, the rate of growth of solar power in Japan has been sluggish. However, the government has set a policy goal of increasing domestic solar power production ten-fold by 2020, has re-enacted its solar power subsidy policy, and has passed a new law requiring electricity generated using PV technology to be purchased for roughly double the current price.

With respect to biomass, generation capacity around the world appears to be increasing, and in Japan electricity from biomass represents a high proportion of new energy supplied, but the biomass power market lacks vitality. However, in June 2009 the Diet promulgated the Basic Law for Promoting the Utilisation of Biomass. In order to comprehensively and systematically promote the use of biomass, this new law sets out basic principles concerning the promotion of biomass and clarifies the responsibilities of the national and local governments for planning and implementing the necessary measures. The law also sets out matters which are deemed to be fundamental to the implementation of measures to promote the use of biomass.

There are other recent market developments in Japan which should be noted, including:

- an increase in demand for light-emitting diode (LED) products, primarily because the retail and restaurant industries have become subject to restrictions on energy use due to the enactment of the Act on the Streamlining of Energy Utilisation (which came into force on 1 April 2010), and have chosen to switch from fluorescent lighting to LED lighting (which is more energy and cost efficient); and
- an increase in demand for the replacement of lighting and air conditioning devices used in office buildings and factories which have energy consumption levels equivalent to 1,500 kilolitres or more of crude oil per year, in response to an obligation under the Tokyo Environmental Protection Ordinance to reduce carbon dioxide emissions.

Interface with other climate change and environmental regulation

One danger that some players have run into is examining individual incentives in isolation from other environmental regulatory measures, particularly where such measures could have an impact on investment returns, or even the commercial viability of a project, to a very material extent. Likewise, it can be critical to understand the interrelationship between existing and proposed incentive mechanisms. An investment that benefits from one particular incentive may not necessarily benefit from other co-existing or future measures, potentially resulting in less favourable returns than might otherwise have been expected.

This has been acutely demonstrated in the UK by the position of renewables under the Carbon Reduction Commitment (CRC) Energy Efficiency Scheme. The CRC is a mandatory UK emissions trading scheme which commenced in April 2010. It covers emissions of carbon dioxide resulting from energy consumption across a range of sectors that fall outside the EU ETS. While consumption of electricity generated by on-site renewables will not be covered by the requirement to purchase CRC allowances, this is strictly on the proviso that ROCs and feed-in tariffs are not claimed. Thus, whilst renewable sources are incentivised through ROCs and feed-in tariffs, claiming these benefits means that CRC allowances must be purchased, at full value, for electricity generated and consumed as if this electricity had been generated from non-renewable sources. Maintaining that the scheme was fundamentally about energy efficiency, irrespective of the low-carbon nature of the energy source, has led to assertions that some plans to develop on-site renewables would be rendered uneconomic and therefore abandoned. Further, the consumption of 'green tariff' electricity supplied by the UK grid is treated no differently from any other tariffs.

Emissions and other environmental controls can also have significant economic and practical implications for renewable energy projects. Controls under the EU Waste Incineration Directive (WID) led to one UK operator of a co-fired coal and biomass power station finding itself subject to the stringent emissions standards imposed by the WID. The costs involved in upgrading the station to comply with these standards would have meant that the project, including a £65 million biomass fuel production plant, would not have been commercially viable[40].

Many jurisdictions have adopted, and continue to adopt, increasingly stringent environmental controls over fossil fuel emissions, particularly those from coal-fired power stations. Such controls increase the competitiveness of renewables and thereby serve as an indirect incentive. In the EU, the most important regulatory pressures on fossil fuel generators are controls established by the Industrial Emissions Directive (IED)[41], which entered into force on 6 January 2011, and the EU ETS. Broadly speaking, the IED applies strict limits on air pollution and lays down rules on the prevention and control of pollution resulting from industrial activities. It also sets

---

40 *Scottish Power Generation Ltd v Scottish Environment Protection Agency* [2005] SLT 641. The plant is still being permitted to operate by the Scottish Environment Protection Agency on the condition that a new biomass plant capable of meeting WID standards is constructed on the same site.
41 The IED recasts seven directives, including the Large Combustion Plant Directive and the Integrated Pollution Prevention and Control Directive.

rules designed to prevent (or where that is not practicable, to reduce) emissions into air, water and land and to prevent the generation of waste. In particular, it sets stricter limits than were previously in place on pollutants such as nitrogen oxides, sulphur dioxide and dust. As a general rule, installations will have until 2016 to comply with the limits. However, the IED permits member states to draw up "transitional national plans" which allow certain large combustion plants an extension until 30 June 2020[42]. The IED also contains a limited lifetime derogation which, whilst limiting the number of hours combustion plants can operate, affords them an opportunity to continue generating beyond 2016[43]. The impact of the derogation will vary according to the particular generation mix of a member state and its future energy policy plans, but it will help to allay concerns over security of supply pending the construction of new generation capacity.

The scale of the economic and operational impact of environmental controls can be considerable. For example, in April 2010, the European Court of Justice ruled that the predecessor to the IED, the Large Combustion Plant Directive (LCPD), applied to a coal-fired combustion plant in the UK that was used exclusively to heat and power an aluminium smelting plant, even though the UK government was of the view that the LCPD did not apply[44]. The operator claimed that adaptations costing at least £200 million would have to be made as a result of the decision[45].

New renewables and related technologies may also need to comply with increasing environmental product regulation, irrespective of the environmental benefits that such technologies themselves may offer. The EU Directive on the Restriction of Hazardous Substances (RoHS) prohibits the use of lead, cadmium, mercury and certain other substances within new electrical and electronic equipment. Many non-EU jurisdictions, including China and some US states, have adopted similar legislation. Some of the prohibited substances are used in renewable technologies and, whilst the EU legislation provides for some exemptions, the legislation can trip up the unwary investor, who may not be aware that restrictions could prevent any future market in the technology. A revised RoHS Directive is undergoing final nego-

---

42 Provided that: (i) they were granted their first permit, or submitted a completed application, before 27 November 2002; and (ii) the plant became operational no later than 27 November 2003.
43 The derogation grants combustion plants an exemption from the revised emissions limits (which replace those that applied under the Large Combustion Plant Directive (LCPD)) and from inclusion in transitional national plans (which replace National Emission Reduction Plans) provided that the following conditions are satisfied: (i) by 1 January 2014 the operator gives a written declaration to the relevant competent authority that it will not operate the plant for more than 17,500 hours between 1 January 2016 and 31 December 2023; (ii) the operator submits a record of operating hours since 1 January 2016 to the competent authority each year; (iii) the emission limits for sulphur dioxides, nitrogen oxides and dust applying to the plant on 31 December 2015 are maintained, and in the case of combustion plants with a thermal input of over 500MW firing solid fuels which were granted a permit after 1 July 1987, the emission limits for nitrogen oxides set out in Part 1 of Annex V to the Directive are complied with; and (iv) the plant has not already been granted an exemption from the old LCPD emission limits, or from inclusion in a National Emission Reduction Plan under article 4 (4) of the LCPD.
44 *Commission v United Kingdom* 2010 C-346/08.
45 The plant is now co-firing coal and biomass.

tiation and is expected to enter into force in 2011. It will extend the scope of RoHS to all electrical and electronic equipment but is expected specifically to exclude solar cells. This exclusion has been contentious and caused division between manufacturers of thin film solar modules (which contain RoHS restricted substances and would not comply with an extended directive absent an exclusion) and manufacturers of crystalline silicon modules (which do not contain any RoHS-restricted substances) and may be removed in the future.

Similarly, the EU Regulation on the Registration, Evaluation, Authorisation and Restriction of Chemicals (REACH), which came into force on 1 June 2007, imposes increasingly extensive controls on the manufacture and supply of chemical substances in the EU. REACH does not cover naturally occurring substances, except where these are chemically modified, but nonetheless may apply to certain renewable fuels manufactured or imported into the EU, or at least to additives contained within them. In the same way that the RoHS Directive inspired similar hazardous substance controls outside the EU, REACH is also driving major developments across the world in chemicals regulation including, notably, in the US.

Conclusion

Despite some of the toughest economic conditions in decades and limited progress towards an international climate change agreement, the political will to ensure further growth and confidence in renewable energy markets has, if anything, sharpened. Soft words and shallow promises of yesteryear have been replaced with ever tougher targets, and incentives reinforced by substantial financial packages. A variety of regulations worldwide, underpinning such initiatives, is forcing markets into new directions – some with greater gain potential than others. From an investors' perspective, the challenge can be put in simple terms: against this regulatory backdrop, which initiatives present good prospects in terms of financial, environmental (and social) performance? The rapid pace of regulatory change means it is easier to pose this question than it is to answer it. But, from a legal point of view, understanding and managing the regulatory drivers and jurisdictional variants means that opportunities in this area can be optimised, and the best means implemented to ensure that risks are spread and otherwise managed. Much of the regulation and fiscal initiatives talked about in this chapter are relatively (or even very) new, but from a regulatory standpoint a clear message is being sent to the market. With time, and continued commitment, quite how effective these measures will prove to be should become clearer.

Chapter 22

An investment portfolio view of the low-carbon world

Professor Michael Mainelli, Z/Yen Group; James Palmer, BP; Liang Shi, University of Edinburgh

A portfolio approach

During 2007, the London Accord, like other climate change investigations, concluded that there is no single solution to the problem of climate change. One thematic paper drawing the London Accord results together was 'A Portfolio Approach To Climate Change Investment And Policy', by Michael Mainelli and James Palmer (Mainelli and Palmer, 2007). Mankind must deploy a diverse range of potential solutions – market solutions, technological solutions and social solutions.

The 'supply side' of potential solutions does not contain one guaranteed single solution, a 'silver bullet'. Pacala and Socolow (2004) note, "Although no element is a credible candidate for doing the entire job (or even half the job) by itself, the portfolio as a whole is large enough that not every element has to be used." On the 'demand side', Stern (2006) highlighted the limitations of cost/benefit analysis where one cannot afford to fail; cost/benefit analysis is of little use in Russian roulette, unless you accept extinction as an option. A portfolio approach to climate change solutions is warranted, given the catastrophic nature of failure – 'don't put all your eggs in one basket'.

Policy is important to portfolio selection; more so is investment. According to the United Nations Framework Convention on Climate Change (UNFCCC), "When considering the means to enhance financial and investment flows to address climate change in the future, it is important to focus on the role of private-sector investments as they constitute the largest share of investment and financial flows (86 per cent)" (UNFCCC, 2007). However, the UNFCCC does not say how that private sector investment will happen (there were attempts, but private sector consultations met with disappointingly little enthusiasm). Both Stern and the UNFCCC worked top-down, macroeconomically.

Investors realise that there is rarely a single winner in any investment field: 'there will be winners and losers'. There is a continuum from portfolio investment to direct project investment where somewhere along the continuum things change from picking a portfolio to picking and supporting a potential winner. Still, long-term investment is about having a range of options. Investors analyse a range of options as a portfolio. For the majority of investors, the 'most effective' portfolio means the most profitable selection of options for a given level of investment and financial risk. Similarly, for policy-makers, 'most effective' is likely to mean a portfolio that delivers a desired level of emissions reduction at the lowest cost and level of social risk. Any single solution may fail or, at the extreme, even increase climate change. But policy-makers have a strong tendency to try and pick winners.

Some shared assumptions among the London Accord participants are:
- climate change is one of the world's great externalities;
- greenhouse gas (GHG) emissions can be internalised through a price mechanism, a cap-and-trade system, a carbon tax or, perhaps realistically, a hybrid cap-and-trade system with auctioned permits;
- the world is looking at its greatest infrastructure transformation;
- private sector investment is not just important to solving climate change, it is essential;
- investors only invest significantly when they can make returns commensurate with risk;
- there will be significant winners and losers;
- policy-makers need to avoid trying to guess the winners but rather develop technology- and solution-neutral market prices within which investors and market participants can select winners; and
- long-term investors – for example, pension funds and larger fund managers – need to take a portfolio approach.

Figure 1 sets out a simplified model of the London Accord perspective on the systems involved in investment and climate change.

In the figure, the supply and demand models stand for the market and policy mechanisms that set prices for energy and for GHG emissions. Given the wide range of investment options sensitive to dynamic factors such as energy prices, carbon prices, policies, standards, regulation, taxation and rates of technology improvement, larger investors with longer-term views participating in the London Accord – for example, investment managers, asset managers and pension funds – sought a top-down Monte Carlo analysis of possible climate change portfolios, a Portfolio Model. Such a Portfolio Model could answer some key questions, not least of which were:
- Can existing investment opportunities solve climate change?
- Are there significant gaps or dependencies in reasonable investment portfolios?
- Where would further investment research have the most impact?

Intergovernmental Panel on Climate Change (IPCC) data and London Accord information, in conjunction with a number of 'heroic' assumptions, can produce an outline Portfolio Model as a starting point for further thinking by investors and

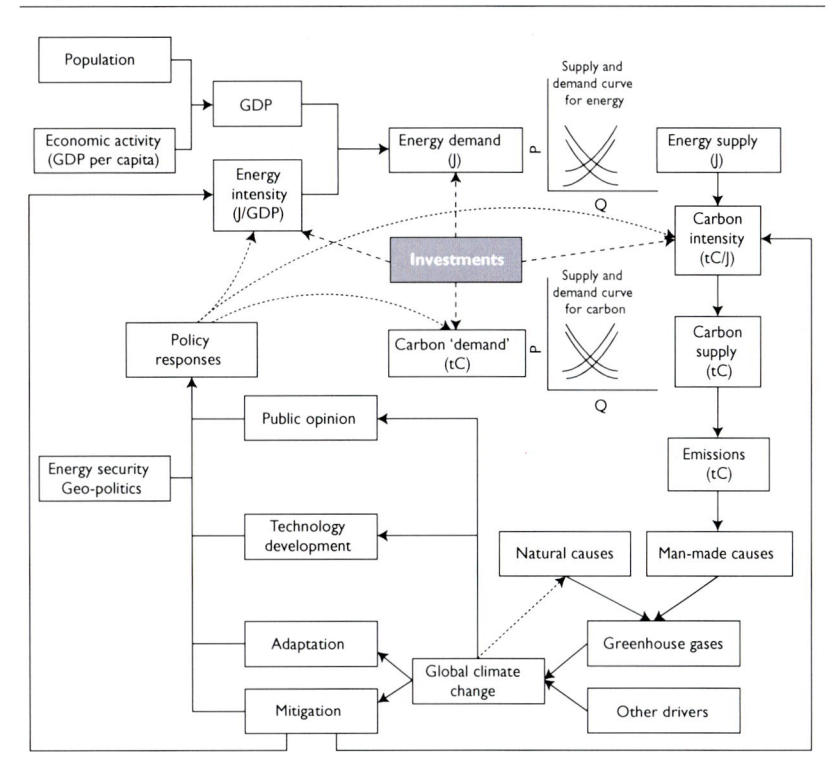

Figure 1. A simplified model

Source: Michael Mainelli and Jan-Peter Onstwedder (2007), Review of the Contents, The London Accord: Making Investment Work for the Climate, A2, City of London Corporation

climate change policy-makers. A bottom-up Portfolio Model differs from much of the IPCC or Stern Report macroeconomic approaches by (1) being closer to how investors often model their choices and (2) examining multiple end-points efficiently. A Portfolio Model on climate change investments can be neither comprehensive nor rigorous at the present time. The data needed for a comprehensive model is not available. There is no consensus view on many important factors. Investors and policy-makers have differing assumptions and opinions about risks, returns, technological improvement, market elasticity, factor interactions and likely scenarios, just to get started. Still, a starter Portfolio Model can at least start to map out the likely risks and returns and begin to answer the three questions listed above.

Modern Portfolio Theory

Harry Markowitz proposed Modern Portfolio Theory (MPT) in 1952, and later shared a Nobel Prize with Merton Miller and William Sharpe for founding a school

Figure 2. Portfolios and efficient frontiers

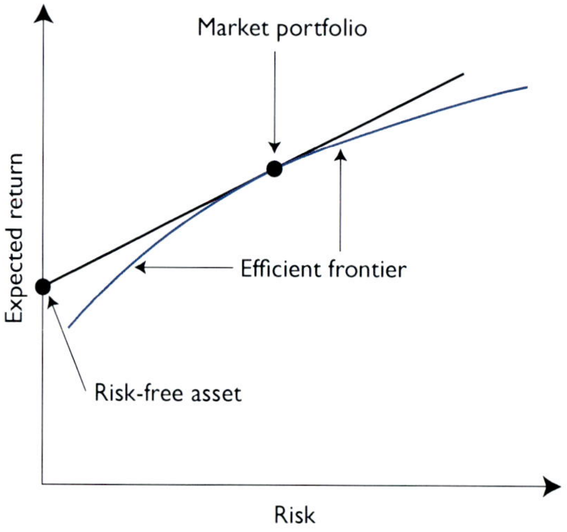

Source: http://en.wikipedia.org/wiki/Modern_portfolio_theory

of thought on the rational selection of investment portfolios. Before MPT, investors assessed the risks and rewards of securities individually with little thought for the overall risk or reward in their portfolios. It was assumed that the best portfolio consisted of the amalgamation of securities with the most opportunity for gain at the least risk. An investor might invest solely in automobile companies because all automobile companies' securities seem to offer better risk/reward than all other industries' securities. In the extreme, an investor might invest solely in the 'best' automobile company, to the exclusion of all other securities. Overall portfolio risk and reward might be ignored. Post MPT, such an approach would be considered crude or even dangerous. Markowitz sets out the mathematics behind diversification, recommending that investors select portfolios based on their overall risk/reward characteristics. Investors should select for their portfolios, not just pick individual securities. In addition, they should select portfolios along the 'efficient frontier'. From Wikipedia: "... for a given amount of risk, the portfolio lying on the efficient frontier represents the combination offering the best possible return. Mathematically, the Efficient Frontier is the intersection of the Set of Portfolios with Minimum Variance and the Set of Portfolios with Maximum Return ...."

Specific risk is the risk associated with individual options. Within a diversified portfolio, the overall specific risk starts to cancel out. From the universe of possible portfolios, certain portfolios will balance risk and reward better than others. James Tobin developed the idea of the 'risk-free asset', permitting the selection of the super-efficient portfolio and introducing the use of leverage. Sharpe developed the

An investment portfolio view of the low carbon world | 321

capital asset pricing model (CAPM), introducing beta as a measure of asset or portfolio expected risk against the market. Sharpe pointed out that the overall market portfolio should intersect the efficient frontier at Tobin's super-efficient portfolio. According to CAPM, investors should mimic the market portfolio, leveraged or de-leveraged with positions in the risk-free asset.

MPT gave a context for understanding systematic risk and reward, led to structured management of institutional portfolios and inspired passive, 'tracker', investment management approaches. Naturally, MPT has been followed by a 'Post-Modern' Portfolio Theory that tries to model more closely a real-world situation where the underlying distributions are non-normal, risks and rewards are non-linear, and where human behaviour matters. In summary, the basic concepts of MPT are diversification, the efficient frontier and the CAPM.

Methodology

The efficient frontier of a Portfolio Model should produce sensible combinations of climate change solutions for further discussion. The model should produce combinations across a range of expenditures and returns. In the case of climate change expenditure, financial returns are not sufficient; the model should also produce returns as a range of GHG emission reductions (abatement). A Monte-Carlo approach can be used to generate possible portfolios using an algorithm outlined in Figure 3.

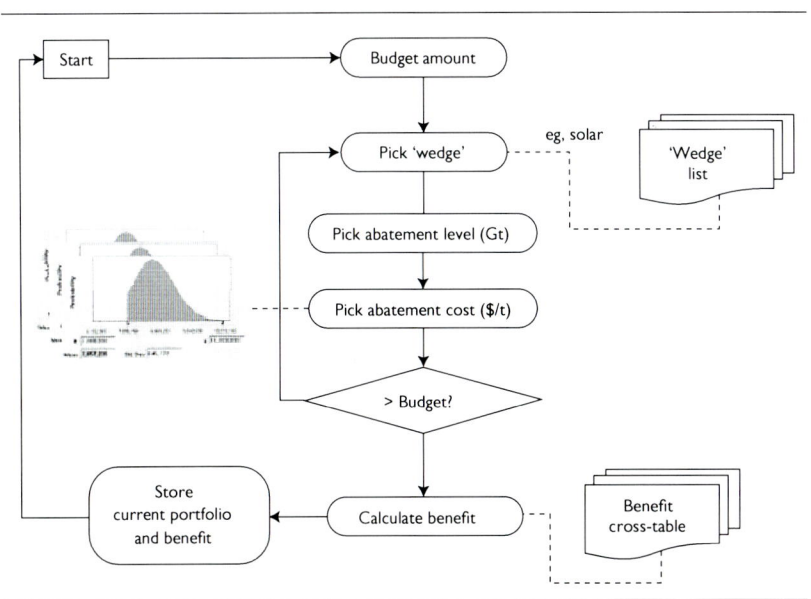

Figure 3. Portfolio generation algorithm

There are two loops in this algorithm. The outer loop is the 'budgetary loop'. In each budgetary loop, the algorithm randomly generates an annual budget up to $850 billion/year (by way of comparison, about 2% of global GDP). Within the inner loop, the 'wedge loop', the algorithm randomly selects an investment option (equivalent to a 'wedge' – eg, 'nuclear', 'hydro'; Pacala and Socolow (2004)) and then selects a random abatement level for the wedge up to the maximum potential of the corresponding technology. The next step generates an abatement cost from the assigned cost distribution. The inner loop ends when the allocated budget is reached, generating one portfolio. The outer loop runs up to the number of portfolios desired for analysis – 10,000, for example.

DATA
The key input data are returns and costs. Returns are investment returns or GHG emission reductions. The primary source of data was the 2007 IPCC Working Group III Report 'Mitigation of Climate Change' and London Accord data. The abatement costs are forecast 2030 incremental costs above the cost of capital for an assumed business-as-usual scenario. For example, geothermal costs represent geothermal power infrastructure being built and operated instead of the reference mix of fossil-fuel fired power. The costs are based on replacing existing infrastructure at the end of its normal economic life, not earlier, which limits the potential of new energy infrastructure.

Abatement by portfolio
The basic portfolio variables consist of an input cost, an incremental investment above business-as-usual and a benefit of annual GHG emissions abatement. In short:

input = annual incremental cost above cost of capital, in 2030 (in 2006 $);
value = annual 2030 GHG emissions abatement (in gigatonnes).

Returns by portfolio
A crude investment 'return' was derived by calculating the incremental income that would be generated from a carbon market with a carbon dioxide (CO_2) price ranging between $30 and $40 per tonne. This price range reflects a general consensus among participants in the London Accord of a realistic social and investment price level for mitigation. In the event, $30–40 per tonne also tended to be close to the point such that half of the portfolios were profitable and half were unprofitable. The return was calculated as the carbon value for each portfolio's abatement level as:

input = annual incremental cost above cost of capital, in 2030 (in 2006 $);
value = annual carbon market returns in a $30–40 per tonne carbon market randomly selected (in 2006 $).

An investment portfolio view of the low carbon world | 323

By the standards of some portfolio models, the Portfolio Model developed for the London Accord is simplistic, but it does illustrate the range of revenue that investors might achieve from technological options combined with carbon markets. Ideally, net investment returns would have been constructed from direct investments, rather than marginal, and contrasted with abatement value for each portfolio, taking into account 25 or more years of risk. The capital requirement, cash flows, discount rates, capital structure, long-term risk-free rate and other risk factors will complicate future investment decisions, but this simple portfolio approach still provides a broad overview.

THE BASE CASE
The following charts show the unfiltered portfolio distributions for the base case scenario. The abatement charts plot each portfolio's emissions reduction against the incremental cost of the portfolio. The radial lines on the abatement charts indicate an average cost of abatement for portfolios on those lines.

By inspection, Figure 4 shows that there are numerous potential portfolios that can achieve abatement up to about 15 gigatonne (Gt) between the $30 per tonne and $40 per tonne radial lines. When interpreting these graphs, it is important to re-

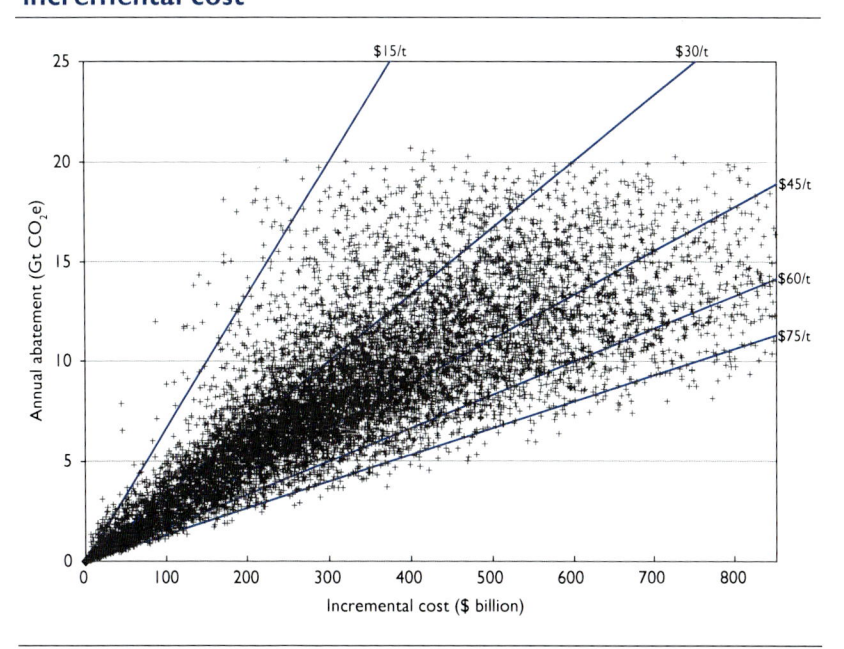

Figure 4. 10,000 portfolios by abatement and incremental cost

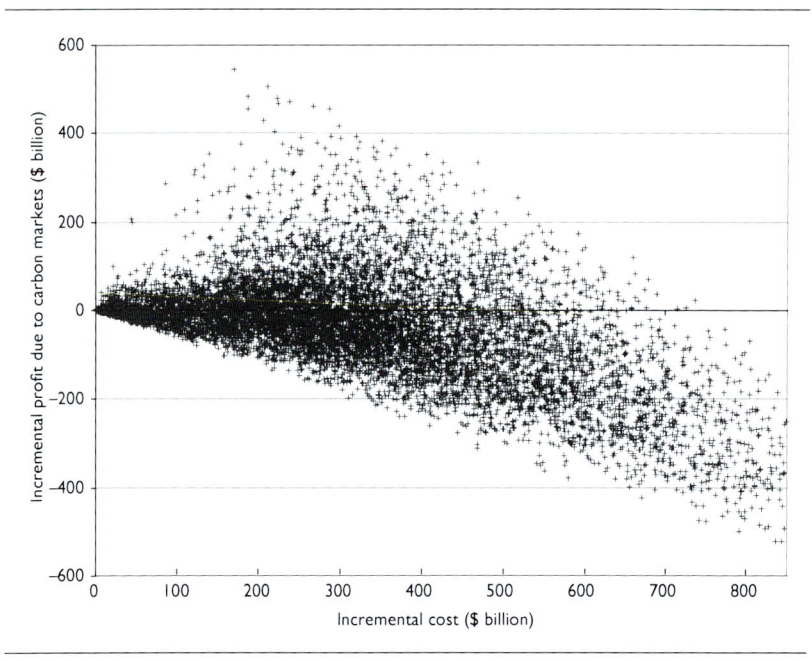

Figure 5. 10,000 portfolios by incremental profit and incremental cost

member that the distributions model the range of possibilities. For example, Figure 4 suggests that it is possible to construct a portfolio that might offset 20Gt carbon dioxide emission equivalent per year for less than $15 per tonne, and a bit more likely from $15 per tonne to $30 per tonne, though a range of $30–45 per tonne is even more likely. Figure 5 illustrates the incremental revenue that could be generated for each portfolio in a world of $30–40 per tonne carbon dioxide emission equivalent avoided.

As noted earlier, a $30–40 per tonne price range for carbon seems to produce a balance of successful investment portfolios and unsuccessful investment portfolios. The portfolio distributions show a wide range of average abatement costs, indicating both uncertainty and the fact that it is possible to construct very bad portfolios. The large proportion of portfolios with negative incremental profits shows that it is rather easy to construct losing portfolios. The wide range of returns, many at significant costs, highlights the perils of policy-makers trying to pick winners rather than allowing markets to learn and 'evolve' towards efficient investment.

The efficient frontier for the base case touches $15 per tonne, potentially indicating that estimates of marginal abatement costs could be on the high side or, more likely, there is a lot of money to be made by selecting an efficient portfolio, given the current uncertainties in the market. Some specific portfolios on the efficient frontier

An investment portfolio view of the low carbon world | 325

have been selected for further examination. Figures 6 and 7 identify six portfolios and their placement on the efficient abatement frontier and on the efficient financial return frontier at prices of $30–40 per tonne of carbon dioxide emission equivalent.

Interestingly, Stern (2006) estimates 1% of global GDP as the likely cost to avoid climate change, in a range from −1% to +3.5% of global GDP at estimates of global GDP from $35 trillion to $45 trillion. Figure 7, where rates of return begin to decline after an incremental expenditure of approximately $300 billion but abatement portfolios are in the range of 10–20Gt, is in line with the Stern Report, at least at prices of $30–40 per tonne of carbon dioxide emissions.

Figure 6. Frontier portfolios by abatement and incremental cost

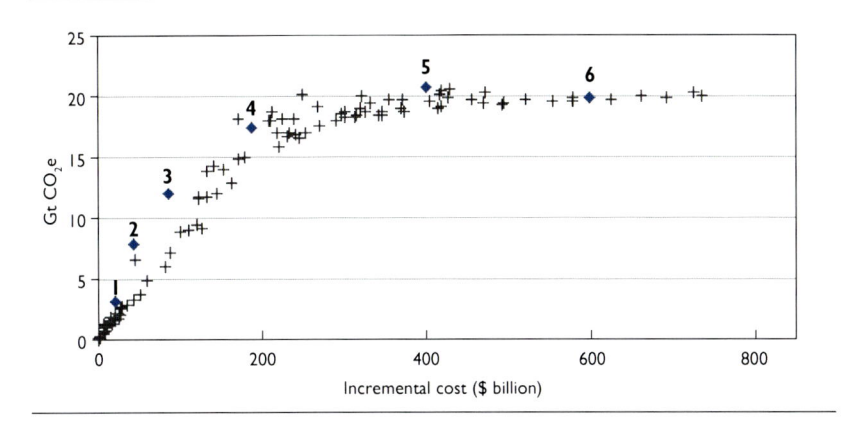

Figure 7. Frontier portfolios by financial return and incremental cost

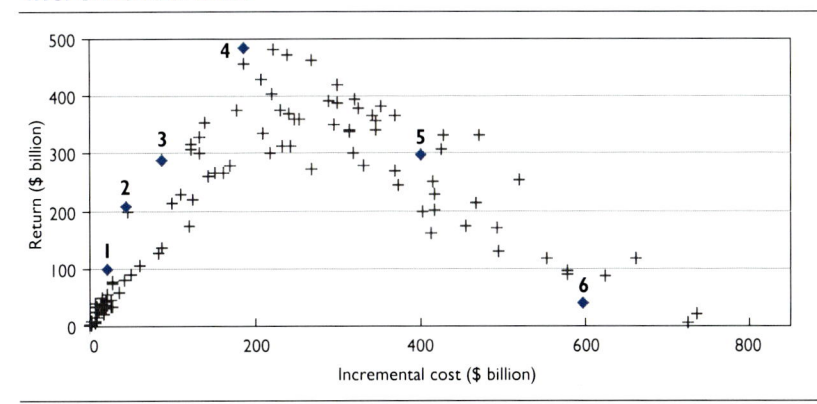

326 | Investment Opportunities for a Low-Carbon World

Figure 8. Breakdown of six frontier portfolios by principal abatement and cost option

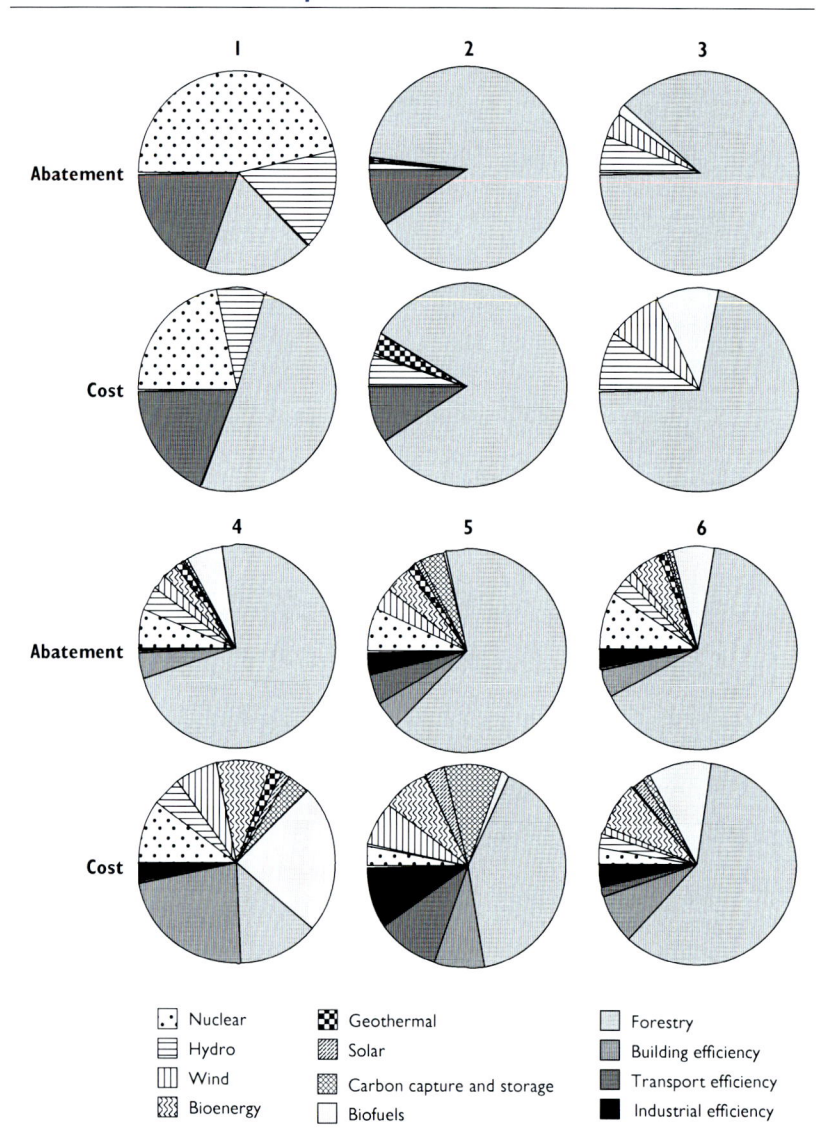

Legend:
- Nuclear
- Hydro
- Wind
- Bioenergy
- Geothermal
- Solar
- Carbon capture and storage
- Biofuels
- Forestry
- Building efficiency
- Transport efficiency
- Industrial efficiency

In Figure 8, each of the six selected portfolios has been broken down by investment option, displayed separately for abatement and cost. For example, in Portfolio 1, nuclear is the biggest contributor to abatement while forestry is the largest contributor to cost.

Figure 9. Analysis of portfolios 4 and 5

Portfolio	Cost $bn	Abatement Gt	Returns $bn	Largest financial components	Implied return %	Abatement efficiency $/tonne
4	200	17.5	500	Biofuels/building efficiency	250	11
5	400	21.0	300	Forestry	−25	19

Contrasting just two of the six portfolios, 4 and 5, in Figure 9 helps to illustrate how abatement and investment do not necessarily align.

The problem is that 'dream portfolios', such as Portfolio 4, are possible, but perhaps not probable. First, a large number of things must go right at once. Second, almost all of the dream portfolios rely on fantastic forestry investments for their superb returns. It can be seen by inspection that:

- forestry is by far the most significant contributor to significant portfolios, essentially because (although more uncertain than other options) forestry has the largest abatement potential. Clearly, more definitive, perhaps urgent, research into forestry cost and abatement would help to produce better portfolio analysis;
- nuclear is a proportionally big contributor in the smaller, efficient frontier portfolios, reflecting its cost parity with business-as-usual options; however, its scale is limited in the IPCC data, reflecting the difficulties associated with new nuclear facilities politically, including planning permission and long-term waste disposal risks;
- solar, carbon capture and sequestration/storage (CCS) and geothermal are not big contributors in the frontier examples. IPCC forecasts their technology cost curves. If technology cost curves change – and this might well be the case for solar – then their importance in an efficient climate change portfolio might alter markedly;
- small abatement portfolios of three or four technologies can be financially rewarding, but achieving large emissions reductions requires a wide range of technologies – there is no silver bullet. This portfolio analysis has not taken account of the risk of failing to solve climate change. Arguably, the risk of failure decreases as the range of options in a portfolio increases.

Conflicting values – policy meets finance

For most investors, the abatement realised from a low carbon portfolio is less important than the return on investment of that portfolio. For most policy-makers, the investment community must invest in abatement, yet simultaneously create wealth. Investors undervalue externalities, by definition. Policy-makers undervalue investors' needs to generate returns within macroeconomic and microeconomic frameworks. The Portfolio Model sets out a crude dual 'returns' approach that can highlight conflicts between abatement value and investment value. This tension may be particularly evident in markets where certain technologies enjoy direct subsidies in addition to a carbon price signal – these technologies are likely to be more attractive in terms of their investment returns than in terms of abatement. What might be best for investors may not result in the best outcome for the environment and vice versa.

Critique and extension

Liang Shi (2008) extended the London Accord work and used two portfolio optimisation models to analyse climate change investments – a stochastic programming model and a Markowitz model. The prime objective of both models was to simulate policy-makers choosing efficient portfolios to achieve as high a carbon dioxide abatement level as possible at the lowest cost. Risk was measured by the variance of the portfolios in each of the two approaches. The advantage of the stochastic programming-based approach is the ability to decide future production and abatement schemes within capacities (decided by the initial investments), while facing different demand and emission limits. The stochastic programming model, like the London Accord Portfolio Model, showed the significant contribution in carbon dioxide reduction made by nuclear and forestry in low and high abatement, respectively.

The Markowitz approach can suggest winning portfolios for policy-makers when targeted abatement levels are given. The advantage of the Markowitz approach is its ability to provide a straightforward view of carbon dioxide emission abatement methods and relevant costs. Using a Markowitz mean-variance model framework, to achieve a 24Gt annual global abatement of carbon dioxide emissions, the theoretical maximum potential and well above scientific estimates of what is required, the model indicated that $800 billion was needed. If negative abatement costs were included, then investors profited at abatement levels starting below 3Gt. Two slightly different models were built under two different assumptions: first, that the abatement costs of each technology are independent; second, that they are correlated. When abatement costs correlated, higher investment costs were needed than under independent abatement costs. In terms of the proportion of abatement of each investment option, forestry, nuclear and biofuels play large roles while solar contributes little. (Eckhard Plinke and Matthias Fawer of Bank Sarasin, in London Accord C1: Solar Energy 2007, believe, contrary to IPCC projections, that solar could be a major contributor – see Chapter 2.)

Plotting the optimised expected cost for abating carbon dioxide emission, excluding negative abatement, against targeted abatement levels of up to 24Gt, it can be observed in Figure 10 that 24Gt abatement implies $820 billion on average, with a variation of approximately $70 billion – that is, $750 billion–890 billion.

Few portfolios can generate significant returns with few 'wedges'. A strong price mechanism is clearly required to lead to abatement above 3Gt (3Gt is where negative abatement – ie, obvious wins such as energy efficiency – dissipates). Figure 11

An investment portfolio view of the low carbon world | 329

Figure 10. Efficient frontier by abatement and cost ranges

Figure 11. Efficient frontier by abatement and cost showing primary option

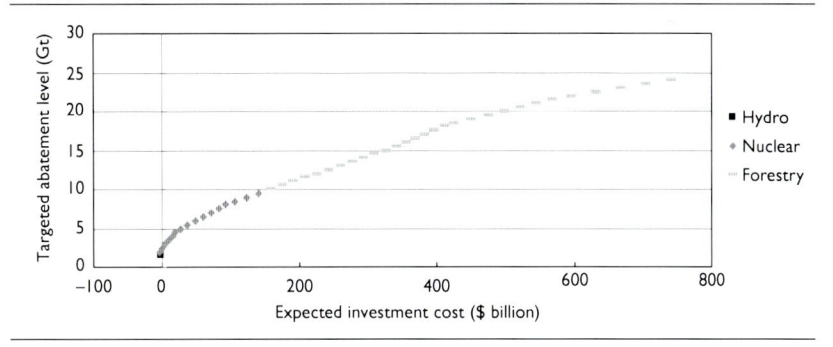

illustrates the prime abatement investment option for 48 efficient frontier portfolios increasing from 1 to 24Gt.

The IPCC report contains two different estimates of the abatement potential of forestry. The IPCC chose to emphasise its lower, more conservative, estimate, but its higher estimate is 13.77Gt. Again, using a Portfolio Model, when the abatement level is less than 10Gt, nuclear or hydro dominates, while at abatement levels of above 10Gt forestry is the biggest contributor.

Results

In summary, Portfolio Model analysis indicates that:
- carbon dioxide emission avoided prices of $30–40 per tonne seem to produce a reasonable number of portfolios that might lead to abatement of up to 20Gt, with positive investment returns in about half of the cases;
- significant private-sector investment is possible, given enough confidence in a carbon price, probably within a largely cap-and-trade system;

- forestry might be the most significant part of any portfolio, investment or policy. If forestry's costs and benefits reflect a real opportunity, it is fantastic; but if they are illusory, it is important to dispel that illusion rapidly through research;
- policy-makers should examine some of the reasons for negative abatement opportunities not being seized today, with a view to considering new policies for abatement.

There are a large number of ways in which this Portfolio Model could be improved and extended. The IPCC's underlying abatement costs are based on relatively low energy prices, approximately $25–30 per barrel (bbl) of oil. The IPCC points out that an additional cost of $50 per barrel for oil is roughly equivalent to a $100 per tonne abatement cost. With higher fossil fuel energy prices, renewable energies and efficiency look much more attractive, whereas forestry and CCS become less attractive abatement options. The Portfolio Model uses abatement costs expressed as costs over and above the use of fossil fuels but, with constant energy price changes and currency market movements, all assumptions bear periodic re-examination. Many model extensions would be technical: calculations of discount rates, cash flow estimation approaches, capital structures, asset life estimates, underlying probability distribution work on volatility calculations, as well as significant improvement to the input data. Some obvious improvement areas include:

- *aggregate limits*: the Portfolio Model ignored the issue of aggregate limits to abatement potential and conflicts between options. For example, if a portfolio contains too much energy efficiency, there will be insufficient demand for new energy sources and lower returns for energy investments;
- *each option as a portfolio*: the Portfolio Model ignored heterogeneity within investment options, which a richer model might handle as options with sub-options exhibiting their own diversification and concentration effects;
- *intra-portfolio correlations*: synergies between technologies could be modelled with a multiplicative approach using benefit cross tables with correlations between different technologies. For example, the solar option might be assumed to benefit from the wind option due to the joint feedback-to-grid technology development;
- *positive feedback and expectations*: expectations on topics as diverse as taxation, political will, elasticity or technology performance curves do affect inputs and returns, and in some way can be self-fulfilling. People observe early failures and invest in previous successes. Further, most investments are made with an eye on the potential for sale to the next investor and then the next. Modelling the evolution of the fitness landscape with positive feedback and expectations would be challenging but interesting;
- *sensitivity*: more complete analysis would analyse the response of portfolio models to external variables, testing portfolios for robustness over a wider range of scenarios.

Implications

Both Liang Shi's 2008 work and the 2007 London Accord work conclude that climate change is preventable using current investment opportunities, but further research would lead to better decisions, particularly research into the abatement potential and costs of forestry. This conclusion may seem a bit 'rosy' or optimistic, but the wide, many inputs do provide optimism. However, the optimism would become more realistic with more realistic research estimates. As investors learn about what works and what does not, as policy-makers learn which policies increase investment and which do not, portfolios will evolve to more optimal levels.

Savvy investors realise that abatement options are not the only investment response to a changing climate. Adaptation projects or biases towards companies with low-carbon exposure are also part of the mix. For savvy policy-makers, there may be a need to incorporate even broader measures of value in the portfolio analysis, beyond just returns and abatement. Forum for the Future's 'Five Capitals' model (see Forum for the Future's contribution to the London Accord – D3: *Investments To Combat Climate Change: Exploring the Sustainable Solutions*) might inform the valuation of portfolios in terms of sustainability.

Portfolio analysis is already an important and powerful tool for investors but it is not a static tool and investors must constantly review their assumptions and forecasts. With the addition of an abatement axis, or perhaps additional sustainability axes, multi-value portfolio analysis can help to highlight contradictions between investment potential and policy. Thus, portfolio analysis should be as important a tool for policy-makers as it already is for investors.

Postscript: The London Accord

The London Accord is a unique collaboration among investment banks, research houses, academics and NGOs, providing an 'open source' resource for investors, policy makers, NGOs and politicians interested in environmental, social and governance (ESG) solutions. The London Accord was launched in 2005, by the City of London Corporation, Z/Yen Group, Forum for the Future and Gresham College. In 2006, the London Accord began joint research into climate change. In 2007, when the London Accord published some 24 reports amounting to over 780 pages, its theme was 'cash in, carbon out'. During 2008, the theme was 'making investment work for the climate' and 13 reports were published ranging from efficient buildings to green information and communications technology (ICT) to 'peak grain'. The London Accord entered 2009 with 26 contributors, 40 reports and the aim of working 'towards better policies through shared investment research'. The London Accord continues to seek research on wider sustainability issues such as scarcity of resources, quality of life, governance and health and hold regular roundtable discussions exploring themes such as investment opportunities in forestry or overcoming barriers to long-term investment.
www.london-accord.co.uk.

THANKS

Our thanks go to Dr Andreas Grothey, Dr Julian Hall, Ian Harris, Tessa Marwick, Professor Ken McKinnon, Jan-Peter Onstwedder, Dr Sotirios Sabanis and Mark Yeandle for all of their comments and assistance.

Further reading

IPCC (2007), Fourth Assessment Report, Working Group III Report, Mitigation of Climate Change, www.ipcc.ch/ipccreports/ar4-wg3.htm.

Lintner, J (1965), 'The valuation of risk assets and the selection of risky investments in stock portfolios and capital budgets', *The Review of Economics and Statistics*, 47(1), pages 13–39.

Mainelli, M and J P Onstwedder (eds) (2007), *The London Accord: Making Investment Work For The Climate*, City of London Corporation – multiple chapters, www.london-accord.co.uk/accord_2007/contents.htm:

Investment opportunities
C1: Solar Energy 2007 – Eckhard Plinke and Matthias Fawer, Bank Sarasin.
C2: Investing in Biofuels – Conor O'Prey, ABN AMRO.
C3: Investing in Renewable Energy – Mark Thompson, Canaccord Adams.
C4: Energy Efficiency: The Global Case for Efficiency Gains – Miroslav Durana, Tanya Monga and Hervé Prettre, Credit Suisse.
C5: Energy Efficiency: The Potential for Selected Investment Opportunities – Asari Efiong, Merrill Lynch.
C6: Carbon Capture and Sequestration – Marc Levinson, JPMorgan Chase.
C7: Emissions Trading: Trends and Opportunities – Andrew Humphrey and Luciano Diana, Morgan Stanley.
C8: Forest Assets for the Future – Stephane Voisin and Mikael Jafs, Cheuvreux.

Cross analysis
D1: Adaptation: Credit Risk Impacts of a Changing Climate – Christopher Bray, Barclays and Acclimatise.
D2: Modelling Carbon Intensity – Valéry Lucas-Leclin, Société Générale.
D3: Investments to Combat Climate Change – Exploring the Sustainable Solutions – Alice Chapple, Vedant Walia, and Will Dawson, Forum for the Future.
D4: Investment in Low-Carbon Technology – the Legal Issues – Lewis McDonald, Herbert Smith (ed).
D5: A Portfolio Approach to Climate Change Investment and Policy – James Palmer and Michael Mainelli, Z/Yen.

Commentary
E1: Dynamics of Technological Development in the Energy Sector – J Doyne Farmer and Dr Jessika Trancik, The Santa Fe Institute.
E2: Toward a Product-Level Standard: Life Cycle Analysis of Greenhouse Gas Emissions – Steven Davis, The Climate Conservancy.
E3: A Commentary on the Product-Level Standard – Hendrik Garz, WestLB.
E4: Cap-and-Trade Versus Carbon Tax: A Comparison and Synthesis – Michael Mainelli, Alexander Knapp, Z/Yen, Jan-Peter Onstwedder.
E5: Carbon Markets: the Forest Dimension – Eric Bettelheim, Gregory Janetos and Jennifer Henman, Sustainable Forestry Management.
E6: A Role for Philanthropy – Davida Herzl, NextEarth Foundation.

Markowitz, H M (1952), 'Portfolio selection', *Journal of Finance*, 7 (1), pages 77–91.

O'Callaghan, M, M Mainelli and I Harris (July 2004), 'Maximum impact', *The Charity Finance Journal*, pages 28–9, www.zyen.com/index.php?option=com_content&view=article&id=129.

Pacala, S and R Socolow (2004), 'Stabilization wedges: solving the climate problem for the next 50 years with current technologies', *Science*, 305 (13 August 2004), pages 968–72, http://ethree.com/downloads/Climate%20 Change%20Readings/Low%20Carbon%20Technology%20and%20Mitigation%20Costs/Pacala%20-%20 Stabilization%20Wedges%20SCIENCE.pdf.

Shi, L (2008), 'Portfolio Approaches to Climate Change Investment and Policy', Dissertation presented for the degree of MSc in operational research with finance, The University of Edinburgh School of Mathematics.

Stern, N (2006), *The Economics of Climate Change: The Stern Review*, Cabinet Office – HM Treasury, Cambridge University Press.

UNFCCC (August 2007), *Investment and Financial Flows Relevant to the Development of Effective and Appropriate International Response to Climate Change*.

Xia, Y *et al* (2000), 'A model for portfolio selection with order of expected returns', *Computers and Operations Research*, 27, pages 409–22.

Chapter 23

Investor case study: investment issues for public pension funds

Winston Hickox, adviser to CalPERS and the FTSE Group

Introduction

Large institutional investors, including public pension funds, as a group, now own nearly 50% of all US corporate stock, up from 30% approximately 20 years ago. This outcome has resulted in new thinking regarding the investment strategies of these funds.

Given their fundamental purpose to manage assets held in trust for their beneficiaries and to make appropriate risk-adjusted investments on their behalf, which in turn will allow them to pay promised benefits over a 'long-term horizon', these pension funds have more recently begun to consider concepts such as 'sustainability' as part of their investment and management strategies.

Because pension funds in general, defined benefit public pension plans in particular, see their overall business plan encompassing more of a long-term horizon, the concept of 'sustainability' is often applied to other aspects of their business, such as health care – for example, is the current health care plan sustainable?

The 'globalisation' of the economy is another driver for change among all investors, but public pension funds in particular. Increasingly, pension fund investment strategy has evolved to recognise the need to modify asset allocation decisions to include international investments, which in turn has created the need to better understand the forces in play, which will affect investment outcomes in the global economy.

Taken together, these two shifts in 'thinking' at the public pension funds have resulted in a gradual increase in the belief that this portion of the institutional investor world can and should operate, at least to a degree, as 'patient money', in addition to their already evolving image as proactive investors.

Many are beginning to see with clarity that, 'the world ahead is highly likely to be different, perhaps very different, from the world we now see in our rear view mirror'. The importance of this realisation is the effect it will have on investment decision-makers. It will not be enough to rely upon highly developed models of past performance, but investors will need to find a way to 'see' risks to the global economy and the resultant 'opportunities' that those risks will bring, as they make an appearance coming 'over the horizon'.

Taken together, this represents a list of the investment issues facing public pension funds and other institutional investors, as we begin our journey through the 21st century, where change, as has been predicted, will come at ever increasing speed. Those that have committed themselves to the effort to understand the agents of change and developed a strategy for taking advantage of the opportunities presented by change will thrive; those that do not will likely be harmed.

Identifying and managing long-term risks and opportunities

Some believe that the global economy is now facing two large risks, which over time will make winners and losers of countries, companies and investors on a scale that is unprecedented in the history of humankind.

Those two 'externalities' or risks to the global economy are climate change and peak oil.

Climate change has the potential to be a disruptive force to global ecosystems and the global economy on a scale that is unprecedented in the history of the planet. Much has been written about the cause and the consequence of climate change, but an increasing consensus is developing that the risks of doing nothing in response to climate change are too significant to bear.

As a result, there is an increasing trend in the investment world, including the public pension funds, to find opportunities to deploy investment capital with this global economic force in mind. From private equity investments in new clean energy technologies, to real estate investments that favour 'green' standards like Leadership in Energy and Environmental Design (LEED), to public equity investments that take into account the 'sustainability' or 'green' aspects of given companies in each sector of the economy, to the increased use of 'governance' tools to communicate investor views on the risks and opportunities of climate change, the investment world is responding to this 'externality' in a productive way.

Because pension funds and other institutional investors are tending to a more expansive view of the investment world (eg, global investments), they are more and more aware of the interconnectivity of their various investment classes and, as mentioned previously, they are more and more tending to act as 'patient capital' (eg, the addition of infrastructure investments as an asset class). As a result, we now have a very important new player in the global effort to address climate change, the institutional investor, particularly public pension funds.

In addition to this requirement for patient money, and investors with a global view of the economy, the investment world needs leaders with the wisdom to develop new investment tools and products to take advantage of the changes that will be necessary to solve this historic challenge to mankind; many believe that technology advancement represents our biggest hope for a successful outcome, hence the need for products like the FTSE ET 50 Index Fund.

Peak oil is a somewhat different story. The phrase is utilised to communicate in the most simplistic sense, but perhaps not the most sensitive way, the realisation that energy from carbon-based fuels is unsustainable. There is an ultimate limit to the amount of carbon-based fuel the world can find, extract and utilise. The date we will 'run out' is still anyone's guess, but the increase in the pace of consumption has begun to affect pricing in a significant way.

In addition, the 'national security' aspect of continuing business as usual in terms of the use of carbon-based liquid fuels is becoming a broadly agreed-upon concern, and as a result increased emphasis is being placed on the need to find technologies that will lead to the rapid development and deployment of alternative sources and supplies of energy, such as wind, solar, biofuels, tidal power, fuel cell/hydrogen, etc.

It is not difficult to see that these two forces for change will result in change on a scale that is unprecedented in our history. The risks associated with not addressing these 'externalities' that are bearing down on the global economy and not seizing the opportunity to invest with purpose are substantial.

Key environmental issues
In addition to a broad review of these topics, climate change and peak oil, it is likely instructive to give some thought to the range of environmental issues that will need to be addressed in conjunction with the development of a response to these 'externalities'.

For example, it is widely understood that climate change will result in potentially significant changes in weather patterns, including rates and location of precipitation. This, in turn, will likely mean droughts in some locations/regions and flooding in others. Water supply systems will be challenged to meet current and future demand, and flood protection systems will have to be re-evaluated and modified to address the consequences of these changes in the patterns of precipitation. New technologies, in turn, will need to be developed to meet these challenges.

Businesses will increasingly be challenged to reduce their 'carbon footprint' as well as their overall environmental footprint. In addition, the resources (commodities) needed to grow the world economy will become increasingly scarce, driving the need to find new ways to substitute different base stock materials or to be more economical with the use of our ever more scarce reserves of these resources. Recycling and reusing materials will become increasingly important in the future; technologies to do so will be favoured in the global economy. Biodiversity will be challenged to an even greater degree and again technologies and regulatory programmes that favour market approaches will likely help address this concern in a more expedient way. Methods of 'adaptation' will need to be found, including ways to address population dislocation on a scale that is unprecedented. Lower-carbon and no-carbon fuels will need to be developed.

Lastly, in an ever more interdependent world, we will need to see ourselves and our neighbours through a different prism. In the investment world, concepts like the 'universal investor' will need to be given full exploration. One source's waste is potentially another's feed stock, but simply to toss a waste 'over the fence', when as a 'universal investor', we may well own a piece of what lies over that fence, will likely be found simply unacceptable and unsustainable.

The CalPERS response

As two of the largest members of the institutional investor community, the California Public Employees' Retirement System (CalPERS) and its sister entity the California State Teachers Retirement System (CalSTRS), have given significant thought to the concepts presented here and have begun to develop clearly articulated strategies to address the challenges facing the global economy and the forces of change also mentioned here.

Both systems have earmarked funds from the private equity portion of their portfolios for the 'clean-tech' space, in order to take advantage of the opportunity presented by the changing world ahead. The funds have selected money managers to deploy this capital in an appropriately diversified way along the continuum from early to late stage venture capital, including project finance. They have also spread their focus to a wide range of areas of clean technology development including materials development, energy load management, wind, solar, biofuels, water supply and treatment, water efficiency and more.

The two systems have asked the managers of their real estate portfolios to accept the challenge to improve the overall energy efficiency of the portfolios they manage by 20% over a five-year period, among other things serving as an increase in the 'demand' for new real estate-related energy efficiency technologies.

In the public equity portion of their portfolios, they have allocated money to invest in companies that have communicated an awareness of the need to better understand their environmental footprint, and made a commitment to reduce it over time. The advancement of environmental technology (ET) will likely be a favoured area of investment on a global scale, and we can look to these investors to favour ET companies in future.

As a further commitment to this area of focus, in November 2010 CalPERS invested $500 million into a new internally managed strategy for investing in global public companies that are actively working to improve the environment and mitigate the adverse impacts of climate change. To be included in the portfolio, companies must derive a material portion of their revenues from low carbon energy production including wind, solar, biofuels and other alternative energy; water, waste and pollution control; energy efficiency and management, including building insulation, fuel cells and energy storage; and carbon trading and other capital deployment and financial products.

In addition, they have begun to utilise their governance tools to remind companies that they are watching and to encourage greater transparency regarding these aspects of the performance of public companies. For example, they have both joined the Carbon Disclosure Project, and both wrote to the auto companies in early 2005, asking why they were suing to overturn a law requiring that cars sold in California beginning in 2009, would need to reduce their greenhouse gas emissions by 30%. More recently, the systems are either exploring or have agreed to add 'commodities' (which will one day hopefully include 'carbon') and infrastructure as new asset classes, both of which have a place among the Environmental Investment Initiatives (or GreenWave) developed by both systems.

Signalling a further commitment to these investment strategies, the CalPERS and CalSTRS CEOs, Anne Stausboll and Jack Ehnes, recently joined the board of Ceres, Stausboll as a co-chair. Ceres is a coalition of investors and environmental groups working to advance sustainable prosperity, which in turn supports the Investor Network on Climate Risk (INCR), a network of institutional investors and financial institutions that promotes better understanding of the financial risks and investment opportunities posed by climate change.

This provides an overview of the new investment strategies that have been developed for a low carbon world.

Chapter 24

Investor case study: an institutional investor approach to 'clean-tech'

David Russell, Universities Superannuation Scheme, UK

Introduction

The Universities Superannuation Scheme (USS) is a pension fund managing approximately £32 billion for some 250,000 UK university staff. As a result, the scheme's primary focus is to make the returns required to fulfil the pension promise to our members. USS, therefore, focuses its attention on assets and asset classes where its managers believe these returns will be made.

As a consequence, USS has been investing in environmental technologies, renewable energy and clean technologies since 2001. Even at this early stage, the fund's investment managers took the view that there was long-term potential for returns in this area. There were a number of reasons for this view:

- environmental impacts of businesses were increasingly being regulated; therefore, companies were looking for solutions to reduce both their costs and their environmental impacts;
- climate change was going up the political agenda and therefore mechanisms to reduce carbon emissions and address climate risks were likely to be needed in the future; and
- carbon cap and trade was an increasingly likely policy tool.

As a result, USS invested in the Blackrock New Energy Investors[1] (formerly the Merrill Lynch New Energy Investors) and Impax Environmental Markets[2] funds in 2001 and 2002, respectively. Since this time, the fund has continued to be positive about renewable and clean technologies as an investment asset class. We have invested in a number of renewable energy infrastructure funds, clean-tech private equity and have taken a direct equity stake in Climate Change Capital[3], a specialist bank in this area. USS, currently, has over €300 million invested in this sector. The fund expects to continue allocating significantly to this asset area on an ongoing basis.

---

1 www.blackrock.co.uk/content/groups/uksite/documents/literature/emea02012178.pdf
2 www.impax.co.uk/funds/listed-equity-funds/impax-environmental-markets-plc
3 www.climatechangecapital.com/

Investment drivers and issues

USS is of the view that the drivers in this area, particularly the policies set by governments, will continue to drive the potential upside in this asset class. Technologies are becoming more efficient at energy generation, with wind and indeed solar closing in on grid parity in some markets. This does not mean that there will not be problems (see below). However, the fund believes that these will be overcome with innovation, investment and political will.

Since USS started investing in this asset class, another driver has been added to the reasons why the fund is positive about the long-term nature of the sector: energy security. This is true not only in the US, where in many ways it has become a key driver, but also in Europe where there have been concerns regarding the probity of hydrocarbon energy supply from some sources.

As indicated above, USS is aware of a number of issues associated with investing in these new assets:

- there has been a rush of capital into the asset class. While this is positive in terms of potentially generating improvements in technology and reductions in emissions, it is not necessarily positive from a long-term investor perspective as asset prices have been pushed up, sometimes to the point where long-term returns may fall below what is expected. These 'bubbles' have the potential to drive investment away from the sector in the future.
- government policy and support is still essential in the area, but it is often changeable – hence adding to the difficulties of investors in calculating long-term returns. A good demonstration of this has been the retrospective capping of solar photovoltaic tariffs in Spain, and the EU discussion regarding exclusion of HFC23 projects from the EU Emissions Trading System. Both are actions which significantly limit investor confidence and trust in policy in this area.

A significant barrier to investment in this asset class has been a lack of awareness of the potential value in the sector from an investment perspective. There are a number of reasons for this, varying from a lack of awareness among pension fund trustees to a lack of information available from pension fund consultants. These consultants are critical in this as they act as 'gatekeepers' for many pension funds, and therefore having these consultants recognise the sectors' potentials is essential.

Whilst a problem in the past, fund sizes are growing, making it easier for large funds (in particular) to allocate capital economically and efficiently.

It should be recognised, however, that whilst pension funds are large and important investors in most markets around the world, they are still only a small part of the capital available; for example, UK pension funds own not much more than 10% of the UK equity market. This means that asset managers, insurers and the retail market also need to play their roles in putting capital into the low-carbon economy.

Role of other asset classes

In addition, while investing in this asset class is one way in which asset owners play a role in the shift to a low-carbon economy, it is critical that we also look at what this means to our other asset classes:

- How are we encouraging our equity investments to manage the issues and drivers?
- How are our real estate assets responding to the challenge?
- How do our other alternative asset investments, particularly private equity, manage these issues?

To address some of these broader issues associated with climate change, renewables and the low-carbon economy, USS has been an active member of the Institutional Investors Group on Climate Change (IIGCC)[4], since we helped establish the group in 2001. Among other things, the IIGCC has produced material to help trustees and others in the investment chain to understand the options associated with investing in the clean-tech and renewables sector.

This includes, in particular, placing investment in this sector into a fiduciary context: occasionally trustees have expressed concerns that investing in 'green' investments may be seen as ethical investment and, therefore, outside the bounds of their fiduciary responsibilities. The group, in collaboration with the Investor Network on Climate Risk (INCR) in the US and the Australia/New Zealand Investor Group on Climate Change, has been pushing policy-makers at the UN climate negotiations, the EU and at national levels to establish appropriate policy support for the switch to a low-carbon economy. This includes appropriate support for the technologies that will be needed in the switch. For example, the investor groups have participated in the UN climate change conferences since 2008, and have submitted investor statements outlining what investors require from climate policy[5].

Conclusion

In conclusion, USS's investments in this area not only have the benefit of reducing environmental, particularly climate, impacts; they also provide the returns we need to pay out pensions. Should clean-tech be treated as a special case? USS's view is no – the fund treats this area as just another investment asset class and, as with all other investments, the fund takes time to ensure that it has confidence in the management of the funds and assets in which it invests. But, through appropriate selection of funds and fund managers, USS believes that this asset class will continue both to pay strong returns and to reduce the impacts of climate change, both of which fulfil our fiduciary duty to our members.

---

4 www.iigcc.org
5 www.iigcc.org/publications/policy-statements

Chapter 25

Investor case study: low-carbon investments and considerations

Marcel Jeucken, Pieter van Stijn, PGGM

PGGM is a leading Dutch pension fund administrator with origins in the care and welfare sector. It provides pension management, integrated asset management, management support and policy advice for pension funds. PGGM currently manages around €105 billion of pension assets of over 2.3 million participants.[1] PGGM manages a diversified investment portfolio with several investment categories, such as commodities, high-income bonds, inflation-linked bonds, infrastructure, liquid equities (listed shares), private equity (unlisted shares), structured credit, real estate, cash and other assets.

Responsible investment is of great importance to PGGM. We are convinced that responsible investment contributes to a high and stable return; financial and social returns go hand in hand. The inclusion of environmental, social and corporate governance (ESG) criteria provides added value to our investment process.

We define responsible investment as the overall investment activities that deliberately and actively take account of the impact of ESG factors. This is translated into various activities, according to a method specified in our and our clients' responsible investment policies. Because we believe that social and financial returns go hand in hand, responsible investment is an integral part of our investment decisions. PGGM developed two methods for implementing responsible investment in investment decisions: integration of ESG factors and thematic ESG investments. In addition to these two methods, PGGM provides a responsible investment overlay service focusing on voting on all shareholders' meetings of companies in our funds and clients' portfolio according to our own voting guidelines, engagement with companies and markets, exclusion of certain companies from our funds and clients' portfolios, and legal proceedings.

Low-carbon investments

Managing assets for pension funds, including one of the largest pension funds in Europe, has both positive and negative implications for the ability of PGGM to pursue low-carbon investments. Size means that, in the strategic asset allocation, we

1 February 2011

have room for alternative, focused investments in low-carbon technology and clean energy. In addition, due to the long-term nature of the investments of our clients – pension funds – PGGM has the ability to invest in less liquid funds that directly invest in low-carbon solutions. Examples of such investments are clean-tech private equity and sustainable energy projects in the infrastructure portfolio.

CLEAN-TECH PRIVATE EQUITY
In 2007 PGGM, which was then still part of what is now Pensioenfonds Zorg en Welzijn, issued a separate mandate to AlpInvest to invest worldwide in clean technology through private equity. Currently, over €200 million has been committed to nine specialist private equity funds in the US and in Europe. In composing the portfolio, the aim has been to achieve a balance between funds focused on innovative technologies and funds investing in more developed and proven technologies. A feature common to both categories is improvement of sustainable and efficient use of natural resources and reduction of the impact of energy consumption on the environment. The aim of these investments is to achieve a high return in the medium to long term. At the end of the first half of 2010, investments were made in 86 companies through these nine private equity funds.

CLEAN ENERGY INFRASTRUCTURE
Sustainable energy infrastructure projects can offer an attractive and stable return and are long-term investments. They can consequently be a good fit with the nature of pension liabilities.

In 2010, investments in sustainable energy made up 9% of the infrastructure portfolio. The portfolio includes three investments in infrastructure funds, which invest exclusively in sustainable energy projects.

One of the three funds is the Dutch Ampère Equity Fund, which invests in projects such as wind farms (on land and at sea), solar energy and biomass plants. The second fund is from Hg Renewable Power Partners. This fund invests mainly in on-shore wind farms in Western Europe and in other sustainable energy technologies, such as small-scale hydropower projects. The third fund is the BNP Clean Energy Fund, which invests in solar, hydro and wind energy across Europe.

But size also limits PGGM's investments in low-carbon technologies. For internal efficiency reasons, we have to look for large investments, mandates of more than several million euros each, enabling us to keep our operational cost low. We ask fund managers to pool many smaller assets and construct funds that meet our requirements. For proven technologies, the number of such suitably large funds has grown. But for newer, limitedly proven, low-carbon technologies, this is still a challenge, which we managed to overcome in the private equity space. As a consequence of our size limitation, however, the majority of our low-carbon investments are directed towards well-established technologies.

Markets and policy-makers are increasingly looking to large pension funds and their asset managers as a source for the large low-carbon investments that are needed to meet their targets in the coming years. Pension funds' large assets under management and longer-term investment horizon, which is required for long-term infrastructure investment, contribute to this attention. For liquidity reasons, however, a large majority of our assets under management is invested in liquid asset classes such as listed equities, government bonds and corporate bonds.

To mitigate risk optimally, PGGM constructed a well diversified portfolio containing many investment categories. Conscious of our shared responsibility for the long-term financial security of millions of (former) workers, we will only invest in low-carbon solutions or other assets with a positive social and environmental impact, if such investments provide a risk/return profile that is at least equal to the other investments in those asset classes. Investments that have a positive environmental or social impact currently make up 3.6% of our assets under management[2].

With risk being an important driver for investment decisions, it is striking that investments in the low-carbon energy area are still exposed to additional risk when compared to conventional energy: regulatory risk. For instance, a recent large study by 14 global institutional investors (including PGGM) and leading climate change economics experts clearly revealed regulatory risk as the largest source of portfolio risk for low-carbon investments. Recognising this additional risk, PGGM decided several years ago to join the Institutional Investors Group on Climate Change (IIGCC). This group of European institutional investors offers an excellent platform for policy engagement. It has proved its added value in collaborative engagement with national and EU policy-makers – for instance, with regard to the proposed policy change in Spain to cut photovoltaic tariffs.

Climate change considered in investment decisions

For PGGM, investment in a low-carbon world is not limited to targeted investments in new technologies and energy. PGGM strives to take environmental effects such as climate change into account in its investment decisions. We call this 'ESG integration'.

A good example of this integration can be found in real estate investments, both private and listed. Buildings account for about 40% of energy consumption and 36% of greenhouse gas emissions in the EU[3]. It is widely recognised, by both policy-makers and investors, that improvement of energy efficiency in buildings is one of the most efficient ways of reducing global emissions of greenhouse gases and of reducing energy costs. Last year, for instance, the European parliament passed a resolution asking for efficient buildings to be a key priority of the EU's Energy Ef-

---

2 PGGM Responsible Investment Annual Report 2010, available at: www.pggm.nl/about_pggm/investments/responsible_investment/responsible_investment.asp.
3 European Commission: ec.europa.eu/energy/efficiency/buildings/buildings_en.htm.

ficiency Action Plan. This demand was supported by IIGCC, which added that the greatest challenge for reducing emissions in the building sector is to find ways for governments to address emissions from existing buildings. To achieve its aims, the EU needs to develop a coherent set of policies to drive mutually reinforcing behaviour and engage all parties over the whole life cycle of a building.

Acknowledging the importance of real estate in achieving substantial reduction of greenhouse gas emissions, PGGM – in partnership with Dutch pension scheme administrator APG and the UK's Universities Superannuation Scheme (USS) – sponsored a survey by the European Centre for Corporate Engagement (ECCE), analysing the environmental management practices of property managers. Based on this analysis, a Global Real Estate Sustainability Index was published, enabling investors, funds and companies to compare sustainability performances and identify necessary improvements. PGGM decided to continue working with this index and became a partner of the foundation that supports and promotes the index.

The main driver for PGGM to participate in this project is the conviction that the link between environmental performance and financial return on investment is particularly strong in real estate. Rental income and occupancy rates of energy-efficient property tend to be higher and less volatile than those of conventional property. Tenants are expected to be more loyal to green buildings, which should also result in better or at least more stable values.

The underlying property and the environmental performance metrics are the same for listed and private real estate. The way in which the decision process is influenced is different, however. With respect to listed real estate, PGGM engages with property managers to challenge environmental performance and, through its membership of the European Public Real Estate Sustainability Committee, it is adding the investor's perspective to the evolving standards in the industry. As of 2011, the indicators are also included in PGGM's reporting requirements and are as such part of the legal documentation of new contracts with external real estate fund managers. With respect to private real estate, PGGM considers the environmental performance indicators in the investment decision-making process.

PGGM's engagement on environmental performance is not limited to real estate investments. As a consequence of the size of our portfolio, PGGM holds equity stakes in more than 2,500 listed companies worldwide, including in companies in the oil and gas and traditional utilities sectors. PGGM pursues an active dialogue on environmental management and climate change-related issues with many of these companies, often in collaboration with other institutional investors with a long-term investment perspective.

With these companies, we discuss their contribution to a low-carbon energy system by investing in clean energy and accompanying infrastructure. As energy companies and utilities play a key role in the energy market and have the knowledge and resources to fundamentally change the system, they are being encouraged to develop a longer-term view on the energy market, accompanied by concrete actions such as substantial investment in R&D and positive lobbying. For PGGM, it is important to show its emphasis on the longer term, in order to provide some counterweight to the short-termism institutional investors often show by focusing on quarterly results.

Conclusion

For universal investors – investing globally and in all sectors – like PGGM, optimising our profit from and contribution to a move towards a low-carbon world involves more than direct investments in clean energy projects. Engagement with policymakers and companies and integration of climate change considerations into our investment decisions are also essential activities in this respect. PGGM reports about this broad range of responsible investment activities in the Responsible Investment Annual Report, which can be found on the PGGM website (www.pggm.nl).

Chapter 26

Company case study: the challenge of moving to mass low-carbon automotive transportation

Nissan Motor Company

Introduction

All indicators suggest that we are on the front edge of the next automotive revolution. The word 'revolution' points to changes that are so sweeping that they engulf us completely and cannot be reversed. The first revolution was probably the shift from horses to horsepower – the mass production of automobiles in the early 20th century. The notion of transportation changed forever.

In the 1980s, we saw a revolution stemming from Japanese Kaizen. (Kaizen means 'improvement'. Kaizen strategy calls for ongoing efforts for improvement, involving everyone in the organisation.) This leap forward in quality and manufacturing efficiency raised consumer expectations and standards rose throughout the industrialised world.

The most recent revolution? The unrelenting effects of globalisation on our industry and the impact this will have on the types of automotive transportation available to consumers in both the developed and developing world.

Although the environmental debate over transportation is not new, in recent years it has taken on increasing significance, with soaring oil prices, political tensions over resource supply and the realisation that the earth's resources cannot sustain forecasted development. These factors have brought a new intensity to the debate over the future of oil-powered transportation.

Governments are pouring funds into 'green' solutions based on a vision. By 2020, according to the Economist Intelligence Unit, the world's cities will contain 1 billion more people than today. There is a growing fear of crisis: congestion, scarce resources, pollution and inequality.

Clearly, societies around the world are seeking a new paradigm, one that elevates today's quality of life to new heights with more convenience, affordability and appeal without jeopardising future generations. Some call this the green revolution.

Low-carbon car technologies

At Nissan, we believe cars do have a future. In fact, we believe that for millions of people, cars have no substitute. They cannot be totally replaced by public transportation because people need and want their autonomy. We see it all the time in emerging markets, where buying a car is both an aspirational and a major life event. As soon as people gain purchasing power, the first thing they want to do is buy a car. Cars will continue to be with us long into the future. But what kind of cars will they be – electric, hybrid, fuel cell, diesel?

As oil prices climbed during the last decade, the hybrid vehicle was embraced as a way to improve fuel economy and reduce emissions. However, as in a game of chess, this seems to be an opening move rather than the end game. After all, a hybrid still has an engine, a fuel tank, a tailpipe and, of course, emissions.

In the short to medium term, since no one can fully anticipate customer preferences, Nissan is investing in a portfolio of transitional technologies, including:

- hybrid,
- clean diesel, and
- improvements to the internal combustion engine, such as lean-burn technologies, downsized turbo-charged engines and the wider use of the continuously variable transmission.

It is likely that all these vehicle types will continue to be in demand for some time to come. It is not Nissan's job to push one technology over another – ultimately the customer will decide what will be successful. However, two particular trends are bringing the challenge of zero-emission transportation to the forefront.

The first trend is the shift in demographics. Today, approximately 6.7 billion people constitute the world's population . By 2050, the world's population is expected to reach over 9 billion. Today, there are 600 million vehicles worldwide. By 2050, there will be 2.5 billion.

Many of those vehicles will be sold to the rising middle classes all over the world – in markets such as China and India, where today there are fewer than 50 vehicles per 1,000 inhabitants, compared to 800 vehicles per 1,000 in the United States. With such rapid population growth in developing markets, it is no wonder that consumers and governments alike are becoming concerned about the 'crowding effect' and the potential for congestion, pollution and scarce resources. Thinking about our planet's ability to sustain a potential 2.5 billion oil-fuelled cars 40 years from now leads to the second key trend – the rising concern over the environment.

Although global warming is sometimes debated, there seems to be broad consensus that we can no longer sustain the levels of emissions and damage to the environment we have seen in previous years. Particularly among younger generations, the demand for cleaner energy solutions is growing.

We have a convergence on the issue – but a divergence on the solutions. As automakers, we answer with a range of technologies – from hybrids to diesels to fuel cell

The Nissan LEAF: launched in the US and Japan in December 2010

vehicles. However, a 20–30% improvement in emissions is not the end game. The end game is zero emissions; the best way to curb emissions is not to produce them at all.

This is why Nissan, together with its Alliance partner Renault, has made zero-emission mobility a key strategic focus over the coming years. In 2007, we committed to launch our first pure-electric car in 2010, in the US and Japan, and to begin mass-marketing electric cars in 2012. To date, we are on track with that objective: the Nissan LEAF was launched in the US and Japan in December 2010.

Nissan has been working on the development of lithium-ion batteries – the most important part of the electric car – since 1992. We own our battery company, Automotive Energy Supply Corporation (AESC), a joint venture we started with NEC in April 2007, which gives us better control of quality and cost. We will bring a smart, substantial alternative to ordinary cars – and not just one car, but a range of different electric vehicles to meet a variety of customers' needs.

The distinction that makes Nissan's zero-emission strategy unique goes beyond the product itself, extending beyond what we can provide on our own. Taking this new technology to mass production will require building up the infrastructure required for its use and securing the economic conditions for success.

Zero carbon mobility

This is Nissan's vision of zero emission mobility. We see the interdependence of the auto-makers, the government and third parties essential to building a zero carbon transportation system. Introducing a zero-emission line-up is good, but it is one piece of a much larger puzzle. People want to know: 'Where will I charge my electric vehicle? Where can I find charging stations when I am away from home? Is there any tax break available to make it more affordable?'

To ensure the adoption of more eco-friendly cars, to provide a good alternative for crowded city driving and to build an infrastructure that gives consumers sufficient autonomy, we need to think in terms of a big-picture vision for the future of mobility.

The good news is, our vision is one that is shared. Ever since we announced the electric vehicle plans for the Renault-Nissan Alliance, we have received calls not just from consumers, but from presidents, prime ministers, governors and mayors. To date, we have more than 100 partnership agreements around the world with organisations and governmental units that are committed to the mass marketing of zero emission mobility.

What are these agreements about? They are about infrastructure system planning. For example, in Israel, customers will be able to plug their cars into charging units in any of the 500,000 charging spots located throughout the country. An on-board computer will guide the driver to the nearest charging spot. We are talking to governments about shaping public policy, designating special rights of way and approving tax credits that can put this new technology within the reach of a wide cross section of consumers.

This kind of involvement is very important. We do not expect at the start that consumers will rush to buy an electric car as soon as it is available. Some early adopters will jump for electric vehicles (EVs). Others may be interested, but they may not buy without some financial incentive. They will look for tax breaks or special privileges for low- or no-emission vehicles or for a lower total cost of ownership, which we believe electric cars will provide.

Challenges

Three challenges, in particular, face the development and acceptance of electric cars:
- concerns about cost and the investment required;
- anxiety about the vehicles' range and the availability of charging infrastructure; and
- the availability of funding for renewable energy.

For auto-makers, any new technology of this scale bears a substantial cost. Together, the Renault-Nissan Alliance will invest over $5 billion into the first phase of its EV project. Scale will be a key factor in determining the success of zero-emission cars in the marketplace. By sharing the risk, sharing investment costs and achieving lower costs per unit, both Nissan and Renault can execute their environmental strategies and make cars more affordable to the mass market. To date, the Alliance has confirmed eight unique electric vehicles will come on to the market over the coming four years.

As we are working with national and local governments, we are also working with electric utility companies and other third parties about building networks of EV charging stations. You can imagine plugging your car into a charging station while you are busy shopping for groceries or watching a movie in your local cinema or just relaxing at home while your car is parked in your garage. Trips to a gas station could become a thing of the past.

However, we need to acknowledge that consumers are sceptical of electric vehicles, driven by a history of mixed success. The first electric carriage, powered by non-rechargeable primary cells, was made in the 1830s. Electric cars were more popular in Europe than in America until the late 1800s, when Americans began to pay attention to the technology. When gasoline-powered cars were introduced in the early 1900s, the shift away from electric cars started. Gasoline was becoming readily available, and gasoline-fuelled cars gave consumers more horsepower and the ability to travel longer distances. Interest in electric cars picked up again in the early 1970s as consumers became concerned about high oil prices. In the mid- to late- 1990s, several manufacturers offered all-electric models. Technological developments in the past few years have brought the affordable electric car within reach.

There is also a perception of a range 'problem', even with the modern generation of electric vehicles. Our first electric car – the Nissan LEAF – will have a range of 160kms per charge. Based on our research, this covers a significant amount of most people's daily driving needs.

Nissan's vehicle will be powered by advanced compact lithium-ion batteries sourced from AESC, the Nissan-NEC joint venture. Battery production will be based in a manufacturing plant at Nissan's Zama facility in Kanagawa Prefecture, Japan. Over the next three years the Alliance will bring on stream more battery capacity than any other auto-maker as we launch production plants in the US, UK, France and Portugal.

Our advanced batteries offer superior performance, reliability, safety, versatility and cost competitiveness, compared to the conventional nickel-metal hydride batteries. The compact laminated configuration delivers twice the electric power of a conventional nickel-metal hydride battery with a cylindrical configuration. Three key points related to the battery are its materials, structure and control.

The battery being developed by Nissan and NEC is focused around safety and uses stable manganese-based materials. The laminated structure controls heat emission and Nissan's battery size is the industry benchmark for compactness. The compact lithium-ion battery pack allows for improved vehicle packaging and a wide range of applications. The pack will be installed under the vehicle's floor, without sacrificing cabin or cargo space.

Additionally, lithium-ion batteries do not experience the 'memory effect', which occurs when incomplete charging cycles lead to a drastic decline in range. Nissan's battery should maintain 80% of its capacity after six years of use. Together, Nissan and NEC engineers are addressing the key challenges of cost, performance, safety and reliability. Through AESC, this battery will be made available to all auto-makers and is expected to help further accelerate the development of future generations of eco-friendly vehicles.

Since 1992, Nissan has been conducting research on lithium-ion batteries for vehicle applications. Nissan introduced the world's first application of lithium-ion batteries in the Prairie Joy EV in 1996, followed by the ultra-compact electric vehicle Hypermini in 2000.

For a customer looking at electric vehicles through today's lens, there is a clear sacrifice of convenience, especially in expansive countries like US. Through tomorrow's lens, it could look more convenient:

- the vehicle 'fills up' while you sleep – no need to wait in line at filling stations;
- it meets your daily needs;
- its cost of ownership is significantly lower; and
- it will be the right size to be a 'real' car but small enough to fit in a crowded city centre.

Finally, we also support the urgent need for more funding for renewable energy. With electricity produced by the sun, wind or water or by nuclear power, the zero-emission cycle would be complete. By 2020, in the EU, 20% of energy consumption must come from renewable sources. In the US, the percentage is much lower, but the new president has expressed interest in developing additional renewable energy sources.

Conclusions

At no time in history has there been so much interest and action focused on sustainable energy, sustainable mobility and how ultimately to move to mass low carbon automotive transportation. It's the chicken-and-egg dilemma: in the past there has been neither a credible mass-produced product, nor the infrastructure to make such a product viable. In 2010, Nissan showed the first fruits of its investments in zero emission mobility, and there is so much more to come. But we cannot operate in isolation with electric vehicles and once again call on private and public partners to work with us to create true clean mobility for all.

Chapter 27

Company case study: desalination's place in the water cycle

Degrémont (part of Suez Environnement)

Introduction

To understand the role of desalination in the water cycle, one needs to confront two false popular myths: one old, one new. The first is that drinking water is a free, one-shot resource, collected from the rain, a spring, a stream or a well and, once used, dumped for nature to recycle into more raindrops. The second is that there is a shortage of water. There is not. Seventy per cent of our planet is made up of water. Much of it just happens to be in the wrong place – that is, not where people live – or unfit to drink.

So in order to ensure that our burgeoning global population has enough water of the right quality in the right place, engineers have had to intervene. Humans have been managing water resources for thousands of years, from ancient Persia via the Roman Empire to the canals and waterworks of Europe's industrial revolution.

Traditionally, we have tended to take water for urban populations from rivers, treat it and deliver it to household taps and industry. In industrial economies, we collect the waste water from homes, factories and city streets, clean it and return it to rivers, ready for use by the next town downstream.

Alternatively, we pump it up from aquifers, treat and distribute it, and return the treated waste water to rivers, or sometimes the aquifer itself.

However, as use of water, and hence abstraction, increases, the capacity of rivers to meet demand, and of percolating rainfall to replenish aquifers, has come under pressure. To make up for the shortfall, desalination is increasingly being seen as an attractive and cost-competitive option. That is a function of technology advance, and the fact that humans are migrating to cities. Some 39% of the world's population, or 2.4 billion people, live within 100 kilometres of the sea. Of the 70 cities around the world with more than 1 million residents, 42 are located beside the sea. Why not use the inexhaustible resource on the beach front?

History and current need for desalination technology

Today, there are 12,500 desalination units in operation in 120 countries, producing 25 million cubic metres a day, 14 million cubic metres of which are produced using sea water. Out of the 25 million cubic metres, 75% are intended for consumption and 25% for industrial uses. The production capacity worldwide in drinking water is about 500 million cubic metres a day.

However, desalination is not just about removing salt from sea water. In fact, 97% of the water on our planet is salty. A further 2% is frozen in glaciers, which only leaves 1% without dissolved salts. Much of the groundwater extracted for farming, industry or consumer use is also brackish, so some desalination plants are inland, purifying groundwater for human consumption.

In California, water management takes a further twist, desalinating seawater to restock underground resources and so prevent the incursion of ocean water into aquifers, depleted of fresher water by over-abstraction.

Distilling freshwater from brine is an old and simple technology. In theory, all you need to do is heat the salty water, capture the vapour and condense it into drinkable, but rather tasteless, distilled water. But it wasn't until the early 1960s that humans started to do this on a widespread commercial scale to produce potable water.

The technology proving ground was the Middle East, thanks to a combination of water scarcity, rising prosperity and abundant cheap fossil energy. Typically, waste heat from oil, gas (or elsewhere coal and nuclear plants) can be used to extract freshwater from brackish water. Since the beginning, Suez Environnement has succeeded in offering innovative solutions to desalination needs through its water treatment specialist and subsidiary, Degrémont[1]. One of Degrémont's biggest ever desalination projects was of this type, involving the simultaneous construction of four desalination plants at Riyadh, Saudi Arabia, in 1975, to produce 200,000 cubic metre a day of freshwater.

Thermal desalination

For countries with plenty of cheap coal, oil or gas, or even those with nuclear plants, which also produce a great deal of heat that would otherwise be wasted, thermal desalination can be an attractive option.

In such cases, Degrémont teams up with Suez Environnement's sister company, GDF Suez Energy International, to build the power plant, while Degrémont provides the desalination technology and can even run the desalination plant for a customer. However, not every region has plentiful fossil energy or nuclear power. In those that do not, unstable energy prices, following an underlying upward trend, can make thermal desalination unattractive. Nor does every community seeking a desalination plant necessarily need or have a thermal power station with a suitable site alongside, or the power and freshwater needs may be imperfectly matched.

Osmotic desalination

The solution to these size and power constraints came with the construction of the first reverse osmosis desalination plant in 1969, by Degrémont on the tiny island of

---

[1] With business in more than 70 countries and nearly 3,700 employees, Degrémont generated sales of €954 million in 2007.

Houat, off the west coast of Brittany in France.

By squeezing salty water against a membrane filled with tiny holes, potable water is captured on the other side of the membrane and becomes available to the island population. Solutions like this can safeguard traditional, local communities and have since been replicated on other Breton islands, allowing them to develop tourism as part of their economy, which would have been impossible without adequate water supplies.

In the past 40 years, reverse osmosis technology has been steadily improved to enhance efficiency and reduce costs. It can be scaled to provide large or small plants that can be located anywhere, can run at times of the day when electricity is cheapest and can be powered by renewable energy.

Today, Degrémont, one of the world leaders in this technology, has completed more than 250 desalination plants worldwide, which together produce 2 million cubic metres of water a day – enough to supply 10 million people. About a quarter of this output is produced by plants that Degrémont owns or operates for customers under contract.

The company has experience with plants in Majorca, such as Bahía de Palma with an output of 65,000 cubic metres a day and Son Tugores with 40,000 cubic metres a day, in Andalusia, Carboneras with 120,000 cubic metres a day, in Málaga, El Atabal, with 165,000 cubic metres a day of brine. The company has also built a plant in Curaçao, in the Dutch West Indies, to replace the thermal stills on the island. It has also built the largest plant in Europe to date; in Barcelona, Spain, with 200,000 cubic metres a day, serving 20% of the population in the region, or 1.3 million people. Degremont has also engineered the Perth desalination plant in Australia – the largest desalination plant in the country and the largest in the southern hemisphere – with 143,000 cubic metres a day.

Socio-economic and environmental issues

As technology improves and costs fall, desalination enables us to make up for the shortfall in water resources in 'stressed' regions. Today, the cost of water produced by reverse osmosis varies from €0.40–0.80/cubic metre, which compares with €0.50–1.10 from thermal desalination. Both are becoming increasingly cost-competitive, with alternative water sources in regions where raw water is scarce and the cost of providing additional water is rising.

In stressed regions, alternatives are costly too. Treating waste water to produce drinking water is technically possible, but few consumers are yet ready to make the psychological leap needed to consume recycled sewage water. Only three countries, Singapore, Japan and Namibia, have managed to cross this cultural barrier.

However, you do not necessarily have to drink recycled waste water for re-use to make sound economic and environmental sense. In many countries, regulations now require waste water to be treated before it is returned to the environment. This treated water, though not necessarily of potable quality, can be used for watering parks and gardens, for irrigating crops or by industry in cooling and air-conditioning plants. This helps ease demand on other water sources in areas where fresh water is in short supply and can be combined with introduction of other new sources of water, including desalination, to provide a complete and sustainable solution to problems of water supply.

Though we each only drink a few litres of water a day, experts at the Stockholm International Water Institute calculate that 1,000 cubic metres of water a year is required, equivalent to two-fifths the volume of an Olympic swimming pool, to keep each of us from thirst and washed and fed. To produce a single tonne of grain, 1,000 tonnes of water is required.

Both over-abstraction from rivers and aquifers, and water diversion give rise to a range of environmental problems, which impact consumers and farmers elsewhere who may be deprived of water as a consequence.

Desalination, too, arouses legitimate environmental concerns. These are essentially three-fold. In the case of sea water desalination, the water has to be sucked in from the sea and treated in an energy-intensive process, before the by-product - concentrated brine - is released back into coastal waters.

Degrémont has tackled all three environmental challenges at its showcase reverse osmosis plant that was opened in 2007 in the coastal city of Perth, Western Australia.

Key features of the technologies

The thermal technology of desalination, which currently accounts for a majority of installed desalination capacity, condenses sea water to form a salt-free distillate. There are two principal technologies. Multi-stage flash (MSF), which dates from the 1920s and uses high-temperature steam, is widely used. In the past 20 years, this has been complemented by multi-effect distillation, which uses steam at temperatures as low as 60–80°C.

The need for vast quantities of steam, nonetheless, restricts applications to locations alongside power generation plants. In addition to the thermal energy needed for evaporation, plants consume a lot of electricity for pumping of raw water, distillate and cooling water. Because both distillate and residual brine are heated in the process, they must be cooled, or allowed to cool, before being, respectively, delivered to consumers and released back into the sea.

Despite these disadvantages, as recently as 2000, thermal desalination accounted for 80% of the market. However, soaring demand for membrane, or reverse osmosis, technology has lifted its market share to 50% today, and this trend should continue.

Reverse osmosis takes advantage of a relatively simple scientific process. Osmosis is the process by which a solvent, in this case water, diffuses through a porous membrane towards a solution that has a higher concentration of solutes. Diffusion halts only when the solute concentration is equalised on each side of the membrane.

Our bodies use this principle - by stocking solutes within the cells from which we are made, they enable them to retain water.

However, if you pressurise the water against the membrane, the process reverses. The solute, in this case salt, is retained on one side of the membrane and pure water is expelled on the other.

Reverse osmosis desalination plants, therefore, pump sea water against membranes, producing potable water and a by-product of concentrated brine, which can be returned to the sea. The pressure required varies from 32 bars in brackish water from an aquifer to as high as 80 bars in sea water.

To achieve up to 80 times atmospheric pressure, the pumps require a lot of electrical energy. Finding ways to reduce the amount of energy consumed per unit of water is thus the key challenge for engineers of reverse osmosis desalination systems.

Energy consumption comes at four phases in the desalination process: (1) sea water has to be pumped to the plant; (2) freshwater and brine pumped from it; (3) as the sea water arrives, it has to be pumped through pre-treatment; and (4) finally pumped at sufficient pressure to overcome the osmotic pressure.

EXAMPLE OPERATION – PERTH, AUSTRALIA

A state-of-the-art plant, such as that in Perth, works as follows. Water is drawn from the sea at low pressure, either via intakes that are covered by a mesh to prevent fish being sucked in or from sand-covered 'wells' on the seabed, which minimise the ingestion of maritime organisms and are sufficiently deep that they do not disturb plankton.

It is then pumped into a pre-treatment process. This is designed to minimise contaminants that might otherwise clog the osmosis membranes. The water is clarified and or filtered typically using a combination of traditional sand and anthracite filters and chemicals. At the Perth plant, the water is acidified with sulphuric acid in the first filter rack; in the second, the contaminants are coagulated with iron chloride.

The impure salty waste water from this process is again clarified and treated to ensure it is cleaner than the sea water initially drawn in, before it is returned to the sea.

The purified sea water desalination feedstock is then pumped into banks of pressure vessels containing the membranes. The ultimate aim is to produce drinkable water containing less than 200 milligrams per litre of salt and a bromide content of less than 0.1 milligrams per litre.

At the Perth plant, reverse osmosis is a two-stage process. First, the salt water is pumped through 12 'trains', each containing racks of 163 cylindrical pressure vessels. The flow rate can reach 14,800 cubic metres of water an hour. The part-desalinated water is then passed through the second stage, again of reverse osmosis, via six 'trains', each fitted with 124 pressure vessels.

From this process emerges potable water, which can be pumped into the distribution network to homes, factories and farms, and a concentrated brine containing 99.9% of the salts that were in the sea water feedstock. Thanks to improvements in membrane technology, the so-called recovery ratios – that is, the proportion of salt water feedstock converted into potable water – have risen from approximately 30% a few years ago to 45–60% today.

In consequence, the brine that has to be returned to the sea contains two to two and a half times as much salt as normal sea water. US regulations, a benchmark, state that the salinity of sea water in discharge areas must not rise by more than 1% above the 'normal' level in the area.

The aim is to ensure the outflow does not harm the marine environment or marine life. So plant designers have to pay very close attention to the outfalls releasing concentrated brine into the sea.

Studies of currents and tidal flows are needed to identify where best to release the brine so that it is quickly diluted and diffused – typically where currents are strongest. Degremont has worked hard to develop diffusion systems that achieve the objectives. The brine has to be released in small doses through a series of outlets along a pipe, at the same temperature as the surrounding sea water.

At Perth, universities carry out independent studies to ensure the necessary standards are consistently maintained.

A new so-called hybrid approach combining both of these techniques was developed for the first time by Degremont in 2003, on an industrial scale at Fujaïrah, in the United Arab Emirates. The technology can be used for additional production of water by the thermal process or reverse osmosis. Depending on the period of the year (high or low demand for electricity), priority is given to one or the other of the processes.

Key features of the desalination processes

The key issue for any reverse osmosis desalination plant is the amount of energy it uses. Typically, electricity accounts for 37–43% of operating costs. Degrémont engineers, therefore, devote considerable effort and ingenuity to reducing electricity use and enhancing plant efficiency.

The central focus is the reverse osmosis process, which consumes 50–80% of the plant's electricity needs. Compressing sea water is energy-hungry. Big advances have been achieved in this area. Since the earliest reverse osmosis systems of the 1960s and 1970s, membrane technology has matured. Modern membranes allow water through more easily, block more salt and last longer, permitting improved recovery ratios.

Since compression stores energy in the residual brine, energy recovery systems have been developed that capture much of that energy as the pressure is released. The first systems used reversed pumps or Pelton turbines, which converted the pressure into mechanical energy that was transmitted to the shafts of the turbo pumps pressurizing the water. These simple and robust systems could capture up to 80% of the stored energy, reducing the power consumption of the turbo pumps. Such systems are still competitive where electricity is cheap.

A second, more efficient technology began to catch on in the 1980s and is becoming commonplace in large plants built since 2000: pressure exchangers. Use of positive and rotary displacement machines can raise recovery efficiency to 94–97%, thereby reducing energy consumption per cubic metre of desalinated water to a range of 0.4–0.7 kilowatt hours. At Perth, this cuts overall plant electricity consumption by a third.

Meanwhile, engineers designed systems to optimise electrical use and minimise electricity bills. Monitoring the consumption of each pump enables plant engineers to adjust their use to get the most water out for the lowest overall price, as well as alerting to any change in pump efficiency.

Installing capacitors, which store power, on the plant distribution network also limit demand surges as pump loads change. So intensive data capture enables power consumption to be optimised, and data can be shared with experts via the internet, thousands of kilometres away.

Nonetheless, a reverse osmosis plant consumes a lot of power. The Perth plant uses 210 gigawatt hours a year to produce 140,000 cubic metres of water a day. In everyday terms, the plant uses as much power as 40,000 homes.

Thermal desalination becomes cost effective when it uses waste heat from another plant, such as a power station, to evaporate fresh water from sea water. But except for nuclear plants, power stations generating large amounts of waste heat run on fossil fuels and release carbon into the atmosphere.

In addition, a reverse osmosis plant just needs electricity to power the process, which means it can be located hundreds of kilometres from a power station. It could run only at night, when household power consumption declines and when power prices fall in many markets.

The power source does not have to be a thermal plant. If desired, the electricity can be generated from renewable resources, which makes it possible to derive drinking water from sea water without contributing to global warming.

Solar power, wave power, biomass and wind power are among possible renewable sources for the energy to drive a reverse osmosis plant. In practice, you would need to cover many hectares with solar panels to generate that much power – though solar generation techniques and photovoltaic conversion ratios and costs are improving rapidly as technologies advance.

At Perth, however, Water Corp has turned to wind power. Construction was coupled with the development of an 18-turbine wind farm generating 80MW at nearby Emu Downs. The company contracted 70% of the wind farm output, a capacity equivalent to the entire needs of the desalination plant.

Future opportunities in desalination technology

Advances in plant efficiency, falling costs and the ability to build desalination plants distant from their power source have helped make reverse osmosis plants the technology of choice in a growing number of regions suffering water shortages.

The high-growth desalination market initially developed in the Arabian Gulf, before spreading to island economies, those in the Mediterranean in particular (Cyprus, Malta, the Spanish islands) and to new states facing fresh water shortages (Cape Verde, Mexico, California, Florida, Israel).

Such factors explain worldwide why development in installed desalination capacity is expected to have a 100% growth rate over the period 2005–15 and why capital expenditure on reverse osmosis plants during this period is expected to reach $17 billion. Use of both thermal and reverse osmosis desalination is rising; but by the end of the forecast period, reverse osmosis is predicted to account for almost half of installed capacity that is set to reach more than 60 million cubic metres a day.

However, such a fundamental change in where and how we source our water supplies can be controversial. The choices we make are laden with environmental consequences.

Many would argue that reverse osmosis desalination powered by renewable energy has become one of the soundest environmental options; but the choice of desalination can still stir vigorous and legitimate debate in communities.

The ongoing discussion over whether Victoria, in southeastern Australia, should source some of its drinking water from the sea provides a good example of the range of issues.

Australia is widely thought to be one of the first countries to be affected by global warming. The country has undergone a prolonged drought, which has left many communities short of water and had a disastrous environmental impact on river systems.

However, communities do not want to solve their water resource challenges by creating new environmental problems. They want simultaneously to improve their water supplies while solving environmental problems.

So, naturally, plant designers have to ensure that sea water abstraction and brine outflows would not affect marine life. Because temperature affects factors such as reverse osmosis efficiency and brine diffusion, key features of each plant have to be tailored to the local environment. That is why the Perth plant has marine life preservation and protection features built into its design and strives to be exemplary in the way it co-exists with sea life.

Clearly, companies that design, build and operate reverse osmosis desalination plants will have to keep on improving their environmental footprint to meet community sustainable development challenges and deliver water at an affordable price. If so, prospects for growth in the desalination market look strong.

Concluding remarks

The contributors to this book have provided an authoritative review of the state and evolution of many of the clean technology and low-carbon service industries that have emerged over recent years and of their investment potential. Although many commentators have proclaimed the dawn of a new 'low-carbon industrial revolution', the reality is that such a revolution is still, at best, in its early stages of development.

As environmental technologies and services continue to improve in terms of their efficiency, reliability and quality, as well as enjoying lower production costs, there are many other factors that may affect their rate of growth and deployment. Key factors that will drive the rate of growth and innovation in environmental markets include:

- climate change and public policy regarding emissions;
- energy security and supply concerns;
- growth in the global population and associated consumption;
- economic development and increasing urbanisation;
- water scarcity, food production and weather volatility; and
- ecosystem degradation and natural resource depletion.

The transition to a low-carbon world is under way around the globe and the evidence is increasingly compelling despite the absence of a global agreement on emissions reductions. In 2010, global investment in renewable power and fuels hit $211 billion, up 32% from 2009; compared with 2004 levels this figure has increased five-fold[1]. Also, the rate of project finance lending for renewables experienced a 24% rebound in deal volume in 2010, with the trend following through in the first half of 2011[2].

The emerging economies, including China, India, Africa and parts of Latin America, are now leading the way, with new investments in renewable energy projects exceeding those in the developed world. China alone was responsible for nearly $50 billion of investment in 2010, up 28% on 2009 and the levels of investment in Africa and the Middle East increased by 104%[3].

Governments have played an important role behind these developments with 120 countries now having some form of renewable energy policy target and/or supporting policy. This number more than doubled between 2005 and early 2011[4]. China's 12th Five-Year Plan, which has also been designed to stimulate employment and reduce the dependence on imported energy, is expected to generate around $770 billion of new investment in low-carbon energy by 2020[5].

---

1 UNEP, *Global Trends in Renewable Energy Investment 2011*.
2 Research by Ernst & Young.
3 UNEP, *Global Trends.*.
4 REN21, *Renewables 2011 Global Status Report*.
5 Impax/ASrIA, *Asian Environmental Markets Report*, September 2011.

In Australia, a new carbon pricing plan was unveiled by the government and now lies at the centre of its energy policy. More than 500 Australian businesses will face a new emissions tax from July 2012. A carbon price will be fixed until 2015, when the government will introduce an emissions trading programme. The scheme aims to cut national emissions by 5% from 2000 levels by 2020. With a set target of generating 20% of Australia's electricity from renewable energy by 2020, a strong level of investment is expected over the coming years.

In the US, despite the uncertainty surrounding energy legislation at a federal level, a large number of states have set standards specifying the amount of electricity that must be generated from renewable or alternative energy sources. By 2010 renewable energy accounted for about 10.9% of domestic energy production, an increase of 5.6% relative to 2009[6]. In terms of the rate of new financial investments, the country saw an increase of 58% during 2010, behind only China; however, the future of support mechanisms for renewables remains unclear.

Europe, badly affected by the financial crisis, saw a decline of 22% in new financial investments in renewable energy in 2010. However, the introduction of feed-in tariff subsidies in many countries has created a new trend, with a surge in small-scale project installations, notably roof-top solar. In 2010 small-scale investments reached $60 billion, up 90% from 2009[7].

Investors have a critical role to play through their ability to provide capital to finance the transition to a low-carbon economy. Bloomberg New Energy Finance estimates that renewable energy projects will require $7 trillion in new capital over the next 20 years. For those investors looking to allocate assets to these sectors, there are several trends and potential developments that may impact the investment outlook that should be consistently monitored and evaluated. These trends are examined below.

Energy

Concern regarding energy security and access is a growing political issue. The world's current supply of energy is not enough to meet the increasing demands of a growing population, particularly in emerging economies. It is estimated that around 20% of the world's population have no access to electricity[8]. In response to this global challenge, many energy utility companies are diversifying both their fuel sources and their power portfolios, and this is beginning to change the shape of the global energy markets. Government concerns about energy security and supply have led to a public debate about the long-term sustainability and costs of fossil fuel-based energy supply versus the economics and cost competitiveness of various forms of low-carbon and renewable energy.

---

6 REN21, *Renewables 2011*.
7 UNEP, *Global Trends*.
8 International Energy Agency, *Energy for All*, 2011.

COST COMPETITIVENESS

Due to the declining cost of solar photovoltaic modules during the past three years, solar power has been, for the first time, in a position to compete with the retail price of electricity in a number of countries[9]. Wind turbines and biofuels also benefited from cost reductions in their processing technologies, which has contributed to their growth. However, many forms of renewable energy still rely on fiscal incentives to enable them to compete with the more traditional forms of energy from coal, gas and oil sources and will continue to do so in the short term.

Sceptics, and proponents of more traditional forms of energy supply, should remember, however, that almost all forms of energy (including coal, nuclear and oil) were also developed with the help of subsidies and incentives. The International Energy Agency (IEA) has estimated that, in 2010, $409 billion was spent supporting the production and consumption of fossil fuels. Furthermore, it also predicted that, without further reform, global subsidies for fossil fuel consumption are set to reach $660 billion in 2020, or 7% of global GDP[10].

Although renewable energy is still a relatively nascent sector, there is much technological innovation, efficiencies and development driving growth. This brings some levels of unpredictability; so, the most attractive companies, from an investor's perspective, are those that have in place long-term power purchase agreements and therefore a source of long-term income.

CLEANING 'DIRTY' CARBON-INTENSE ENERGY SOURCES

There is no doubt that technologies for reducing carbon emissions at source and for reducing other pollutants from the atmosphere, land and water are gaining political support, funding and momentum. Energy companies are investing capital into research and development for carbon capture and storage (CCS) systems, supported by increasingly sympathetic government policies.

As the capacity served by renewable energy grows, there remain the environmental impacts from the high global use of oil and, in particular, coal, which is predicted to be the main source of power production in non-OECD Asian countries over the next 20 years. IEA analysis suggests that, without CCS, overall costs to reduce emissions to 2005 levels by 2050 would increase by 70%. It also predicts that, to cut 2005 levels of greenhouse gas emissions by 50% by 2050, it will be necessary to develop 100 projects by 2020 and 3,000 by 2050[11]. Currently, there are eight large-scale integrated projects in operation around the world, with a further six under construction. The total CO_2 storage capacity for these 14 projects is only 33 million tonnes a year[12].

---

9 UNEP, *Global Trends*.
10 IEA, *World Energy Outlook 2011*.
11 IEA, *Technology Roadmap – Carbon capture and storage*, 2009.
12 Global CCS Institute, *The Global Status of CCS: 2011*.

Although the carbon capture technology has been shown to work in a number of demonstration sites and operations, the industry still faces the challenge of demonstrating commercial scale and addressing the concerns of environmental NGOs regarding suitable storage sites. Government policy and substantial financial support is required to support the deployment of CCS; for investors, the immediate investment opportunity is as yet unclear.

International policy

Following the high expectations and widespread disappointment of the outcome of the UN Climate Change Conference in Copenhagen in 2009, there was an unexpected success at Cancún in 2010. For the first time, it was acknowledged in a UN document that global warming must be kept below 2°C compared to pre-industrial temperatures. The outcomes of the talks held in Durban in December 2011 were considered by many as a progressive step in the direction towards a global climate change agreement. Whether this progress can underpin emission reductions in the timeframe necessary is questionable. According to the IEA, global emissions need to peak and be in a marked downward trend by 2020, yet the new UNFCCC roadmap foresees the 'coming into force' and implementation of a new global agreement on climate change only from 2020 onwards.

The central achievement of the Durban talks, however, lay in the agreement on establishing a process toward a global agreement that – unlike the Kyoto Protocol – will cover a significant fraction of global, man-made emissions. When the Protocol came into force it covered roughly 30% of such emissions. Today it covers about 13%, mainly because the two largest emitters, the US and China, are not part of it.

While the agreement that both developed countries and large emerging emitters should be required to commit to emission reductions is a landmark step, the timeframe envisioned for the roadmap is long and makes the achievement of the needed reductions within this decade unlikely. The Durban outcomes foresee a global agreement being reached by 2015, with it being implemented from 2020.

With the end of the first commitment period under the Kyoto Protocol almost in sight, this delay in policy action and the slow process to an agreement can only add to the sense of perceived risk for investors.

Domestic policy risks

Greenhouse gas emission reduction targets, renewable energy targets, and energy and climate change policies including buildings, waste and transport, all provide potential policy risks for investors in the environmental technology sectors. Many renewable energy technologies still enjoy policy privileges that have helped maintain their continued development. When clear consistent policy exists, the confidence of investors to deploy capital in the sector is higher. The debate about climate change and the challenges governments face in seeking to meet their Kyoto commitments have also encouraged and sustained generally favourable policy and incentive frameworks in many countries. It is hard to imagine that broad political support will diminish for sustainable, renewable, low-carbon energy sources as the issues of energy security and supply feature high on many government agendas over the coming decade. However, the strain of recession caused abrupt and unwelcome policy changes in some countries, adding to the many challenges for the sector, especially in the short term. Domestic policy, therefore, poses a material risk to investors, particularly in the renewable energy generation sector, that will need to be monitored.

Emerging markets

Emerging economies have, in many instances, been leading the adoption of climate policies in the past few years. China has been a highlight, becoming the leading country in terms of new financial investment in renewable energy in 2010. Other developing economies have also shown an impressive level of growth in renewable energy markets. Developing countries now represent more than half of all countries with a policy target and renewable policy support. As policies and/or targets spread around the globe, the use of renewable energy also increases. Commercial wind power now exists in at least 83 countries; solar PV capacity was added in more than 100 countries in 2010[13]. Excluding China, Brazil and India, regional economies in the developing world now represent 9.7% of global financial new investment[14]. Emerging economies have therefore become important players in the transition to a low-carbon world.

CHINA

China's environmental markets have offered a very attractive investment opportunity in recent years. The country now leads in several indicators of market growth: in 2010, it was the top installer of wind turbines and solar thermal systems and was the top hydropower producer[15].

The government has put into place favourable policies and legislation, as detailed in the 12th Five Year Comprehensive Work Plan for Energy Conservation and Emission Reduction, which provides insights as to the key targets and strategies to achieve a greener Chinese society. Its objectives and policy actions have a focus on, for example, improving energy efficiency, encouraging the development of renewable energy and establishing market mechanisms for emissions and carbon trading.

Economic growth in China has also come with environmental challenges, such as air and water pollution. Water scarcity is also an increasing issue; water resources per capita in the country are only a quarter of the global average, but water consumption (per unit of GDP) is more than five times this amount. Consequently, supplies

---

13 REN21, *Renewables 2011*.
14 UNEP, *Global Trends*.
15 REN21, *Renewables 2011*.

are declining and more than 400 cities in the country suffer from water shortages[16]. A study undertaken by HSBC Climate Change Global Research[17] emphasises this issue, by identifying the importance of increased investment by local governments in water conservation and water infrastructure as the availability of water is essential to so many industries. It suggests that investors should begin to look at climate change as a key business risk, carefully examining their portfolios to identify risk exposure to specific provinces and policies, as there is a vast variation in terms of economic activity, water resources, water productivity and energy intensity between the provinces. In this context, location matters for industries, for individual companies and, therefore, for investors.

INDIA

India has also seen extraordinary growth in its renewables sector. In 2010, new financial investment increased 25% to $3.8 billion[18]. The country is now fifth worldwide in total existing wind power capacity and is rapidly expanding many forms of rural renewable energy such as biogas and solar[19].

The Indian government has also implemented a series of schemes designed to limit future environmental degradation and to support the accelerated development of cleaner, more efficient technologies. It plans to add 17GW of renewables-based power generation capacity between 2012 and 2017, aiming to reduce the amount of CO_2 emitted per unit of economic output by between 20 and 25% (from 2005 levels) by 2020. Furthermore, India's 2010/11 budget proposes a levy of $1 on every tonne of coal produced or imported.

However, as in China, with India's rapid population growth and rising affluence, it is expected that the demand for water will exceed overall supply within the next two decades[20]. The country already suffers from water scarcity due to poor planning and constrained local government budgets. This has created an urgent need for expansion and modernisation of the water infrastructure network, including both supply and sanitation.

BRAZIL

Brazil generates approximately 80% of its electricity from hydropower. It produces almost all of the world's sugar-derived ethanol and has been adding new hydropower, biomass and wind power plants, as well as solar heating systems[21].

The Brazilian government has committed to reducing the country's CO_2 emissions by between 36% and 39% by 2020; however, electricity use is growing strongly

---

16 Impax/AsrIA, *Asian Environmental Markets Report*.
17 HSBC, *China's rising climate risk*, October 2011.
18 UNEP, *Global Trends*.
19 REN21, *Renewables 2011*.
20 Impax/AsrIA, *Asian Environmental Markets Report*.
21 REN 21, *Renewables 2011*.

and in the next decade demand for energy is expected to increase by around 60% as a consequence of the country's economic growth. Brazil's dependence on hydropower also makes the country especially vulnerable to power supply shortages; in 2010 the country suffered 91 major blackouts. It is therefore a key objective to expand the country's power generation capacity rapidly.

Investor knowledge and education

The deployment of 'patient' capital – that owned by long-term investors such as pension funds – into the low-carbon economy is critical to its growth.

Allocations by pension funds to low-carbon sectors have historically been low. This is in part due to many of the issues discussed in this book, such as a lack of policy support and the shortage of suitable appropriately and transparently priced investment vehicles. One key element, however, is the limited knowledge and expertise within pension funds and their investment advisers regarding environmental market investment opportunities, the key market drivers and the risk and return assumptions and expectations. This particularly applies to environmental or 'green' infrastructure investments, which are often an ill-defined sub-group within the wider infrastructure sector and therefore challenging to identify. Increasing the flows of private capital into such projects is critical to the advancement of the low-carbon economy and in meeting environmental and climate goals. Advisers will therefore be required to do more in terms of data collection, analysis and reporting for pension fund managers and to provide them with more training, education and support.

Whilst a majority of pension funds are still on the sidelines, some leading investors and visionaries are creating and investing in financial instruments that are designed to overcome medium-term investment barriers and achieve economies of scale in low-carbon industry sectors. An example is the development of green or climate bonds. The growth of this green debt market may well provide institutional investors with a low-risk and financially attractive instrument to enable an increased exposure to the infrastructure assets that will ensure the growth of the low-carbon economy.

The 'generation game'

In schools and colleges all over the world, a new generation of environmentally aware students is emerging. Children are being taught from an early age the importance of our ecosystem, of the rainforests, of the need to conserve water, not waste energy and recycle. This trend will continue to develop awareness of the fragile status of our environment and the importance of environmental markets. This phenomenon, and increasing public and media interest and awareness of environmental issues, should continue to influence both individual and corporate behaviour. Ignorance will no longer be a credible defence for complicity in polluting our environment. It should also mean a greater awareness of, for example, the financial and environmental benefits of reducing energy consumption and adopting energy efficiency measures.

Individuals should also ask themselves and their pension providers how climate and environmental issues are being integrated into the management of their pension fund assets. By now the reader should be well aware that environmental issues pose both opportunities and risks. For those who have a choice, via membership of defined contribution schemes, the same questions apply.

Summary

The transition to a low-carbon global economy is critical to helping tackle the damaging effects of anthropogenic climate change and containing global temperature rises. From this pressing and, many would argue, 'moral' imperative beckons a range of exciting investment themes and opportunities for those investors with the foresight to utilise their capital to generate market rate returns and actively contribute to a sustainable and low-carbon future. There are estimated to be around 1,400 investible companies operating in environmental markets, comprising around 8% of the global stock markets[22], providing a significant and growing investment universe.

Those investors seeking to marry commitments as responsible investors with the desire for long-term sustainable growth, should demand of their investment advisers that they research, monitor and report on the most appropriate approaches to manage environmental risks across asset classes and strategies to increase exposures to environmental markets. They should also be able to identify managers that exhibit the most innovative ideas and are best able to capture above-market benchmark returns over the medium to long term from environmental and climate trends and drivers.

The more these discussions take place in governance forums, whether they be investor, trustee or investment committee meetings, the more significant a role the owners of long-term capital will play in financing and delivering a sustainable lower-carbon economy. For the beneficiaries of pension funds and the environments in which they and their dependents will live, this is an investment well worth making.

Will Oulton
December 2011

---

22 Impax, *Environmental Markets, A compelling investment for 2011.*

Glossary of terms

Adaptation Changes in policies and practices designed to deal with climate change threats and risks. It can refer to changes that protect livelihoods, prevent loss of life or protect economic assets and the environment.

Autogeneration Generation of electricity by companies for their own use, where their main business is not power generation.

Abatement Reducing the degree or intensity of greenhouse gas emissions.

Afforestation Planting of new forests on lands that historically have not contained forests.

Annex I Parties The industrialised countries listed in this annex to the UNFCCC which were committed to return their greenhouse gas emissions to 1990 levels by 2000, as per Article 4.2 (a) and (b). They have also accepted emissions targets for the period 2008–12 as per Article 3 and Annex B of the Kyoto Protocol. They include the 24 original OECD members, the European Union and 14 countries with economies in transition. (Croatia, Liechtenstein, Monaco and Slovenia joined Annex 1 at COP 3, and the Czech Republic and Slovakia replaced Czechoslovakia.)

Annex II Parties The countries listed in Annex II to the UNFCCC that have a special obligation to provide financial resources and facilitate technology transfer to developing countries. Annex II Parties include the 24 original OECD members plus the European Union.

Baseload capacity The power output that generating equipment can continuously produce.

Baseload demand The minimum demand experienced by an electric utility, usually around 30–40% of peak demand.

Baseload plant The generating plant normally operated to meet requirements for energy on a round-the-clock basis.

Biomass fuels or biofuels A fuel produced from dry organic matter or combustible oils produced by plants. These fuels are considered renewable as long as the vegetation producing them is maintained or replanted, such as firewood, alcohol fermented from sugar and combustible oils extracted from soy beans. Their use in place of fossil fuels cuts greenhouse gas emissions because the plants that are the fuel sources capture carbon dioxide from the atmosphere.

Cap and trade An approach to limiting greenhouse gas emissions that sets a maximum emissions level (a cap) for regions or nations and requires participating emitters to obtain permits to pollute. Companies or governmental jurisdictions with extra pollution permits can sell or trade them to parties whose permits are insufficient to cover their full emissions.

Carbon cycle The process of removal and uptake of carbon on a global scale. This involves components in food chains, in the atmosphere as carbon dioxide, in the hydrosphere and in the geosphere. The major movement of carbon results from photosynthesis and respiration.

Carbon dioxide (CO_2) A colourless, odourless, incombustible gas present in the atmosphere and formed during the decomposition of organic compounds – eg, burning of fossil fuels.

Carbon monoxide (CO) A colourless and poisonous gas, produced by incomplete burning of carbon-based fuels, or many natural and synthetic products.

Carbon sink A pool (reservoir) that absorbs or takes up released carbon from another part of the carbon cycle. For example, if the net exchange between the biosphere and the atmosphere is towards the atmosphere, the biosphere is the source, and the atmosphere is the sink.

Carbon tax A tax levied on carbon dioxide emissions that aims to reduce the total amount of greenhouse gas emissions by setting a price on pollution.

Carbon sequestration The process of removing carbon from the atmosphere and depositing it in a reservoir.

Certified emission reduction (CER) A Kyoto Protocol unit equal to 1 tonne of CO_2 equivalent. CERs are issued for emission reductions from CDM project activities. Two special types of CERs, temporary certified emission reductions (tCERs) and long-term certified emission reductions (lCERs), are issued for emission removals from CDM afforestation and reforestation projects.

Chlorofluorocarbons (CFCs) Synthetically produced compounds containing varying amounts of chlorine, fluorine and carbon. Used in industrial processes, refrigeration and as a propellant for gases and sprays. In the atmosphere they are responsible for the depletion of ozone and can destroy as many as 10,000 molecules of ozone in their long lifetime. Their use is now restricted under the Montreal Protocol.

Clean Development Mechanism (CDM) A mechanism under the Kyoto Protocol through which developed countries may finance greenhouse gas emission reduction or removal projects in developing countries, and receive credits for doing so which they may apply towards meeting mandatory limits on their own emissions.

Climate (green) bonds Asset-backed or ring-fenced bonds, issued by governments, multinational banks or corporations, designed to raise finance for climate change mitigation projects that deliver genuine reductions in emissions, or for climate change adaptation measures.

Climate Bonds Initiative An international network, comprising a group of more than 50 leading finance and climate experts, together with some of the world's largest institutional investors, which promotes the development and use of climate bonds.

Climate change The long-term fluctuations in temperature, precipitation, wind and all other aspects of the Earth's climate that are attributed directly or indirectly to human (anthropogenic) activity.

Combined cycle gas turbine Power plant that combines gas and steam turbines in the same operation. The gas turbine produces mechanical power to drive the generator and heat in the form of hot exhaust gases that are fed to a boiler, where steam is raised to drive a conventional steam turbine also connected to the generator. Uses gas as the primary fuel, with heat recovered from the turbine exhaust utilised in a steam turbine.

Combined heat and power Simultaneous generation of usable heat and electrical power in a single process. A generating facility that produces electricity and another form of useful thermal energy (such as heat or steam) used for industrial, commercial, heating, or cooling purposes.

Conference of the Parties (COP) The supreme body of the UNFCCC. It meets once a year to review the convention's progress. The word 'conference' is not used here in the sense of 'meeting' but rather of 'association'.

Conference of the Parties serving as the Meeting of the Parties (CMP) The UNFCCC's supreme body is the COP, which serves as the meeting of the parties to the Kyoto Protocol. The sessions of the COP and the CMP are held during the same period to reduce costs and improve coordination between the convention and the Kyoto Protocol.

Conventional thermal power station Power station generating electricity by burning fossil fuel to produce heat to convert water into steam, which then powers steam turbines.

Declared net capacity The maximum power available from operating a power station on a continuous basis, less any power from the network used to run the station.

Demand A country's requirement for power.

Demand-side management The planning, implementation and monitoring of activities designed to encourage consumers to modify patterns of electricity usage, including the timing and level of electricity demand.

Density The mass per unit volume (kg/m^3) of a substance under specified conditions of pressure and temperature.

Distributed generation Generation by a plant connected to a distribution system rather than to a transmission system.

Distribution system The local wires, transformers, substations and other equipment used to distribute and deliver energy to end-use consumers.

Energy A measure of the amount of 'work' that can be done by, or is needed to operate, an energy conversion system. Measured in joules (J) or kilowatt hours (kWh).

Embedded generation Generation that is connected to the local (distribution) grid, rather than the national (transmission) grid. This locates supply closer to demand, which reduces transmission losses and can make the grid more robust.

Emission reduction unit (ERU) A Kyoto Protocol unit equal to 1 tonne of CO_2

equivalent. ERUs are generated for emission reductions or emission removals from Joint Implementation projects.

Emissions trading A system that allows countries that have committed to targets to 'buy' or 'sell' emissions permits among themselves, as detailed by the Kyoto Protocol. It provides participating parties with the opportunity to reduce emissions where it is most cost-effective to do so.

Environmental impact assessment (EIA) A process for identifying the potential impacts of development and communication of these to the competent authority prior to a decision being made on development.

EPC (Equip, procure and construct) A contract for the delivery of a major construction project that specifies the results and not necessarily the process.

Feed-in tariff Feed-in tariffs, which are commonly used across Europe, guarantee a payment for any renewable electricity fed into the grid and are readily available to any power plant.

Fossil fuel A collective term for coal, petroleum and natural gas, which are used for energy production through combustion. They are called fossil fuels because they are made of fossilised, carbon-rich plant and animal remains. These remains were buried in sediments millions of years ago and, over geological time, have been converted to their current state. Fossil fuels can be extracted from the sediments by humans millions of years after their deposition and their stored energy can be used as fuel when it is burned.

Gigawatt (GW) A unit of power equal to 1 billion watts, 1 million kilowatts or 1,000 megawatts.

Gigawatt hour (GWh) A unit of energy equal to 1 million kilowatt hours.

Global warming Strictly speaking, the natural warming and cooling trends that the Earth has experienced through its history. However, global warming has become popularised as the term that encompasses all aspects of the global warming problem, including the potential climate changes that will be brought about by an increase in global temperatures.

Global warming potential (GWP) The concept has been developed to compare the ability of each greenhouse gas to trap heat in the atmosphere relative to another gas.

Greenhouse effect Warming of the atmosphere due to the reduction in outgoing solar radiation caused by greenhouse gases.

Greenhouse gases (GHGs) Carbon dioxide (CO_2), methane (CH_4), nitrous oxide (N_2O), perfluorocarbons (PFCs), sulphur hexafluoride (SF_6) and hydrofluorocarbons (HFCs). These gases absorb the earth's radiation and warm the atmosphere. Some greenhouse gases occur naturally but are also produced by human activities, particularly the burning of fossil fuels. When greenhouse gases build up in the atmosphere, they have an impact on climate and weather patterns. They are usually measured in carbon dioxide equivalents.

Grid supply point A point of supply from the national transmission system to the local system of the distribution network operator.

Hydro-electric power plant A plant that uses natural water flows to turn turbines.

Hydro-electric pumped storage A plant generating electricity during peak loads by using water previously pumped into an elevated storage reservoir during off-peak periods when excess generating capacity is available to do so.

Hydroflurocarbon (HFC) A compound consisting of hydrogen, fluorine and carbon, which is used as a replacement for CFCs. Because the compound does not contain chlorine or bromine, it does not deplete the ozone layer and has an ODP of zero. Some HFCs have a high GWP.

Installed capacity The total capacity of generation units installed at a power station.

Interconnector A connection or link between power systems that enables them to draw on each other's reserve capacity in times of need.

Intergovernmental Panel on Climate Change (IPCC) Established in 1988 by the World Meteorological Organization and the United Nations Environment Programme (UNEP), the IPCC is the authoritative international body charged with studying climate change. The IPCC surveys the worldwide technical and scientific literature on climate change and publishes assessment reports. Its widely quoted 1995 report found that "the balance of evidence suggests that there is a discernible human influence on global climate".

Joint Implementation (JI) The concept that, through the UN Framework Convention on Climate Change, a developed country is involved in emissions projects that result in a real, measurable and long-term reduction in net greenhouse gas emissions in a developing country.

Kilowatt (kW) A standard unit of electrical power equal to 1,000 watts, or to energy consumption at a rate of 1,000 joules per second.

Kilowatt hour (kWh) A unit of energy. A typical home uses around 3,300kWh of electricity per year.

Kinetic energy The energy possessed by a body because of its motion, equal to one half the mass of the body times the square of its speed.

Kyoto Protocol Legally binding agreement between developed countries to reduce emissions of six greenhouse gases to tackle the threat of climate change.

Kyoto mechanisms Three procedures established under the Kyoto Protocol to increase the flexibility and reduce the costs of making greenhouse gas emissions cuts: the Clean Development Mechanism, emissions trading and Joint Implementation.

Load (electric) The amount of electric power delivered or required at any specific point or points on an electricity system. The requirement originates at the energy-consuming equipment of the consumer.

Load factor The ratio of the actual energy output of a generating plant to the maximum possible energy output over a time period.

Megatonne of carbon (MtC) One million tonnes of carbon. Emissions of carbon dioxide are often expressed in terms of their carbon content. 1MtC is equivalent to 3.67 million tonnes of carbon dioxide.

Megawatt (MW) Standard measure of generating plant capacity equal to 1,000 kilowatts, or 1 million watts. Medium to large power stations have capacity typically in the range of 500–2,000MW.

Megawatt hour (MWh) A unit of energy. Used to measure usable or 'active' power. Equal to 1,000 kilowatt hours.

Mitigation In the context of climate change, a human intervention to reduce the sources or enhance the sinks of greenhouse gases. Examples include using fossil fuels more efficiently for industrial processes or electricity generation, switching to solar energy or wind power, improving the insulation of buildings, and expanding forests and other 'sinks' to remove greater amounts of carbon dioxide from the atmosphere.

Peak demand The highest level of demand recorded on a transmission system.

Power The rate at which energy is produced or consumed.

Power purchase agreement (PPA) A (typically) long-term contract to buy power.

Photovoltaic (PV) The use of semi-conductor material to produce electricity

REDD A United Nations collaborative initiative on Reducing Emissions from Deforestation and forest Degradation (REDD) in developing countries. REDD is a mechanism to create an incentive for developing countries to protect, better manage and wisely use their forest resources, contributing to the global fight against climate change. REDD strategies aim to make forests more valuable standing than they would be cut down, by creating a financial value for the carbon stored in trees. Once this carbon is assessed and quantified, the final phase of REDD involves developed countries paying developing countries carbon offsets for their standing forests.

Registered capacity Full load capability of a generating unit as declared by the generator, less the energy consumed through the unit transformer.

Renewable energy Energy derived from resources that are regenerative. This includes solar power, wind, wave and tide and hydroelectricity. Wood, straw and waste are often called solid renewable energy, while landfill gas and sewage gas can be described as gaseous renewable.

Renewable energy target An official commitment, plan or goal by a government (at local, state, national or regional level) to achieve a certain amount of renewable energy by a future date. Some targets are legislated while others are set by regulatory agencies or ministries.

Rio conventions Three environmental conventions, two of which were adopted at the 1992 Earth Summit in Rio de Janeiro: the United Nations Framework Convention on Climate Change (UNFCCC), and the Convention on Biodiversity (CBD). The third, the United Nations Convention to Combat Desertification (UNCCD), was adopted in 1994. The issues addressed by the three treaties are related – in particular, climate change can have adverse effects on desertification and biodiversity. Through a joint liaison group, the secretariats of the three conventions take steps to coordinate activities to achieve common progress.

Rio + 20 A United Nations Conference on Sustainable Development to be held in Brazil in 2012. Its main objective is to secure renewed political commitment for sustainable development, assess the progress to date and the remaining gaps in the implementation of the outcomes of the major summits on sustainable development, and address new and emerging challenges. The conference will focus on two themes: a green economy in the context of sustainable development and poverty eradication; and the institutional framework for sustainable development.

Sinks Natural systems, such as forests and wetlands, that absorb and store greenhouse gases.

Turbine Any of various machines in which the kinetic energy of a moving fluid is converted to mechanical power by the impulse or reaction of the fluid with a series of blades arrayed about the circumference of a wheel or cylinder.

UN Framework Convention on Climate Change (UNFCCC). An international treaty to consider what can be done to reduce global warming and to cope with whatever temperature increases are inevitable.

UN Green Economy Initiative 'Green Deal' Announced in October 2008 and supported by funding from the EU, Norwegian and German governments, the Green Economy initiative has three pillars – valuing and mainstreaming nature's services into national and international accounts; employment generation through green jobs; and laying out the policies, instruments and market signals to accelerate a transition to a green economy.

Sources: Editor, UNFCCC, Cannacord Adams.

Appendix

The FTSE Environmental Markets Indices

FTSE Environmental Markets Classification System Service

EMCS SECTOR/SUB-SECTOR	Constituent name	Country
ENERGY EFFICIENCY		
BUILDINGS ENERGY EFFICIENCY	Acuity Brands Inc	US
	Aixtron	Germany
	Apogee Enterprises	US
	Bright Led Electronics Corp	Taiwan
	Carlisle Cos Inc	US
	Chigo Holding	Hong Kong
	Chofu Seisakusho	Japan
	Comfort Systems USA	US
	Cree Inc	US
	CSR	Australia
	Epistar Corp	Taiwan
	Everlight Electronics	Taiwan
	Formosa Epitaxy	Taiwan
	Genesis Photonics	Taiwan
	Harvatek Corp	Taiwan
	Hubbell Inc CL B	US
	JM	Sweden
	Johnson Controls	US
	Kingspan Group	Ireland
	Koninklijke Philips Electronic	Netherlands
	Legrand	France
	Lennox Intl Inc	US
	LG Innotek Co. Ltd.	South Korea
	MITIE Group	UK
	NIBE Industrier B	Sweden
	Noritz Corp	Japan
	NVC Lighting Holding Ltd.	Hong Kong
	Opto Tech	Taiwan
	Owens Corning	US
	Peab B	Sweden
	Rational	Germany
	Recticel	Belgium

EMCS SECTOR/SUB-SECTOR	Constituent name	Country
ENERGY EFFICIENCY (continued)		
BUILDINGS ENERGY EFFICIENCY	Rinnai Corp	Japan
	Rockwool Int B	Denmark
	Sanki Engineering	Japan
	Seoul Semiconductor	South Korea
	SIG	UK
	Skanska B	Sweden
	Smith (AO)	US
	St Gobain (Cie De)	France
	Stanley Electric	Japan
	Taiwan Surface Mounting Technology	Taiwan
	Takasago Thermal Engineering	Japan
	Unity Opto Technology Co Ltd	Taiwan
	Veeco Instr Inc	US
	Zumtobel AG	Austria
DIVERSIFIED ENERGY EFFICIENCY	Chung-Hsin Electric & Machinery MFG	Taiwan
	Exide Technologies	US
	GrafTech International	US
	IMI	UK
	Invensys	UK
	Linear Technology Corp	US
	OM Group	US
	SKF B	Sweden
	Sumitomo Electric	Japan
	Wartsila B	Finland
INDUSTRIAL ENERGY EFFICIENCY	Alfa Laval	Sweden
	ATS Automation Tooling	Canada
	Belimo Holding N	Switzerland
	China Automation Group	Hong Kong
	China High Precision Automation Grp	Hong Kong
	Chroma Ate	Taiwan
	CIRCOR Intl	US
	Daifuku	Japan
	Daihen Corp	Japan
	Daikin Industries	Japan
	Delta Electronics	Taiwan
	Eaton Corp	US
	EMCOR Group	US
	Fairchild Semiconductor	US
	Fanuc	Japan
	GEA Group AG	Germany
	Hisaka Works	Japan
	Hitachi Zosen	Japan
	Honeywell International Incorporation	US

EMCS SECTOR/SUB-SECTOR	Constituent name	Country
ENERGY EFFICIENCY (continued)		
INDUSTRIAL ENERGY EFFICIENCY	Infineon Technology	Germany
	Ingersoll-Rand	US
	Intl Rectifier	US
	Kaydon Corp	US
	Keyence Corp	Japan
	Lite-On Technology	Taiwan
	Maxwell Technologies	US
	Middleby	US
	Minerals Tech	US
	Miura	Japan
	Murata Manufacturing	Japan
	Nat Semiconductor	US
	Nichias Corp	Japan
	Nidec Corp	Japan
	NSK	Japan
	NTN Corp	Japan
	ON Semiconductor Corp	US
	Outotec Oyj	Finland
	Power Integrations	US
	Power One	US
	Regal-Beloit Cp	US
	Richtek Technology	Taiwan
	Rockwell Automation	US
	Rogers Corp	US
	Rohm	Japan
	Samsung Electro	South Korea
	Schulthess N	Switzerland
	SFA Engineering Corp	South Korea
	SGL Carbon	Germany
	Siemens AG	Germany
	Silicon Graphics International	US
	Simplo Technology	Taiwan
	Spirax-Sarco Engineering	UK
	SPX Corp	US
	THK	Japan
	Tokai Carbon	Japan
	Universal Display Corp.	US
	Vacon	Finland
	Vicor Corp	US
	VMware Inc.	US
	WEG Ord	Brazil
	Yamatake Corp	Japan
	Yaskawa Electric	Japan

EMCS SECTOR/SUB-SECTOR	Constituent name	Country
ENERGY EFFICIENCY		
INDUSTRIAL ENERGY EFFICIENCY	Yokogawa Electric	Japan
POWER NETWORK EFFICIENCY	A123 Systems	US
	ABB	Switzerland
	ABB India	India
	Alstom	France
	Cooper Industries	US
	Crompton Greaves	India
	Echelon Corp	US
	Emerson Electric	US
	Ener1 Inc.	US
	EnerNOC Inc.	US
	ESCO Technologies	US
	GS Yuasa Corp	Japan
	Itron Inc	US
	LS Corp	South Korea
	Nexans SA	France
	Osaki Electric	Japan
	Polypore International	US
	Powercom	Taiwan
	Quanta Services	US
	Saft Groupe SA	France
	Samsung SDI	South Korea
	Schneider Electric	France
	Sensata Technologies Holding	US
	Siemens India	India
	Taiwan Cogeneration	Taiwan
	Taiyo Yuden	Japan
	TDK Corp	Japan
	Von Roll I	Switzerland
	Wasion Group Holdings	Hong Kong
	Woodward	US
TRANSPORT ENERGY EFFICIENCY	Aisin Seiki Co	Japan
	BorgWarner	US
	China ITS Holdings Co Ltd	Hong Kong
	Clean Energy Fuels	US
	Denso Corporation	Japan
	Faiveley Transport	France
	Fuel Systems Solutions	US
	Innospec	US
	Landi Renzo	Italy
	Modine Manufacturing Co	US
	Stella Chemifa	Japan
	Tianneng Power International Ltd.	HK

EMCS SECTOR/sub-sector	Constituent name	Country
ENERGY EFFICIENCY		
Transport Energy Efficiency	Westport Innovations	Canada
ENVIRONMENTAL SUPPORT SERVICES		
Diversified Environmental	3M Company	US
	Advanced Energy Industries	US
	Air Liquide	France
	Air Products And Chemcom	US
	Air Water	Japan
	Atlas Copco A	Sweden
	Bekaert	Belgium
	Charter International	UK
	Chugai Ro	Japan
	Doosan Heavy Industries and Construction	South Korea
	Dover Corp	US
	Ellaktor	Greece
	Flowserve Cp	US
	Fomento De Construc Y Contra	Spain
	GS Engineering & Construction	South Korea
	GWA Group	Australia
	Halma	UK
	Hera	Italy
	Hexcel	US
	HKC (Holdings)	Hong Kong
	Hyosung Corp	South Korea
	Intertek Group	UK
	Kawasaki Heavy Industries	Japan
	KNM Group	Malaysia
	Kubota	Japan
	Kyocera Corp	Japan
	Linde	Germany
	Maharashtra Seamless	India
	Meidensha Corp	Japan
	Mersen	France
	Metso Corporation	Finland
	MKS Instruments	US
	Mota-Engil Sgps	Portugal
	Nitto Denko Corp	Japan
	OCI Materials	South Korea
	OSAKA Titanium technologies	Japan
	Parker-Hannifin	US
	PPG Industries	US
	Praxair	US

EMCS SECTOR/SUB-SECTOR	Constituent name	Country
ENVIRONMENTAL SUPPORT SERVICES		
DIVERSIFIED ENVIRONMENTAL	Rhodia	France
	Rotork	UK
	Sekisui Chemical	Japan
	SembCorp Industries	Singapore
	Sharp Corp	Japan
	Shin-Etsu Chemical	Japan
	Sulzer AG	Switzerland
	Taeyoung Engineering & Construction	South Korea
	Thermax-A	India
	Toda Kogyo	Japan
	Toyo Tanso	Japan
	Tyco International	US
	Vinci	France
	Weir Group	UK
	Xinyi Glass Holding	Hong Kong
	Yingde Gases Group Co. Ltd.	Hong Kong
ENVIRONMENTAL CONSULTANCIES	Aecom Technology	US
	Arcadis	Netherlands
	Atkins (WS)	UK
	Cardno	Australia
	Coffey Intl	Australia
	Foster Wheeler	US
	Grontmij Cert	Netherlands
	IHS Cl A	US
	Keller	UK
	Mouchel Group	UK
	Oyo Corporation	Japan
	Poyry Oyj	Finland
	RPS Group	UK
	Shaw Group	US
	Shimizu Corp	Japan
	Stantec Inc	Canada
	Tetra Tech Inc	US
	URS Corporation	US
	WSP Group	UK
POLLUTION CONTROL		
ENVIRONMENTAL TESTING & GAS SENSING	Campbell Bros	Australia
	Ecolab	US
	Eurofins Scienti	France
	Horiba	Japan
	Perkinelmer Inc	US
	Pfeiffer Vacuum	Germany

EMCS SECTOR/sub-sector	Constituent name	Country
POLLUTION CONTROL		
Environmental Testing & Gas Sensing	SGS S.A.	Switzerland
	Shimadzu Corp	Japan
	Spectris	UK
	Thermo Fisher Scientific	US
Pollution Control Solutions	Beijing Enterprises (Red Chip)	China
	China Gas Holdings	Hong Kong
	Clarcor Inc	US
	Donaldson Co Inc	US
	ENN Energy Holdings	Hong Kong
	Ibiden	Japan
	Johnson Matthey	UK
	Kunlun Energy (Red Chip)	China
	NGK Insulators	Japan
	Perusahaan Gas Negara	Indonesia
	SMC Corp	Japan
	Team Inc	US
	Tenneco	US
	Towngas China	Hong Kong
	Umicore	Belgium
RENEWABLE & ALTERNATIVE ENERGY		
Biofuels	Abengoa	Spain
	Bajaj Hindusthan	India
	Balrampur Chini Mills	India
	China Agri-Industries Holdings (Red Chip)	China
	Cosan S/A Industria e Comercio	Brazil
	CropEnergies AG	Germany
	Novozymes A/S	Denmark
	Praj Industries	India
Diversified Renewable & Alternative Energy	Unison Ind	South Korea
Other Renewables Equipment	Andritz	Austria
Renewable Energy Developers & IPPs	Aboitiz Power	Philippines
	AES Tiete Pref	Brazil
	Avista Corp	US
	BKW FMB Energie	Switzerland
	Cemig PN	Brazil
	China Longyuan Power Group (H)	China
	China Power International Development (Red Chip)	China
	China Power New Energy Development (Red Chip)	China
	China WindPower Group	Hong Kong

EMCS SECTOR/sub-sector	Constituent name	Country
RENEWABLE & ALTERNATIVE ENERGY		
Renewable Energy Developers & IPPs	Contact Energy	New Zealand
	EDF Energies Nouvelles SA	France
	EDP	Portugal
	EDP Renovaveis	Portugal
	Enel Green Power	Italy
	Energy Development	Philippines
	Enersis	Chile
	Fersa Energias Renovables S.A. New	Spain
	First Gen Corp	Philippines
	Fortum	Finland
	GCL Poly Energy Holdings	Hong Kong
	Geodynamics Ltd	Australia
	GPO Acciona	Spain
	Gpo Empresarial Ence	Spain
	Iberdrola	Spain
	Iberdrola Renovables	Spain
	Idacorp Inc	US
	Infigen Energy	Australia
	Infratil	New Zealand
	Jaiprakash Associates Limited	India
	Martifer SGPS	Portugal
	National Hydroelectric Power Corp	India
	Ormat Industries	Israel
	Ormat Technologies	US
	Portland General Electric	US
	Rural Electrification	India
	Sechilienne	France
	THEOLIA	France
	Tractebel Energia	Brazil
	Verbund Oesterreich Elektrizitats	Austria
Solar Energy Generation Equipment	AMG Advanced Metallurgical Group N.V.	Netherlands
	Apollo Solar Energy Technology Holdings	Hong Kong
	centrotherm photovoltaics AG	Germany
	China Singyes Solar Technologies Holdings	Hong Kong
	Conergy	Germany
	E-Ton Solar Tech	Taiwan
	First Solar Inc	US
	Gintech Energy	Taiwan
	Green Energy Technology	Taiwan
	GT Solar International Inc.	US
	Jusung Engineering	South Korea
	Manz Automation	Germany
	MEMC Electronic Materials	US

EMCS SECTOR/sub-sector	Constituent name	Country
RENEWABLE & ALTERNATIVE ENERGY		
SOLAR ENERGY GENERATION EQUIPMENT	Meyer Burger Technology AG	Switzerland
	Mosel Vitelic Inc	Taiwan
	Motech Industries	Taiwan
	Neo Solar Power Corp.	Taiwan
	OCI	South Korea
	Phoenix Solar AG	Germany
	Pv Crystalox Solar	UK
	Q-CELLS	Germany
	Renewable Energy AS	Norway
	Roth & Rau AG	Germany
	Shenglong PV-Tech Investment	South Korea
	Shin Kobe Electric Machinert	Japan
	Sino-American Silicon Products Inc.	Taiwan
	SMA Solar Technology AG	Germany
	Solar Applied Materials Technology	Taiwan
	Solar Millennium AG	Germany
	Solaria Energia y Medio Ambiente S.A.	Spain
	Solartech Energy	Taiwan
	SolarWorld AG	Germany
	STR Holdings	US
	SunPower Cl A	US
	SunPower Corporation Class B	US
	Tokuyama Corp	Japan
	Topco Scientific	Taiwan
	V Technology	Japan
	Wacker Chemie	Germany
	Wafer Works Corp	Taiwan
	Woongjin Energy	South Korea
WIND POWER GENERATION EQUIPMENT	American Superconductor	US
	China High Speed Transmission Equipment Group	Hong Kong
	Dongfang Electric (H)	China
	Gamesa	Spain
	Gurit Holding AG	Switzerland
	Hansen Transmissions	UK
	Hyunjin Materials Co Ltd	South Korea
	Nordex	Germany
	Pyeong San	South Korea
	Suzlon Energy	India
	Taewoong Co Ltd	South Korea
	Vestas Wind Systems	Denmark
	Xinjiang Goldwind Science & Technology (H)	China

EMCS SECTOR/SUB-SECTOR	Constituent name	Country
RENEWABLE & ALTERNATIVE ENERGY		
WIND POWER GENERATION EQUIPMENT	Zoltek Cos Inc	US
WASTE MANAGEMENT & TECHNOLOGIES		
DIVERSIFIED WASTE & TECHNOLOGY	Progressive Waste Solutions	Canada
GENERAL WASTE MANAGEMENT	A2A	Italy
	Derichebourg	France
	Falck Renewables	Italy
	Lassila & Tikanoja	Finland
	Republic Services	US
	Seche Environ.	France
	Shanks Group	UK
	Suez Environnement	France
	Takuma Co Ltd	Japan
	Waste Connections	US
	Waste Mgmt Inc	US
HAZARDOUS WASTE MANAGEMENT	Clean Harbors	US
	Daiseki	Japan
	Darling International	US
	EnergySolutions	US
	Headwaters Inc	US
	Stericycle Inc	US
	Transpacific Industries	Australia
	US Ecology	US
RECYCLING & VALUE ADDED WASTE PROCESSING	Asahi Holdings	Japan
	Chiho-Tiande Group	Hong Kong
	China Metal Recycling Holdings Ltd	Hong Kong
	Commercial Metals	US
	Copart Inc	US
	Covanta Holding	US
	Daido Steel Co	Japan
	Dowa Holdings	Japan
	Fook Woo Group Holdings Ltd.	Hong Kong
	Gerdau	Brazil
	Indah Kiat Pulp & Paper	Indonesia
	Insun Ent	South Korea
	Interface Class A	US
	Lee & Man Paper Manufacturing	Hong Kong
	LKQ	US
	Matsuda Sangyo	Japan
	Mayr Melnhof	Austria
	Nine Dragons Paper Industries	Hong Kong
	Nucor Corp	US
	Recylex SA	France

EMCS SECTOR/SUB-SECTOR	Constituent name	Country
WASTE MANAGEMENT & TECHNOLOGIES		
RECYCLING & VALUE ADDED WASTE PROCESSing	Rock-Tenn Co	US
	Sao Martinho	Brazil
	Schnitzer Steel	US
	Sims Metal Management	Australia
	Smith (DS)	UK
	Steel Dynamics	US
	Tokyo Steel Manufacturing	Japan
WASTE TECHNOLOGY EQUIPMENT	Goodpack	Singapore
	Krones Ag	Germany
	Tomra Systems	Norway
	Zhongde Waste Technology AG	Germany
WATER INFRASTRUCTURE & TECHNOLOGIES		
DIVERSIFIED WATER INFRASTRUCTURE & TECHNOLOGY	Arkema	France
	Crane Co	US
	Danaher Corp	US
WATER INFRASTRUCTURE	Aalberts Industries	Netherlands
	Ameron Intl Cp	US
	Badger Meter	US
	Beijing Enterprises Water Group (Red Chip)	China
	Boskalis Westminster	Netherlands
	China Liansu Group Holdings Ltd.	Hong Kong
	Fischer (Georg)	Switzerland
	Franklin Elec	US
	G.U.D. Holdings	Australia
	Geberit N	Switzerland
	Gorman-Rupp Co	US
	Guangdong Investment (Red Chip)	China
	Hyflux Ltd	Singapore
	IDEX Corp	US
	Insituform Technologies - Cl A	US
	IVRCL	India
	Jain Irrigation Systems	India
	Jindal Saw	India
	Kitz Corporation	Japan
	Layne Christensen	US
	Lindsay Corporation	US
	Maezawa Kyuso Industries	Japan
	Mueller Water Products	US
	Nagarjuna Construction	India

EMCS SECTOR/sub-sector	Constituent name	Country
WATER INFRASTRUCTURE & TECHNOLOGIES		
WATER INFRASTRUCTURE	Patel Engineering	India
	Pentair Inc	US
	PICO Holdings	US
	Puncak Niaga Holdings	Malaysia
	Sacyr-Vallehermoso	Spain
	Sound Global	Singapore
	Tianjin Capital Environmental Protection (H)	China
	Torishima Pump MFG	Japan
	Transfield Services Ltd	Australia
	Tsukishima Kikai	Japan
	Tsurumi Manufacturing	Japan
	Uponor	Finland
	Valmont Inds	US
	Watts Water Technologies	US
	Wavin N.V.	Netherlands
	Welspun Corp	India
WATER TREATMENT EQUIPMENT	Arch Chemicals	US
	Asahi Kasei Corporation	Japan
	Ashland Inc	US
	BWT	Austria
	Calgon Carbon	US
	Ebara	Japan
	Entegris Inc	US
	Kemira	Finland
	Kurita Water Inds	Japan
	Nalco Holding	US
	Organo	Japan
	Pall Corp	US
	Roper Industries	US
	Woongjin Chemical	South Korea
	Woongjin Coway	South Korea
WATER UTILITIES	Acea	Italy
	American States Water	US
	American Water Works Company	US
	Aqua America	US
	Athens Water Supply & Sewerage	Greece
	California Water Service Group	US
	China Everbright International (Red Chip)	China
	China Water Affairs Group	Hong Kong
	Companhia de Saneamento de Minas Gerais Ord	Brazil
	Inversiones Aguas Metropol	Chile

EMCS SECTOR/SUB-SECTOR	Constituent name	Country
WATER INFRASTRUCTURE & TECHNOLOGIES		
WATER UTILITIES	Manila Water	Philippines
	Metro Pacific Investments	Philippines
	Northumbrian Water Group	UK
	Pennon Group	UK
	Ranhill Bhd	Malaysia
	Sabesp ON	Brazil
	Severn Trent	UK
	SJW Corp	US
	United Utilities Group	UK
	Veolia Environnement	France

As at December 2011. Source: FTSE

FTSE Environmental Opportunities 100 Constituents

EMCS SECTOR/SUB-SECTOR	Constituent name	Country
ENERGY EFFICIENCY		
BUILDINGS ENERGY EFFICIENCY	Johnson Controls	US
	Koninklijke Philips Electronic	Netherlands
	Legrand	France
	Skanska B	Sweden
	St Gobain (Cie De)	France
DIVERSIFIED ENERGY EFFICIENCY	Linear Technology Corp	US
	SKF B	Sweden
	Sumitomo Electric	Japan
	Wartsila B	Finland
INDUSTRIAL ENERGY EFFICIENCY	Alfa Laval	Sweden
	Daikin Industries	Japan
	Delta Electronics	Taiwan
	Eaton Corp	US
	Fanuc	Japan
	Honeywell International Incorporation	US
	Infineon Technology	Germany
	Ingersoll-Rand	US
	Keyence Corp	Japan
	Murata Manufacturing	Japan
	Nidec Corp	Japan
	Rockwell Automation	US
	Rohm	Japan
	Samsung Electro	South Korea
	Siemens AG	Germany
	VMware Inc.	US
	WEG Ord	Brazil

EMCS SECTOR/sub-sector	Constituent name	Country
ENERGY EFFICIENCY		
Power Network Efficiency	ABB	Switzerland
	Alstom	France
	Samsung SDI	South Korea
	Schneider Electric	France
	Sensata Technologies Holding	US
	Siemens India	India
	TDK Corp	Japan
Transport Energy Efficiency	Aisin Seiki Co	Japan
	BorgWarner	US
	Denso Corporation	Japan
ENVIRONMENTAL SUPPORT SERVICES		
Diversified Environmental	3M Company	US
	Air Liquide	France
	Air Products And Chemcom	US
	Atlas Copco A	Sweden
	Doosan Heavy Industries and Construction	South Korea
	Dover Corp	US
	Flowserve Cp	US
	Kubota	Japan
	Kyocera Corp	Japan
	Linde	Germany
	Metso Corporation	Finland
	Nitto Denko Corp	Japan
	Parker-Hannifin	US
	PPG Industries	US
	Praxair	US
	SembCorp Industries	Singapore
	Sharp Corp	Japan
	Shin-Etsu Chemical	Japan
	Tyco International	US
	Vinci	France
Environmental Consultancies	IHS CI A	US
POLLUTION CONTROL		
Environmental Testing & Gas Sensing	Ecolab	US
	Eurofins Scienti	France
	SGS S.A.	Switzerland
	Thermo Fisher Scientific	US
Pollution Control Solutions	Johnson Matthey	UK
	Kunlun Energy (Red Chip)	China
	Perusahaan Gas Negara	Indonesia
	SMC Corp	Japan
	Umicore	Belgium

EMCS SECTOR/sub-sector	Constituent name	Country
RENEWABLE & ALTERNATIVE ENERGY		
BIOFUELS	Cosan S/A Industria e Comercio	Brazil
	Novozymes A/S	Denmark
RENEWABLE ENERGY DEVELOPERS & IPPs	Cemig PN	Brazil
	China Longyuan Power Group (H)	China
	EDP	Portugal
	Enel Green Power	Italy
	Enersis	Chile
	Fortum	Finland
	GPO Acciona	Spain
	Iberdrola	Spain
	National Hydroelectric Power Corp	India
	Tractebel Energia	Brazil
	Verbund Oesterreich Elektrizitats	Austria
SOLAR ENERGY GENERATION EQUIPMENT	OCI	South Korea
	Wacker Chemie	Germany
WIND POWER GENERATION EQUIPMENT	Dongfang Electric (H)	China
WASTE MANAGEMENT & TECHNOLOGIES		
GENERAL WASTE MANAGEMENT	Republic Services	US
	Suez Environnement	France
	Waste Mgmt Inc	US
HAZARDOUS WASTE MANAGEMENT	Stericycle Inc	US
RECYCLING & VALUE ADDED WASTE PROCESSING	Nucor Corp	US
WATER INFRASTRUCTURE & TECHNOLOGIES		
DIVERSIFIED WATER INFRASTRUCTURE & TECHNOLOGY		
WATER INFRASTRUCTURE	Beijing Enterprises (Red Chip)	China
	Geberit N	Switzerland
	ITT	US
WATER TREATMENT EQUIPMENT	Asahi Kasei Corporation	Japan
	Pall Corp	US
	Roper Industries	US
WATER UTILITIES	Sabesp ON	Brazil
	Severn Trent	UK
	Veolia Environnement	France

As at December 2011. Source: FTSE

Answers to the quiz

1	B	7	C	13	C	19	B
2	B	8	D	14	B	20	A
3	D	9	A	15	A	21	D
4	C	10	C	16	D	22	B
5	C	11	D	17	B	23	D
6	B	12	C	18	All D	24	A